Globalization and I

Also by M. Panić

CAPACITY UTILISATION IN UK MANUFACTURING INDUSTRY

ECONOMIC INTEGRATION IN EUROPE AND NORTH AMERICA
(*co-editor with A. Vacić*)

EUROPEAN MONETARY UNION: Lessons from the Classical Gold
Standard

NATIONAL MANAGEMENT OF THE INTERNATIONAL ECONOMY

PRODUCT CHANGES IN INDUSTRIAL COUNTRIES' TRADE: 1955–1968
(*with A. H. Rajan*)

REFORM OF THE INTERNATIONAL FINANCIAL SYSTEM (*with A. E. Astapovich and
others*)

UK AND WEST GERMAN MANUFACTURING INDUSTRY 1954–72 (*editor*)

Globalization and National Economic Welfare

M. Panić
Fellow of Selwyn College
University of Cambridge, UK

First published in hardcover 2003
First published in paperback 2005 by
PALGRAVE MACMILLAN
Houndmills, Basingstoke, Hampshire RG21 6XS and
175 Fifth Avenue, New York, N.Y. 10010
Companies and representatives throughout the world

PALGRAVE MACMILLAN is the global academic imprint of the Palgrave
Macmillan division of St. Martin's Press, LLC and of Palgrave Macmillan Ltd.
Macmillan® is a registered trademark in the United States, United Kingdom
and other countries. Palgrave is a registered trademark in the European
Union and other countries.

ISBN 0–333–77283–0 hardback
ISBN 1–4039–4343–5 paperback

This book is printed on paper suitable for recycling and made from fully
managed and sustained forest sources.

A catalogue record for this book is available from the British Library.

Library of Congress Cataloging-in-Publication Data
Panić, M.
Globalization and national economic welfare/M. Panić
    p. cm.
Includes bibliographical references and index.
ISBN 0–333–77283–0
    1. International economic relations. 2. Globalization 3. National state. I. Title
HF1418.5.P364 2003
337—dc21
                                                            2002030796

10   9   8   7   6   5   4   3   2   1
14 13 12 11 10 09 08 07 06 05

Printed and bound in Great Britain by
Antony Rowe Ltd, Chippenham and Eastbourne

To the memory of my parents

Contents

List of Tables

List of Figures

Foreword

The past decade has seen an outpouring of books on globalization. Relatively few of their authors, however, have been studying the subject for more than a quarter of a century. The publication of this collection of essays by Mića Panić, bringing together his thinking over past decades, is therefore especially welcome.

As the author notes in Chapter 1, debate about globalization has generated a great deal of heat. Books on this topic tend to be polemical, with authors concerned to take positions with regard either as to the desirability of globalization or as to its theoretical underpinnings. In contrast, the present book provides a calm, dispassionate analysis of the origins of globalization and its implications for economic policy. The book also stands in contrast with the view that globalization raises no issues that cannot be treated within the standard theory of international trade as a reduction in the barriers to trade and capital (but not labour) flows, or that it is simply a further development of the international division of labour. To quote, "it is a mistake to treat globalization as just another term for international economic integration" (p. 10).

The essays span the period since 1976 but are woven together in the fifty-page introductory chapter. A key linking element is that the author, like those writing from a political economy perspective, stresses the endogeneity of institutions and organizations, including the important fact that the degree of economic integration is itself the product of decisions by, on one side, national governments and, on the other, individual firms. One consequence is that today's increased integration, while it may have similarities with earlier epochs, has to be seen in the light of its own historical context. The context includes the lengthy period of national economic sovereignty after 1945, the creation of the European Union, and the collapse of Communism. Moreover, the evolution of institutions reflects a mixture of interest and ideology. On the former, one of the many strengths of the present book is that the author has always in mind the question regularly posed by Joan Robinson 'cui bono?' Even if the capitalist playing field were a level one, those who start well endowed, whether individuals or countries, can retain an enduring advantage.

The author sees multinational companies as key 'missionaries' in the promulgation of the ideology of liberalism. The prominence given to transnational enterprises is a refreshing feature of the essays. The typical textbook on international trade only introduces multinationals after a hundred pages or more. Yet their student readers start from a position of wanting to know about the activities of the companies whose products they buy and which help fund their universities. From the present book, they will learn about the role of transnational corporations in linking national economies and their contribution to the spontaneous integration of the world economy. These are crucial to understanding the patterns of trade and investment, and the likely evolution of the global economy. They are essential to understanding the distributional implications. Attention has tended to focus on the impact of out-sourcing on the wages of the unskilled – the delocalization of jobs – but it could be the upper end of the wage hierarchy that is most affected by globalization. A striking feature of the United States income distribution is the rise in the share of the very top groups: the share of the top 1% in total gross income more than doubled between 1980 and 2000. To the extent that this is driven by the remuneration of CEOs, the pay policies of multinationals is of central importance for the distributional outcome.

The domination of the world economy by transnational enterprises raises key policy questions. The relationship with national economic policy is the subject, in particular, of Chapter 6; and Chapter 11 takes up the question as to whether the nation state will be superseded by a supranational state. The author argues that supranational ideals are difficult to put into practice, even in the EU, on account of the problems of mobilizing consensus because of the important differences in national values, institutions and priorities. But the process of reaching such a consensus will undoubtedly be easier if this book is widely read.

A. B. ATKINSON
Nuffield College
Oxford
June, 2004

Preface

The most difficult and dangerous periods in history are those which involve systemic change. The existing framework of rules, conventions and laws that guide the actions of economic and other organizations becomes ineffective, even counterproductive. Risks and uncertainties, which are always present in economic decision making, become more serious and prevalent. As a result, in some cases the pace of economic progress slows down. In others, growth gives way to stagnation. Employment and income – in other words, economic welfare – are either increasingly insecure or experience a sharp decline. A gulf opens up between people's needs and aspirations and their ability to realize them. Sooner or later economic activity is increasingly seen as a zero-sum game, where it is possible to maintain or improve economic welfare for some only at the expense of others. The longer this persists, the greater the danger of bloody conflicts both within and between countries.

This description of the economic problems and risks normally associated with fundamental economic and political change has again become highly relevant because of two major developments that began in the closing decades of the twentieth century. Both involve far-reaching systemic change of uncertain duration and outcome. The first of these, caused by the collapse of communism, is obvious enough. It represents a concerted effort to alter radically the economic, social and political systems of the countries concerned.

The other transition currently in progress, globalization – the result of growing international economic integration and interdependence spearheaded by transnational enterprises – does not appear to involve anything resembling such a fundamental, systemic change. Superficially, globalization seems to amount to nothing more than the accelerated evolution of the division of labour within one particular system, capitalism, from the national to the supranational level – in principle no different from the progression from regional to national specialization that happened in the early phases of the Industrial Revolution. In fact, it involves much more than that. For reasons analyzed in the chapters that follow, the long-term effects of globalization – assuming that the trend is not reversed – may well bring about even more profound changes than the transition from socialism to capitalism. Unlike the latter, they are already affecting most countries, irrespective of the exact nature of their economic and political predilections and forms of organization.

The 11 chapters in this volume therefore give prominence to an important aspect of economic change that is normally ignored by economists.

Instead of taking economic and political institutions and organization as given, they are fully integrated into the analysis. In other words, they are treated as endogenous variables. Drawing on the experience of many countries the interaction between economic organization and performance, and its wide-ranging sociopolitical effects are examined in relation to one of the key issues raised by globalization: the conflict between economic interdependence and sovereignty.

As both systemic transitions and international economic integration have occurred before, the chapters combine economic analysis with historical experience when considering a number of crucial issues raised by growing international economic interdependence. This combination is of critical importance. Sir John Hicks, one of the most influential theoretical economists of the twentieth century, frequently made the point that economic theory 'must be the servant' of applied economics.

The analysis in the chapters that follow therefore incorporates applied or historical experience into the analysis of some of the basic changes in the institutions, policies and economic organization needed to create a viable, lasting international economic order. This is essential for one very important reason. Considerable progress in the international division of labour was achieved on more than one occasion in the past only to disintegrate into a universal retreat into autarky and economic warfare. Twice in the twentieth century inappropriate economic institutions, policies and organization caused serious losses in economic welfare that affected millions of people around the world, and, as a result, became one of the factors that led to the two world wars.

All the chapters are primarily concerned with economic problems and their possible solutions. However, the issues that they cover transcend economics. They are also of vital importance to the social harmony and political stability of individual countries and to the international community as a whole. Not surprisingly these issues have stimulated global interest and debate. I have therefore tried to ensure that the analysis is accessible to other social scientists as well as to the interested non-specialist who is concerned about some of the most complex problems (and their potentially unpredictable consequences) that the world has yet experienced.

The forces that set the process of globalization in motion are unquestionably economic. No serious analysis of the process can ignore this fact. At the same time the reasons behind this process may or may not be entirely economic; and their consequences certainly extend well beyond purely economic considerations. The close link between economic, social and political transformations, especially in the long run, ensures this – something that we economists must bear in mind if we are to make a constructive contribution to the debate on the possible consequences and long-term sustainability of globalization.

I have tried to overcome at least some of these problems by integrating and, where necessary, extending different aspects of macro- and microeconomic theory, practice and organization, as well as by incorporating into the analysis non-economic considerations of importance to the central argument.

As most of the chapters were written and published over the past decade or earlier, I have, where relevant, made small changes to the text to update the analysis in the light of subsequent developments or important new information. In two cases it also seemed appropriate to alter the title either completely (Chapter 7) or partly (Chapter 2) to ensure that it reflected the contents of each chapter more accurately and clearly.

At the same time, after careful consideration and discussion with other economists, I have decided to leave the statistical data and their analysis as originally published. The reason for this is that using more up-to-date data would not have altered either the original analysis or the conclusions and policy recommendations in any of the chapters.

Part I consists of a single chapter, a general introduction to the subject of globalization. It is one of the two essays published for the first time in this volume. (The other is Chapter 9.)

Chapter 1 provides an overview of the concept and extent of globalization, including the economic, institutional and cultural developments that make greater long-term integration of nation states difficult to avoid for dynamic capitalist economies. In other words it examines the causes and consequences of globalization and their implications for economic and political organization. The chapter concludes with an analysis of the institutional and policy approach that is most likely to ensure that the current process of international economic integration does not end in failure yet again.

The three chapters in Part II analyze the dynamics of macroeconomic organization: the role of important changes in macroeconomic organization and policies in determining, among other things, the outcome of greater economic specialization and interdependence. The chapters cover three major issues: why macroeconomic management becomes essential during the advanced stages of industrialization; the conditions required for the state to perform this function effectively; and the extent to which the objectives that governments set themselves and the complexity reached by the division of labour define the limits of the state's ability to bring about improvements in economic welfare.

Chapter 2 traces analytically the evolution of the relationship between economic progress and organization from a small firm in a highly competitive new industry to supranational forms of organization at the industry and state levels. It shows why economic progress is brought to a halt, or even reversed, in the absence of changes in the institutions and forms of organization appropriate to each stage of development.

Chapter 3 examines the most effective form of macroeconomic organization and management achieved so far: the model of active government involvement adopted by the most industrialized countries after the Second

World War. The chapter first develops and then applies to the most advanced economies an analytical framework that explains why some countries are much more successful than others in achieving and sustaining high levels of economic welfare. Equally important, it shows why the same country may be markedly more successful in improving the standard of living of its population in some periods of its history than in others.

Chapter 4 considers an equally important issue, with specific reference to the experience of the socialist economies in Eastern Europe (including the USSR): the problems that arise when the ends bear little relation to the means available. The result, among other things, was in this particular case a rigid and inefficient form of economic organization under the control of a totalitarian political regime. This combination meant that the whole experiment was doomed to failure from the beginning. It also imposed appalling social costs on the countries in question. Their experience provides important lessons for the role of the state in modern economies.

The two chapters in Part III are concerned with the relationship between levels of economic development, forms of economic organization and globalization. Some of these are determined by the deliberate actions of governments (that is, from above), while the others are the result of spontaneous long-term developments and actions at the level of individual firms and industries (that is, from 'below'). These actions are normally highly interdependent, as the two chapters show in their analysis of the origins of globalization: institutional and spontaneous.

Chapter 5 examines the long-term relationship between changes in the level of development and trade policy. Until the late 1970s most countries tended to adopt trade policies that they regarded as appropriate to their level of industrialization and economic performance relative to the rest of the world. That was very much what the corpus of knowledge in this field, developed since the eighteenth century, suggested they should do. The chapter pays special attention to the important distinction between 'economic openness' and an 'outward-looking economic strategy'. This has become highly relevant since the 1970s, as the two concepts are wrongly treated as synonymous in policies that are advocated and imposed from outside, especially by the 'Bretton Woods' organizations.

Chapter 6 focuses on the main channel through which international integration has taken place since the 1960s, and the driving force behind the pressure for universal liberalization of international trade and capital flows: the transnational enterprise. The analysis covers the economic and other developments that have led to the rise of transnationals in virtually all spheres of economic activity, and their role in the process of globalization, with special attention to the effect of these enterprises on national economic policies and, consequently, on national economic welfare.

The logic of globalization points to supranational forms of organization – at both the macro- and the microeconomic level – as the most effective form of decision-making framework for an internationally integrated and inter-dependent system. The five chapters in Part IV therefore consider the links between globalization, cooperation and supranationalism. More specifically, they analyze the factors that reduce the ability to pursue effective macro-economic policies at the national level and the problems that a suprana-tional approach to macroeconomic economic management would have to overcome to perform such a function at least as efficiently as the most suc-cessful national authorities.

Chapter 7 adopts an unusual approach to the problem of global infla-tionary pressures of the kind experienced since the 1970s by analyzing their origins rather than the mechanics that have received so much attention, especially in the economic literature. It traces the process by which irrecon-cilable claims on limited resources in one part of a highly integrated system can lead to an inflationary spiral that engulfs the whole system. The analy-sis demonstrates why the question of income distribution – within and between countries – is, as David Ricardo pointed out almost two hundred years ago, 'the principal problem of Political Economy'.

Although the analysis in Chapter 8, which was written jointly with Manmohan Kumar in early 1983, deals specifically with the 1982 Debt Cri-sis, it also identifies the main reasons for the global financial crises that have occurred with increasing frequency and magnitude ever since – highlight-ing weaknesses in the existing international institutional framework. The analysis of the shortcomings of the IMF and the World Bank anticipated by almost two decades the criticisms that became common at the end of the 1990s.

The lending policies of transnational banks have been a major factor in all these crises. Chapter 9 analyzes some of the problems created by dereg-ulation and globalization for the prudential regulation and supervision of banks. The analysis distinguishes clearly between the needs and problems that arise at each of the three levels at which banking supervision is of cru-cial importance: the level of individual banks, and the national and inter-national levels. Unlike most of the literature on the subject, which deals predominantly with supervision at the national level, the chapter considers the various forms of action that are most appropriate to each level and the extent to which the effectiveness of one of them depends on the success of the other two.

By analysing the origins, history and demise of the Bretton Woods System, Chapter 10 takes a critical look at the institutional requirements and problems that are common to all attempts to create a global financial order. It shows why, even when the setting up of supranational institutions enjoys widespread international support, such institutions are unlikely to be effective if their existence threatens powerful economic interests in the dominant economy of the time. Contrary to the Bretton Woods blueprint, the system agreed in 1944 operated in exactly the way that those who created it wanted to avoid.

Finally, Chapter 11 shows why supranational ideals are difficult to put into practice even in the European Union, which has been so far the most successful attempt ever by a number of independent, sovereign states to create an economic union. The obstacles are formidable, despite the fact that it is generally recognized that a highly integrated international economic system will be fundamentally unstable as long as the nation state remains the most effective form of macroeconomic management. In analyzing these difficulties, this chapter identifies some of the problems that those who share the cosmopolitan ideal in Europe and elsewhere must solve if they are to achieve their objective.

As pointed out earlier, most of these chapters were commissioned and published in the 1990s in response to some of the key policy issues raised by the rapid pace of globalization in the closing decades of the twentieth century. They have been selected for this volume because they all deal with subjects that are even more topical and relevant now than when they first appeared in print. Moreover, together they present a unified and rounded analysis of some of the most complex and difficult economic and political problems that confront the international community at the beginning of the twenty-first century, and sketch broad policy recommendations to deal with them.

Acknowledgements

I am grateful to the following for permission to reprint essays included in this volume: Macmillan Press Ltd (Chapters 2, 4, 6 and 8), Oxford University Press (Chapters 3 and 10), the Department of Applied Economics, University of Cambridge (Chapter 5), Elsevier Science (Chapter 11), Lloyds Bank plc (Chapter 7) and the Department for International Development (Chapter 9).

I am also grateful for their comments on some or all of the chapters in this book to Tony Atkinson, Ha-Joon Chang, Ian Clark, Ken Coutts, John Dunning, David Ford, Charles Goodhart, Geoff Harcourt, Geoff Ingham, Angus Maddison, Colin Miles, Alan Milward, Ann Newton, Maurice Peston and Robert Rowthorn. Responsibility for the views expressed and any remaining errors and omissions is, of course, entirely mine. Beth Morgan prepared the two indexes with the usual speed and efficiency.

MIĆA PANIĆ

Part I
Introduction

1
Globalization: The Meaning, the Claims and the Reality

1.1 Introduction

Few international developments have received as much attention since the closing years of the twentieth century as 'globalization'. Yet it is clear from the rapidly growing literature on the subject, and the increasingly heated debate which it has stimulated, that there is little agreement about the meaning of the term, even less agreement about the processes that bring globalization about, and no agreement at all about its effects. As a result, the international community appears to be in the middle of major economic, cultural and institutional changes that are imperfectly understood despite the general feeling that their potentially far-reaching consequences deserve special attention.

Not surprisingly, it is difficult to give convincing, authoritative answers at the moment even to some of the basic questions about the observed changes. For instance, is globalization something that refers to rapid improvements in international communications brought about by the extraordinary growth of information technology, to economic processes such as deregulation and free trade, or to political actions that may eventually lead to the loss of national sovereignty? Are these developments inevitable – in the sense that they evolve 'naturally' from economic progress, technical advances and their interaction with socio-political changes? Do they affect some countries only or, as the term seems to imply, the whole world? Are the consequences of globalization going to be as beneficial and benign as the Bretton Woods institutions claim, or as sinister and costly as those who disrupt the annual meetings of these organizations fear? Above all, are we ready to deal with the adjustment costs of globalization, especially when it becomes clear that they are going to vary significantly between countries, and between economic and social groups, as well as regions, within countries?

As an introduction to the chapters that follow, this chapter considers some of these and similar questions.

Finding answers to these questions is essential for two very important reasons. First, economic theory suggests (see Chapters 5 and 6) that left to the uncoordinated actions of microeconomic agents in the pursuit of their frequently irreconcilable aims, international economic integration – one of the key aspects of globalization – is a process of uncertain duration and outcome. In particular, there is no guarantee that the outcome will satisfy the expectations of all those who participate in it; or that the transitional costs, economic and social, will be politically acceptable. That immediately raises doubts about long-term prospects for globalization, at least in its current form and objectives.

Second, the international community made two concerted attempts between the middle of the nineteenth century and the Second World War to achieve greater international integration of national economies. Neither could be sustained for long (see Panić 1988, Bairoch and Kozul-Wright 1998). The first of these (after 1860) was reversed in less than two decades; and the second (in the 1920s) collapsed after only a few years. The important question is, why? Equally important, why has the current wave of international economic integration survived for almost 40 years globally and even longer in case of the European Union? Does this mean that, unlike in the past, the process of deregulation and liberalization currently in progress is not going to end in yet another acrimonious and costly economic disintegration and military conflict?

1.2 Globalization: its meaning and domain

The mere mention of 'globalization' raises two important questions. First, does it mean anything more than economic integration and interdependence, two concepts – though not the terminology – that have formed a major part of economic analysis since the eighteenth century? Second, whatever the answer to the first question, does the word describe something that applies only to a relatively small number of countries or, as it appears to imply, to the whole world?

Those who write and speak about globalization may not have the same definition in mind. Nevertheless, they invariably agree about one thing: the process that it describes, and which has gathered momentum since the 1970s, is dominated by *economic* considerations and developments. As a scholar in international relations concluded after reviewing the literature on globalization: "The vast majority of globalization theorists present it as a characteristic of economic activity" (Clark 1997, p. 21). More specifically, the process is associated first and foremost with the economic aspects of what many observers regard as an irreversible trend towards greater international integration and interdependence.

The economic changes that have attracted so much attention in recent years can easily be explained, as Chapter 6 shows, by two interrelated developments. One of these, widespread liberalization of international trade and capital flows, has been initiated by governments. It represents, therefore, *institutional integration*. The other, and in many ways much more relevant in any analysis of globalization, is *spontaneous integration*: the international division of labour achieved mainly through the actions of transnational enterprises in pursuit of their corporate interests and objectives. (See also Panić 1988, Chapter 1.)

The first of these developments, as economic historians have been quick to point out, is not new. As already mentioned, there have been two other attempts since the middle of the nineteenth century to increase international trade and specialization by opening up national economies.

What makes globalization significantly different from these earlier attempts is the second development – which *is* new. The extent to which the world economy is dominated now by transnationals – which according to Dunning (see Chapter 6) constitute one of the most powerful forms of economic organization developed by the capitalist system – is far greater than either before 1914 or between the end of the First World War and the 1970s. The growth of transnationals in virtually every sector of modern economies, especially since the 1970s, has added a completely new dimension to global specialization and exchange, their scope and extent. However, transnationals are frequently hindered in their search for new, more profitable markets by the diversity of national cultures and institutions. It is hardly surprising, therefore, that the latter are receiving so much attention from all those concerned with the international division of labour and its consequences. In other words, as transnationals overcome traditional barriers to trade and capital mobility (see Chapter 6), it is increasingly realized that the process of economic integration cannot become truly global unless all countries develop the attitudes and institutions needed to create a single world market.

As a result, the impact of transnationals on the international economy is felt in two ways. First, because of the contribution that they make to national output and employment they are in a position to exert considerable influence on national economic and social policies and, consequently, on national economic welfare. This enables them to ensure that national governments, and international organizations in which these governments are represented, actively promote the liberalization and deregulation of economic activity globally. Second, as a result of the greater freedom that such changes in national policies give them, transnationals are able to spread and rationalize their operations internationally – becoming in the process the main channel through which world production, trade, investment, capital flows and the diffusion of technology take place. The outcome is an increase in international economic interdependence. This, in turn, requires further liberalization and deregulation in order to harmonize national economic environments and policies. The cycle of policy changes, integration, interdependence and further policy changes assumes in this way a dynamic of its own that is increasingly difficult and costly to reverse.

It goes without saying, of course, that close economic links between countries can evolve over time through the specialization and trade carried out by national enterprises – that is, enterprises that, unlike transnationals, do not operate outside their country of origin. That, after all, is how the growth of the international economy was largely achieved in the nineteenth century and for most of the last hundred years. However, international specialization and exchange of this kind tend to be hampered by risks and uncertainties that can be reduced significantly by the concentration and diversification of economic activity within transnationals. Hence, it is extremely unlikely that, without transnationals, international economic links could ever achieve the scale, diversity and complexity made possible by specialization and trade within these enterprises.

It is also highly unlikely that national firms could have given rise to some of the non-economic developments that are now firmly associated with globalization. (See the sections that follow, and Panić, 1988.) These include: technological integration (UNDP 1999); ideological uniformity, which has been imposed on many countries by those promoting the 'Washington Consensus' (Williamson 1994, Stiglitz 2001); institutional harmonization, which is increasingly advocated by international organizations (for example EBRD 1999); pressure for cultural conversion to a standard, Western pattern (Huntington 1997); weakening of the nation state and the question of accountability and governance (Giddens 1998, Gray 1999, Korten 1995, Ohmae 1990 and 1995); the growing inability of governments to deal with increases in income inequality, poverty and the social problems that these inequalities generate (Atkinson 1999, Milanović 2002, UNCTAD 1997); and the threat to globalization posed by growing international opposition to these developments in the form of militant nationalism (Gellner 1998), as reflected in what one writer has called "the clash of civilizations" (Huntington 1997).

As this list suggests, globalization is widely seen as embracing far more than the kind of issues normally considered by economists in the context of international integration: comparative advantage, trade policy, division of labour, and the gains from trade that the opening up of national economies is expected to generate. The prevailing view is, clearly, that globalization was set in motion by the economic dynamics of the international division of labour. However, an increasing number of scholars in different fields are suggesting that these initial, purely economic developments have evolved into a much more complex process. This involves nothing less than a *long-term* fusion of national economies, cultures and institutions into a completely new world order: a single global market operating within the framework of a common global civilization that is increasingly supervised and regulated by supranational institutions. In short, according to this view, globalization is a process of continuous change – driven by the interaction of economic integration and cultural harmonization – that will eventually engulf every single country in the world. That may not be what many of those involved in different aspects of the process are seeking to achieve. However, for reasons that will be considered below and in the chapters that follow, this is what globalization means, and if sustained indefinitely this will be its eventual outcome. Driven both directly and indirectly by unfettered 'market forces', it is a virtually inexorable process towards ever greater economic integration, cultural universalism and the institutional uniformity of sovereign nation states – making them ultimately "an anachronism", as Robert Schuman, one of the architects of the European Union, used to argue (see Chapter 11).

However, like all dynamic processes, globalization can also be viewed as a state of affairs at a particular time: the extent to which economic interdependence, cultural integration and institutional harmonization have progressed up to that time. This provides an opportunity to measure at least some of the economic and technological aspects involved in the process in order to assess the degree to which economic integration has become a global rather than a regional phenomenon. The problem is that these measurements are frequently based on data of varying quality, cover different periods and countries and, consequently, lead either to different results or to different interpretations of the same results. Not surprisingly, many scholars have expressed serious doubts about the degree to which the concept of globalization accurately captures the state of international economic and other relations at the beginning of the twenty-first century.

Hence, to answer the second question raised at the beginning of this section, whether globalization is really a *global* phenomenon, it is necessary to examine briefly what the indicators traditionally employed for this purpose show – including their implications for the non-economic aspects of globalization.

For instance, one of the standard criticisms of the 'novelty' of globalization can be found in Hirst and Thompson (1996). They argue that, as a proportion of GDP, both international trade and capital flows were more important before 1914 "than they are probably today" (*ibid.* p. 32). The problem with this criticism is that it is not supported by the available data, which clearly show that the ratios of exports and imports to GDP are higher now than before the First World War (cf. Maddison 1991 and 2001). Moreover, many more countries are now involved in international trade than was the case a hundred years ago. As for the relative size of international long-term capital flows before and since 1914, the conclusion reached by Hirst and Thompson depends very much on whether the data include the period since the mid 1980s. Up to that time, what they say is essentially correct (see Panić 1988, p. 172). But the picture has changed radically since then (see UNCTAD 1994 and 2000). For instance, in 1998 stocks of inward foreign direct investment accounted for around 14 per cent of world GDP compared with a little over 5 per cent in 1980 (UNCTAD 2000, p. 319). Also, as in the case of trade, there is no reason to doubt that this capital is now located in more countries than before the First World War.

It seems much more relevant, therefore, when considering the economic aspects of globalization, to examine the frequently quoted fact that as, for instance, Weiss (1998, p. 176) points out, "world trade, production and investment remain highly concentrated in the wealthy northern countries of the OECD". Various indices, such as those of 'transnationalization' (UNCTAD 1999) and 'financial integration' (World Bank 1997), confirm this. The same is also true of the benefits derived from the most recent technological advances, such as information technology, where by far the greatest beneficiaries have been the industrialized countries (UNDP 1999). Judged by these indicators alone, globalization appears to be something of a misnomer. At best, it seems to refer to economic and technological integration among industrial countries.

The problem with these and similar measures is that they show only certain, rather narrow aspects of international integration and as such cannot provide a reliable picture of the true extent of economic interdependence between the countries and regions of the world. Moreover, they are not designed to show the non-economic aspects of globalization.

It is true, of course, that the industrialized countries account for most of world trade – around 68 per cent of the total, with three-quarters of the exchange representing trade between countries in this group (United Nations 2000, pp. 260–2). However, most exports from developing countries go to the developed economies: 60 per cent on average, over 70 per cent in the case of Latin America (*ibid.*). Exports also account for a high proportion of GDP in many of these countries (UNDP 1999, table A1.1). This, plus the fact that their exports tend to be highly concentrated in a relatively small number of mainly primary commodities, indicates that changes in industrial countries' policies and levels of activity are likely to have a particularly strong effect on the welfare of developing countries. The members of OPEC have paid a heavy price in economic welfare, since they agreed on two large increases in the price of oil in the 1970s, for ignoring this simple fact (see Panić 1988, Part IV). Furthermore, although exports from developing countries account for only a small proportion of total imports into industrial economies, the effect of these imports on employment in the latter is far from negligible (Wood 1994).

Indirect links between national economies make it even more difficult to determine accurately the extent of global integration. When international economic interdependence reaches a certain level, what happens in one group of economies may have a major impact on another group – even when the volume of direct trade between the two is small – through the effect on a third group with which both these groups trade heavily. For instance, the countries of Eastern and South Eastern Asia trade relatively little with those in Western Asia, and even less with African and Latin American economies. Yet it is estimated that the East Asian Financial Crisis of 1997 had a major effect on the export earnings of countries in the other three regions, reducing them by 20 per cent in Venezuela and by 25 per cent in Kuwait and Angola. According to UNDP estimates, this contributed a year later to falls in the GDP of the three countries, ranging from 6 per cent in Venezuela to 14 per cent in Kuwait and 18 per cent in Angola (UNDP 1999, p. 42).

The economic dependence of the rest of the world on the industrial countries is even greater when one takes financial flows into account. Developing countries cannot raise their efficiency and income levels without imports of capital, technology and technical expertise from the most advanced economies. As their savings are insufficient to generate the export surpluses needed to finance these imports, they have no alternative but to borrow heavily from the exporting countries and international organizations. The result is that many of them accumulate large external debts, often within a short period. In a number of countries the debts are much larger than their GNP. This means that a high proportion of developing countries' exports has to be used to service and repay these debts (cf. UNDP 1999, pp. 49–52 and 193–6). In addition, official development assistance from the most advanced economies accounts for a significant proportion of GNP in the least developed countries: 11 per cent on average and, of course, much more than that in many of them (*ibid.*).

What is more, the involvement of foreign transnationals – predominantly from industrial countries – in the productive capacity of developing countries has increased significantly. In 1998 foreign direct investment (FDI) accounted for 11.5 per cent of the gross fixed capital formation in developing countries, ranging from 4.6 per cent in Africa to 17.5 per cent in South America and 28.3 per cent in Central Asia (UNCTAD 2000, table B.5). As a proportion of GDP, stocks of FDI (again predominantly from the most advanced economies) amounted to 12 per cent in developed and 20 per cent in developing economies (*ibid.*, table B.6). These figures indicate that although most of the world's FDI is located in industrial countries (see UNCTAD, 1994), it accounts for a higher proportion of the productive capacity in developing than in developed economies.

Moreover, the unprecedented activity in cross-border mergers and acquisitions since the early part of the 1990s has increasingly involved developing countries. There were 6,233 such deals in 1999. Out of these, 1,042, or 16.7 per cent, consisted of foreign mergers with or acquisitions of enterprises in developing countries. In 1990, the equivalent figure was 7.6 per cent (UNCTAD 2000, p. 232). As the foreign firms in this case also come predominantly from the most advanced economies, the figures suggest a marked increase in the control of productive capacity in developing countries by transnationals from the developed world.

Such heavy *economic* dependence by the rest of the world on the most advanced economies makes developing nations vulnerable to more than changes in economic policies and performance in the highly industrialized countries. Given their very limited resources, the greater the development ambitions or the need for external assistance in order to cope with the problem of absolute poverty, the more difficult it becomes for developing nations to resist pressure from the donors for ideological uniformity and the harmonization of national institutions and policies. Hence, if they wish to reduce poverty and social deprivation they have no alternative but to accept these demands, irrespective of whether the conditions imposed by the donors are appropriate to their national preferences, history or needs.

For instance, following the debt crisis in 1982, 18 developing countries with external financial problems had to liberalize their trade. In the 1990s 16 developing countries with similar problems were forced to do the same. In both cases, trade liberalization was part of a programme of reforms imposed by the IMF and the World Bank as a precondition for external assistance (Rodrik 1993 and 1994). Similar conditions also formed part of the package of reforms that the transition economies in Central and Eastern Europe had to adopt in order to qualify for economic and technical assistance from international organizations (Lavigne 1999). After its financial crisis in 1997, South Korea had to implement wide-ranging, free market reforms prescribed by the IMF – even though, as Feldstein (1998, p. 27) pointed out at the time, these reforms were "not needed for Korea to gain access to capital markets".

For all these reasons, it is a mistake to treat globalization as just another term for international economic integration. The external pressure for ideological and institutional uniformity to which independent, sovereign countries are now being subjected – as part of the drive for a broader cultural uniformity – goes well beyond anything attempted in the past.

In that sense, the globalization currently in progress represents the most significant, sustained advance towards the realization of the free-trading, *laissez-faire* ideals of those nineteenth-century liberals who dreamed of a "single, more or less standardized world where all governments would acknowledge the truth of political economy and liberalism would be carried throughout the globe by impersonal missionaries more powerful than those of Christianity and Islam had ever been; a world … from … which, eventually, national differences would disappear" (Hobsbawm 1977, p. 83).

So far, at least one part of the dream has come to pass. The ideals, as pointed out earlier, are carried to different parts of the globe by a relatively small number of extremely powerful 'missionaries': transnational enterprises in pursuit of narrow corporate objectives, with the support of their national governments and the international organizations that these governments control. The combination of nineteenth-century liberal ideals and twenty-first century corporate resources represents a powerful force for change. As John Stuart Mill, one of the most eminent nineteenth-century liberals, observed: "A good cause seldom triumphs unless someone's interest is bound up with it" (quoted in Semmell 1970, p. 207).

1.3 Capitalism and the origins of globalization

1.3.1 Globalization: a distinctive feature of capitalism

The problem now, as in Mill's time, is that such cosmopolitan ideals invariably come up against formidable obstacles that make their realization virtually impossible. One of these is the sheer scale and complexity of the transformation required and the time that it would take. The degree of international integration may be greater now than at any other time in history. But it is still very far from resembling anything like a global economic, cultural and political union. That being the case, what guarantee is there that the process of globalization can continue for much longer?

This raises an important question which, like so many of the questions on globalization, has yet to produce a generally agreed answer: is globalization inevitable? Is it a 'natural' development in the process of industrialization (spontaneous integration) or a consequence of policies imposed by the state (institutionally generated integration)? This distinction is important because the former is likely to propel international economic interdependence into a much higher degree of intra-firm specialization and trade (see Chapter 6). This means that, given that national economies are more self-sufficient in the latter case, it would be relatively easy, despite the considerable social costs, to reverse institutionally generated integration – as was demonstrated by the socialist economies in the early 1990s. Spontaneous integration, on the other hand, would be potentially much more costly and risky to disentangle because of the extent and complexity of the international economic linkages involved. The available evidence (see Part II) makes it clear that it is this form of economic integration that is at the root of the globalization process.

One thing that stands out from economic analysis and the historical experience of international economic integration and, more recently, of globalization is that the origins of these processes lie in the nature of the economic system within which they have evolved: capitalism. (The traditional terms of 'capitalism' and 'socialism' reflect far better the all-embracing complexity and distinctiveness of the two systems than the labels currently in vogue: 'market' and 'centrally planned' economies.) It is under capitalism that the two forms of international economic integration (spontaneous and institutional) flourish to an extent unknown in alternative economic systems. In pre-industrial societies, the international division of labour is restricted partly out of necessity (low levels of development and specialization, rudimentary means of transport and communications, low levels of income and small markets) and partly out of choice (autarky to protect static levels of production and income, most of which belong to those who also control political power). Under socialism, international trade and factor movements are controlled by the state in order to maximize various social and political objectives that are given priority over private preferences and net benefits. This is most likely to be achieved in conditions of self-reliance – in other words by autarky, which keeps foreign interference to a minimum.

Under capitalism, it is exactly the reverse: private preferences and priorities take precedence over social needs and aspirations; and it is this distinctive approach to the production, exchange, distribution and accumulation of material wealth that has shaped the values, aims and behaviour of the societies that have adopted it. In turn, the system has been shaped by different cultures and forms of economic and political organization created for the specific purpose of achieving wider *national* social and political objectives.

The important question in this context is, therefore: what is it in the nature of capitalism that makes globalization an integral part of its long-term dynamic? The answer is to be found in the three important, closely related features of the system: property *rights*, the incentive to *create* wealth, and the *means* with which to do so. It is a combination of these three factors that accounts for the extraordinary capacity of the system to amass *productive* wealth – something that distinguishes it from all other economic systems, including socialism.

1.3.2   The right to withdraw productive resources from social use

The fact that property, including the means of production, is privately owned has been traditionally regarded as one of the defining characteristics of capitalism. However, what really counts in this as in other systems is not so much the legal ownership of property (the nominal right) as what the owners are allowed by law, defined and enforced by the state, to do with their property as a matter of *right* (the effective right).

The advantage of possessing property does not stem from the owners' freedom to do with it whatever they like. No modern state is prepared to grant or tolerate such a freedom. That would mean anarchy, and no complex economic system can operate under disorderly, unpredictable conditions. *The advantage that really matters under capitalism comes from the right guaranteed by law that entitles those who own productive property (that is, the means of production) to withhold it from use by society as a whole.* The fact that they can withhold the use of their property by society gives those who own it considerable influence and power over collective action. Hence, the more property they own the greater will be the influence and power that they exercise as well as the social prestige that they command. Not surprisingly, it is this particular right and the conditions under which it can be exercised most effectively that set in motion the whole complex chain of events that are unique to the system and which ultimately lead to the process of globalization.

Although wealth has been desired and acquired throughout history for the benefits that go with it, the form of affluence that is particularly valued under capitalism is productive wealth – that is, command over the resources that generate prosperity – rather than wealth to be used for ostentatious purposes. The advantage of the former is obvious. Ownership of the means of production under a dynamic economic system represents both wealth in the short run, and the capacity to perpetuate and increase it (together with the privileges that go with it) in the long run. Wealth acquired solely for direct use and enjoyment is, like the advantages that it brings, ephemeral.

The reasons that drive people to acquire wealth and, in this way, be able to determine how it is to be used are the same under industrial capitalism as in pre-industrial societies: the desire for prestige and personal dominance (influence and power) that property rights enable them to exercise. The right to withdraw resources from social use – directly affecting the well-being of large numbers of people – makes it possible for those who control the means of production to influence the political structure of the societies in which their resources are employed. As a result, by shaping the values and behaviour of these societies according to their preferences and interests they will, as a group, have a major influence on the way that the societies are organized and controlled.

Individually, however, the extent to which they can exercise such power and influence will, *ceteris paribus*, depend on the size and quality of the resources under their control compared to the resources controlled by others. In other words, what matters is the *relative* size of the resources that they command. This is equally true of individuals, corporations and countries.

There is bound, therefore, to be intense competition for the acquisition and accumulation of scarce productive resources – with the largest share of the existing or new wealth going to those who possess uncommon advantages over their competitors. In this sense, success and dominance under industrial capitalism appear to rest, as they did in pre-industrial societies, on the competitive advantage of those engaged in the struggle for greater wealth.

1.3.3 Individualism as the ideology of wealth creation

There is, however, a fundamental difference. In pre-industrial systems, where the capacity to create new productive resources was limited, the acquisition of wealth was basically a zero-sum game. It depended on success in the continuous redistribution of existing wealth through war and plunder. Social prestige and political power depended on military advantage and prowess.

It needed the unprecedented brutality and destruction of the Second World War to demonstrate finally, even to those with a pre-industrial mentality, that military conflict is not an option that is open to modern industrial societies – at least in their relations with each other. Their wealth-creating capacities are so interdependent that the destruction of productive resources in one country is bound to have an adverse effect on economic welfare and social well being in other countries. The larger the country the greater the loss of international welfare. Observing the consequences of the early stages of the Industrial Revolution, John Stuart Mill was one of those who realized this already in the first half of the nineteenth century. As he put it, before industrialization, when international trade and interdependence were limited, "the patriot, unless sufficiently advanced in culture to feel the world his country, wished all countries weak, poor, and ill-governed, but his own: he now sees in their wealth and progress a direct source of wealth and progress to his own country" (Mill [1848] 1965, p. 594).

Hence, under capitalism, especially industrial capitalism, the competitive code of behaviour, defined and enforced by the state, differs in a number of major respects from that in economic systems based on private property in pre-industrial societies. (Socialism and communism are, of course, fundamentally different from capitalism, in that their *modus operandi* is determined by the collective ownership of the means of production and, in theory at least, by co-operation instead of competition.)

First, although the law protects property from expropriation by force, it does not protect it from loss through negligence, obsolescence, inefficiency or commercial takeover by more successful competitors. In other words, property ownership and the privileges that go with it are ultimately determined under capitalism by *relative* economic performance. Second, the threat to established property owners is increased by the fact that it is open in law to anyone to acquire and accumulate productive resources – provided that this is done according to socially approved rules and conventions. In practice, those who own such resources will always be at an advantage compared with those who do not. However, this does not protect them in the long term from newcomers with superior knowledge, the capacity to innovate or managerial ingenuity. Third, the divorce of economic activity from direct political power ensures that no factor of production can be forced to work for another factor of production. (Exceptions to this are national emergencies such as war, or under an autocratic plutocracy such as fascism.) Society cannot force the owners of productive resources to act in its collective interest. Equally important, unlike in slavery and feudalism, the owners of capital cannot force labour to work for them.

As society cannot force those who control productive resources to use them in its collective interest, it has to make it worth their while to act in a way that will maximize their own material and social benefits and, in so doing, enable society to realize *its* objectives. However, to be acceptable as a guide for social action this, in turn, requires a convincing system of ideas, an ideology, that promises to enhance the economic welfare of all rather than a small minority only. In the case of capitalism such an ideology has been available since the publication of Adam Smith's *Wealth of Nations* in

1776. Not surprisingly, in one form or another – and ignoring Smith's unease about the social consequences of unregulated capitalism – this has been the ruling ideology in all the countries that have embraced the system. What Smith did in his attack on the static, corrupt, over-regulated feudal system was to elevate the pursuit and maximization of private wealth into a major social good. Through hard work, thrift and enterprise, individuals can increase not only their own command over productive resources, with the accompanying social privileges, but also the wealth, influence and power of their country relative to those of other nations. In this way, individuals and nations become free from the constraints imposed by poverty, making it possible for them to choose the kind of life that gives them the greatest satisfaction. What Smith could not do, because it was not so obvious in his time, was to point out that this also happens to be essential as a motive for action in a secular society that has no 'other life' to look forward to. The present and *only* life has, according to the view increasingly taken by subsequent generations, to be lived as long as possible and enjoyed to the full. The prevailing ideology offers the promise that this can only be achieved by continuous increases in personal and public affluence through *private* action.

It is not surprising, therefore, that the quest for greater efficiency and higher personal and corporate gains tends to take precedence over social considerations, especially in unregulated, 'free market' forms of capitalism. This happens even when the outcome may be higher unemployment, poverty, social friction, irreparable damage to the environment and the possibility of political instability. The ideology of free private enterprise as the key to continuous economic progress, social well-being and political stability provides the foundations on which the whole programme of social and political organization and action rests under capitalism.

1.3.4 The institutions

As a result, one of the most important tasks in any country that adopts capitalism is to translate the ideology of individualism, or 'private enterprise', into a legal code of rules and regulations that define the institutional framework and behaviour according to which economic activity is to be carried in the country. The basic code will refer to property, including intellectual property (ownership, rights, contracts, and obligations); labour (hiring and firing, wages, hours and conditions of work); trade (competition, fair trade and advertising); banking and capital market regulations; accounting practices; and others.

The objective is to ensure that all of these are observed in every region of the country so that there are no legal barriers to the development of national, rather than purely regional, enterprises and trade. As a result, no individual or enterprise can be legally prevented from engaging in an economic pursuit that is open to any other individual or enterprise. Economic activity can therefore be located and pursued in any part of the country according to purely commercial criteria in order to maximize net private gains, especially profits. In this way, the law, backed by the coercive power of the state, removes inter-regional obstacles to trade and factor movements – unifying the whole country into a single market. The unification is completed with the creation of a single currency, the only one that is permitted to act as legal tender within the country.

There is an important reason for this. The larger, national, market enables firms to specialize in order to make full use of economies of scale and, consequently, maximize profit to an extent that would be impossible if their activities were confined to the region in which they originated. Greater factor mobility, specialization and economies of scale also raise the level of labour productivity and, with it, wages and salaries. When spread across the country, this further increases the size of the national market and, together with higher profits, stimulates investment in new products, production methods and productive capacity in general.

In other words, mass production, made possible by economies of scale, requires mass consumption which, in turn, is determined by increases in efficiency and income levels, cultural harmonization and the upward 'equalization' of personal income. Cultural harmonization involves the spread of knowledge through education and the mass media, bringing a greater uniformity of beliefs, tastes, values and aspirations. Higher income levels diffused widely raise the purchasing power of the population – especially the lower income groups who tend to have a high marginal propensity to consume.

To oversee, foster and enforce all these developments the country obviously needs a framework of *national* legal, commercial and political institutions – all within a system that is supportive of the nature and *modus operandi* of capitalism. The exact character of the political system that determines such a framework will depend essentially on the extent to which the values and practices of capitalism enjoy widespread support in the country. In general, this will tend to be determined by the system's ability to satisfy as widely as possible the individual and social aspirations of the population. In other words, if capitalism is successful in meeting widely desired material and social needs the country is likely to enjoy a genuinely democratic form of government, with the full support of its powerful corporate interests and the majority of the population. That, in turn, will provide the system with the vitality required to reconcile the future demands of a diversity of interests by adapting its institutions in a way that is most likely to achieve them.

Where this is not the case, there are likely to be important divisions of interest between those who own and control productive wealth (capital) and those who do not (labour). This makes a truly democratic form of government much more difficult, as each side will try to gain power in order to use existing institutions to impose its values and objectives on the whole country. Ultimately, it is those who control productive resources that will prevail, especially if they can exercise the right to withdraw these resources from social use by moving them to another country. In that case, what outwardly appears to be a democracy – with a 'free' press and elections in which the candidates appeal to the whole population for support – may well, in fact, be an elective plutocracy. When this happens, the economic system is likely to lose much of its dynamism, as the ruling oligarchy will become preoccupied with the distribution and protection of existing wealth rather than with wealth creation. This sclerosis will be even more extensive if the threat to the oligarchy is so great that the political system degenerates into an autocratic plutocracy, in which those who own and control productive resources also assume control of political power, either directly or through their surrogates. That enables them, effectively, to force labour and owners of capital dependent on the ruling plutocrats to work for them on their terms in what amounts to a form of neo-feudalism.

National cultural differences ensure in practice that the basic institutional aspects of capitalism vary considerably between countries. The importance of these cultural differences to an understanding of the process of globalization stems, therefore, from the fact that once powerful national oligopolies begin to operate globally on a large scale, they will use their economic power to impose on other countries those non-economic features of the system that are particularly favourable to them. That is when what appears to be no more than a relatively familiar aspect of international economic specialization and trade begins to evolve into something much more complex: globalization.

1.3.5 Science, technology and the role of inequality

With property rights defined by law, supported by a distinctive ideology and enforced by a complex framework of institutions, including the power structure, the system is ready to set in motion a sequence of developments that will eventually lead to globalization.

The problem is that, although it may be legally open to everyone to acquire productive resources and wealth, some corporations and individuals will be at a clear advantage if the resources are unequally distributed at the beginning of the process. Their resources, their knowledge of the existing industry or profession and their reputation, secured and nurtured over time, are difficult to challenge seriously, especially by those attempting to enter the industry or the profession. Similarly, a large corporation, with a major share of the market, normally has sufficient financial resources either to take over or to underprice and drive out of business a small or less successful competitor. A newly qualified surgeon cannot command the eminence, fees and influence of an acknowledged expert in the field.

The only way that a small or new firm can effectively challenge enterprises with greater experience and resources is to develop an important invention or innovation that enables it to introduce new or superior products and/or production methods, giving it a clear advantage over existing products and processes. If the potential market is judged to be large, the novelty and/or superiority of what it has to offer will attract sufficient financial backing in the expectation of high profits. In this way, the existing small firm or a new entrant will be able to grow rapidly either by dominating sales of the new product or by increasing its share of the existing market through superior efficiency and lower prices that the competitors cannot match. Similarly, the only way that a newly qualified surgeon can hope to enjoy at least the same reputation and remuneration as someone who is already pre-eminent in the field is to acquire equal or superior knowledge and surgical skill. In both cases it is the *scarcity*, the uniqueness of what they have to offer, that makes it possible for the surgeon and the firm to earn exceptional returns on their investment in education, research and development. Long-term survival and success under capitalism are, therefore determined, by the resources devoted to scientific research as well as by the development and application of new discoveries.

As a result, scientific and technical progress are of critical importance for the dynamics of capitalism. They enable newcomers to exploit a new area of activity profitably or to enter and do the same, through lower costs and prices, in an existing industry. The threat of this, in turn, forces established firms or individuals to adapt continuously to the latest developments in science and technology in order to protect their dominance or, in most cases, to survive the threat posed by more enterprising competitors.

Moreover, if they make full use of the opportunities available to them, the long-term advantages open to successful innovators may be even greater than the preceding analysis suggests. *Ceteris paribus*, excess demand – generated by the relative scarcity of their product – will ensure high returns on their investment, enabling firms to finance new R&D and further expansion of their productive capacity from internal resources. Alternatively, high actual or expected profits also make it easier for these firms to raise additional capital on the financial markets. Access to external finance is likely to be assisted further by the fact that successful, rapidly growing firms will attract managerial, technical and administrative staff of high calibre. Such firms can normally offer higher remuneration and other benefits than their competitors – in addition to the greater social status associated with working for a successful enterprise with highly promising long-term prospects. As many of these employees are likely to come from less successful firms, the gap between dynamic and stagnant enterprises is bound to open up, accelerating the process of cumulative success at one end and failure at the other.

Technical advances in transport and communications are equally important, as they reduce the cost and time needed to obtain information or to reach distant markets. They also make cheaper or higher-quality inputs more accessible. The combined effect of these improvements is to enable firms to maximize profits further by spreading and diversifying their operations geographically within the country in order to utilize fully their engineering, financial, marketing and managerial advantages.

Implicit in this brief sketch of the dynamics of capitalism is an important, though frequently neglected, feature of the system: the extent to which it depends for its energy, its vitality and, ultimately, its survival on its capacity to create and sustain *inequality* of opportunity through advances in science and technology. It is this characteristic, unique to the system, that enabled capitalism to demonstrate its superior wealth-creating potential over feudalism and, more recently, to see off the challenge from socialism.

1.3.6 The search for new markets

Traditionally, changes in the international division of labour have been analysed from the standpoint of individual countries: the extent to which specific official policies either enhance or retard the trend towards greater integration and harmonization of national economies, institutions and policies. The underlying assumption, irrespective of the nature of the economic system, is that each state is in full control of the relationship between its own and other economies and that it will try to use this power (economic sovereignty) to advance whatever it believes to be in the 'national interest'.

With the growing ubiquity and power of TNEs this particular approach becomes increasingly inappropriate if it fails to take into account their role in the process. After all, as they are the main channel through which international integration takes place, transnationals are in a position to influence the economic, social and political environment in which they operate. Government actions are still important. But the intricate knitting together of national economies, cultures and institutions is difficult to understand without considering explicitly corporate behaviour (the motives, aims and actions that bring this about), both directly and through the influence that it has on government policies.

Following the preceding analysis, it is not difficult to see why the systemic characteristics of capitalism are sooner or later going to force firms – especially those in industries that are subject to economies of large scale production – to engage, in the absence of trade barriers, in international trade and investment. The continuous search for a larger market, as already pointed out, arises from the need to gain and maintain competitive advantage over other firms. Initially, a firm will acquire such an advantage by having superior products and/or production methods and, as a result, earn a higher rate of return on capital invested than do its domestic competitors. Superior profit performance will, in turn, enable it to improve its relative performance further by increasing its investment in R&D and productive capacity in order to exploit economies of scale. This will open up even more the gap between successful firms that are experiencing the virtuous circle of growth and those firms which fail to match their performance. The latter will end up with higher unit costs and, as they cannot raise prices to compensate for the cost disadvantage without experiencing even greater contraction of their market share, their profits will be squeezed further. The falling rate of return on their investment will make it even more difficult for them to make a significant improvement in their relative performance. Consequently, sooner or later they will be either driven out of business or taken over by more efficient rivals.

There is a limit, however, to the growth that firms can achieve within their domestic market through internal improvements in efficiency relative to that of other firms, or through mergers or takeovers. If they reduce production they will sacrifice profits by failing to utilize economies of scale fully; and if they expand it rapidly in order to maximize profits by reducing unit costs the market will be saturated at the prevailing capacity and prices. It will take longer to reach saturation point in large than in small economies, but eventually the outcome will be the same in both cases.

From that point on, growth at higher or even the existing rates of profit is possible only if the firms succeed in one or more of the courses of action open to them. First, they can spend more on R&D in search for radically new products or for methods of production that will reduce their costs significantly. The former will in effect create a new market. The latter, as a result of lower unit costs and prices, will expand the existing market. The problem is that the closer they are to the frontiers of knowledge, the greater their expenditure on R&D will have to be and the longer it will take to achieve a significant improvement in either methods or products. At the same time, the risk is also greater that, whatever the expenditure, the effort may either fail or result in unsatisfactory returns on the resources invested.

Second, mergers and takeovers can be used to reduce existing capacity in an industry and, in this way, the volume of output relative to the level of demand. The smaller the number of firms left, the more successful they are likely to be in pursuing this particular strategy of maintaining a high level of prices and profits. This can delay saturation point. But it cannot avoid it indefinitely. Anti-monopoly legislation prevents firms from growing beyond a certain size; and most countries have legislation that forbids the remaining firms to form cartels.

Third, they can, especially if there is a good deal of unemployment, keep increases in wages below those in prices. A few firms, even a few industries, can pursue such a strategy successfully in order to prevent their rates of return from falling. But if the practice becomes successful across the whole economy, or even a significant part of it, the decline in real wages, combined with greater uncertainty about future employment and income prospects, will affect aggregate demand adversely and, in this way, profits. The adverse effect on the rate of profit may be further aggravated by the various social problems that tend to follow closely economic stagnation.

Given these limitations on their long-term growth, firms producing internationally tradable goods and services will turn to exports as the most effective way of avoiding the decline in profits caused by the saturation of their domestic market.

1.4 From international economic integration to globalization

The advantage of foreign trade from the point of view of individual firms is clear enough. It enables them to maximize profits in three ways: by avoiding saturation of the domestic market, by being able to sell in markets where their products command the highest price, and by enabling them to buy raw materials and other inputs at the lowest price.

However, the extent to which they are able to benefit from these advantages will depend on a number of factors: levels of protection in foreign markets, the size of those markets, technical progress in transport and communications and the cost of these services, the international competitiveness of their products, and the sophistication of their internal forms of organization and control.

Consequently, as long as they depend on *national* firms, the scope for international specialization and trade will be limited by important developments outside the control of these firms. The most prominent among these are the actions of foreign governments, the rate of growth of individual economies, and the rate of technical progress in the sectors over which the vast majority of trading firms have no direct influence. The only effective course of action open to them is to lobby their government to liberalize trade, stimulate the economy or assist R&D in transport and communications in order to encourage other governments to reciprocate.

They are most likely to succeed in this in periods of sustained growth of the domestic and foreign economies when there is relatively little spare capacity in the economies concerned and unemployment is low. As these also happen to be periods of investment booms embodying important technical advances, including those in transport and communications, a combination of economic progress, technical improvements and trade liberalization will result in the rapid growth of international specialization and trade.

The growth of international markets enables national firms to differentiate increasingly what they produce by utilizing their country-specific natural resource endowments, skills and tastes. There will be an expansion, therefore, of *intra-* as well as *inter-*industry specialization and trade. These changes in the character of international trade indicate that national firms are capable of achieving a high degree of international division of labour despite the fact that they have no production facilities outside their own country.

Moreover, even under these conditions international economic integration will be accompanied by a certain degree of international cultural assimilation – in other words, 'globalization'. The growth and deepening of international trade are closely related to the spread of industrialization (see Panić 1988); and industrialization inevitably involves the borrowing from highly industrialized countries of ideas, values, beliefs, systems of education, technical and managerial knowledge, legal codes and practices, even forms of political organization. Historical experience shows that truly independent sovereign states normally adopt some or all of these at the pace at which they can manage such a profound transformation of their economies, societies and cultures in a way that will increase rather than diminish their national economic welfare. Globalization under these conditions will, therefore, be adapted to suit their national ideological and cultural tradition, preferences, priorities and capacity for change.

An important reason for this is that national firms ultimately have to conform to the socially acceptable practices and aspirations that exist in their country. They will, of course, enjoy the wider power and influence that go with their property rights; and they will do their best to use these to ensure that the country's economic and social values and behaviour are not in conflict with their own long-term interests and objectives. However, as long as their operations are confined to one country, their use of the power that command over productive resources gives them has to be exercised within the constraints imposed by what is socially and politically acceptable in that country. Economic progress in general and the profitability and growth of individual firms require long-term social and political stability. Neither can be achieved and sustained unless the distribution of the benefits that they bring about is regarded by the majority of the population as 'fair'.

Attempts by firms to disregard these long established rules of socially acceptable behaviour by withdrawing their resources from social use under these conditions would impose serious costs not only on society at large but also on the firms themselves. Consequently, they will have little alternative but to make their contribution to the maintenance of harmonious industrial relations and, more generally, to play their role in helping the state achieve its economic and other objectives, all of which are essential to the pursuit of their own self-interest.

The limits on what national firms can do to 'globalize' the world are even greater outside their own country. As they do not have production facilities in their export markets they are unable to use the threat of withdrawing them from social use in order to achieve a particular objective. The only threat open to them is to stop exporting to a particular country. The problem is that, unless a firm enjoys a world monopoly, other firms will step in and supply the market. Alternatively, hostile or unreliable behaviour by important foreign suppliers will encourage the importing country to develop domestic substitutes. If the country has a strong comparative advantage in the industry concerned, the long-run effect of this may well be that domestic firms will drive foreign competitors out of the home market before expanding their operations internationally by penetrating and taking over the markets of many of these competitors as well.

Moreover, the range of institutional and policy issues in their export markets that are of direct relevance to national firms is also limited. What matters to them is free access to foreign markets, and that the countries to which they export honour international agreements and contracts so that exporters can be sure of receiving payment for their goods and services. Provided that these two conditions are met, other institutional aspects of the importing countries – such as their ideological preferences, legal systems, cultural values or the nature of their economic and political systems – are of no direct concern to foreign national firms.

There are two important reasons for this. First, what matters to foreign exporters is that trading with a particular country is profitable. If it is, they are not going to sacrifice these profits because they dislike the country's economic or political system. Second, there is very little that they can do themselves directly about the institutions and policies in the country concerned even if these affect their business interests adversely. They cannot force the country to reduce either its tariffs or its non-tariff barriers to trade. That will depend on the bargaining power of their national government in international negotiations. Improvements in transport and communications, as already pointed out, are outside their control. As for their competitive position in external markets, this depends on how long they can sustain their initial advantage through improvements in R&D in the face of similar or greater efforts by other firms, especially those located in the export markets.

All this changes fundamentally as soon as national firms begin to set up production facilities in other countries, thus transforming themselves into *transnational* firms. When this happens the competition for resources, power, influence and prestige also transcends national borders and becomes international. It, therefore, affects radically the behaviour of those who own and/or control productive resources. What is more, it affects also radically consumer behaviour. Relative wants and competitive position are now measured against behaviour and achievements in other countries (see Chapter 7).

As a result of these changes the process of international economic integration accelerates. Transnational enterprises (TNEs) locate both similar and different stages of production in different countries to exploit those countries' absolute and relative advantages. This changes the character of both international production and trade: a high proportion of intra-industry trade now becomes intra-firm trade (see Chapter 6). Even more important, as they have committed productive resources in a number of countries, the economic, social and political environments in all these countries are now of great concern to TNEs as they affect directly their ability to achieve their corporate objectives, both overall and in each of the countries concerned.

Moreover, by controlling productive resources in different countries TNEs, unlike national firms, are in a position to use the power and influence that property rights give them to reshape many of the factors that affect their performance. The greater their importance to the national economy of a country, the greater will be their ability to do this. This ability is increased further the less they are dependent on any one country to achieve their overall objectives either because of the country's size or because of the uniqueness of its resources.

There are several reasons why national firms transform themselves into TNEs. All of these are intended to give them a competitive advantage, or at least to ensure that they are not put at a competitive disadvantage in the long term. First, as TNEs they are able to internalize various activities across national frontiers in order to gain and maintain competitive advantage by reducing transaction costs and making full use of economies of scale. Second, as already mentioned, expansion into new markets enables them to sustain rapid growth and high rates of profit even after their national market becomes saturated, making further expansion both difficult and costly. Third, their presence in other countries increases the cost of entry into these markets, especially for national firms in the countries concerned. In the absence of TNEs, governments are likely to give special assistance to domestic firms to develop substitutes for imports, thus increasing national economic welfare. If there are TNEs that are willing and ready to set up production facilities in a particular country, the government is likely to assist them instead, as they have the resources, know-how and access to international markets that would take national firms years to acquire. Finally, the transnationalization of their activities is also driven by a desire to escape from national restrictions on the ability of firms to externalize as many costs as they can – particularly those concerned with new investment, labour and the environment.

The exact location of activities by transnationals is therefore determined by their assessment of the relative potential to achieve these objectives in different countries. Hence, although many governments may be keen to attract TNEs, only a relatively small number of them will be able to do so on a scale that will make a significant long-term contribution to their economies. The reason for this is that, with the exception of firms in the primary sector whose geographic mobility is limited, TNEs prefer to invest in countries with large and/or rapidly growing markets, a sufficiently advanced economy for them to be able to make full use of external economies, an educated labour force, and political stability. As these conditions are most likely to be satisfied in countries with a high level of industrialization, and as TNEs originate predominantly in such countries, it is hardly surprising that four fifths of the world's foreign direct investment is located in the most advanced economies.

Implicit in the previous paragraph is one of the key factors behind the growth of transnational activities since the 1960s: the convergence in efficiency and income levels among industrial and a few other nations. The greater the proportion of countries that are converging to the level of affluence in the country from which a TNE comes, the greater its potential market and hence its scope to expand its activities globally. In other words, the close relationship between equity (within and between countries) and efficiency is as important internationally as it is nationally. Yet the myopic pursuit of self-interest by those who run transnationals ensures that few of them, or their political supporters, have any awareness of the full significance of this relationship and its policy implications for the long-term prospects of their own businesses.

What both these groups do appreciate fully is the extent to which institutional and policy differences even between capitalist countries can affect the ability of TNEs to achieve their corporate objectives. Given that transnationals are in a position to use, usually with the support of their governments, the economic power at their disposal to eliminate these differences, they are bound to make a concerted effort to do precisely that. This is how the process of international economic integration becomes transformed into a drive towards comprehensive globalization, something that would be virtually impossible without transnationals.

The process of international harmonization is likely to start at the economic level and initially to involve mainly industrial countries. If national firms and TNEs are to exploit fully the opportunities offered by international trade and investment it is essential for the barriers to entry to various countries to be eliminated, or at least reduced to negligible levels. Hence, there will be strong corporate pressure on governments to remove quotas and reduce tariffs significantly. When this is achieved, attention will switch to the need to remove non-tariff barriers to trade by harmonizing national technical, health and safety standards.

The problem is that even if the barriers to trade are brought down to uniformly low levels or even removed completely, the 'optimum' allocation of international resources, from the corporate point of view, cannot be achieved so long as governments use exchange controls to prevent the free flow of capital between countries. If they are to allocate their activities in a way that will maximize their profits and growth, TNEs need to be able to transfer profits from country to country to finance new investment or, quite simply, to exploit international tax and interest rate differentials. Hence, having liberalized trade, governments will come under increasing pressure to allow free mobility of capital between countries.

However, even deregulation and liberalization will remain 'sub-optimal' as long as they are confined to industrial economies. To maximize profits internationally trading companies need to have access to cheap or high quality inputs, many of which are located in developing countries. The liberalization of trade by these countries enables foreign firms in general and TNEs in particular to use their monopsony power to acquire the inputs they need at the lowest possible price. In addition, although relatively small within each developing country, the combined size of the more affluent consumer market in all these countries is far from negligible. The governments of developing countries will, therefore, be under great pressure to liberalize trade and capital flows even though this may be against the long-term interest of their countries (see Chapter 5).

It would look too much like neo-colonialism, however, if leading industrial countries were seen to force on developing nations institutional changes and policies likely to be against the long-term interests of the latter. The alternative, less transparent, strategy is to use their influence to achieve the same aim by altering radically the main responsibilities of some of the world's most prominent international economic institutions. This explains the perceptible change in the way that these organizations, such as those created at Bretton Woods in the 1940s, and their regional equivalents operate. Instead of concentrating, as originally intended, on resource transfers to countries in need, irrespective of their economic systems, they are increasingly using the means at their disposal to impose on the international community a particular ideology that suits the corporate interests of their most powerful members.

Few international organizations are in a better position to promote the 'Washington Consensus' (a modern euphemism for the *laissez-faire* form of capitalism) than the IMF and the World Bank. As developing countries depend heavily on them for financial assistance, it is relatively easy for these institutions to insist on wholesale deregulation and liberalization of the countries' economies as a pre-condition for receiving international assistance. Furthermore, when developing countries receive external loans they have to increase their exports in order to service and repay them. They cannot do this unless they have free access to the markets of other nations – especially those of the industrial countries, as these provide most of the funds at the disposal of the two organizations. That gives the World Trade Organization (WTO) the opportunity to re-enforce the 'reforms' imposed by the IMF and the World Bank. Developing countries are highly unlikely to secure preferential treatment from industrial nations unless they join the WTO; and they will be granted membership only if they liberalize their external trade as part of wider 'free market' reforms.

As in national economies, implementing laws favourable to TNEs and other corporate interests is the most effective means of putting the ideology of 'free markets' into practice. It is hardly surprising that laws on property rights, including intellectual property, have become a highly topical issue internationally. The same is also true of competition laws: partly to take into account the effect of opening up national economies and partly to ensure that national laws do not discriminate against foreign TNEs. Labour law is receiving considerable attention and undergoing important changes, even in industrial countries. The aim is to enable transnationals and other firms to earn 'satisfactory' rates of return on their capital by giving managers greater freedom to hire and fire labour, increase the hours of work, bring down labour costs by lowering health and safety standards, and reduce the power of trade unions to reverse these changes. According to the 'Washington Consensus', laws that increase 'labour flexibility' are the only way to ensure high employment in conditions of globalization. Laws that allow firms to fire labour at short notice with little or no compensation, and to offer employment at low, internationally competitive wages are expected by the proponents of the 'Washington Consensus' to improve national economic welfare by attracting TNEs. The implicit threat is that failure to implement such laws will lead to an exodus of these enterprises, with their advanced technology and know-how, to countries with more compliant laws.

More generally, there is a very important reason why adherence to the ideology of unfettered individualism requires the proliferation and greater uniformity of national laws. If individuals pursue their own desired goals – in competition with each other and the rest of society – with little or no restraint, the bonds of trust and loyalty between them will diminish rapidly. This will weaken social cohesion and, in so doing, make collective action at all levels highly uncertain, especially in the long run. Recourse to law becomes then the only means of ensuring that promises, contracts and other obligations are honoured. This helps to explain why the United States, where social links are weak, has proportionally far more lawyers and lawsuits than any other industrial country (Gray 1999, pp. 118–19).

The next step in the process of globalization is even more sensitive because of its wide ranging implications: international pressure on governments to undertake fundamental reform of their public finances by reducing and harmonising taxes. Other things being equal, in conditions of international factor mobility, high taxes will encourage capital – physical, financial and human – to migrate (or to threaten to do so) to countries where the general level of taxation is low. As a result, unless they enjoy important advantages that offset unfavourable tax differentials, countries that wish to keep the existing TNEs and highly skilled labour have little alternative but to bring down their taxes to the levels prevailing elsewhere. This immediately reduces the resources available to governments to finance welfare provision or to assist the restructuring and modernisation of their economies.

This has several important consequences. First, there is an increase in poverty and social hardship. Second, as the level of inequality increases so do also social problems such as crime (see Chapter 3). Third, emasculation of the welfare state, especially if combined with high unemployment, forces those who do not possess human capital of the kind demanded internationally to work for low wages in order to survive, thus increasing the ability of those who control productive resources to maximize their income. In other words, one of the major consequences of (downward) international tax harmonization is to strengthen the property rights of those whose who own and control productive resources by increasing significantly the power of capital over labour.

Furthermore, tax harmonization, like deregulation and liberalization, is also designed to fortify this power further by reducing the role of the state – the only form of collective organization with the power to mobilize the resources needed to safeguard and improve social welfare by redressing the balance of power between society and its dominant corporate interests. With the shrinking of the resources at its disposal, the state is in no position to threaten the growth, power and influence of large corporate interests. The result is that the state becomes increasingly dependent on these interests to realize the collective needs and aspirations of its citizens, with profound changes in the nature of national political systems. With large financial resources donated to political parties and governments that support the interests of those who control productive resources, corruption becomes endemic internationally, right-wing dictatorships become entrenched and, where it exists, democracy slowly begins to give way to elective plutocracy. These trends help to explain the fact that even in long-established democracies a rapidly growing proportion of the electorate is refusing to participate in a political process that they feel is failing to represent and protect their interests.

Finally, the analysis in the last two sections makes it possible to give a partial answer to an important question raised at the beginning of the previous section: is globalization inevitable? Clearly, the necessity to unify the world economy, culture and the political process is an essential, integral part of the dynamic of capitalism. As a result, the quest for 'globalization' *is* inevitable. The process may stall or go into reverse, as in the 1930s. However, once the problems that caused this are resolved, and the system regains its momentum, the sequence of developments from growth to deregulation, liberalization and international economic integration leading ultimately to globalization will continue – until the next crisis.

Consequently, an even more important question is whether realization of the ultimate goal of a 'globalized' world is feasible. The reason for this is that, as historical experience shows, more than economic welfare may depend on the answer. The problem of sustaining the process of globalization is, therefore, considered briefly in the following two sections and at greater length in the chapters that follow.

1.5   The benefits and costs of globalization

Despite the overall complexity of globalization, the most important argument in its favour remains economic: the role of greater openness of national economies in increasing national economic welfare through international specialization and improvements in efficiency. In that sense, little has changed, apart from the terminology, since the eighteenth century when the doctrine of free trade was first developed in France and Britain.

For instance, according to the OECD (1998, p. 36): "More open and outward-looking economies consistently outperform countries with restrictive trade and [foreign] investment policies." This view tends to receive unqualified support from senior economists in international organizations that actively promote the 'Washington Consensus'. Thus, Anne Krueger (1998, p. 1514) has "no doubt" that the countries that liberalized trade "grew faster". The IMF (1997, p. 84) is of the same opinion, though it tends to express it more guardedly: liberal "[p]olicies towards foreign trade are among the more important factors promoting economic growth and convergence in developing countries."

The problem with generalizations of this kind is that they are difficult to justify analytically (except under highly restrictive, fictitious assumptions) or to demonstrate empirically. The OECD ignores the fact that an economy need not be open in order to pursue successfully an outward looking economic strategy (see Chapter 5). As for the relative performance of economies with different degrees of openness, their claim, like Krueger's assertion, is not supported by empirical evidence (cf. Chapter 5, Rodrik 1997, Deraniyagala and Fine 2001). The same is also true of the second part of the IMF's statement in support of free trade (see below). It requires much more than a simple, single policy instrument to explain something as complex as the relative economic performance of nations!

Even the World Bank frequently ignores the important conclusion reached in one of its own reports after examining economic crises in a number of developing countries: "there are large potential costs if [international economic] integration is not carefully managed" (World Bank 1997, p. 3). That, in a nutshell, is the real challenge of globalization!

Ceteris paribus, trade liberalization and the international division of labour are neither as beneficial as the optimists claim nor as costly as the pessimists fear. The outcome depends critically on the conditions under which such policies are pursued; and conditions vary even more now between countries and within the same country over time than when the doctrine of free trade was first developed. Hence, it is impossible to conclude purely on the basis of *a priori* reasoning that international economic integration will be either beneficial or costly to a particular country. The actual outcome will be determined by economic and political developments in the rest of the world, the level of development and international competitiveness of the country concerned, the length of time over which it liberalizes its trade, the range and success of its other policies, and its ability to bring about the socio-economic changes that successful integration into the world economy requires.

The classical economists were aware of this. In fact, the most influential economists have always been careful, after arguing the case for free trade, to state the conditions under which trade liberalization is either the wrong policy option or has to be managed very carefully (cf. Panić 1988, Chapter 7). Subsequent analysis has developed these arguments further. In particular, contributions to the theories of growth and trade developed over the last 20 years confirm the need for the caution advocated by the classical economists.

The most appealing argument in favour of international economic integration and, therefore, globalization lies in the promise that *all* countries participating in the process will 'gain' – in the sense that they will be better off than if they persist with economic isolationism. The promise stems from Ricardo's theory of comparative advantage, one of the most original and important theoretical contributions in the history of economics. Even if country *A* is more efficient in every branch of production than country *B*, the welfare of both will be improved if they eliminate barriers to trade and specialize: *A* in those goods and services in which its comparative advantage is greatest and *B* in those activities in which its comparative disadvantage is the smallest.

There are, however, a number of problems with this theory when applied in practice, not least because the world has changed beyond recognition since the beginning of the nineteenth century when Ricardo formulated it.

One difficulty arises from his use of a two-country model to prove that the principle of comparative advantage will enable all countries to gain from free trade, a practice that trade theorists have followed to this day. The gains might well be shared if there were only two economies in the world. But there is no guarantee that everyone will benefit from international specialization and trade when there are many countries, so that there is a great diversity of national differences in resource endowments, institutions and policies. Davis (1998a, 1998b) shows that extending the analysis to a three-country model already produces an outcome in which there are winners and losers! For instance, the measures advocated by neoliberals to make European labour markets flexible may have adverse effects on developing countries (see Atkinson 2002). In fact, even if there are only two countries both of which gain from trade, if one specializes in activities in which rapid technical progress and economies of scale are important and the other in activities where this is not the case, the former will gain significantly more from trade in the long run than the latter. Sideri (1970) shows this by analysing the effect that international trade and specialization have had since the early nineteenth century on the two countries actually used by Ricardo to illustrate the gains that trade makes possible: Britain (industry) and Portugal (agriculture).

This conclusion is hardly surprising once the assumptions of perfect competition and full employment, adopted by Ricardo and most economists after him, are abandoned. This is essential for the very simple reason that such an assumption bears no relation to a world dominated by imperfect – especially oligopolistic – competition. Perfect competition implies *equality* of opportunity. There is no technical progress, the cost of entry into an industry or occupation is low and all those who do so have perfect (or at least equal) knowledge and foresight. All the goods or services produced by an industry and all the factors of production that it employs are homogeneous and, therefore, perfect substitutes. Moreover, decreasing returns to scale ensure that all firms remain small. As a result, no firm or individual can acquire unique advantages that would enable it to dominate the market in which it operates.

Most of this may have been true, or nearly true, of the world just before the Industrial Revolution. But, as the earlier analysis in this chapter shows, none of these assumptions describes even remotely what actually happens under advanced industrial capitalism. (See also Porter 1990.)

Not surprisingly, as the next section shows, the institutional and policy implications of perfect competition are at complete odds with reality, and are therefore dangerously misleading as a guide to action. In conditions where equality of opportunity is the rule, there is no reason for the government to assist economic growth and restructuring with industrial and other policies that accelerate R&D and raise the level of human capital. Perfect competition would ensure the convergence of economic performance and welfare both nationally and internationally through the actions of private individuals and firms, all taken in the pursuit of self-interest.

This conclusion follows from the neoclassical growth model developed by Solow (1956) and others. Without institutional changes or assistance from the state, neither of which plays any part in the model, competitive microeconomic agents absorb 'exogenously' determined technical progress. In the process they ensure that low-income countries grow faster than highly industrialized nations, until they too reach their 'steady state' rate of growth. Hence, thanks to 'market forces', the result is international convergence in efficiency and income levels in the long run.

However, as the theory of endogenous, or self-sustained growth (see Romer, 1986) shows, if one takes into account the three conditions under which modern economic activity actually takes place – imperfect competition, positive externalities and the fact that technical progress is endogenous – the outcome is quite different. First, oligopolistic competition is common in most industries, especially those which depend on advanced technology, because of the importance of increasing returns to scale. Second, one of the most important features of this type of competition is that it is technical progress and superior organization rather than prices that determine the long-term success of firms. Third, large oligopolies are located predominantly in advanced industrial economies that have large markets and high levels of human and physical capital – all of which provide the foundations for further technical progress. Finally, as technical change is one of the key endogenous variables in the economic development of capitalist economies, the theory leads to the conclusion that there is no reason for the rate of economic growth in developing countries to converge with that in the advanced economies.

This conclusion obviously has very important policy implications for developing countries. Unless they can develop appropriate institutions and policies, and mobilize the resources that will enable them to sustain long-term rates of growth above those in the highly industrialized countries, there is no mechanism in capitalist economies that can automatically produce international convergence in economic performance and in standards of living. On the contrary, as Myrdal (1957) has argued, other things remaining the same, the cumulative wealth-creating capacity in industrial countries, which the rest of the world cannot match, will ensure that the gap between the rich and poor countries grows over time.

One of the reasons for this is that, given the extent and complexity of the modern division of labour, the location of industrial activity is influenced by much more than the relative abundance and costs of natural resources, capital and labour. External economies – a combination of human capital, the range and sophistication of existing industries and institutions, and quality of the infrastructure – tend to encourage clusters of economic activity in certain parts of the world, invariably those which are already highly advanced. The 'new economic geography' attributes these clusters to the importance of economies of large scale in modern economic processes (see, for instance, Krugman 1991). In this way, it provides a partial theoretical explanation (Martin 1999) of something observed over the years by students of TNEs.

Transnationals are, of course, not unique in their preference for industrial economies. In the absence of exchange controls, private financial capital tends to flow in the same direction: partly because of the range and quality of financial services that exist in these economies and partly because the risks are lower. Human capital will follow the same route if there are no barriers to labour mobility: the material rewards are greater and the quality of life generally superior in countries with highly advanced economies. Equally important, human capital, like other forms of capital, also derives important benefits from positive externalities: by being in close contact with people of similar educational background, interests and achievements, and by enjoying similar opportunities and facilities for work. The cumulative effect of all these movements is to reduce, because of their 'small knowledge' base (Grossman and Helpman, 1991 and 1994), the pace at which the transfer of technology to developing countries takes place, slowing down their rate of economic growth relative to that in industrial countries. This will, of course, perpetuate and widen international inequality in per capita incomes.

Consequently, although TNEs have the resources and the know-how to act as important 'engines of growth' (UNCTC 1992), the logic of oligopolistic competition ensures, *ceteris paribus*, that the benefits of this will be much greater over time in core (industrial) than in peripheral (developing) countries. The same is also true of regions in individual industrial countries: clusters will tend to form in the most advanced and prosperous of them.

Applying this kind of analysis to the European Union, Bertola (1993) shows that the greater mobility of capital and labour within the Union will lead to a more pronounced concentration of production. As a result, some regions and countries will prosper at the expense of others.

In other words, endogenous growth theory, the 'new economic geography', and studies of the organization, preferences and profit maximizing behaviour of oligopolies, both national and international, all lead to the same conclusion: there is nothing in the competitive dynamics of capitalism that can ensure convergence in economic welfare. The more open national economies are, the greater the scope for TNEs to rationalize their operations by concentrating their activities in those countries which provide the best opportunity for internal and external economies of scale and, therefore, for profit maximization. Few developing countries fall into that category. Strategic trade theory (see below) comes to the same conclusion.

It is hardly surprising, therefore, that there has been a marked increase in income inequality between and within many countries since the 1970s – a period of active deregulation and trade liberalization for a large number of economies, both developed and developing (Atkinson 1999, United Nations 2001, Milanović 2002). Far from generating the convergence of national economies, globalization appears to be responsible for a growing divergence in their performance (see, for instance, Pritchett 1997). Moreover, there is no evidence that unregulated, profit maximizing actions at the microeconomic level (i.e. the 'market forces') tend to reverse these trends even in the long run. On the contrary, the gap between rich and poor countries is much wider now than at the beginning of the Industrial Revolution (Jones 1997, Williamson 1998, Bourguignon and Morrisson 1999).

In fact, in the almost two centuries since the Revolution spread from Britain to other parts of the world only one country, Japan, has managed to close the wide gap that separated it originally from the most advanced economies and to join the ranks of the world's wealthiest nations. The Japanese have achieved this unique transformation thanks to a combination of factors: social cohesion and team effort, the capacity to absorb successfully best practice techniques from other countries, the radical reform of institutions and policies, and generous external assistance. As a result of all these factors, they were able to achieve and sustain a long-term rate of growth that no other country has managed to equal. (See Tsuru 1994.)

Japan's success was so remarkable in its scale and the relatively short period over which it was achieved that it inspired strategic trade theory (Brander and Spencer 1983, Krugman 1986). According to the theory, the prevalence of imperfect or oligopolistic competition in modern capitalist economies – in other words the prevalence of *inequality* of opportunity – justifies protectionist policies as well as an industrial policy that makes development of strategic industries possible. Without these policies, developing countries are in no position to close the growing gap between them and the most advanced economies, as only strategic industries are able to generate external benefits to the whole economy. Hence, although formulated within a modern analytical framework and based on modern experience, strategic trade theory reaches conclusions that are no different from the case for protection put forward by Hamilton, List, Mill, Marshall and others. Similar concerns also prompted Adam Smith and Ricardo to argue for the gradual liberalization of trade and against capital exports from their country (Panić 1988, Chapter 7).

Implicit in all these theories, old and new, is the importance of institutions and government policy in economic development and performance – a historical fact that emerges from the experience of individual economies. Different regions within a country form parts of 'open', nationally integrated regional economies with a single currency, exchange rate and monetary policy. The most important aspects of their fiscal policy are also decided at the national level. They share the same, nationally determined, laws and institutions. They are guided in their actions by a common ideology that incorporates many of the cultural traits that they have developed jointly over time. Together, these are the characteristics that define and distinguish individual 'nation' states.

As the preceding analysis shows, the ultimate goal of globalization is to reproduce a similar institutional framework, similar aspirations and similar behaviour globally. That being the case, the existing multi-regional states provide ready-made models of what a global economic and political union might look like under *different* conditions, institutions and policies. (See Panić 1988, Part V.) These differences are of crucial importance, as experience shows that some of these models have been much more successful in maximizing both social and private welfare. Many countries are still struggling with the problem of absolute poverty. At the other extreme, a small number of nations enjoy to an unprecedented extent all those benefits that optimists expect from globalization: affluence, social cohesion and political stability under democratic forms of government. It is also clear from historical evidence that in the case of individual countries all these characteristics tend to be much more in evidence in some periods of their history than in others.

For instance, income distribution was more equal in most industrial countries between the late 1940s and the early 1970s than either before or since. The same period also saw a significant, lasting convergence in efficiency and income levels between these countries and, to a lesser extent, between them and a number of rapidly growing economies at lower levels of development (Panić 1988, Dowrick and Nguyen 1989). Examples of international economic convergence among members of "The Club" were also in evidence during the classical gold standard (1880–1914). (See Panić 1992, Williamson 1998.)

All these developments coincided with periods of rapid economic growth in some parts of the world and increases in international economic integration.

It would be wrong, therefore, to conclude, as pessimists do, that greater international economic specialization and closer economic links between countries inevitably lead to economic stagnation and a widening gap between rich and poor. At the same time, it is also evident from the available evidence that these improvements in relative economic performance were experienced by a small group of countries during certain periods only. What all of them had in common is the fact that, in each case, the major improvements in the relative position of lower income groups and the less developed countries involved important institutional changes and large transfers of resources within and between countries, invariably with the active participation of the state. As Rodrik (1996) shows, there is a close relationship between the degree of openness and the size of the government sector. This relationship holds for both industrial and developing countries.

Nevertheless, despite theoretical analysis and empirical evidence that question or even deny its relevance, it is the neo-liberal approach, with its blend of the ideology of individualism and neoclassical economics, that now dominates the policy agenda. The 'Washington Consensus' advocates and promotes it; and international economic and financial institutions are imposing it on the countries under their influence with complete disregard for their level of development, beliefs, institutions and aspirations.

This raises an important question about the future course and sustainability of globalization. Neo-liberalism rests on a number of specific assumptions about the way that a completely decentralized economic model of capitalism operates, that is, the model in which all key economic decisions are made at the microeconomic level. How realistic are these assumptions when applied to the most important decision-making unit at this level: the business corporation? In other words, can corporations, with the vast resources under their control, ensure that the neo-liberal approach solves the highly complex economic and social problems that globalization creates by resolving conflicts of interest between different groups and countries to the benefit and satisfaction of all concerned?

The next section considers briefly these two questions with specific reference to the responsibilities and behaviour of modern business enterprises. It has little to say about the alternative approach in which the state plays a crucial role because some of the most important aspects of this for economic policy are analysed in the chapters that follow. The relevance of the next section is that it shows why it is necessary for the state to assume an active economic role in the process of globalization. The form of state organization most likely to perform such a function effectively is explored in the rest of this book.

1.6 Conflict resolution: the critical role of the state

A dynamic economic system such as capitalism, in which the creation and distribution of wealth is the outcome of continuous competition for scarce resources, power and prestige, is bound to generate conflicts of interest. This is true of individuals, corporations and countries – including social, racial and ethnic groups within individual states. The reason is that competition for command over productive resources, like any other form of competition, produces winners and losers. Some of the competing units end up being relatively worse off, despite the fact that the level of their real income and wealth is higher than before. Others experience absolute losses in economic welfare. What is more, the gains and losses are not necessarily of a short-term nature. The purpose of the competitive process is to enable the winners to secure command over productive resources (physical and human) that will give them a *long-term* competitive advantage.

The fact that the most dynamic of economic systems can generate both absolute and relative decline in economic well-being has its origin in three important aspects of its dynamics. Each will be exacerbated by globalization as it locks into the competitive process countries at different levels of development, with different cultures, problems, priorities and capacity for change.

First, capitalism is unique among economic systems in its wealth-destroying as well in its wealth-creating capacity. In fact, the process of creating new wealth involves the 'destruction' of many of the existing goods and services and the resources, including skills, that produce them. Some of these are made obsolete by important new inventions and innovations, the process that Schumpeter ([1943] 1961) called "creative destruction". But that is not the only reason. The need to maximize profits in order to survive and prosper in the competitive struggle means that relatively new, profit-making products and productive capacity are frequently scrapped and replaced by marginally improved alternatives. The hope is that the latter will generate higher profits, as their relative novelty and scarcity are expected to stimulate a significant increase in demand for existing products. The liberalization of trade speeds up the process of "creative destruction" by making it easier for superior foreign products and more efficient foreign firms to enter national markets, displacing domestic products and firms. This invariably creates structural problems that can be eliminated only in the long term. Even then, there is no guarantee that the losers will be re-absorbed into the economic system by uncoordinated actions at the microeconomic level in a way that will restore their well-being in either an absolute or a relative sense.

Second, macroeconomic shocks to the system, caused by unequal command over highly heterogeneous productive resources, conflicts of interest, imperfect information and poor co-ordination of interdependent actions at both the micro- and the macroeconomic levels (see Chapter 2), can result in even greater losses and waste of productive resources. Avoiding that, as Keynes (1936) demonstrated, requires stabilization policies to minimize short-term welfare losses and, more important, to prevent short-term instability and crises from turning cyclical disequilibria into long-term structural and political problems through their effect on investment and growth. Economic liberalization and deregulation make it increasingly difficult, for reasons analysed in the chapters that follow, to stabilize national economies. The result is higher risks and uncertainty, lower investment and, consequently, slower growth – all of which exacerbate structural problems.

Third, the system's dependence on the continuous creation of relative wants and the improvement in relative performance needed to sustain the profit maximizing rate of change through economic and social inequality, means that despite its enormous potential to produce wealth, capitalism can never satisfy the expectations and aspirations which it generates. Relative wants and standards, unlike their absolute equivalents, have no clearly definable upper limit. As Easterlin (2001) shows, aspirations grow with income. Hence, the fact that people are better off materially does not necessarily mean that they will be happier, more satisfied with their lot, than before. Other things remaining the same, widespread deregulation and liberalization will increase existing inequalities, partly because their benefits and costs will not be spread equally between different sectors and countries and partly because some skills are much more mobile internationally than others. Persistent inequalities require the redistribution of income and wealth through resource transfers in order to reduce them to socially acceptable levels.

Clearly, the dynamics of the system, with its competitive, uncoordinated nature, are bound to produce a far from insignificant number of losers, especially in periods of rapid technical or institutional change. (See Foster and Kaplan 2001.) Globalization requires both.

What is more, it tends to make the problems just described worse by promoting a similarity of wants in conditions under which there is great inequality in the capacity to satisfy them. International comparisons of social attitudes and aspirations show little difference between countries in the economic goals that their populations desire: high levels of employment and job security, sustainable growth, price stability and an equitable distribution of income. More broadly, as Goodin *et al.* (1999, p. 23) put it: "Low poverty rates, social stability, social integration and – most important – high economic growth rates are all goals that are internalized by [capitalist] welfare regimes of all sorts. So too are freedom and equality."

The prevailing, neo-liberal view (supported by the 'Washington Consensus') is that these goals can be achieved efficiently only if the business corporation, the most important unit of microeconomic organization in modern capitalism, is allowed to operate with the minimum of social restraint within, to borrow Ohmae's description, "a borderless world". The underlying assumption is that if the state retreats into a 'neutral' role, or becomes no more than a 'night watchman', business enterprises, especially TNEs, will employ their resources in ways that maximize individual, national and international welfare.

Given the resources at their disposal, there is little doubt that, collectively, TNEs in particular have the potential to make a significant contribution to economic growth – especially to the transformation of developing economies. As the UNCTC (1992) points out, they can do this in a number of ways. First, they can make a significant contribution to the levels of savings and investment, both of which are severely suboptimal in developing economies. Second, they are one of the most effective channels for the international dissemination of technical knowledge and information, as this kind of activity at the industry level tends to originate within individual enterprises and, consequently, tends to be firm specific. Third, by training their employees in superior technical, managerial, financial, marketing and administrative skills they can make a significant contribution to improving a country's human capital and, in this way, contribute to sustainable, long-term, increases in its productivity and standard of living. Finally, they can enhance the country's economic welfare by enabling it to participate on advantageous terms in the international division of labour. (All these arguments assume that TNEs will observe the rules and regulations designed to protect the environment, so ensuring that economic progress is sustainable.)

There are, however, a number of serious shortcomings in the neo-liberal approach to economic policy. To begin with, it confuses the partial with the general. TNEs and other privately owned 'free enterprises' can and do improve, often significantly, the well-being of a particular group of individuals directly associated with them. But that does not mean that their actions will be sufficient to improve the economic welfare of all. The reason for this is that the approach ignores the institutional framework, constraints and limited social obligations under which such enterprises operate. It is only by ignoring these factors that the neo-liberal policy prescriptions can be justified in conjuring up the perfectly competitive (equal opportunity) economic model, even though those who advocate these policies could hardly dispute the existence of TNEs and other oligopolies that dominate modern economic activity.

In order to argue that it is unnecessary, even counter-productive, for states to become involved in the management of their economies, neo-liberals have to rely on a number of heroic assumptions (in addition to those listed in the previous section) that underpin neoclassical economics. Together, these assumptions describe a 'perfectly competitive' world from which negative externalities, 'monopoly' (that is, market) power and public goods are absent, all individuals are fully informed about the choices open to them, capital and labour are perfectly mobile, and property rights are perfectly defined and costlessly enforced. (See Helm 1990.)

Yet, by admitting the existence of 'market failures' (cf. Bator 1958), mainstream economic theory implicitly recognizes that none of these conditions is satisfied in practice. The reason for this becomes obvious even from a brief consideration of the institutional responsibilities and constraints, invariably ignored by the theory, under which modern privately owned business enterprises operate.

The most effective way to do this is to employ an analytical framework that incorporates the four factors that determine the nature of all types of collective action by defining their *raison d'être*, form of organization and *modus operandi*. These are: **accountability** (in whose interest is an organization required to act and to whom it is, therefore, ultimately responsible for its decisions); **domain** (the area or sphere over which it has direct control); the **resources** (human, material and financial at its disposal, which define its capacity to undertake a specific course of action); and **governance** (the system of effective authority and control exercised by those who run the organization and those to whom they are directly accountable).

In principle, the question of *corporate accountability* under capitalism could not be more straightforward: unless they happen to be the same individuals, those who control and run a business enterprise are accountable to its legal owners, the shareholders. Their main responsibility – and, therefore, the most important corporate objective – follows directly from this: to maximize total return (capital value plus income) on the shareholders' equity, as that is the reason why the stockholders have invested their savings in the company. (Failure to achieve the main objective will encourage the shareholders to switch their investment elsewhere, thus threatening the very existence of the enterprise as an independent entity, including the employment, remuneration and future prospects of its management.) At the same time, provided that the main objective is achieved within the laws of the land, that is as far as corporate responsibility for wider economic welfare goes. In other words, it is not the duty of business enterprises to look after the losers produced by the competitive process. To impose such a requirement on them would be an infringement of the owners' effective property rights and would, therefore, be incompatible with the nature and *modus operandi* of the system.

Not surprisingly, neo-liberals regard the idea that private enterprises should be responsible both to their owners and to society as being, in the words of Milton Friedman (1962, p. 133), "fundamentally subversive". In Friedman's view: "Few trends could so thoroughly undermine the very foundations of our free society as the acceptance by corporate officials of a social responsibility other than to make as much money for their stockholders as possible" (*ibid.*). International organizations might not go that far, but most of them would, no doubt, agree with the OECD (1999) that the main responsibility of business corporations is to their shareholders. (UNCTAD 1994, Chapter viii, takes a wider, more inclusive view.)

The problem with these definitions of corporate accountability and responsibility is that there is more than one way to maximize profits; and not all of them improve social well being, despite the fact that they may greatly enhance private economic welfare. Those that fail to do so raise serious issues of both equity and efficiency.

For instance, the return on shareholders' investment can be maximized by improving efficiency through investment in physical and human capital, which will also raise real wages. Provided that all costs of production are internal to firms and that real wages and salaries rise while employment either remains the same (under full employment) or grows, there will be an improvement – in absolute, though not necessarily in relative terms – in both private and social welfare. (Imperfect competition in product and factor markets, unequal bargaining power, and differences in labour productivity will ensure that, *ceteris paribus*, the gains are unequally distributed. See Goodin *et al.* 1999 for empirical evidence.)

However, the outcome is radically different if high profits depend predominantly, as has increasingly been the case since the early 1980s, on reducing costs by passing them on to the community – that is, by externalizing them. This can take different forms: higher unemployment, ecological degradation, the lowering of health and safety standards, a reduction in real wages to levels that are too low to maintain basic health standards, dismissal of employees whose health is affected by these changes without proper compensation, and so on. In this case, the winners achieve both absolute and relative gains in their real income and wealth at the expense of the losers – a classic example of the zero-sum game outcome.

In a world of closed economies the extent to which firms can externalize their costs would depend entirely on the willingness and ability of the state to prevent such practices. Globalization diminishes the effectiveness of state action by making it possible for TNEs to transfer their operations to a country where the regulatory authorities are either weak or non-existent. This obviously increases the return on shareholders' investment and managers' incomes – achieved by imposing higher net social costs on the countries concerned.

In fact, the widespread practice of externalizing costs creates a difficulty of fundamental, systemic importance for advocates of the neo-liberal approach to globalization. Their argument, rooted in neoclassical economics, rests on the proposition that once firms are freed from the shackles of national regulation they will be able to maximize economic welfare by allocating global resources more efficiently. The reason for this is that the price of their products will now reflect the *real* costs of production – *all* of which are assumed to be *internal* to the firm. What happens, however, if this important condition is not satisfied? The very same neoclassical analysis shows that the outcome will be exactly the reverse of that suggested by the neo-liberals! Other things remaining the same, the greater the freedom to externalize costs, the greater the likelihood that scarce global resources will be irreversibly misallocated, as prices will reflect the private rather than the full social costs of production!

The importance of the *corporate domain* (that is, the area of economic activity over which a firm has full control) stems directly from the nature of a firm's accountability and responsibility.

The ability of a business enterprise to achieve the objective of maximizing profits depends, in addition to its relative efficiency, on its market power: its size relative to other firms in the market and the uniqueness of its products. The concentration and diversity of resources at the disposal of large firms gives them considerable influence over their suppliers, developments in their own and related industries, as well as over economic and social policy in general. The uniqueness of a firm's brand of products, on the other hand, increases its freedom to manipulate their price and quantity in order to maximize profits. The more distinct (differentiated) its products, the lower is their price elasticity of demand – enabling the firm to keep its prices unchanged, or even to raise them, in a recession in order to protect its profits. As a result, the firm will have considerable market power that can be exploited to increase narrow personal or sectarian income and wealth by restricting output in order to keep prices and profits high. Adam Smith warned against the danger of this long before Marx.

The freedom to pursue goals of personal wealth, influence and prestige under capitalism, analysed earlier, and the scope for misusing it make it essential for the society to control the size of the domain over which corporate power can be exercised directly. The result is national laws and regulations designed to promote competition by forbidding cartels and restricting the growth of large firms in order to prevent them from gaining monopoly power. Provided that the state is willing and able to use its own power, such rules and laws may be enforced effectively in a world of closed economies, since those who control productive resources are prevented from transferring them to other countries.

Globalization reduces the effectiveness of such controls for two reasons. First, an enterprise that is large by national standards, exercising considerable market power within its own country, may turn out to be no more than a small to medium-sized participant in a unified international market. As a result, governments will tend to relax the existing competition laws and regulations, as many of them have done since the 1970s, to enable national firms to increase in size in order to survive and compete effectively against much larger foreign competitors. Second, even if national governments continue to enforce their laws against monopolies and cartels rigorously, globalization makes it possible for individual firms to increase greatly the size of their overall domain. They are able to do this through international mergers, acquisitions and 'green field' investments while, at the same time, strictly observing the laws and regulations in each of the countries in which their activities are located. In this way, TNEs can continue to grow by exploiting the large size of the world market while retaining full control over their specific comparative advantages.

The sheer size of resources that transnational oligopolies can accumulate in this way, and the cost in lost output, employment, trade and income if they move their operations to another country, gives them the power to influence national policies that affect their interests. When necessary this influence can be used to prevent national governments from dealing effectively, through taxation and regulatory activities, with the kind of negative externalities described earlier. As a result, the acquisition of market power, made possible by the deregulation and liberalization of trade and capital movements, is likely to exacerbate further the impact of negative externalities on the efficiency of global allocation of resources and on both national and international income distribution.

The size of a firm's domain is clearly not in itself an end or even the means to achieving the end of maximizing the return on shareholders' investment. Its importance lies in the unified organization and control of the means, *corporate resources*, in the way that is most likely to bring about such an outcome: by internalizing as many of the strategically important resources and activities as those who run the firm are able or allowed to do. If they succeed they will reduce transaction costs and acquire the capability to respond more rapidly and effectively to unanticipated actions of competitors or governments.

Most of the issues and their policy implications raised by the unequal distribution of corporate and other resources have already been covered in this chapter. They are also analysed much more fully in the chapters that follow. It is therefore sufficient here to summarize some of them briefly. Their relevance to the main argument in this section is that they (a) contradict the assumptions on which the neo-liberal analysis rests, and (b) make it extremely unlikely that, in the absence of active government assistance, TNEs will act as 'engines of growth' in developing countries.

For example, the combination of corporate accountability and the predominance of oligopolistic competition makes the existence of asymmetric information unavoidable. Success in the competitive struggle depends on the ability of an enterprise to acquire, at substantial cost, knowledge and R&D capabilities that are exclusive to that enterprise. It is therefore perfectly rational for firms, having secured such an advantage, to make a considerable effort to protect it through patents, secrecy about their true performance and long term plans, trademarks and other intellectual property rights (see Cornish 1999). As experience since the 1980s shows, such efforts intensify when technical progress reaches the frontiers of existing knowledge, increasing sharply the cost of R&D and the risk of failure. This restricts the dissemination of commercially valuable information between individuals, enterprises and countries – with an adverse effect on the efficiency of the global allocation of resources.

Such inequalities in corporate and national capacity to achieve their objectives are re-enforced by the fact that in complex, highly industrialized societies it is impossible for individuals, firms and consequently countries to be fully informed of the choices open to them. The disparities arise partly because of differences in the existing levels of human capital and partly because of differences in the ability to attract and keep individuals with the required knowledge and skills, especially if the latter are in short supply.

Large corporations and highly industrialized countries have a clear advantage in this respect thanks to their ability to offer a level of remuneration, opportunities for work and further development, and quality of life that small firms and developing countries cannot match. As a result of all these differences, labour mobility, far from being perfect, is restricted by differences in knowledge and skills as well as by significant disparities in conditions of employment. Globalization re-enforces these differences by widening the gap between net private returns to internationally mobile labour and net social returns to the countries affected by its movement. The reason for this is obvious: those with scarce knowledge and skills will tend to move to those occupations and countries where the private return on their labour is relatively high. As these happen to be the countries in which such labour is 'abundant', the social return on their services will be lower than it would be in developing countries.

The same, private welfare maximizing, type of behaviour also ensures that the global allocation of scarce capital resources follows the same pattern, with even greater consequences for the short-term stability and long-term development of national economies. As in the case of labour, the conflict between private and social interests arises despite the fact that the enterprises involved are acting both rationally and legally in the pursuit of their corporate goals – that is, within the rules of behaviour demanded and sanctioned in a capitalist economy. Hence, far from reflecting 'market failures' caused by microeconomic agents disregarding the basic tenets of capitalism, the failure to maximize social welfare stems directly from fundamental deficiencies in the nature and *modus operandi* of the system.

There are several examples of this in the allocation and use of capital resources, one of which has already been analysed: the tendency of TNEs to concentrate their productive capacity predominantly in the most advanced economies. Such an allocation of resources may be sub-optimal from a social, global point of view. But it is the most efficient way of maximizing the welfare of those who own and run these enterprises. It is therefore hardly surprising that most global saving is generated in these countries and that most global investment takes place in them.

The timing of investment decisions within an economy creates a similar divergence of interests. No rationally managed firm will increase its productive capacity in conditions of low capacity utilization and return on capital, high unemployment and uncertainty about long term economic prospects. If these problems are widespread, lower investment will reduce aggregate demand, plunging the economy into even deeper recession. As the Japanese experience since the early 1990s has shown, a reduction in demand for loanable funds and lower interest rates will fail to reverse corporate investment behaviour unless there is a dramatic change in business expectations. If this happens there will be a frantic race to increase investment – with the 'herd' behaviour generating higher levels of employment, income and expenditure and leading eventually to an unsustainable investment boom.

There is nothing in corporate behaviour, therefore, to guarantee automatic economic stabilization, for the simple reason that in conditions of uncertainty and instability it becomes essential for the survival and long-term competitive advantage of firms to adjust their operations in a way that exacerbates that instability!

In fact, the destabilizing effect of the allocation and use of capital resources is even greater if one extends the analysis to include financial as well as real assets. All firms invariably hold a certain proportion of their assets in liquid form. Some of this 'liquidity' is required for transaction purposes. The rest is needed for precautionary reasons, as liquidity provides firms with the freedom to react rapidly to unforeseen threats and opportunities. Not surprisingly, its importance increases in conditions of uncertainty, as the lower the volume of investment in productive capacity, other things remaining the same, the higher will be the volume of liquid assets held by firms. It is then the task of management to protect and, if possible, increase their real worth by investing in those financial instruments which offer and/or promise the highest returns, provided of course that the risks are comparable. If economies are open but do not share a single currency within a unified monetary system, the funds will move between assets in different currencies, frequently creating international financial instability and crises followed by large, permanent losses in economic welfare. (See Chapters 6, 8 and 9, and Kindleberger 1978b.)

Finally, there is a whole range of goods and services ('public goods') of strategic importance for economic development and social well being in which the vast resources under corporate control will either not be invested at all or they will be invested in a socially sub-optimal form. The first group includes the so-called 'pure' public goods such as defence, law enforcement, street lighting and clearing up air pollution. The reason why no firm will undertake to provide such a good is that its domain is too small to enable it to force those who enjoy the benefits to pay for them. Equally, it cannot exclude those unwilling or unable to pay from 'consuming' the good. The second group consists of the quasi public goods (for example, healthcare, education and housing) the provision of which can be restricted to those who are willing and able to pay for them, thus excluding those who cannot or refuse to pay. The problem is that if these goods are provided only by private investors, their quality and/or quantity will invariably be insufficient to meet social needs. (See Atkinson and Stiglitz 1980.)

The neo-liberal case is weakened further by changes in the ideology and effectiveness of *corporate governance* since the early 1980s that·raise serious doubts about the extent to which modern corporate businesses are run in the shareholders' interests.

An important assumption behind the neo-liberal case for the superior performance of deregulated, 'free' enterprises is that senior corporate executives will maximize the return on shareholders' investment because two important aspects of corporate governance ensure that they do so. First, shareholders are able to monitor and supervise executives, and to dispense promptly with their services if they are unsatisfactory. Second, there is an effective system of internal control that makes it possible for the executives to monitor and supervise the actions of the staff, dismissing those whose performance is not up to the required standard.

The problem of internal control is a surprisingly neglected aspect of managerial diseconomies of scale, as economists have concentrated their attention on the rising costs of bureaucracy and co-ordination that accompany the growth of firms. Yet the cost of corporate failure caused by deficiencies in internal control is ultimately likely to be much higher to all concerned: employees (who will lose jobs), shareholders (who may lose their life savings) and society at large (as it will have to deal with consequences of the failure). The risk is particularly high in the financial sector, as shown by the increasing incidence in recent years of bank failures, or near failures. (See Chapter 9.) There are two important reasons for this, both of which can be traced to financial deregulation and the liberalization of international capital flows. First, the proliferation of financial instruments and the speed of computerized transactions give considerable scope to relatively junior members of staff to misuse investors' funds for personal gain. Second, the transnationalization of international finance makes it difficult for executives to monitor and control the actions of staff in their overseas branches and affiliates.

In contrast, the fact that the separation of corporate ownership from control provides business executives with the opportunity to maximize their own rather than the owners' utility has received a good deal of attention since Berle and Means (1932) drew attention to the problem. The most obvious reason for this is that the two sides are not equally informed about the true performance and future prospects of the enterprise. Shareholders have neither the time nor the resources to monitor closely what executives are doing. Even if they could, the sheer number of shareholders, each of whom is likely to own no more than a small fraction of a large corporation, would make it virtually impossible to mobilize quickly sufficient support for the prompt censure or sacking of senior executives. To complicate matters further, the proliferation of equity sharing, corporate alliances and joint ventures makes it increasingly difficult to be sure who exactly owns what. By encouraging corporate growth and operations across national frontiers, globalization increases these problems and hence the risk of capital losses if shareholders fail to respond quickly to an expected deterioration in corporate performance by selling their shares.

The reason why executives tend to hold back information at their disposal is usually either because it is commercially sensitive or in order to protect their own position, especially if the firm's performance is deteriorating relative to that of its competitors. To make matters worse, outsiders who are aware of the true financial position of a large corporation (for example auditors and financial institutions) may be reluctant to reveal this because it could cost them lucrative business. With the rise of plutocracy, politicians who owe their office to the financial support of large enterprises may put considerable pressure on the regulatory authorities to ignore corporate malpractice. The collapse of ENRON in 2001, resulting in the largest bankruptcy in US commercial history, revealed all these weaknesses in corporate governance and the danger that they pose to the interests of both employees and shareholders.

The alternative, (for example the German model, which has been adopted in a number of countries, including Japan) is to involve large creditors such as investment banks directly in monitoring and supervision of corporate performance. Empirical studies show that this approach to corporate governance tends to produce a better long-term performance than the Anglo-American system described above, which relies on the stock market (cf. Cosh *et al.* 1990, Porter 1992). The danger is that either through negligence or "corporate cronyism" (also common in the Anglo-American system) supervisors may fail to discharge their responsibilities, leading to the sudden collapse of long-established and highly successful corporations (for example Swissair in 2001).

The danger of such weaknesses in corporate governance is that they can set in motion a vicious circle of decline and failure that extends beyond the individual firm. The risk of this is particularly great in the conditions of instability and uncertainty that are common in *laissez-faire* capitalism. A combination of instability and imperfect information encourages shareholders to take a short-term view, selling their equity at the first sign that the return on it may fall below market expectations, thus bringing down share prices and the value of the capital invested. The greater the number of investors who react in this way, the greater the fall in equity prices, with consequences that may extend far beyond the shareholders' immediate concerns.

If the fall is significant it will increase the risk of takeover, threatening the employment and income of the executives. This threat, together with uncertainty about long-term prospects and the rising cost of R&D – both of which have increased markedly since the 1980s – will, in turn, make it too risky to take a long-term view by investing heavily in physical and human capital. (See Hayes and Abernathy 1980, Stein 1988.) Hence, instead of increasing productive capacity, they will engage in corporate 'downsizing' by shedding labour and less profitable capacity to reduce costs and maximize short-term profits (Lazonick and O'Sullivan 2000). Apart from keeping the shareholders contented, this also suits their own personal interests as a high proportion of senior executives' remuneration consists of share options in the company they run.

The problem is that this strategy cannot be pursued for long without putting corporate viability and long-term survival at risk. It is hardly surprising, therefore, that senior executives in particular not only operate with short-term horizons but also increasingly tend to make only a short-term commitment to the corporations that employ them. The fact that their contracts usually include 'loyalty bonuses' ensures that, unlike the employees and shareholders, they cannot lose – irrespective of what happens to the firm during their tenure!

As a result, with the growth of corporate domains vast productive resources are increasingly entrusted to a small number of individuals who are pursuing their own interests and effectively are accountable to no one! The transnationalization of corporate businesses inevitably reduces the ability of both shareholders and national governments to monitor and supervise their actions. According to Lazonick and O' Sullivan (2000, p. 33): "The experience of the United States suggests that the pursuit of shareholders' value [via short-term profit maximization through downsizing] may be an appropriate strategy for running down a company and an economy. The pursuit of [a different] kind of value is needed to build up a company and an economy."

Clearly, there is nothing in the way that modern business enterprises operate to ensure that, in the absence of government involvement in economic activity, their actions will improve national economic welfare permanently. In fact, recent developments in corporate governance raise serious doubts about the ability of the neo-liberal approach promoted by the 'Washington Consensus' to improve, or even maintain, shareholders' income and wealth in the long run. As in the case of labour, changes in the way that capitalist economies operate, brought about by deregulation and liberalization, are not necessarily in the interest of 'capital' – only some forms of it.

This raises an important question for the long-term success and survival of capitalism and, therefore, of globalization: is it possible to correct the serious flaws inherent in the system (described briefly in this section) by reconciling its economic dynamics with social needs and aspirations?

Neo-liberals have a standard, ready-made answer to this question, provided by neoclassical economics. Actions by microeconomic agents will achieve such an outcome automatically if the government ensures that there is a high degree of competition. The snag is that a 'high degree' of competition is not enough to eliminate market failure unless all economic agents have at their disposal no more than a small amount of resources – both physical and intellectual – relative to the total available. (See Roberts and Postlewaite, 1976.) It is only if this condition is satisfied – that is, the condition that would exist under perfect competition – that 'price makers' become 'price takers' unable to manipulate the market and the general economic environment to their advantage. In other words, as already pointed out, it is a utopian world in which equality of opportunity reigns ensuring, through the competitive process, equality of outcome in the long run.

It requires little reflection to realize that to implement such a policy prescription literally at the present level of industrialization would require corporate fragmentation/ atomization and intellectual amnesia on a monumental scale. Moreover, as such a policy would have to be applied by force, the result would be a form of government that was no less oppressive than that which destroyed the socialist experiment in Eastern Europe. (See Chapter 4.) As a highly successful financier and self-made billionaire has observed: "…the misuse of scientific theories for political purpose is not confined to totalitarian ideologies; it applies to market fundamentalism with equal force. Classical economic theory is as easily misused for political purposes as…Marxist theory" (Soros 2000, p. 45).

Realistically, this leaves only one course of action that can ensure that capitalism will realize widely desired economic and social objectives: for government to manage and regulate the economy in a way that maximizes both private and social welfare. The experience during the third quarter of the twentieth century when industrial countries, especially those in Western Europe, managed to achieve this has been called nostalgically, though justifiably, "the golden age of capitalism". (See Maddison 1995, Boltho 1982, Marglin and Schor 1990, Chang 2002.) Goodin *et al.* (1999) show in their analysis of a unique set of panel data from Germany, the Netherlands and the United States that the superiority of economic and social performance of the social democratic over the liberal model continued into the 1980s and 1990s. This is indirectly confirmed also by surveys of economic literature that show how inequality has an adverse effect on economic volatility and growth by increasing social and political instability (see for example Alesina and Perotti 1996, Aghion *et al.* 1999).

The fact that the executive arm of the state, the government, has to play a crucial role in the socio-economic development of nations does not mean, of course, that all governments will undertake such a responsibility or that, if they try, they will do so successfully. As in the case of business corporations, their performance will be determined by four factors: accountability, domain, the physical and human resources at their disposal, and the form of governance adopted by individual countries.

However, as the extent of their accountability is vastly different, the relationship between the size of state and corporate domains and resources is of vital importance. The state cannot fulfil its socio-economic responsibilities, and in this way ensure that the existing economic order is sustainable, unless its political domain is at least equal in size to its economic domain. That is why no international economic system has been able to survive for long when, as a result of actions at the microeconomic level, the economic domain expands significantly beyond the boundaries of the individual states that comprise it. If this happens, the only way to achieve lasting economic, social and political stability is either to expand the political domain (by creating a supranational state) or to reduce the economic domain (by reverting to economic insularity, as in the 1930s).

The institutional and policy aspects of all these factors are analysed in the chapters that follow (especially in Part II and Chapters 10 and 11). However, it is only natural that in essays written by an economist, exploiting his comparative advantage, the emphasis is on *economic* organization, policy and performance. At the same time, it is impossible to analyse these issues in a meaningful way if one ignores the extent to which governments take into account the 'general will' of the population when formulating and implementing their economic and social policies. "Whether and how a government responds to needs and sufferings may well depend on how much pressure is put on it, and the exercise of political rights (such as voting, criticizing, protesting, and so on) can make a real difference" (Sen 1999a, p. 92. See also Frey and Stutzer 2000, Swank 2002). Empirical studies suggest that the form and quality of governance are highly significant in explaining why even among democracies and elective plutocracies some countries have much more successful economies than others. (See Sen 1999b, Dollar and Svensson 2000, Olson *et al.* 2000, Persson *et al.* 2000.)

For all these reasons, one of the key issues in any analysis of globalization must be the extent to which the conditions and institutional frameworks that have been successful in minimizing the systemic flaws and social costs of capitalism within countries can be recreated internationally. Unless this can be achieved, the costs of globalization will exceed the benefits, making it unsustainable in the long term.

1.7 Conclusion

Globalization is much more than the relatively simple concept of international specialization and trade that has received so much attention since the eighteenth century, for the process currently in progress involves nothing less than a combination of international economic integration *and* cultural (in the broadest sense) harmonization. It may be driven now, as in the past, primarily by economic considerations. The important difference stems from the dominant role that transnational enterprises play in globalization. As they operate in different countries, it is essential for them that the uncertainties and risks posed by national differences in beliefs, values and institutions be removed; and unlike national firms they have the bargaining power to ensure that governments introduce the necessary changes. Hence, it is the rise of transnationals, made possible by rapid advances in transport and communications, that makes globalization a genuinely new phenomenon that in one form or another affects virtually every country in the world.

To understand what is happening it is imperative, therefore, to understand the dynamics of capitalism, as both transnationals and, through them, globalization are essentially a spontaneous outcome of long-term changes that take place within the system. The reason for this is that although international specialization, trade and cultural assimilation take place under all economic systems, the forces that generate *globalization* are possible only under capitalism. Among all the major economic systems that have existed so far, capitalism is the only one in which economic activity is separated, as a matter of principle, from direct political control. This separation ensures that the private interests of powerful economic agents take precedence over wider social interests; and it is this pursuit of private interests that provides almost limitless scope for globalization. The snag is that, in absence of major institutional changes to the system, it also makes it unsustainable in the long term.

Globalization promotes a similarity of wants in conditions where there are vast differences in the capacity to satisfy them. Far from removing these differences, the competitive process unleashed by globalization exacerbates them, widening the gap between winners and losers, making it unsustainable in the long run. In other words, the very processes responsible for the extraordinary dynamics of capitalism are also responsible for making it highly unstable in the absence of institutional reforms to reconcile its competitive dynamics with wider social needs and aspirations.

The great challenge of globalization is therefore to reproduce *internationally* a form of socio-political organization that is similar to those in the countries that have achieved a high level of individual and social well being, by reducing the conflict of interests inherent in the system. This is possible only through a more equitable distribution of the gains from economic progress. As Keynes ([1926] 1972, p. 33) wrote in a different context, although "in itself it is in many ways extremely objectionable ... capitalism, wisely managed, can probably be made more efficient for attaining economic ends than any alternative system yet in sight ..." The problem is "to work out a social organization" that will reconcile a high level of efficiency with "a satisfactory way of life" (*ibid.*)

Historically, failure "to work out" such a form of organization internationally has been extremely costly. In 1912 a respected economist argued that the international economy had become so interdependent that national independence was an anachronism. As this interdependence was achieved by markets rather than governments, war between modern industrial states would inflict such heavy costs on all the combatants that it would be "futile – useless even when completely victorious" (Angell 1912, pp. v–vi). Angell's book, translated into many languages, met with general approval, even acclaim, in countries such as Britain, France, Germany, Russia and the United States. Less than two years later, these and other industrial countries were locked in what at the time was the most savage and destructive military conflict in history!

Part II

The Dynamics of Macroeconomic Organization

2
Economic Progress and Organization in Capitalist Economies*

2.1 Division of labour and the need for collective action

As economic processes become more and more specialized and divided, people become increasingly separated, both geographically and in their understanding of each other's problems, aspirations and skills. It is, therefore, in the very nature of the continuous specialization and segmentation of production and distribution processes that they increase the problem of communication and, thus, the risk of failure. The ability to achieve a particular economic objective depends increasingly on the compatibility and timing of a vast number of seemingly unrelated actions carried out by a large number of people. Yet most of these people frequently have no idea that they are working towards the same goal for the very simple reason that they are not even aware of each other's existence! To complicate matters further, in the absence of coercion no objective can be attained unless it is, first of all, accepted by those whose participation is essential for its realization.

For all these reasons, the division of labour is bound to create a good deal of uncertainty; and under these conditions "the actual execution of activity becomes in a real sense a secondary part of life; the primary problem or function is deciding what to do and how to do it" (Knight 1921, p. 268). In other words, in an uncertain world it becomes essential to find ways of: (a) securing agreement about the type of action required to deal with unanticipated events; and (b) ensuring that those involved in the activities which form part of an integrated chain in the wealth-creating process have some idea of what other groups participating in the same chain are doing, as well as of what they intend to do.

It is preoccupations of this kind that give rise to different forms of administrative control, the main aim of which is to reduce uncertainty and the risk

---

* This chapter was previously published (without sub-headings) in M. Panić, *National Management of the International Economy*, Macmillan, London, and St Martin's Press, New York, 1988, pp. 261–82.

of failure. As the size and complexity of the production chain grows, those in charge of various economic entities within the chain will try to minimize uncertainty by assuming control over an increasing number of factors which are of strategic importance in the pursuit of their long-term objectives. The form that this control takes, and the flexibility with which it responds to the needs for co-ordination created by technical and economic change, will determine in the end the success or failure of an economic strategy. It is for this reason that the organization of economic activity will have an important effect on economic performance (Chandler 1962 and 1977, Davis and North 1971); and continuous success in economic performance will, eventually, require a reorganization of economic activity. Under dynamic conditions, the very success in solving a problem and attaining a particular objective will give rise to new problems and, consequently, new objectives.

This is why there are important similarities at all levels of economic activity in the evolution of their economic organization. Each of them ('micro' and 'macro') represents a particular form of *collective* action, the only way in which economic activity can take place once people begin to specialize so that different individuals and groups perform different tasks.

2.2   Growth and organization at the firm level

Organizational problems which result from the complexity and uncertainty created by the division of labour are apparent already at the level of the 'firm', the micro-economic unit of collective action. The firm accomplishes its objectives through a fairly intricate division of labour that in many ways represents a microcosm of modern industrial society. Hence, an understanding of developments in its internal organization, of the structure of its industry, and of the way that these two determine the pattern of its behaviour, makes it easier also to appreciate the evolution that much more complex forms of economic organization, such as those at the national and international levels, have to take.

New industries usually start with a relatively large number of producers, all offering slightly different varieties of the same type of product. However, with time, some of them will prove to be much more resilient than others as a result of their engineering, marketing, financial or managerial superiority. Consequently, they will expand their operations both by internal growth and by taking over their less successful competitors. The increase in the scale of output of successful companies will be accompanied by increased specialization within them, within the industry in which they operate and within the industries closely related to it. The reason for this is that the "capacity to buy depends upon the capacity to produce", or in other words, "the division of labour depends in large part upon the division of labour" (Young 1928, p. 533). As the proliferation and complexity of production grows, the number of functions that have to be performed in order to ensure the success of the production process (engineering, research and development, marketing, finance and others) multiply. The problem of co-ordinating these numerous activities becomes acute. It is in the process of such changes that personal contacts will give place increasingly to impersonal, legal contracts. This becomes essential in order to ensure the required flow of goods and services that the firm needs if it is to achieve its objectives. However, the success of the contractual arrangements will depend on the frequency with which transactions between different producers take place; the extent to which these transactions depend on long-term investment made especially for the purpose; and the uncertainty to which such transactions are subject (Williamson 1975 and 1979). The greater the uncertainty the more difficult it becomes to incorporate a wider range of possible outcomes into a contract so that it remains acceptable to the parties over a long period. The alternative is short-term contracts, which would make the contractual arrangements much more flexible. Their most serious disadvantage, however, is that they make long-term corporate planning and, consequently, long-term investment decisions extremely difficult.

These problems multiply as the complexity of an industry increases and different stages of production are carried out by a multitude of highly specialized, independent producers. For instance, there is the growing problem of obtaining information about the past performance and future intentions of individual enterprises. More and more time has to be spent in bargaining. The risk that contracts might not be fulfilled, or that they might not be completed on time, increases. At the same time, there is a lack of machinery for resolving quickly the conflicts between different organizations.

The result of all these complications is an increase in delays, uncertainty and, therefore, production costs. Even worse, from the point of view of a firm, these developments restrict its freedom of action, its ability to respond rapidly to the changes and shocks that take place continuously in a dynamic environment.

It is in order to avoid many of these problems that, as the division of labour increases, firms will begin to 'internalize' more and more of the functions and production processes which are of strategic importance for the achievement of their objectives (Coase 1937, Williamson 1971). That is, to minimize the transaction costs, internal organization and planning will take the place of market exchange. The integration of different activities within one firm harmonizes conflicting interests – or at least reconciles the differences, by fiat if necessary – and in this way makes it possible for the firm to initiate innovations and changes, as well as to react promptly to changes introduced by its competitors.

How far the process can continue will depend to a significant extent on the development and efficiency of the system of transport and communications. Writing in the 1930s Austin Robinson suggested that uncertainty would limit the size of a firm because communications – and, thus, a quick response to unforeseen developments – would be more difficult in a large than in a small firm (Robinson 1935). The immense progress in this area since then, especially since the 1950s, has reduced greatly the 'uncertainty barrier' to the growth of firms. In fact, recent developments in transport and communications have enabled firms to internalize not only different types of activity but also activities located in different regions of a country as well as in different parts of the world. This is one of the main reasons for the phenomenal growth of transnational enterprises since the 1950s. In other words, industrial firms, banks and other corporate entities have been able to grow by exploiting the large size of the world market, while at the same time remaining in full control of their 'ownership specific' advantages, notably their technical, financial and managerial superiority.

Another development that has enabled firms to diversify their activities across industries and countries has been the evolution of the multidivisional structure of organization, a result of the growth of individual firms described above (Williamson 1975 and 1981). Beyond a certain level of growth and specialization in a firm, managerial diseconomies of scale set in. Those responsible for running the enterprise have to make an increasing number of highly complex decisions, while at the same time becoming more and more removed from the levels of, say, the production and marketing processes at which these decisions have to be implemented. If the hierarchical structure is highly centralized, the efficiency of the whole enterprise will be reduced by the delays and mistakes, as the problems which require attention, and the subsequent decisions, pass through numerous levels of the hierarchy. The shortcoming is particularly serious in a rapidly changing and uncertain environment when top management is required to deal with all sorts of novel problems that require prompt decisions and actions. The cost of overcentralization is reduced greatly by decentralizing the decision-making process along divisional lines.

However, functions which firms rarely, if ever, decentralize are those that involve fixed capital expenditure above a certain nominal sum. The main reason for this is that the decisions made about:

> the long-term uses of capital are both the means and the determinants of the directions the overall enterprise will be taking. It is a matter of the prospective best use of the corporation's capital resources in which the planning horizon involves a decade or more.... No division has the appropriate scope or the time perspective to make these decisions. (Hefleblower 1960, p. 13)

In other words, the board of directors of a modern corporation is concerned with the long-term strategy of the enterprise, not the day-to-day management and administration. As the responsibilities become narrower, down the hierarchical structure of a corporation, the time horizons of the decision-making process also becomes shorter.

The main advantage of this kind of executive division of labour is that it enables a firm to 'internalize' a large number of different activities, and in this way to co-ordinate them within a coherent, long-term strategy which reduces at least some of the uncertainty and risks that its decision makers have to face. The firm becomes able, therefore, to react speedily to a changing environment. This ensures its survival as well as its long-term success and growth. At the same time, its subdivisions also derive an important advantage from these arrangements by:

> being able to draw on the overall resources of the corporation [so] that the division can, if its case is strong, get more capital than it would generate internally were it an autonomous enterprise. Indeed, from the common fund it may be able to obtain more funds than it would acquire in the market and on more favourable terms. (*ibid.*)

2.3 Oligopolies and *intra*-industry co-ordination of corporate activity

However, while one firm can internalize some highly integrated operations, both across industries and national frontiers, it cannot internalize all of them. The huge scale of most modern industries, managerial diseconomies, the limited resources at the disposal of a firm and anti-monopoly legislation combine to ensure this. Hence, most modern industries will tend to end up with a fundamentally oligopolistic structure: a few large enterprises surrounded by numerous entities of small to medium size highly dependent on one or two of the 'giants'. This means that although internalization may solve the problem of co-ordination within a firm, it still leaves a good deal of uncertainty concerning the behaviour of other firms in the same industry.

Consequently, oligopolists have had to develop a number of alternative ways of co-ordinating their activities to enable them to attain their corporate objectives. In each case, a general realization and acceptance of their interdependence is the most important precondition for co-ordinating their corporate strategies.

All oligopolists are aware of the fact that, given the overall economic environment, the most as well as the least favourable course of action open to each of them depends on actions taken by his rivals. It would not make sense, therefore, to provoke them into actions detrimental to all members of the industry. This is why oligopolists will be careful to avoid doing something that promises short-term gains at the cost of breaking the accepted code of behaviour within the industry thus increasing uncertainty and, with it, the problem of achieving their own long-term objectives.

The emphasis is, therefore, on achieving a long-term competitive advantage rather than on gains of a purely short-term nature. Price competition, in which all oligopolists can engage at short notice, and from which none of them can gain any lasting advantage, will be avoided. Oligopolistic competition instead relies heavily on various 'non-price' factors that involve long-term improvements in the firms' technical, marketing, financial and managerial performance. It is in this way that each of them hopes to acquire certain 'ownership specific' advantages which, unlike short-term price changes, cannot be reproduced easily by his rivals.

The success of oligopolists' attempts to co-ordinate their activities in a way that is beneficial to each and, therefore, all of them will depend critically on two factors. First, the more comparable are the levels of efficiency (in other words, the cost conditions) attained by oligopolists the more similar are also likely to be their price preferences and, consequently, their patterns of behaviour. Second, the smaller the number of oligopolists in an industry the better they are likely to be informed about their rivals' prices, output and profits – which, again, reduces the risk that any one of them will act in a way which is detrimental to everyone's interest. In other words, the more similar the conditions under which oligopolists operate the greater the chances that they will act in such a way as to maximize their own as well as the industry's profits.

There are a number of alternative methods used by oligopolists to co-ordinate their actions. What they all have in common is that, by accepting in the management of their own firms certain rules of behaviour which restrict each firm's autonomy, oligopolists end up, in fact, managing collectively both the short-term behaviour and the long-run progress of their industry. That is, in accepting constraints imposed by their interdependence, oligopolists surrender a certain degree of their corporate independence. But, in return, they acquire an important influence over the allocation and use of productive resources considerably wider than those which are under their direct control!

Cartels provide the most obvious example of this. In establishing a cartel oligopolists reach an open, formal agreement about overall output and prices. However, the success of this joint strategy depends on *each* of the members: (a) accepting a price that brings all of them the highest return obtainable without encouraging new entrants which could destroy the cartel's cohesion; and (b) adjusting their output, if demand conditions change, in such a way that the agreed price can be sustained.

An awareness of oligopolistic interdependence and the extent to which each oligopolist's actions can influence developments in his industry are equally important, though less apparent, in those cases in which cartels are either difficult to organize or forbidden by law. In the absence of such an awareness both formal and informal attempts by firms in an industry to co-ordinate their actions will be broken by 'chiselling' (price undercutting).

On the other hand, once interdependence is recognized and accepted, firms will strive to observe certain generally desirable rules of behaviour which minimize uncertainty within their industry. Where one firm is dominant it will act as the 'leader', indicating by its own behaviour the course of action that the rest of industry should take in response to external developments. In the absence of a clear leader, the largest firms in an industry can alternate in providing similar signals.

Whatever the form that oligopolistic co-ordination within an industry takes its key aspect remains the same: by accepting that orderly pricing is in their common interest, firms will adjust output and stocks to prevailing prices and *not* the other way round. But the real significance of the oligopolistic type of behaviour is that it forces firms to recognize their interdependence and, consequently, to look for lasting solutions to their problems, instead of engaging in competitive skirmishes which result in transient gains for some of them and long-term losses for all.

2.4 *Inter*-sectoral co-ordination through macroeconomic management

However, reduction of uncertainty and risk within an industry is not enough to guarantee its long-term progress. This can still be impeded – given the interdependence of various sectors of an economy – by uncertainty to which developments outside the industry give rise. One of the tasks of national economic management is, therefore, to promote *inter*-sectoral co-ordination of activity by reducing uncertainty in ways that are external to individual sectors but internal to the economy as a whole.

National economies are much more diverse and, therefore, much more complex – both in economic and social terms – than a firm or industry. Yet the basic policy issues concerning their levels and patterns of activity, and methods of organization required to deal with them, are not fundamentally different in the three cases. In fact, as the size of firms increases and the activities in which they engage become more and more diversified, their problems of organization and management become similar to those experienced at the macroeconomic level.

One of the reasons for this is that there is a common factor that ensures that both modern firms and modern states attach so much importance to 'growth'. In most modern industries, firms have to grow in order to preserve their corporate identity. It is much more difficult for outsiders to take over a large than a small firm. The process of 'internalizing' productive activities plays an important role in this by giving a firm the resources needed to deal with outside threats.

For similar reasons, given the threat of foreign interference and domination, usually associated with economic backwardness in an increasingly industrialized world, most countries will make an effort to industrialize in order to preserve their national identity by strengthening the capacity to defend their sovereignty. Hence, once a country starts to industrialize, its major trading and territorial rivals will have no alternative but to do the same. The longer they delay their industrialization the greater will become the gap between them and their more dynamic rivals. As a result of this, the rate of their economic growth will have to be appreciably higher than that of the leading rivals if they are to re-establish the *status quo ante* within a reasonable period of time. However, as experience of many countries since the beginning of the Industrial Revolution shows, rapid and sustained recovery of this kind is not something that developing and declining economies can achieve easily.

Modern industrial processes rely heavily on increasing returns to scale, in other words, on mass production. The two key features in this process are the division of human labour and the heavy use of machines and tools in the production process. The first presents great problems of organization and management: (a) in processing and absorbing highly complex information; and (b) in co-ordinating and controlling a wide range of highly interdependent activities. The heavy dependence of modern production processes on fixed capital creates the need for large volumes of investment in education and in productive facilities – as both skilled labour and productive capital stock are in short supply in the early phases of industrialization.

Not surprisingly the state will tend to play a very important role in the early stages of economic development, irrespective of whether the means of production are owned privately or collectively. One reason for this is that it has the power to create – by fiat if necessary – the consensus for change without which the desired economic transformation cannot take place. Moreover, in many cases, only the state can mobilize scarce national resources and channel them into the sectors that will produce the fastest rate of growth. This will be achieved by 'internalizing' within the state apparatus (that is, by bringing within government control) the power to direct the generation of savings and allocation of investment. In some cases, a particular outcome will be ensured by public ownership of the means of production. In others, governments will use fiscal and monetary policies, and the whole legislative framework available to them, in order to obtain the distribution of income that is both socially acceptable and produces a large volume of savings – most of which will then find their way into the infrastructure, education and basic industries.

The highly centralized, 'planned', form of national economic management can produce a high rate of investment and growth for some time. Technical change is one of the ways in which the volume of new investment, in which it is embodied, raises the productive potential of an economy. At the same time, the change generates a more complex division of labour that, in turn, requires organizational adaptations in order to increase productive efficiency to the levels required by the new technology. At this point, those responsible for national economic management face problems akin to those that directors of a firm experience when the size and complexity of its operations reach the level at which managerial diseconomies set in. The economy simply becomes too complex for a centralized body to co-ordinate its numerous operations, especially in times of rapid or unforeseen change.

The only way to avoid the rigidities and inefficiencies which centralization produces at higher levels of development is to decentralize (i.e. deregulate) the decision-making process. The exact form that such decentralization takes will be influenced greatly by historical experience and the degree of social cohesion that exists in a country. In the end, it is these factors that will determine not only the future path of an economy but also the means by which the desired results are achieved, or whether they are achieved at all.

In the countries that have attained a high degree of social cohesion governments and the representatives of industry, finance and labour unions play a role not dissimilar to that of the board of directors in a large corporation. The institutional framework within which they operate is not designed to 'direct' or 'administer' the economy. Its main purpose is to promote sectoral coordination either by a combination of income and price policies (designed to minimize the uncertainty about future movements in costs and prices, and thus promote investment by reducing the risk premia); or by industrial policies (the aim of which is to assist new investment, as well as technical and organizational changes, in both new and declining industries).

In other words, national economic management in such economies consists of bringing key economic sectors together in order to enable them to coordinate their actions in a way that promotes rapid adjustments to both internally generated changes and external shocks. As in the case of a multidivisional firm, the economy as a whole benefits from the direction provided by a widely accepted long-term strategy; and firms in key sectors gain from being able to acquire larger financial resources, and on more favourable terms, than they could obtain on the market in the absence of such a strategy. It is for this reason that, thanks to their ability to produce a flexible and broadly coordinated response, 'corporate economies' are much more successful in dealing with large external shocks than either their 'planned' (highly centralized) or 'market' (high decentralized) counterparts.

As 'market economies' lack the cohesion to develop a corporate form of organization, their governments will try to use the combined weight of the sectors which they control directly to provide the kind of economic leadership which is analogous to that of the dominant firm in an oligopolistic industry. By altering its revenue, as well as its current and capital expenditure, a government will signal to the rest of the economy the 'required' short-term response to economic changes which are taking place either inside or outside the country. Moreover, the government also hopes to influence in this way the long-term development of the economy by stabilizing the level of effective demand. The macroeconomic management of a 'market economy' has, therefore, two purposes: to maintain high levels of output and employment in the short run; and to reduce uncertainty, and thus make firms and industries more confident and optimistic about future economic prospects. Hence, if successful, stabilization policies should increase the volume of private investment and, in this way, the long-term rate of economic growth.

Sectoral interdependence is recognized in this form of macroeconomic management by the importance that is attached to price stability: the 'signals' are given in terms of quantities, not prices. This also increases the effectiveness of the 'multiplier' process. Changes in the aggregate propensity to consume, or save, will have much greater impact if prices are stable – so that the adjustment to changes in the volume of demand has to be made in quantitative terms (such as stocks, output, investment and employment).

This is, of course, the most important organizational aspect of the Keynesian attempt to improve the performance of capitalist economies by using their government sector to provide a form of intersectoral coordination and, in this way, raise their investment and employment levels. A 'free-for-all' competitive approach can be dangerously counterproductive in an oligopolistic environment; and, as pointed out earlier, the structure of most modern economies is, basically, oligopolistic.

2.5   International economic interdependence and national sovereignty

The main weakness of even the most successful Keynesian and 'corporate' approaches to national economic management is that their effectiveness diminishes progressively as a country becomes integrated into the world economy and its economic agents begin to receive signals from their own as well as from other governments, often of a conflicting nature.

Yet, under dynamic conditions, the opening up of a capitalist economy is unavoidable in the long run. As its national division of labour reaches higher stages of specialization, limitations imposed by the size of the domestic market will become a serious barrier to further progress. More and more tradable sectors will, therefore, require free access to the much larger world market in order to utilize fully economies of scale. The impetus that trade liberalization gives to international specialization will expand each country's exports *and* imports relative to its total national output – making all of them increasingly dependent on developments in the rest of the world.

In this way, the division of labour will lead to a spread of oligopolistic economic relationships from industry to national and, ultimately, international levels. Consequently, the extent to which a country can achieve its main objectives will depend on its own as well as other countries' actions. In an interdependent world economy, the level and stability of effective demand, output, investment and employment become international, rather than purely national, problems. Nevertheless, most countries, especially those of medium and large size, are likely to refuse to accept the constraint that these changes place on their ability to pursue independently their national objectives and policies. After all, this is what they have always done. Their ideology and institutional framework have evolved, therefore, for the specific purpose of preserving and promoting their national interests, frequently at the expense of other countries.

As a result, international economic integration, especially when it is rapid, will tend to create conditions which resemble those that occur in an industry before the firms comprising it develop a code of behaviour that recognizes their interdependence and uses it to mutual advantage. The structure of the industry at this stage is such that it consists of firms of different sizes. None of them is sufficiently large to dominate it. However, several firms have grown to such a size that each of them can have an appreciable effect on the market for the industry's products and thus on its competitors. The problem at this stage is that the firms have not yet learned to appreciate the real significance of their interdependence. Each continues, therefore, to pursue its own objectives independently, irrespective of the effect that they might have on its competitors, in the belief that it will be able to increase and sustain its share of the market even in the short run. The result is a period of cut-throat competition damaging to all.

'Beggar-my-neighbour' policies are the international equivalent of this type of competition. Underestimating the extent to which they are dependent on one another, each country tries to solve its economic problems at the expense of other countries. As the latter invariably retaliate, no one solves anything and everyone is worse off in the long term!

There are at least three reasons why, *ceteris paribus*, rapid international integration may lead to a beggar-my-neighbour type of competition and general economic stagnation. First, as levels of efficiency and incomes vary considerably from country to country, the nature and size of their problems and policies will also vary a good deal. It will be impossible, in the circumstances, to achieve a co-ordinated policy response spontaneously. Second, the task of achieving an international consensus on any important issue will be made even more difficult by the fact that as the number of participants in the international division of labour increases their understanding of other countries' economic positions and likely policy responses is likely to diminish. The larger a group the more difficult it is to reconcile the members' needs, objectives and actions. Third, structural changes that destabilize national economies are usually followed by government actions that define the rules and encourage modes of behaviour consistent with the new economic environment. More specifically, governments may allow, or even encourage, mergers and takeovers in one or more industries, making it easier for the remaining firms both to rationalize existing capacity and to create new one. It is also easier for a relatively small number of firms to foresee the consequences of their own actions as well as those of their competitors, something that should normally prevent costly outbursts of cut-throat competition. No one can perform such a role in relation to sovereign nation states.

Hence, if nation states wish to maintain and improve their economic welfare within an economically integrated framework, they have to organize their relationships in a way that enables them to achieve these objectives. They can do this only if (like firms within an oligopolistic industry) they accept that genuine political independence – the power to take actions irrespective of their effect on other countries and irrespective of developments in the rest of the world – diminishes progressively with every increase in international economic integration.

The way that countries react to limitations which international integration imposes on their sovereignty will determine the character and future progress of the world economy. There are, at least in theory, a number of arrangements that can be used to ensure that they co-ordinate their actions and, in this way, achieve mutually desirable goals. Virtually all of them closely resemble the forms of collective action employed by firms within a large, multi-product, oligopolistic industry.

2.6 Regional political unions

To begin with, two or more countries with highly integrated economies can merge into a political union. The union provides their economic agents, already highly interdependent, with a uniform framework of institutions, rules, regulations and macroeconomic policies. The uniformity reduces the uncertainty and risks normally associated with incompatible institutional arrangements and conflicting policies. The change enables economic agents to pursue their long-term objectives, instead of devoting all their energies and resources to ensuring short-term survival in an uncertain, crisis-ridden environment.

There are two serious obstacles to such a solution of international economic problems at the beginning of the twenty-first century, one political, the other economic.

Sovereign nation states are reluctant to lose their national identity, invariably a matter of great national pride, born in a different age and nurtured ever since in the struggle for collective survival. In other words, the reluctance has a practical side: the safeguard and promotion of specific national needs and aspirations that may become impossible within a larger political union. The dream of a 'United States of Europe' is as far from realization in the 2000s as it was in the 1950s when the European Economic Community, around which the 'States' were to evolve, was created. For similar reasons, not one of the attempts to create a 'United Arab Republic' has survived for very long. However, even if changes in political organization of this kind were possible, the nature and complexity of contemporary international economic relationships are such that it is very doubtful that political unions involving a few countries, whatever their other merits, would provide an optimum policy area. They would do little, for instance, to improve the existing, informal 'arrangements' between a large economy and its small 'dependencies'. In this case, the small countries are too dependent on the large country, despite their political independence, to have institutions and policies that are radically different from its own. The relationship that they have evolved corresponds, therefore, to that of the dominant country model analysed in Section 2.8. Political unions involving countries with large economies are more likely to create an optimum policy area. However, for reasons to be analysed in Section 2.9, the resistance to such an arrangement is likely to be very strong, as their nationals will tend to regard the political and economic costs of such a union as being far greater than any foreseeable benefits.

2.7 Imperialism

For a long time after the start of the Industrial Revolution, the most common method of achieving a political union was by military conquest (a violent equivalent of industrial 'takeover') rather than by peaceful negotiations. In this way, the country with sufficient military power could 'internalize' factors that were of strategic importance for its economy but happened to lie outside its frontiers. The purpose of such an action, as the mercantilists had been quick to recognize, was to minimize the uncertainty and costs of economic development by ensuring adequate supplies of foodstuffs and raw materials, and securing captive markets for the country's surplus products. Although economic factors were not the only reason for colonialism, it is considerations of this kind that provided the main driving force behind colonial expansion. (See, for instance, Fieldhouse 1981.)

However, as no nation has ever been big enough, or strong enough, to conquer the whole world and keep it permanently subjugated, a country adopting this strategy will, sooner or later, come into conflict with other countries determined to pursue the same course of action. Abundant supplies of raw materials and foodstuffs are available only in certain parts of the world; and there are relatively few potential colonies with a large capacity to absorb imports. National conflicts and wars become, therefore, an inescapable outcome of the 'colonialist' strategy for dealing with unpredictable externalities on a global scale.

The military resolution of international economic conflicts involves high human and material costs at all levels of development. With industrialization, the costs become prohibitive. The growth of a country's technical and productive potential increases its capacity to invent and manufacture highly destructive weapons. The main purpose for making these weapons is to deter other countries from threatening a country's 'vital interests' – including attempts on their part to secure exclusive access to foreign raw materials, foodstuffs and markets. The immense human and material costs of the two world wars demonstrate better than any analytical argument the awesome power for mutual destruction available to highly industrialized nations.

Moreover, the process that makes the cost of military conflict among industrial countries prohibitive gives rise also to the need to look for alternative solutions to problems of general interest. As countries industrialize, their economic structures and institutions become increasingly similar. The first is the product of a growing resemblance in their tastes and factor prices, and ensures that most of each industrial country's trade is with other industrial countries. Most of their investments abroad are also located in the industrialized part of the world. This, obviously, reduces the need for, as well as the feasibility of, the military option open to an industrial country for 'internalizing' strategic economic factors located in other industrial countries. The growing institutional and behavioural similarity also helps to avoid the risk of accidental conflicts by ensuring that the reactions of different countries to a particular change in the economic environment, though far from uniform, become more predictable.

The irrelevance of the colonial model applies also to the relationship between industrial and developing countries. The rivalry among industrial nations protects developing countries from conquest by an industrial power. At the same time, the international division of labour makes industrial countries increasingly dependent on raw materials and energy sources, many of which are produced by less developed countries, while the latter can industrialize only with the help of the industrial countries' technology, expertise and capital.

Consequently, as the energy crises of the 1970s have shown, there is an increasing need for a co-ordination of economic activities not only between industrial nations but also between industrial and developing countries. The colonial model does not provide a realistic solution to this problem – even if one ignores the ethics of military conquest.

2.8   The dominant economy model

There is an alternative arrangement, however, under which a country can assume effective control and management of the world economy without resorting to military conquest. It achieves this position as a result of its size, resources and more rapid economic advance than the rest of the world. In the long term, these advantages combine to create a productive potential so large, relative to those of other nations, that the country dominates world output and trade for the simple reason that it accounts for a large share of each. Its financial sector plays a similar role in international finance.

In other words, the country develops all those characteristics normally associated with a dominant economy.

Once a country achieves this position of pre-eminence in international economic affairs, its institutions, through their domestic and external policies, are bound to have a major effect on output and employment in the rest of the world in both the short and the long terms. Other countries will, therefore, have to respond to these policies and, in doing so, they will (collectively) influence the dominant country's ability to achieve its own economic and other objectives. Hence, willy-nilly, to the extent that it tries to ensure the stability and growth of its own economy, the dominant country will find itself managing the world economy as well.

There is no evidence that in the nineteenth century the British Government and the Bank of England ever set out to manage the international system in order to promote world economic welfare. Their actions were prompted purely by the pursuit of national self-interest. Yet, as the British economy was both much more industrialized than the rest of the world and very open, these actions could not avoid having a major effect on the stability and growth of the world economy. Britain accounted for a large share of world output, and London was the most important international financial centre. At the same time, the country was dependent on imports of food and raw materials and the limited size of its domestic market forced British industry to rely heavily on exports. This introduced a high degree of complementarity and interdependence between the British economy and the rest of the world, making it possible for the country to 'manage', by accident rather than design, the world economy.

The attitude of the United States after the Second World War was quite different. Unlike their British counterparts, the Federal Government and the Federal Reserve Board of Governors undertook the task of managing the international economy consciously. They were forced to act in the late 1940s by the apparent inability of the International Monetary Fund and the World Bank to assist European countries in their urgently needed post-war reconstruction which, in turn, resulted in the growing threat of political upheaval in Western Europe (see Chapter 10). The latter was clearly against US long-term interests. (See, for instance, Acheson 1969, Kennan 1967.) Subsequent US policies – fiscal, monetary and commercial, as well as Marshall Aid and other assistance to industrial and developing countries made, for almost quarter of the century, a major contribution to the unprecedented stability and growth of the world economy.

Although many experts have tended to look back with nostalgia to the periods of British and American domination, there are, in fact, serious long-term weaknesses in an international economic order which depends largely on the correct perception of self-interest and benevolence of one country. Unlike a dominant firm in an industry, a dominant country cannot prevent other sovereign states from developing their economies. Indeed, many of those actions that enhance its own long-term economic welfare and political influence, such as exports of capital and technical knowledge, also assist economic development in other countries. These changes in the relative performance and position of countries may result in the long term either in the emergence of a new dominant economy which has neither the institutions nor the global perception of self-interest to manage the international economy, or in a world in which no economy is capable of performing such a task.

The first problem appeared after the First World War when Britain became incapable of managing the international system and the United States was unprepared and unwilling to do so. The absence of an appropriate global institutional framework led to a period of *'laissez faire'* in international economic relationships – with disastrous world-wide economic, social and political consequences. The important lesson from the inter-war experience, so far as the organization of international economic activity is concerned, is that the emergence of a dominant economy does not necessarily guarantee the existence of an international order which promotes global economic welfare. On the contrary, the world economy is likely to go through a period of great instability and crises until the new dominant power becomes able and willing to 'manage' the system.

The absence of a dominant economy and the extremely remote possibility that, barring some unforeseen global disaster, any one country will ever again be in the position to assume such a role is a development that has become apparent since the late 1960s. The decline of US economic influence, brought about by rapid economic progress in other countries, signifies therefore the end of a particular phase in world economic history, the phase during which an international economic order could be imposed by a dominant *national* economy. Given the current configuration of international economic and political relationships, it is, therefore, inconceivable that another country could 'manage' world economy in the twenty-first century in the way that it was managed for a time accidentally by Britain in the nineteenth century and deliberately by the United States in the middle of the twentieth century.

2.9   A universal, cosmopolitan state?

As international economic integration has reached a very high level and no single country appears to be in a position to 'manage' the system, some form of supranational organization seems to be the only way to ensure the required co-ordination of regional or global economic activity without which the maladjustments accumulated since the early 1970s cannot be solved. The problem is that a 'supranational' framework of economic institutions cannot function effectively unless it is backed up by a similar form of organization at the political level – in other words, a regional or world government. Such a government is needed to decide on supranational priorities and then let the various institutions initiate and oversee their translation into practice. Using modern means of transport and communications, the whole edifice could be constructed in such a way as to replicate at the international level the institutional framework developed in various forms in advanced economies.

In theory, all this is both rational and feasible. What is more, modern technology has probably reached a level at which such a framework of supranational institutions could operate successfully. The problem, as usual, is that, whatever the level at which they evolve, institutions can function effectively only if they reflect accurately existing power relationships. At the international level, this means that a supranational form of organization can be developed only if nation states, especially large ones, become convinced that loss of national independence and sovereignty will increase their economic welfare, influence and power. Moreover, as absolute improvements in these respects are unlikely to be regarded as advantageous if they are spread unequally, each nation will also have to be convinced that it will not enjoy any of these gains to a lesser extent than other nations. These two conditions are extremely important under a highly integrated system operated by supranational institutions because, having given up its sovereignty, no country has the means with which to reverse by retreating into autarky a deterioration in its position, either absolute or relative, without incurring heavy economic and social costs.

As no form of regional or global economic and political authority could possibly guarantee either of these conditions, it is unrealistic to expect nation states to surrender willingly their sovereignty to a supranational authority. It is not simply a matter of historic traditions and cultural differences. At stake is nothing less than their ability to influence events in a way that is in the interest of powerful economic and political groups within each country.

Citizens of a small country, tied economically to a large neighbour, may not lose much, apart from their national pride, in a process of transferring sovereignty to a supranational authority. Those of a large country are in a quite different position. They know from experience that the size of the country and the resources at their disposal give them an important advantage in international negotiations and bargaining. The demise of the nation state would deprive them, therefore, of an important advantage. Hence, even if small countries were willing to surrender their sovereignty to a 'world government', large countries would be most unlikely to do so in the foreseeable future; and their refusal to participate in supranational organizations would deprive the latter of any ability to deal effectively with global economic problems.

It was because of its inability to overcome these fundamental problems that the much more modest attempt made at Bretton Woods in 1944 failed to create a system of stable and sustainable international economic relationships (see Chapter 10). Two of the three organizations originally planned, the

International Monetary Fund and the International Bank for Reconstruction and Development (the 'World Bank'), were established at Bretton Woods, but they were given totally inadequate resources to assist member countries with their stabilization and adjustment problems. Not surprisingly, the two have proved time and again to be in no position to provide more than marginal assistance in situations in which a large number of countries find it increasingly difficult to reconcile their internal (high levels of employment and low rates of inflation) and external (balance of payments) balances: in the post-war reconstruction period, in assisting developing and transition economies, and in dealing with the effects of the two oil shocks. The third institution planned at Bretton Woods, the International Trade Organization (with the task of promoting international economic integration through trade and of stabilizing world commodity prices) did not materialize until 1995 because the US Congress was concerned that its powers would encroach on US sovereignty. The General Agreement on Tariffs and Trade (GATT), which promoted trade liberalization from 1948 until 1995, was much more modest in its scope and powers.

Hence, although a good deal has been written about the 'Bretton Woods System', or even the 'IMF System', the simple fact is that, as Chapter 10 shows, the system created at Bretton Woods never operated in the form intended by its founders. The important organizational point, normally overlooked, is that although major world powers were to play an important role in the institutions created at Bretton Woods *none* of them was intended to manage the system on its own. The main purpose of creating the supranational organizations was to avoid the risks associated with world dependence on changes in the attitude and policies of a single country. The intention behind the institutional framework created at Bretton Woods was, therefore, that major policy decisions were to be taken collectively, in a way not dissimilar to that employed in a 'corporate economy'.

The problem was that there was one country, the United States, which had both the resources and institutions to help other nations with the stabilization and development of their economies; and, as any other country would have done in similar circumstances, it was not prepared to let some supranational organization disburse the resources on its behalf. Instead, when it did decide in 1947 to play an active role in international economic affairs it did so unilaterally and in its own national interest.

However, in doing this, the United States embraced the two guiding principles of the Bretton Woods System, which, after all, it had helped formulate: the spirit of international co-operation and the desire for some form of centralized co-ordination of international economic activity. Both were exemplified, among other things, in a rigid adherence to fixed exchange rates. But in realizing these 'Bretton Woods objectives', the United States bypassed international organizations and became directly involved in the international stabilization and adjustment process.

As a result, the post-war international economic system was managed not 'supranationally' as intended at Bretton Woods, but by one country, according to the principles of the dominant economy model described earlier. In other words, the system was managed, in effect, in US national interest by the US Treasury, the US Federal Reserve and the US Department of Commerce according to the rules laid down by the US Government. It would be more appropriate, therefore, to call the international system that operated so successfully from the late 1940s until the beginning of the 1970s the 'Washington System'.

2.10 Conclusion

In conclusion, like firms and industries, countries operating in an internationally integrated environment have to evolve a system of organizing their activities according to some generally recognized and acceptable set of principles and rules. In other words, they have to establish a code of behaviour appropriate to their level of interdependence if they are to achieve and sustain a desirable level of economic welfare.

There are a number of ways both formal and informal in which nations can organize their relationships in order to reduce the risks and uncertainties present in a dynamic economic environment. The major possibilities were considered in this chapter and found wanting. In fact, not one of them appears to provide a realistic, viable model of organizing international economic activity at the beginning of the twenty-first century.

The political union of a few countries is neither feasible nor adequate to provide an optimum policy area. The colonial solution, even if it were morally acceptable, would lead to military conflicts that could engulf the whole world. Its peaceful alternative, the dominant country model, is unworkable for the simple reason that no country is in a position to undertake such a role. Finally, as nation states are not prepared to give up sovereignty, a supranational political solution to international economic problems – managed by what Immanuel Kant ([1784] 1984) called a universal, cosmopolitan state – appears to be highly unlikely even in Western Europe, which has achieved by far the greatest progress in this respect.

Nevertheless, the international community has to find a satisfactory answer to the central question in contemporary international economic relationships: how to reconcile the fact that while economic problems are becoming increasingly international the only form of organization available for dealing with them remains national? The chapters that follow analyse some of the key conditions that have to be satisfied, and the ways in which this might be done, if current economic problems are to be solved within an organizational framework in which the 'nation state' continues to be the most effective decision-making unit at the macroeconomic level.

3
International Economic Integration and the Changing Role of National Governments*

Arguments concerning the role of government in economic change have been at the centre of economic debate since the eighteenth century. Yet, if anything, they are probably even further from producing a consensus now than they were more than two hundred years ago when two eminent Scots championed the familiar, diametrically opposed views: Sir James Steuart ([1767] 1966), that the state had a critical role to play in economic development and Adam Smith ([1776] 1976), that the role would be performed much more effectively by markets guided by the invisible hand of self-interest.

As far as the history of economic thought is concerned, Smith appears to have won the argument convincingly. Every economist is aware of his work, though few have actually read it. Most economists have never even heard of Steuart. However, when it comes to the policies actually pursued by individual countries since the beginning of the Industrial Revolution, it is arguable that the approach advocated by Steuart has been at least as influential.

Britain adopted some of Smith's key policy prescriptions, such as free trade, in the middle of the nineteenth century, long after his death and not before it had achieved global pre-eminence of a kind emulated only by the United States for a short period after the Second World War. But even this qualified adherence to the doctrine of *laissez faire* did not last long. Many of the policies were abandoned early in the twentieth century, as problems associated with the two world wars and the country's relative economic decline mounted. Elsewhere in the industrial world, the state played an even more active role in promoting and sustaining economic development (Brebner 1962, Gerschenkron 1966, Supple 1973, Cain and Hopkins 1980, Mathias and Pollard 1989).

The extent of state involvement in national economic management has tended to fluctuate over time, depending on whether the governments or

* This chapter was previously published in H. J. Chang and R. Rowthorn (eds), *The Role of the State in Economic Change*, Clarendon Press, Oxford 1995, pp. 51–78.

the markets were held to be responsible for a major and prolonged loss in economic welfare (see Chapter 4). Nevertheless, there is no industrial country in which government has failed to play an influential role in promoting and supporting economic change.

This is hardly surprising. Even Adam Smith agreed that the state should bear full responsibility for the external security and internal order of a country; and since the beginning of the Industrial Revolution, both of these have become increasingly dependent on the level of development and economic performance – including the way that the benefits of economic progress are shared within the state. Consequently, whatever their ideological preferences, governments have been forced to act as the allocator of last resort (underwriting or financing directly large or risky investment projects that the private sector is unwilling to undertake); the distributor or reconciler of last resort (reducing disparities in income and wealth, and with them the risk of social conflicts and political instability); the stabilizer of last resort (smoothing out the instabilities inherent in a market economy, a phenomenon analysed by a number of influential economists from Malthus to Keynes); and, finally, the coordinator of last resort (influencing through its own actions the expectations and behaviour in the rest of the economy).

The extent to which governments have done this has varied from country to country and, in the long run, within the same country – depending on its level and structure of economic development, economic performance, and socio-political conditions. Nevertheless, the question whether governments have an important role to play in macroeconomic management is superfluous. As Dr Erhard, who presided over the creation of the German social *market* economy, pointed out: "In modern times a responsible government cannot resign itself merely to being a night watchman. Such a perverted form of liberty would contain the seeds of disaster" (quoted in Oules 1966, pp. 320–1). The important issue, therefore, is not whether governments should have overall responsibility for the economic performance of their countries but under what conditions they are likely to discharge it most effectively.

This chapter analyses a number of key conditions that have to be met, and the way that changes in some of them have been responsible for the apparent success of government policies at the *national* level in the 25 years before 1973, especially in the post-war reconstruction period, and for their equally apparent failure since then.

3.1 Why some governments are more successful than others

It is customary, both in economic analysis and in public debate, to attribute the success or failure of a government's economic strategy to its competence and, occasionally, its integrity. The judgement may refer either to the government's choice of priorities or to its choice and/or implementation of particular policies.

There is a serious problem with such a simplistic approach to the analysis of the economic performance of governments. In the very short run, it is not inconceivable for a government, like anyone else, to make a mistake, even a serious mistake, especially when confronted with an unfamiliar problem. However, if a government continues to act 'incompetently' over a longer period despite changes in its membership and advisers, or, even more puzzling, if a succession of different, democratically elected governments continue to do so – as in the inter-war period and since the early 1970s – it is surely time to ask a rather obvious question: why do so many governments, not all of the same political persuasion or economic philosophy, have one characteristic in common – incompetence? Equally relevant, why do electorates keep electing apparently incompetent politicians? Or, if they have no other choice, why do competent people keep out of politics?

The problem is that questions such as these take us into the realm of the non-economic determinants of economic performance, a field of exploration in which we, modern economists, rarely feel at ease. Yet they cannot be avoided if we wish to examine seriously the reasons responsible for the success or failure of government economic policies. Once we do this, however, the whole issue assumes a different, much more intricate complexion.

Table 3.1 lists a number of factors that normally determine whether or not economic policies pursued by a government are likely to have the desired effect. Political independence (1a) is clearly one of the key factors. No government can have an effective economic policy, still less a mix of such policies, if its decisions are either imposed by some outside authority or can be changed by it with little or no regard for the country's problems and needs.

For obvious reasons, governments of large countries (1b) are less likely to find themselves in such a position than are those of small ones. Their capacity to pursue much more independent economic policies stems from the fact that the degree of self-sufficiency is far greater in large than in small economies – especially at higher levels of industrialization (Panić 1988, Chapter 2). Consequently, they are less affected by external developments.

However, whatever the size, level of development, or nature of the economic system, governments of countries with lower barriers to trade and financial flows (1c) will have less control over their economies than those whose economies are well protected. *Ceteris paribus*, the more open an economy is the higher will be the level of its international specialization and, therefore, its dependence on developments in other countries. As a result, the short-term stability and long-term progress of such an economy will be affected not only by the policies of its own government but also by the actions of governments in the countries with which it has close economic ties.

Over time, the economic sovereignty of a country and the effectiveness of its government's policies will diminish if it becomes party to international economic treaties and agreements that reduce its political independence. The same will also be true if its barriers to trade are lowered, increasing its

Table 3.1 Factors which determine the effectiveness of government economic policies

---

1. Economic sovereignty
   (a) Political independence
   (b) Size of country (national self-sufficiency)
   (c) Degree of openness (international specialization):
      tariffs
      quotas
      exchange controls
2. Institutional framework
   (a) Constitutional responsibilities/limitations
   (b) Institutional arrangements at the national level
3. Degree of economic consensus
   (a) National
   (b) International
4. A feasible economic strategy
   (a) Realistic priorities
   (b) Applicable, effective policies
5. Competence in implementing the strategy
   (a) Constrained by (1)–(3) above
   (b) Dependent on the ability and political skill of those in power

---

economic links with other countries. The effectiveness of the policies pursued by national governments will obviously increase if these trends are reversed.

Whatever the degree of a country's economic sovereignty, the ability of its government to influence economic performance significantly in either short or long run will depend also on its institutional framework. For instance, the parliament (2a) may empower government to discharge specific economic responsibilities – such as the objective of full employment that was incorporated into the US Employment Act of 1946. Alternatively, parliaments may limit the ability of national governments to use a particular policy instrument. West German and Japanese governments were prevented from pursuing an active fiscal policy for twenty years after the Second World War because the victorious allies insisted that each country should make it obligatory by law for the government to balance its budget.

A highly decentralized form of government, as in Germany and Switzerland, will also limit the ability of *national* authorities to employ an active fiscal policy, forcing them instead to make much greater use of monetary policy. However, even this option may be limited if, as in Germany and the United States, the constitution gives a good deal of autonomy to the central bank, making it largely responsible for the country's monetary policy.

The way that economic institutions are traditionally organized in a country (2b) may make it possible for the government to increase the range of policy instruments at its disposal. Highly centralized forms of wage bargaining, as in Sweden and Austria, enabled the governments to employ incomes policies as an additional, and for a long time very effective, anti-inflationary weapon (Romanis Brown 1975, OECD 1979). They were able to do this by participating in the income determination process either directly (Austria) or indirectly (Sweden). A long tradition of co-operation between industry, banks, and government (as in Japan) will enable the government to play an important role in promoting rapid modernization and restructuring of industry (Magaziner and Hout 1980, Dore 1986). The result is a rate of transformation that countries that are in no position to replicate that kind of co-operation find impossible to match.

However, both these instruments (incomes and industrial policies) require more than an appropriate institutional framework to produce the desired results: they need to be supported by a strong national consensus (3a), which is impossible without a high degree of social harmony. In a democracy this is also true of other economic policies and objectives, though not to the same degree. No matter how imaginative or theoretically sound a particular course of action may seem, it is bound to fail unless there is widespread national support for it. In other words, whatever a country's economic potential, serious social division and the political instability that normally accompanies it will ensure that its rate of economic progress lags markedly behind that of the nations with a more favourable socio-political environment, even though the latter may be at a considerable disadvantage in terms of natural resources. The remarkable success of Japan, and the equally remarkable failure of countries such as Argentina and Brazil to realize their potential provide classic examples of this kind.

Achieving a national consensus is never an easy task, especially in the absence of obvious external threats. The more remote or unlikely the threats are the less urgent it becomes to resolve internal conflicts between sectional interests and, consequently, the more difficult it is to mobilize the consensus for a course of action which is for the benefit of the country as a whole.

The problem becomes even more acute at the international level (3b). Yet a 'harmony of interests' between countries is essential when their economies become integrated and interdependent. The higher the degree of interdependence the more difficult it is for the government of one country to achieve its national objectives unless the governments of the other countries are prepared to co-operate. They are more likely to do so if their national problems and priorities are the same than if they differ. However, even in the former case, there are bound to remain serious limits to such co-operation – set by differences in national constitutions, institutional frameworks, history and culture.

As a result, it will not be always easy for governments representing different national interests to agree on the same or similar priorities; and even if they manage to do so it may not be possible – for reasons mentioned earlier – for them to pursue similar, let alone identical, policies. Realistically, therefore, the co-operation may not extend in practice beyond the pursuit of *compatible* policies.

In the same way that individual economic policies are not applicable to the same extent in all countries, no economic policy or policy mix can be expected to be equally effective in both the short and the long run within the same country. The economic and social characteristics of countries change over time; and, as a result, priorities and policy mixes have to be altered to reflect these new conditions and needs (4a and b). In most cases, it is the very success of a particular economic strategy that will make it essential to adopt new objectives and policies. That, in turn, may require new institutions. The success or failure of individual economies is largely determined by the ease with which their institutions and policies can be adapted to the new realities and problems.

In other words, economic and institutional dynamics are closely related and will, therefore, progress and stagnate together. As the peaceful transformation of increasingly outdated outlooks and institutions is more difficult the more entrenched they become (Olson 1982), it is not surprising that countries often rediscover their economic dynamics after losing a major war which discredits the old institutions and practices.

Finally, the scope and ultimate success of an economic strategy will depend on the conditions described earlier (5a) and on the ability, inventiveness, and political skills of those in power (5b), with the former usually as the dominant factor. A government whose involvement in economic management of the country is strictly limited by law or external factors is unlikely to achieve much, no matter how skilful and able its members may be.

Consequently, what a government can do and the ability of those doing it will tend to be closely related. The more important and effective is the role that national government can play in the economic life of the country, the more likely is it to attract people of high calibre, both at the political and the administrative level. This will be particularly true when economic policy is accorded a key role – exercising a major influence on virtually all aspects of government. In contrast, decline in the ability of governments to achieve economic and, through them, other important objectives will lead to frustration, a fall in the prestige with which government employment is held, and an exodus of able politicians and civil servants. Their successors are then increasingly regarded as second- and third-rate opportunists of limited ability, incapable of understanding the complex issues confronting them, and little or no feeling of social responsibility.

This explains the often observed paradox that a country is least likely to have a government of high calibre precisely at the time when it needs it most, for the simple reason that its most able people will prefer other occupations which provide them with a much greater opportunity to use fully their professional, organizational, and executive talents. Only an exceptional crisis, such as war, makes it possible to alter this imbalance by giving government the power to mobilize these people to work in the national interest.

In conclusion, some governments are more successful than others mainly because they operate in conditions that make it easier for them to discharge their responsibilities effectively and to general satisfaction – assisted by the fact that it is these very conditions that will attract people of high calibre who will then use them to full effect. Virtuous and vicious circles are as common here as in most areas of human activity.

3.2   The success of government economic policies before 1973

Whatever else we may disagree about, no serious economist or economic historian would dispute the fact that, as Table 3.2 shows, the economic performance of the most advanced industrial economies between 1950 and 1973 was quite unique historically. (See also Rostow 1978, Maddison 1989 and 1991.) Rates of growth of output, productivity, investment, and trade were markedly higher and more stable than during any comparable period since the beginning of the Industrial Revolution. At the same time, unemployment levels were considerably lower than either before the Second World War or since 1973. The average rate of inflation, at 4.2 per cent, though higher than in the inter-war period, was low compared with that recorded subsequently, with many countries achieving remarkable price stability. In addition, although some of them experienced crises, no country had persistent difficulty in balancing its current external accounts. Finally, available evidence indicates a clear reduction in income and wealth inequalities during the period, both within and between the countries (Atkinson 1973 and 1975, Sawyer 1982, Panić 1988) – a trend that has been reversed significantly since the early 1980s (Atkinson 1999, UNCTAD 1997).

Unlike the statistical record, which is unambiguous, the underlying causes are difficult to disentangle, let alone quantify, so that the economic performance of the industrial countries between 1950 and 1973 is subject to different interpretations. However, most experts would probably agree on a list containing the following: post-war recovery; the movement of labour from agriculture and other sectors of the economy where productivity was low to those where it was high; liberalization of trade which stimulated international specialization and, in doing so, accelerated growth by increasing opportunities to exploit economies of scale; a backlog of technical inventions and innovations accumulated during the inter-war and war years; low commodity prices, including those of petroleum, which encouraged worldwide substitution of oil for other primary sources of energy; and the international financial stability provided by the Bretton Woods System, which, through the regime of fixed exchange rates, acted as an important external constraint on domestic inflationary pressures.

Table 3.2 Long-term economic performance of 16 leading industrial countries, 1870–1989

				Annual averages (%)				
	Growth of GDP	Amplitude of recessions in total output[1]	Growth of GDP per man-hour	Average rate of unemployment	Average rate of inflation (consumer prices)	Growth of non-residential fixed capital	Growth of exports (volume)	Current account balance as % of GDP at current prices
1870–1913	2.5	−5.6	1.7	n.a.	n.a.	3.4	3.9	n.a.
1920–38	2.2	−12.4	1.9[2]	7.5	−0.6	2.0[2]	1.0	n.a.
1950–73	4.9	0.2	4.5	2.6	4.2	5.8	8.6	−0.2[3]
1973–89	2.6	−1.8	2.3	5.7	7.5	4.2	4.7	−1.1
1974–81	2.4	–	1.9	4.6	10.0	–	–	−2.0
1982–89	3.2	–	2.4	6.8	5.0	–	–	−0.1

Notes
[1] Maximum peak – through fall in GDP or lowest rise (annual data).
[2] 1913–50.
[3] 1961–73.

Sources: Maddison (1989) and the author's calculations.

There is little doubt that all these factors made an important contribution to the extraordinary economic performance of the advanced industrial economies between 1950 and 1973. But can they really account for all of it? The problem is that most of them were also present in the other three periods shown in Table 3.2 (1870–1913, 1920–38 and 1973–89). For instance, there have been important opportunities in each of the three periods to 'embody' technical change in new investment, to catch up with the leading industrial country of the time, and to provide employment for a sizeable proportion of the labour force made redundant by structural changes. Moreover, before 1914 the Classical Gold Standard made even less allowance for inflationary indiscipline than did the Bretton Woods System half a century later. The period of floating exchange rates since 1973 has been much less demanding in this respect. Nevertheless, many of the countries in Maddison's sample have been members of the European Exchange Rate Mechanism since 1979, fixing their exchange rates to each other's currencies either officially or by 'shadowing' the Deutschmark. As for barriers to trade and capital flows, the 1930s are the only decade during the three periods when such policies became a serious obstacle to international specialization and exchange. Finally, although sharp increases in primary commodity prices in the 1970s, above all the two oil crises, gave a structural shock to the international economic system, commodity prices presented no greater problem before the Second World War or after the early 1980s than they did between 1950 and 1973.

The one factor that is missing from the list given so far, and one which also happens to be unique to the 1950s and 1960s, is that of deliberate peacetime control and macroeconomic management of the highly industrialized capitalist economies by their governments – designed specifically to achieve certain clearly defined national objectives. The success with which this was done varied from economy to economy. Moreover, whatever the degree of success, it would obviously be wrong to attribute it entirely to government action. Modern economies are too complex for their performance to be explained in terms of one factor, or by the actions of one economic agent.

Nevertheless, the importance of the role played by national governments during the period 1950–73 cannot be denied. For instance, Samuelson (1967, p. 581) captured the general feeling of confidence in the ability of governments to deal with major economic problems, which existed in the 1960s, when he reassured would-be economists that: "By proper use of monetary and fiscal policies, nations to-day can successfully fight off the plague of mass unemployment and the plague of inflation." Almost a quarter of a century later, Maddison (1991, p. 173) was even more explicit in attributing the exceptionally rapid, widely diffused improvements in economic welfare between 1950 and 1973 to government action based on a "clear bias in favour of growth and employment, the lowered attention to risks of price increases or payments difficulties, and the absence of crassly perverse deflationary policies". His historical analysis led him to single out these aspects of national economic management as "the most important features differentiating post-war from pre-war domestic policy".

In contrast, there has been growing discontent with government economic performance since the early 1970s, reflected in an increase in political instability in most industrial countries. Can this be explained by changes that have taken place since the 1960s in the conditions listed in Table 3.1?

One conclusion which emerges clearly from even the most cursory reading of post-war economic history is that national governments enjoyed considerable control over their economies in 1945 (cf. Chester 1951, Maddison 1964, Cairncross 1985, Milward 1987a, Panić 1991a). Many of the controls were not dissimilar to those introduced during the First World War. The difference was that on this occasion they and the administrative apparatus that enforced them were dismantled only gradually – a completely different approach to that adopted after 1918 (see, for instance, Lowe 1978).

An important consequence of this was that after 1945 the industrialized countries enjoyed a considerable degree of economic sovereignty, mainly thanks to the strict restrictions on trade and capital flows. With the exception of a few countries (West Germany, Japan, and Austria) in the early postwar period, there was no significant change in the ability of national governments in the industrial countries to act independently, despite some limitations on their actions imposed by membership of various international organizations. West Germany apart, there was also little change in size of the countries. Hence, it was their greater control over economic links with the outside world that was largely responsible for the ability of national governments to manage their economies without foreign interference. For although committed to a more liberal trading system, few governments were in a hurry to implement it until they were confident that lower trade barriers would not prevent them from achieving their major economic objectives. Quotas were phased out during the 1950s and tariffs reduced significantly only in the second half of the 1960s. But exchange and other controls on capital flows in many cases remained in force until the 1980s.

The ability of West European countries and Japan to act independently was not diminished by their heavy reliance on the United States for postwar reconstruction (Milward 1987a, Panić 1991a). The reason for this was that the aid generously provided by the Americans determined the speed of the post-war reconstruction and minimized its social cost. But the United States did not interfere with the character of the economic policies pursued by these countries, or insist on imposing a rigid timetable on them (Panić 1991a). Hence, it was the actions of national governments that determined the pace of the reintegration of these countries into the world economy as well as the policy mixes that they adopted domestically.

Moreover, where necessary, institutional frameworks were changed to enable the governments to acquire greater control over the stability and growth of their economies. In the United Kingdom and France a number of sectors and firms were nationalized, giving their governments direct control over decisions concerning output, investment, employment, prices, and wages; and in Italy the size of the public sector, already large, was increased further (Robson 1960, Einaudi *et al.* 1955). France, the Netherlands, and Norway, all with highly centralized policy-making institutions, were able to resort to indicative planning of a kind unique in capitalist economies (cf. Cohen 1969, UN 1965). Sweden, Austria, and the Netherlands, as already mentioned, developed highly centralized systems of wage bargaining which enabled them to pursue incomes policies that were the envy of other countries. In the mid-1960s, West Germany and Japan changed their 'stabilization laws', enabling their governments to engage in more active fiscal policies (Kaspar 1972, Nakamura 1981). All these governments were also empowered to reintroduce or tighten certain measures, if these were required, to deal with a particular problem. Thus in the 1960s most industrial countries brought back exchange controls on short-term capital movements, or tightened those already in existence, in order to reduce the pressure of speculative flows on their exchange rates (Swoboda 1976).

The main reason that governments were able to retain such wide-ranging powers in peacetime was the consensus in favour of active government involvement in national economic management that developed during the Second World War. The collapse of largely unregulated capitalist economies in the 1930s – causing massive unemployment, social unrest, the rise of political extremism, and, ultimately, the most destructive global war in history – produced a widely based consensus that economic failure on such a scale could not be allowed to happen again (cf. Chapter 10, Polanyi 1944, Milward 1987b). To avoid it, general economic welfare had to be maintained and, if possible, improved; and the only economic entity with command over sufficiently large resources to help achieve such an objective was the state.

Hence, throughout the industrialized world, governments of different political complexions accepted the responsibility of managing their economies in order to achieve a number of important objectives. Among these, five were given particular prominence: full employment; a satisfactory rate of growth (that is, the rate needed to sustain a high level of employment in the long run); price stability; external – current account – balance (partly to allow each country the freedom to pursue its domestic objectives without foreign interference and partly to avoid the adverse effects of external imbalances on growth, employment, and price stability); and an equitable distribution of income (to ensure the consensus without which the other objectives could not be reconciled in a democracy).

The fact that all these countries were committed to the same objectives meant that the consensus was not only national but also international. The desire to work towards the same goal was reinforced by two important factors: the Cold War which compelled powerful vested interests in the capitalist economies to co-operate in order to protect the existing economic and political systems on which their wealth, influence, and power depended; and the clear division between countries such as those in Western Europe and Japan, that needed urgently to rebuild their economies and societies, and the few countries in North America and Oceania – dominated by the United States – that were in a position to help them. Consequently, so long as the Americans were willing to provide the necessary assistance, there was no danger that the key economies would follow different objectives, thus making it impossible for any one of them, and economies dependent on them, to achieve their economic and social goals.

However, although the objectives were the same, the emphasis given to any one of them varied from country to country, determined by the nature of the problems confronting them. An important characteristic of economic policy in the industrialized countries until the 1970s was the extent to which, as Myrdal (1960) observed at the time, it was guided by their needs rather than by the ideological preferences of those in power. Thus, exceptionally rapid growth and the threat of overheating made it necessary for West Germany to give high priority to price stability. In contrast, the experience of social divisions and political instability – held responsible for the country's rapid collapse in 1914 and 1939 – led French governments to pay less attention to inflation and give high priority to economic growth in the hope that it would produce greater social harmony (Sautter 1982). The United Kingdom was unique among the industrial countries in experiencing frequent balance of payments problems and currency crises, both in effect self-imposed, as the country desperately insisted on continuing to play a major military and financial role on the world scene despite its apparent lack of the required resources. Nevertheless, although the emphasis varied, the basic objectives remained the same in all these countries.

At the same time, economic policies differed, often appreciably, reflecting differences in the countries' institutions and the degree of social harmony and political consensus. The United Kingdom, Sweden, and Austria – all with strong central relative to regional authorities – made active use of demand management, with monetary policy playing a subordinate role to fiscal measures. West Germany and Switzerland, both with strong regional authorities, relied much more on monetary policy. In all these, as in the other cases, the exact policy instruments varied from country to country (Panić 1991a). As already mentioned, Japan pursued a uniquely active and successful industrial policy. West Germany lacked the institutional set-up, or indeed the need, to replicate the Japanese model. But its government had sufficient authority and enough policy instruments to play an important role in influencing the volume and pattern of private investment, helping to remove bottlenecks in a number of key sectors with remarkable speed (Roskamp 1965). Direct government involvement in investment allocation was even greater in France where the state owned large financial intermediaries, enabling it to channel their investment funds into the sectors given high priority by the planners. Finally, although all the countries greatly improved their welfare provisions, they were much more extensive and generous in Western Europe than elsewhere (Wilensky 1975, Sawyer 1982). This was especially true of the countries that had to rebuild their social harmony and political consensus, both shattered by the war. Many of them were also vulnerable to the threat posed by the Cold War because of their geographic proximity to the Soviet bloc.

Lastly, the war and the apparent success of these policies enabled the state in all these countries to attract politicians and technocrats of high calibre. Many of them had lived through the horrors of the two world wars and the Great Depression. As a result, they were determined – irrespective of their ideological preferences – not to allow something similar to happen again; and the best way to ensure this was to create economic and social conditions that would make a repetition of such events virtually impossible. Equally important, the close links between government, industry, the financial sector, and labour unions developed during the war provided those in positions of responsibility in all these sectors with experience of working together towards a common objective. The need for co-operation diminished once the war was over. But the Cold War ensured that the ties would continue to be cultivated and the government allowed to co-ordinate national economic activity through macroeconomic policies.

As usual, it was the extraordinary success of all these institutional adaptations and policies, as well as the passage of time, that altered the basic conditions under which the governments of industrial countries operate. In the process, the changes have made it much more difficult for governments to cope at the *national* level with the shocks that have altered the character and performance of the world economy since the early 1970s.

3.3   What has gone wrong since 1973?

It is clear from Table 3.2 that the economic performance of the most advanced industrial countries has been far less impressive since 1973 than during the preceding 25 years. The difference would be even more pronounced if the latter period included the 1990s. Contrary to what one might expect from countries at this level of development (Panić 1988), all of them have been struggling continuously, and in most cases unsuccessfully, to reconcile their internal and external balances – in other words, to achieve simultaneously all the major policy objectives mentioned earlier. Following the preceding analysis, the question which immediately poses itself is: what has prevented governments of these countries from promoting economic stability and progress since the early 1970s as successfully as they managed to do in the early post-war period? The best way to answer this question is again to analyse changes in the factors (listed in Table 3.1) that determine the effectiveness of government policies. The first important change to note is the extent to which *national* economic sovereignty has weakened over the period. This has had nothing to do with the political status (1a) or size of the countries (1b), as both were the same in 1989 as in 1950. The changes – caused partly by deliberate government decisions and partly by developments at industry and firm level which were frequently contrary to government wishes and policies – have thus come entirely from the opening up of national economies and, consequently, from the growing dependence of individual economies on the actions of governments and economic agents operating outside their borders (1c).

The need for greater international economic co-operation in order to avoid a repetition of the inter-war experience, to which those participating at the Bretton Woods conference committed themselves in 1944, and the success in achieving full employment and the other objectives after the war encouraged the governments of industrial countries to liberalize first international trade and then capital flows, with the most successful economies, as one would expect, in the forefront of initiating these changes.

Thus, in the late 1940s, when it dominated the world economy, the United States, normally one of the most protectionist countries (see Chapter 5), unilaterally reduced its duties on imports (Anderson 1972). Moreover, the dollar was the only major currency to be fully convertible. Other industrial countries abolished most quantitative controls and reduced some tariffs in the 1950s – with the successful economies, such as those of West Germany and Switzerland, leading the way (Patterson 1966). By the end of 1958, West European countries were confident enough to allow convertibility of their currencies for current account transactions – a step for which Japan did not feel ready until the mid-1960s.

The process accelerated in the 1960s and early 1970s with worldwide reductions in tariffs under the Dillon, Kennedy, and Tokyo Rounds of GATT. In addition, there was regional liberalization of trade in Western Europe, following the formation of the European Economic Community and the European Free Trade Association. Consequently, although there was some increase in non-tariff barriers to trade in the 1970s, levels of protection in international trade are probably lower now than at any time since the middle of the nineteenth century (cf. Bairoch 1989a, OECD 1985). The same is not true of controls on capital flows – though most of these have been either reduced or abolished in industrial countries since the 1970s. The two oil shocks made this necessary in order to finance the large current account deficits, a process that intensified with the election of governments committed to economic deregulation, both national and international.

This liberalization also produced important innovations in international finance (Bank for International Settlements 1986, Eiteman and Stonehill

1989) which expanded the volume of transactions even further. For instance, the combined share of exports and imports in GDP was significantly higher in the 1980s than in the 1960s even in the three largest industrial economies, as the following figures show (average percentage shares per decade, with the 1960s figures in brackets): United States 19 (10), Japan 24 (19), West Germany 56 (36) (EC, *European Economy*, December 1990). With the exception of Japan, the extent of international specialization and exchange has become particularly large in manufacturing. This can be seen by comparing import penetration (imports as a percentage of manufacturing value added at current prices) in the largest industrial economies in 1960 and 1987 (with the former figures in brackets): United Kingdom 72 (16), West Germany 43 (25), United States 35 (5), and Japan 10 (8) (Walter 1993, p. 232). As all these shares are normally higher in smaller economies, it is not surprising that by 1990 the annual value of world trade had risen to over $5 trillion, roughly comparable to the size of US GDP in that year (*ibid.*, p. 196).

The growth of international financial markets has been even more remarkable. For example, in 1964 the value of gross deposits (that is, including inter-bank deposits) on Eurocurrency markets was $19 billion, rising to $86 billion in 1970. Ten years later, in 1980, it stood at $1,574 billion, with a further, almost three-fold increase over the next seven years to $4,509 billion in 1987 (Pilbeam 1992, p. 312). Daily turnover on world foreign exchange markets was estimated at $1 trillion at the end of the 1980s – considerably greater than the combined foreign exchange reserves of central banks which amounted to $800 billion (Walter 1993, pp. 197 and 198).

Moreover, a high proportion of international transactions is controlled by a relatively small number of transnational corporations and financial institutions – with a good deal of it taking place, in fact, *within* the transnationals (TNEs). (See Chapter 6.) This, plus the growing importance of joint ventures even among the giant TNEs, makes it increasingly difficult to disentangle who exactly is producing a particular product and how much of it originates in any one country.

All these changes have invariably reduced the scope for unilateral government measures by increasing the degree of uncertainty associated with any particular course of action. Unlike in the early post-war period, the outcome now depends on the reactions of a large number of powerful decision-making entities, governments, and TNEs, many of them with different problems and objectives. As a result, uncertainty, never absent from economic activity, has grown to the point where it stifles investment and growth, giving rise to permanently underutilized productive capacity and high levels of unemployment. Events since the early 1970s have shown the extent to which even the economic sovereignty of the United States has been eroded by the opening up of national economies.

At the root of all these difficulties is the fact that the rapid increase in international economic integration and interdependence has made the existing institutional framework inadequate for dealing satisfactorily with problems most of which are now international in character. Under these conditions, no government is in a position to react effectively to unfavourable developments, irrespective of the range of policy instruments at its disposal, for the simple reason that in many cases they originate outside the area of its jurisdiction.

That leaves four options for adjusting the existing institutional framework to the new economic environment. They have all been tried since the early 1970s – hesitantly, cautiously, and therefore not very successfully.

The first option consists of reversing the process of international integration by insulating individual economies – a precondition for enabling national governments to engage actively in economic management, as they did after the Second World War. Selective attempts were made in this direction in the 1970s and 1980s, with the governments of industrial countries employing for the purpose non-tariff barriers to trade and competitive devaluations. (See Chapter 5.) However, international production, distribution, and financial networks are too interwoven and complex now for industrial countries to risk economic warfare of the kind that became common in the 1930s. As for devaluations, Table 3.3 shows that the economic performance of those countries which resorted to them was not superior in the long term to that of countries whose currencies appreciated in nominal terms.

Secondly, governments can co-operate in such a way that the overall effect of their policies is similar to the one that could be achieved by a supranational economic authority (Panić 1988). However, in practice, this is possible only if their problems, objectives, and institutions are so similar that the chosen policy options can be confidently expected to work with more or less equal effectiveness in all of them. As already emphasized, although they share many characteristics, industrial countries are far from being identical – which explains why their attempts at international cooperation have tended to be short-lived. The existing national differences and the diffusion of economic power have made it very difficult to sustain such initiatives even when national governments are willing to coordinate their policies.

Thirdly, economic integration can be accompanied by political integration, with nation states transferring sovereignty to a supranational authority. Although perfectly feasible in theory, no attempt of this kind has produced an outcome in which supranational institutions have been able to discharge their responsibilities as successfully as their national counterparts. The IMF and the World Bank have been of marginal importance in the post-war international system; and it is increasingly unlikely that the even more ambitious attempt to centralize EC institutions, proposed in the Treaty of Maastricht in 1991 (EC Council 1992), will be able in the foreseeable future to overcome the mounting opposition to greater political integration in member countries.

The final option is to deregulate, privatize, and thus let the markets reconcile internal and external balances – in other words, achieve the five

Table 3.3 Exchange rate changes and overall economic performance of selected industrial countries, 1976–89

| | Effective exchange rate changes (%)[1] | | Growth of GDP | Unemployment rates | Inflation rates | Current balance of payments as % of GDP | Growth in volume of trade in goods and services | |
	Nominal	Real[2]					Exports	Imports
Japan	130.1	0.3	4.2	2.4	3.5	1.7	7.1	5.2
West Germany	52.4	−6.5	2.3	4.9	3.2	1.7	5.2	4.5
Switzerland	50.4	6.5	2.0	0.5	3.0	4.2	4.3	5.9
Austria	31.6	−19.1	2.4	2.7	4.3	−0.9	5.9	5.8
Britain	−7.7	25.7	2.5	8.3	8.9	−0.1	3.6	3.8
France	−11.2	−0.8	2.6	8.0	8.0	−0.4	4.7	5.0
USA	−12.3	12.1	3.0	7.1	6.0	−1.4	5.4	7.3
Sweden	−31.4	−8.8	1.8	2.0	9.1	−1.4	4.2	3.4

Notes
[1] Plus sign denotes appreciation; minus sign denotes depreciation.
[2] Nominal exchange rates adjusted for changes in relative export prices.

Sources: IMF, *International Financial Statistics*; OECD, *Economic Outlook*.

major objectives. The problem is that, as already pointed out, it was precisely the failure of unregulated markets to achieve this in the inter-war period that produced in the 1940s the international consensus in favour of greater state involvement in economic management. There is little doubt that Keynes was speaking for most of his contemporaries when he expressed the view that: "To suppose that there exists some smoothly functioning automatic mechanism of adjustment which preserves equilibrium if only we trust to methods of *laissez faire* is a doctrinaire delusion which disregards the lessons of historical experience without having behind it the support of sound theory" (quoted in Van Dormael 1978, p. 32).

The main reason that it has proved so difficult to create the right kind of institutional framework is the breakdown of both national and international consensus since 1973. The early post-war period achieved conditions which were, basically, conducive to greater social harmony: as a result of rapid economic growth and full employment, the standard of living of the less well off sections of the population in the industrialized countries could be improved significantly without making the rest worse off. This factor, the fear of a repetition of what had happened in the 1930s and 1940s, and the Cold War enabled the newly created welfare state to undertake a major redistribution of income which, in turn, ensured widespread support for the economic system and the policies that made it function so successfully.

In contrast, the slowing down in economic growth after the first oil shock in 1973, the sharp increases in unemployment, and the historically unprecedented peacetime inflation rates brought with them a return of 'zero-sum' economic preoccupations and behaviour, and the inevitable weakening of social cohesion that such behaviour brings about. The second oil shock simply accentuated these tendencies.

Unemployment affects different occupational groups, sectors, and regions unequally, as does an accelerating inflation rate. The internal disequilibrium caused by the first oil shock, and its persistence, were bound, therefore, to lead sooner or later to a breakdown in the national consensus built up after the war. Some groups began to favour deflationary policies because they were in their interest, and others continued to support expansionary policies either for the same reason (see Frieden 1991) or because they were concerned about the social and political effects of economic stagnation. This division was exacerbated by internal deregulation and external liberalization, as they intensified the conflict of interest between capital (which became highly mobile internationally and, consequently, less concerned with the long-term effects of its actions on any one country) and labour (which remained largely immobile internationally, with its well-being, therefore, closely tied to economic, social, and political developments in its country of residence). As a result, there has tended to be a sharp division of opinion since the early 1970s in many countries between the priorities and policies advocated by employers' associations and those favoured by the labour unions.

The apparent dependence of their economies on TNEs, and the realization that these corporate entities feel no particular allegiance to any one country, has forced governments to give TNE owners and managers tax concessions and subsidies in order to make it less attractive for them to move elsewhere (Reich 1991). Those aspiring to political power have also increasingly had to buy support by promising to ease the tax burden of those in employment. This has opened up further divisions in society by making it difficult for the state to provide adequate welfare for the growing number of elderly, unemployed, and poor, or to cope with the rapidly growing demand on the social services and the law-enforcing agencies created by the adverse effect of greater economic and social inequalities on health and crime (Patrick and Scambler 1986, Burchell 1992, Field 1990).

Not all industrial countries have experienced these problems to anything like the same extent. This explains why Japan and a number of small states in Western Europe managed to cope remarkably well in the 1970s and 1980s with the energy and other crises by using a combination of industrial, incomes, and social policies made possible by their strong social and political consensus (cf. Pekkarinen *et al.* 1992, McCallum 1983 and 1986). Elsewhere, governments have had little success in mobilizing a broadly based national support in favour of the institutions, objectives, and policies required to solve their countries' economic and social problems – especially as the easing of Cold War tensions in the 1970s and 1980s removed the only serious external threat to the prevailing socio-economic order.

This last factor has also made it very difficult to recreate the international consensus that contributed so much to post-war economic recovery. However, although important, this was by no means the only development that weakened the readiness of industrial countries to work towards the same objectives.

The demise of the Bretton Woods System encouraged governments to ignore the interdependence of their economies and pursue 'independent' macroeconomic policies in the belief that the floating exchange rates would enable them to reconcile their internal and external balances. It did not take long for at least one of the advocates of this policy approach to describe the whole idea as 'a chimera' (Kaldor 1978). Nevertheless, so long as they are confronted with serious economic problems and there are no international mechanisms for solving them collectively, governments under pressure will tend to resort to policy instruments which, although incapable of producing permanent solutions, will at least make the problems manageable in the short run.

The tendency to do this has not been helped by the fact that there have been important differences in the kinds of difficulty experienced by both large and small countries, with no country in the position that enabled the United States after the Second World War to secure international consensus and manage the system (Panić 1988, Walter 1993).

For instance, some countries have been earning persistent and fairly large surpluses on their current balances of payments since the early 1970s (Japan, West Germany, Switzerland, and the Netherlands), making it less necessary for them to frame their policies in accordance with the requirements of foreign and domestic capital. Others (the United States, the United Kingdom, France, and Sweden) have had to do precisely that for most of the period because of their persistent current account deficits. There has also been a similar divergence of experience concerning countries' internal disequilibria – with some of them maintaining low unemployment for most of the time since the 1970s thanks to the flexibility of their institutions and policies (Japan, Norway, and Sweden) and others because they were able to pass the problem on to other nations by sending back immigrant workers (West Germany, Switzerland, and Austria). At the same time, many industrial countries have had to cope with high and rising unemployment (Italy, the United Kingdom, Canada, and Belgium).

With no country in a dominant position, it is virtually impossible to agree on a common course of action, or to be confident that, if agreed, it will be followed for long by all those who approved it. It is clearly difficult to avoid such an outcome when industrial countries – including the key members of the international economic community – are experiencing different problems, as this will influence their priorities which, in turn, will determine their choice of policies.

After the war, when, with a few exceptions, most industrial countries were confronted with similar difficulties, it was relatively easy for them to agree on a common course of action. With time, the unequal success in achieving the objectives that they had set themselves made it necessary for individual countries to alter their priorities in a way that was consistent with the new problems. The two oil crises sharpened these divisions as, suddenly, it became much more difficult for every single industrial country to achieve any one of its major aims of economic policy.

Thus, the governments of the United Kingdom, Sweden, and Italy, alarmed by the levels of unemployment that could result from the first oil crisis, reacted to it by attempting to avoid deflation, arguing, not unreasonably, that short-term stabilization measures were inappropriate to deal with a problem that was clearly of a long-term structural nature. The United States, in the grip of the monetarist counter-revolution, and West Germany and Japan, with low unemployment levels for reasons described above, took exactly the opposite view and introduced deflationary policies. The response to the second oil crisis was no more harmonious. For instance, the newly elected socialist government in France gave high priority to faster growth and lower unemployment, while the new conservative governments in the United Kingdom and the United States were determined to ignore all other objectives in order to achieve the single goal of a low and stable rate of inflation.

Unfortunately for the industrialized countries and the world economy, these differences have become pronounced precisely at a time when they are likely to inflict maximum damage on all concerned.

The extraordinary international harmony of interests in the early post-war period occurred at a time when, because of their relatively high degree of insularity, most industrial countries could have set themselves economic objectives that were radically different from those pursued by the rest of the world. It would, no doubt, have taken longer to get there and the outcome would have been less impressive than the one they actually achieved. Nevertheless, there was a reasonable chance that they would have improved their standard of living by pursuing an independent course of action. That, after all, is what happened in socialist economies. In contrast, with their economies open and closely linked to those of other countries, it is now virtually impossible for an industrial country to adopt a radically different, independent macroeconomic policy stance for long without experiencing serious welfare losses. As a result, even governments of medium and large economies have been forced to reverse their policies for reasons such as: a socially and politically dangerous level of unemployment (the United Kingdom), sharply rising inflation rates (Italy and France), and an unsustainable increase in external indebtedness incurred in order to finance current account deficits (the United States).

At the same time, it is both too easy and misleading to exaggerate the impotence of governments by focusing exclusively on macroeconomic policies and *national* governments. After all, regions within individual countries differ, often significantly, in the nature of their economic problems and priorities and have even less scope for independent macroeconomic policies than do the national governments of countries with open economies. Nevertheless, a combination of industrial and regional policies, pursued jointly by national and regional governments, played a major role in enabling industrial countries to achieve their remarkable economic successes after the Second World War (Nicol and Yuill 1982, Armstrong and Taylor 1985). International integration does not diminish the ability of regional governments to pursue polices that are normally within their domain. In fact, as Japan, Austria and Sweden have shown, it need not necessarily reduce the capacity of national governments to promote highly successful industrial and incomes policies.

However, economic and political developments since the early 1970s have combined in most countries to create a serious obstacle to the successful application of such policies in the absence of closer international collaboration.

There are, basically, three reasons for this. First, as already mentioned, the breakdown of national consensus has made it extremely difficult for political parties to be elected to power unless they commit themselves to a policy of low taxation. Consequently, once elected, national governments have tended to find that they have inadequate resources to promote major industrial and regional adjustments without foreign borrowing. The greater the need for external funds the higher will be the cost of raising them (as the risk premiums will go up). That is bound to set a limit to the adjustment process, unless the country or region in question can attract official transfers from either foreign governments or, more likely, supranational institutions. As experience within the European Community shows, the need for external assistance is likely to be particularly serious in the countries and regions where the need for adjustment is greatest.

Secondly, given the extent to which they dominate international production and trade, a successful application of industrial and regional policies increasingly requires the active co-operation of TNEs. The problem is that the objective of these corporations is to maximize their shareholders' income, and not to assist any one country to achieve its objectives. (See Chapter 6.) Indeed, if they are to operate internationally without interference from national governments they cannot afford to appear to make their decisions on the basis of anything other than purely commercial criteria. The result has been an increase in competitive bidding for their investment, involving national and regional authorities, which has raised the cost of attracting TNEs – working, again, to the advantage of wealthier regions and countries (Reich 1991).

Finally, international agreements, such as the Single Europe Act, are making it increasingly difficult for national governments within the European Community to assist their industries and regions (EC Commission 1991). The intention is that industrial and regional policies should be administered by regional and supranational authorities, with the EC Commission in the latter role. There is much to be said in favour of this idea, as the preceding analysis shows, except that member governments have never given the Commission sufficient resources to play such a role effectively (EC Commission 1977, Kowalski 1989).

Hence, as in the case of macroeconomic policies, the national governments of industrial countries have introduced institutional changes that deprive them increasingly of adequate policy instruments at the microeconomic level. Not surprisingly, in the absence of an alternative authority to take over the task of allocator and co-ordinator of last resort, economic failure, social problems, and political instability are on the increase in most of these countries, with the esteem in which governments and politicians in general are held at unusually low levels.

This is not difficult to understand. The objective of improving national welfare was adopted slowly by governments from the middle of the nineteenth century as a result of the growth of democratic ideas and institutions. The inability of governments to ensure this objective becomes, therefore, a direct threat to these institutions which is why – with their experience of the rise of political extremism in the inter-war period – politicians of different ideological persuasion attached so much importance after 1945 to achieving the five economic objectives listed earlier. In other words, governments of both the left and the right realized that if their countries were to avoid the horrors of the 1930s and 1940s they had to pursue policies that were in the national rather than in any purely sectional interest. Given the inherent inequalities of wealth, influence, and power in modern industrial societies, the state had to step in to achieve these objectives, since, given their past performance, sectional interests could not be trusted to act for the good of all.

The problem is even more acute now with the opening up of national economies and the growth of TNEs in every tradable sector. For instance, a policy of lower taxes may, as intended, increase the volume of savings. However, as the analysis in Chapter 6 shows, there is no guarantee that these savings will be invested in the country, raising its rate of growth and employment. Hence, contrary to government expectations, the result may be a deterioration in the country's economic performance, government revenues, and the quality of essential social services, thus increasing political dissatisfaction and instability. Emasculating labour unions in order to reduce wage levels and thus attract TNEs by promising to raise their profits is likely to have a similar effect in the long run. TNEs tend to operate predominantly in prosperous countries with a record of social and political stability.

As these are precisely the policies that governments in many industrial countries have been adopting since the early 1980s, it is hardly surprising that the voters have been turning away from the established parties (cf. Mackee and Rose 1991, Taylor 1992). This may not pose a serious threat at the moment to existing institutions and social order. But German experience in the early 1930s shows how quickly economic failure can be translated into a massive support for an extremist national party. (See Mackee and Rose 1991 and, also, Moore 1967.)

3.4   Conclusion

The institutional framework that defines the nature of an economic system, its *modus operandi*, is determined by the state. This is as true of *laissez faire* as of the most rigid form of central planning. To the extent that economic performance is influenced by the institutional framework (that is, the way that economic relationships and processes are defined and organized), other things being equal, changes for the better or for the worse will be the outcome of state action.

The reforms introduced after 1945 were obviously a major improvement, as they led to the most remarkable period of economic growth and prosperity achieved by the industrial countries since the beginning of the Industrial Revolution. Their strength is that, unlike the changes brought in since 1973, they were designed to deal with the realities and aspirations of the time. National governments can play an active and effective role in relatively closed economies. Open economies, as I have argued elsewhere (Panić 1988), require a different, supranational form of political organization and economic management to satisfy the same aspirations – unless nation states are prepared to risk a return to the economic warfare of the 1930s. The failure of national governments and parliaments to agree on one of these two courses of action has been a major reason why, since the early 1970s, industrial countries have found it much more difficult than before to achieve their economic objectives.

4

The Future Role of the State in Eastern Europe*

4.1 The need for pragmatism

Many people, not least economists, would probably find it difficult at present [1991] to believe that the state has any useful role to play in the economic reconstruction and long-term development of Eastern Europe (including former members of the Soviet Union). After all, is it not the all-pervasive power and incompetence of governments that is responsible for the economic and, in some cases, political disintegration that has taken place in these countries since 1989? The main task facing 'centrally planned economies' is, surely, to wrest power from the state, leaving it as little responsibility as possible (see, for instance, Kornai 1990).

There is, of course, a good deal of truth in such an argument. Nevertheless, it would be as big a mistake for the East in the 1990s to ignore the importance of the economic role of the state as it would have been for the West in the 1930s to adopt a similar attitude towards 'markets' when their spectacular failure led to the Great Depression. If there is one lesson that emerges clearly from the historical experience of a large number of countries – especially those with the most successful economies – it is that a sustained process of industrialization depends on close collaboration between these two forms of economic organization:

> No market economy has ever existed without a public sector which takes care of collective wants. In addition, the governments of market economies see to it that the private sector operates in an orderly fashion, reasonably stable prices and adequate aggregate demand being assured through monetary and fiscal policies. ... There is no fixed boundary line between the public and private sectors. (Halm 1968, p. 21)

---

* This chapter was previously published in D. Crabtree and A. P. Thirlwall (eds), *Keynes and the Role of the State*, Macmillan, London, and St Martin's Press, New York, 1993, pp. 176–203.

In spite of this, a vast amount of time and effort has been devoted over the last two centuries to attempts to prove exactly the opposite: mostly, that when it comes to economic decision-making, markets are superior to governments. The fact that the debate is still in progress indicates the futility of much of the analysis. There are clearly important limits to what either markets or governments can do, limits that are traditionally recognized in the literature on their 'failures'. But all that the literature does is provide important warnings about the tasks that each of these two forms of economic organization cannot perform either adequately or at all. There is quite simply no convincing way of proving theoretically the superiority of unregulated markets over central planning or the other way round (Helm 1986, Inman 1987, Stiglitz *et al.* 1989, Gordon 1991).

A perfect market or a perfect planner – both rational, knowing all that they ought to know and being able to foresee everything that they ought to foresee – will each produce optimum results. It does not require all that much ingenuity, therefore, to show that a perfect model of one against an imperfect model of the other will inevitably lead to policy recommendations in favour of the perfect model. Whatever the political value of this kind of 'scholarship', it is dangerously misleading as a guide to economic policy.

It was their awareness of this that was, no doubt, responsible for the fact that even leading classical and neo-classical economists generally had a rather pragmatic attitude towards the role of the state (Robbins 1952, Gordon 1991). Unfortunately, in their determination to rid society of mercantilist attitudes and practices which they regarded as a serious obstacle to economic progress, they concentrated so much on analysing 'government failure' and 'efficient markets' that they are associated to this day with the idea that the role of the state should be confined to that of a 'night watchman'.

As a result, they failed to set economics on the much more relevant and productive course of analysing not just the division of labour between the private and government sectors but also the dynamics of this relationship. The literature on government and market 'failures' – 'limitations' would be a much more appropriate term – makes it quite clear that each has distinct comparative advantages in certain areas of economic activity. Hence, the extent to which efficiency can be increased by greater competition or by replacing markets through greater government involvement will vary from sector to sector. It follows from this that 'optimum' solutions to economic problems are likely to result in appreciable differences in the relative importance and role of the state *both* between countries at any one time and within each country over long periods.

In other words, implicit in the literature is an important conclusion that has so far tended to be ignored: that the balance between the private and public sectors, between market- and state-initiated responses to change are no more static than the economic processes of which these forms of organization and decision-making are an integral part. Far from being fixed, 'the boundary' between the public and private sectors or, more precisely, their role in the running of an economy has to be redrawn continuously in response to internal developments and external shocks. Moreover, the change is not always in the same direction, as economic crises reveal that one or the other sector has taken on tasks that are beyond its limits of competence. The difference between successful and unsuccessful economies lies largely in their capacity for institutional adjustment and, occasionally, for radical change (Olson 1982).

This explains also why, periodically, there are marked shifts in public attitudes towards the role that the state and the markets should play in an economy. It all depends on which of the two is held responsible for major losses in economic welfare caused by a serious economic crisis. If it is the state (as in socialist and, to a lesser extent, capitalist economies in the 1970s) the generally perceived 'government failure' will create widespread demand for greater freedom to be given to 'the markets'. Alternatively, if it is the markets that are held responsible for a deep and prolonged crisis (as in the 1930s), 'market failure' will produce a strong consensus for the state to play a more active role in economic management.

The risk is that in time of particularly severe crises – when disillusionment with the existing system is widespread and the desire for change, any change, strong – public preference is likely to swing too far in the opposite direction, sowing the seeds of the next crisis and equally radical changes in national economic management. The result, as Hirschman (1982) has pointed out, is a long-term cycle rather than stability. When people become disillusioned with the ability of the state to achieve their economic objectives they turn to the market, whose failure then swings the opinion back in favour of the state, and so on.

The cycles are probably unavoidable. But their amplitude can be greatly reduced by making as clear a distinction as possible between three different kinds of persistent market or state failure to achieve socially desired objectives: those caused by corruption and incompetence, those that originate in unrealistic expectations and inappropriate policies, and those that are the result of inherent systemic defects. This is obviously easier said than done, as all of them will be at the root of every major crisis. Nevertheless, a careful assessment of each is essential, as otherwise serious mistakes are likely to be made in designing and implementing new institutions and policies.

Considerations of this kind are particularly relevant now [1991] in Eastern Europe, where a mixture of extraordinary economic ignorance, *naïveté* and dogmatism, combined with intense power struggles, is making it increasingly difficult to introduce the kind of reforms that these countries really need. For instance, it is one thing to diagnose correctly that corruption and incompetence have been one of the reasons for the poor performance of certain enterprises and sectors in Eastern Europe. It is, however, something quite different to claim that they will be eliminated with the introduction of market relationships based on private property, with the state involvement in the economic life of the countries reduced to a bare minimum. All that such claims do is raise expectations that no alternative economic system can satisfy, for the simple reason that these particular problems are common to all of them. Other things being equal, corruption and incompetence can be minimized by stricter laws, more effective regulatory bodies and measures that improve educational standards and occupational mobility. A systemic change may help by dislodging entrenched interests. The problem is that there is no guarantee that those who replace them will be more competent, or less prone to corruption.

That is likely to depend largely on the level of economic development and sophistication reached by a society. Unfortunately, this is an area in which Eastern Europe lags significantly behind Western Europe. The difference is most apparent in their efficiency and income levels. But it would be a serious mistake to attribute this entirely to the difference between the two economic systems. The reason for this is clear enough to any impartial observer familiar with the economic and political history of the two parts of Europe. Since the beginning of the Industrial Revolution no country in Eastern Europe has matched the levels of industrialization and affluence achieved by the most advanced countries in the world, most of which are in Western Europe (cf. Bairoch 1976a and 1982, Aldcroft and Morewood 1995). Hence, while a good deal of the difference in the existing standards of living, and managerial and administrative competence, may be systemic, a significant proportion is likely to be the result of different levels of economic development achieved by these two groups of countries.

The important thing is not to raise unrealistic expectations about the power of systemic changes to close this gap. The reforms now in progress in Eastern Europe may improve the countries' economic performance in the long run, perhaps even raise their standards of living to those prevailing in the world's leading economies. However, there is, of course, no guarantee that they will do anything of the kind. Most of the world is inhabited by nations that have always had 'market economies'. Yet only a relatively small number of them have managed to utilize fully their productive potential and thus eliminate widespread poverty, social deprivation and corrupt, totalitarian governments. It takes a good deal of technical ingenuity, economic enterprise, social cohesion and political maturity to ensure that a capitalist economy travels down the Scandinavian rather than the Latin American road.

None of this is intended to imply that there are no serious weaknesses in the economic system developed by the Soviet Union after its revolution and exported to other East European countries after the Second World War. However, the mistakes and faults specific to command economies have to be distinguished from those common to all economic systems if these countries are to achieve their economic, social and political objectives.

It is for this reason that the next section will consider some of the systemic and other failures common to socialist economies, in order to distinguish the functions that the state should not have undertaken in the past from those (analysed in the penultimate section) that it should learn to perform in the future. At the same time, the rest of this chapter will have little to say explicitly about the government or market 'failures' which have attracted so much attention in the economic literature. Apart from the fact that they are well known, it is impossible to generalize about the exact nature of goods and services that should be produced by either the state or the private sector. That is bound to be determined in practice by a country's resource endowments, economic structure, level of development and the ideological preferences of its population. In contrast, irrespective of the exact mix at the micro-economic level, there are certain key functions that the state has to perform in the management of all highly industrialized, modern economies – though, as already pointed out, they are likely to differ from country to country, or even within the same country at different levels of its development.

A careful consideration of these issues in relation to Eastern Europe is imperative at present, as there is a real danger that these countries will rush to replace one unworkable system (central planning) with another (unregulated markets) which has, historically, proved to be an even greater failure. The speed with which they are implementing their reform under the pressure from leading industrial nations and the major international organizations that these nations control suggests that their main purpose is political: to destroy the old system, whatever the cost, with little, if any, thought being given to building a realistic, viable alternative. Yet, there is, of course, a highly successful model from which such an alternative approach could be developed. The countries of Western Europe and Japan, with full US support, adopted a completely different approach to the liberalization of their economies after the Second World War when they found themselves in a rather similar situation to that which exists now in Eastern Europe (Panić 1991a).

4.2   Pitfalls outside the boundaries of government economic competence

Whatever weaknesses the socialist economies in Eastern Europe (including, as in the rest of this chapter, countries that formed the USSR) are exhibiting in the early 1990s, it is difficult to form an objective view of their causes if one ignores the considerable successes recorded by all of them over the preceding 40 years. Available evidence indicates that during this period they managed to narrow the gap which had existed between them and the most advanced economies in Western Europe in the 1930s in the levels of industrialization (Bairoch 1982) and per capita incomes (Bairoch 1976a, Summers and Heston 1988). They were also successful in maintaining full employment and an equitable distribution of income (Atkinson and Micklewright 1992), and in avoiding the kind of waste common in market economies as a result of planned obsolescence, unnecessary product differentiation, conspicuous consumption and the need for large advertising and promotional networks.

These are no small achievements. Yet the economic system that produced them is now being dismantled in all East European countries and for exactly the same reason: its failure to match the performance of West European economies, let alone live up to anything resembling the even more ambitious aspirations of a communist society. Although it is the former that has received a good deal of attention, it is the impossibility of creating a 'communist' system in conditions of economic scarcity that is at the root of economic and political problems experienced by all countries that have tried to reconcile the two.

One could argue *ad infinitum* about the meaning of 'communism', what Marx thought that it would look like and whether the countries that adopted the system were following his 'blueprint' (cf. Wiles 1962, Gordon 1991), assuming that what he had to say on the subject justifies such a label. Whatever the precise nature of the system, it appears to be feasible only if one of two basic conditions is satisfied. First, it seems to be attainable and sustainable in a country whose economy has abolished the problem of economic scarcity so that it can "meet [all] requirements at zero price, leaving no reasonable person dissatisfied or seeking more of anything (or at least anything reproducible)" (Nove 1983, p. 15). Second, failing this, communism, as a socio-political system, appears to be consistent with a society in which all needs are absolute, "finite and saturable" (*ibid.*) rather than relative. In this case, general abundance is created the moment an economy eliminates absolute poverty, something that can be achieved with a very simple division of labour.

These two conditions are important because it is only when one of them is realized that a government committed to creating a communist society can realize, *without coercion*, its professed goal of building a system that is more humane, more harmonious and, therefore, superior to any other. It can do this because it is in a position to avoid all those problems that lead to instability and conflict in other systems: poverty (because the economy can meet all material needs); inequality of income and wealth (because there are no factor scarcities); classes and exploitation (because the division of labour is either very simple or non-existent in a highly advanced, automated economy kept going by an economic version of *perpetuum mobile*); and, finally, the coercive power of the state (because the state itself is made redundant by the absence of classes and vested interests).

Clearly, any government that assumes power by promising to achieve these objectives in a world in which human needs are neither static nor absolute and whose productive capacity is totally inadequate to satisfy existing needs will encounter from the start strong resentment from a significant proportion of the population. This is inevitable, since the government will now be able to achieve its proclaimed objectives only by enforcing measures that make part of the population worse off, in many cases markedly so. Greater equality of income is realized and absolute poverty reduced by massive redistribution and tight control of incomes. Classes and exploitation, if not exactly abolished, are separated from private control over productive resources by transferring the ownership of property from individuals and families to the state. To ensure that those adversely affected by these changes are in no position to retaliate and thus threaten its existence, the state, far from 'withering away', finds it necessary, as in Eastern Europe, to assume even more coercive powers than those it has inherited.

Contrary to intention, it is the need for coercion to protect the system that lays the foundations for the economic difficulties that make it unviable in the long term. As the 'losers' include most of the professional, managerial and administrative classes, a newly founded 'communist' state quickly discovers that the people who are of critical importance if it is to function effectively and achieve its economic and other objectives are opposed to the very principles and goals that justify its existence. That being the case, it dare not trust them to act in the national interest (as defined by the government) rather than in their sectional interests, which are diametrically opposed to it. The result, apart from a highly authoritarian political regime, is the ubiquitous state involvement in every layer of economic decision-making: national central planning, facilitated at the level of the individual enterprise by the creation of large production units, often far too large to be run efficiently (Hare 1990).

Moreover, if such a highly centralized form of economic organisation is to exercise full control over resource allocation effectively, it becomes necessary for the system to dispense with prices as an indicator of relative scarcities and of the direction in which productive resources should be allocated. This is essential for two reasons: (a) to ensure that the markets do not override the priorities set by the government, and (b) to make such extensive planning feasible – something that would be impossible if prices were left to fluctuate freely and widely. Prices and wages are, therefore, not only fixed but also allowed to remain unchanged over long periods. As a result, planning targets can be determined and implemented entirely in quantitative terms.

By removing from individual enterprises the freedom to react to changes in their markets and in the general economic environment, the government takes over from their managers, in effect, the responsibility for the four basic economic decisions: what is to be produced, how, in what quantity and within what time horizon. Following the priorities set by the government, the planners decide on the targets to be met by individual sectors and enterprises, and allocate the resources that the latter can employ to achieve these targets. The managers, whose main responsibility is to ensure that the plan for their enterprise is fulfilled within a clearly specified period, are not allowed to alter or modify the task set by the planners. Only a higher, political authority is allowed to do that.

As the experience of East European countries shows, central planning can be an effective form of national economic management in the early stages of economic development, or in times of major post-war reconstruction. One of the reasons for this is that the state has the power to ensure the consensus for change, by force if necessary, without which it is difficult to achieve rapid economic progress. Equally important, it can mobilize scarce productive resources on a large scale and direct them towards projects of key national importance. In other words, it is in a position to undertake and co-ordinate large investment projects in infrastructure and industry by bringing together financial, managerial and other resources. In the same way, it can invest heavily in education, both generally and in those areas that are of particular importance for economic growth.

Yet, it is this very success early on that makes the whole system unsustainable in the long term. It is in the nature of economic development to increase continuously the division of labour and, in this way, the complexity of decision-making at both national and firm levels. This requires, as Chapter 2 shows, institutional flexibility and the capacity for change, requirements that are incompatible with a rigid, highly centralized form of economic organization. Ironically, it is the form of economic management created by the state to secure its long-term survival that becomes a major obstacle to its ability to achieve the high levels of efficiency and income that would make this possible.

The reason for this is that, apart from its disapproval of any change that may threaten its authority, a highly centralized form of decision-making is likely to give rise to a number of developments that are detrimental to a country's long-term economic progress. Particularly relevant in this respect are the failure to provide a system of incentives that would generate continuous improvements in economic performance; a degree of national insularity that extends well beyond the need to protect infant or strategic industries; and an acute shortage, despite considerable expenditure on education, of people with the managerial and administrative skills required at advanced levels of industrialization. It all adds up to a fundamentally static system, incapable of reforming itself. The obvious question is why?

The great danger with any form of economic organization whose *raison d'être* is political is that it will determine its priorities on the basis of considerations that bear little or no relationship to economic realities. Hence, a higher proportion of resources is likely to be used, especially if the state feels insecure, for unproductive purposes: defence, policing, propaganda and a large administrative apparatus with the task of producing and implementing the central plan. Moreover, as policies are determined according to a single view of the world imposed from above, and vast resources are committed towards implementing them, there is always the possibility of waste on a large scale if the original decision proves to be wrong.

The risk of this is likely to increase at every stage of industrialization, simply because of the system's inherent failure to train people in the administrative and managerial skills needed to run increasingly complex forms of economic organization, especially at the microeconomic level. If all that those managing an enterprise have to do is to make sure that the part of the overall plan for which they are responsible is carried out, there is no need for them to acquire the art of managing human, financial and other resources to anything like the extent that would be needed if they were responsible for the survival of the firm within a decentralized, competitive system. Not surprisingly, key positions in a command economy will be occupied by people with a proven allegiance to the aims and survival of the system rather than with the ability to run an industrial enterprise or farm. Consequently, these industrial bureaucrats are in no position to anticipate change, or even to notice it when it is already taking place, and act accordingly before it is too late. Moreover, as their position and further advance depend on carrying out conscientiously the instructions formulated at higher levels, they are likely to discourage and ignore warnings from their subordinates about impending difficulties. Knowing this, the latter may withhold the information at their disposal in order not to jeopardize their own careers.

A highly centralized economic system, therefore, fails (a) to create an effective system of communications which would enable it to detect the appearance and spread of serious weaknesses at the microeconomic level before these reach epidemic proportions, and (b) to encourage individual enterprises to innovate and improve efficiency in a way that would solve the problems and thus avoid a crisis in the whole system. The difficulty is that, in the absence of competition, it is far from easy to judge the efficiency of individual producing units. So long as each satisfies the only criterion available – the fulfilment of quantitative targets set by the planners – its performance will be regarded as satisfactory, irrespective of the quality of goods and services and the efficiency with which they were produced. To make things worse, individual enterprises have no incentives to economize on the use of various inputs, as these are allocated to them by the central authority. In fact, given the uncertainty created by the system's rigidity (Erickson 1983) that normally surrounds the supply of raw materials, parts and components, each enterprise will tend to hoard as many of its inputs as it can.

All this will magnify a problem that is present in all complex economic systems: that of the availability of relevant information and the speed with which it is relayed between those who make decisions and those who have to execute them. The larger the organization, the more difficult such a dissemination of knowledge becomes. Hence, in very large organizations there is always the danger that information reaching decision-makers may be inadequate, irrelevant, incorrect or out of date. The same applies also to the way that their decisions filter down to those who have to carry them out.

This explains the practice in capitalist economies of decentralizing decision-making processes within large organizations by allowing a greater degree of autonomy to individual departments, subsidiaries and affiliates. For obvious reasons, the channels through which information has to flow in command economies are very long. Output quotas are set by planners who lack detailed technical knowledge rather than by managers who have it. The former cannot, therefore, produce the plan without the information provided by individual enterprises. Clearly, it is of critical importance that they receive as accurate information as possible – which is precisely what may not happen. It makes sense for managers to supply deliberately incorrect data in order to be allocated lower quotas than their enterprise is capable of producing, thus making their task much easier. As a result, the economy may well operate with a good deal of excess capacity; and the irregular supply of inputs is likely to encourage corrupt practices and transfers of resources between enterprises of which planners are not aware. This in itself would be sufficient for the failure to reach planned targets in certain sectors and exceed them in others.

In addition, it is not unusual for unrealistic objectives to be set in certain areas and then achieved by switching resources to them from low priority sectors such as services and consumer goods. The result is a growing imbalance in the growth between heavy industry, which is relatively easy to plan and supervise, and consumer goods and services, which are not. The latter normally consist of a great variety of products and require an attention to quality that the planners, who are too distant to observe the great diversity of consumer preferences and tastes, cannot easily take into account. The result is a narrow range, poor quality and an inadequate supply of many services and consumer goods. The shortages, common to all these economies, provide even less incentive for managers to improve the quality and increase the range of their products.

Although they are real enough, these problems would probably not cause general dissatisfaction with the system if the world consisted entirely of socialist economies, all at more or less similar efficiency and income levels. Their governments could then point to the undoubted success that they have achieved so far and the fact that their system was offering the highest standard of living available at the existing level of technical knowledge. It is obviously much more difficult to make claims of this kind when there are economies in close proximity, such as those in Western Europe, which have quite clearly achieved, under a completely different economic system, a much higher standard of living and social welfare as well as a far greater degree of political freedom than anything available in Eastern Europe. One way of avoiding widespread dissatisfaction with the command economy and the unrest that could destroy it is to adopt a policy of national insularity by keeping contacts with the more successful countries to a minimum. Information about these countries is suppressed and permission to travel to them given only to a privileged minority who have an interest in preserving the existing system.

Leaving aside its socio-political implications, there is a high economic price to be paid for such insularity in the long term. The insularity deprives the socialist economies of the chance to improve their efficiency by copying the technology, organization and practices of the most successful enterprises and economies in the more advanced market economies. Japan has shown what can be achieved over a relatively short period by pursuing an outward-looking development strategy behind protective walls until its firms became ready to compete successfully on international markets. Industrial enterprises in centrally planned economies – lacking the kind of internal competition that helped 'select' the most successful Japanese firms – could have been exposed in this way to *indirect* competition. The planners could have set, after observing the best-practice techniques abroad, quality and efficiency targets for each enterprise to achieve and then apply sanctions against those firms that failed to reach them.

That, however, is precisely what governments in Eastern Europe found it virtually impossible to do. It is difficult for a system that claims to represent the highest form of economic and political organization to admit its inferiority without undertaking fundamental reforms that would alter it beyond recognition. This is never easy, especially if it is likely to threaten – as it would have done in Eastern Europe – the whole power structure of these countries. No wonder that the numerous reforms attempted since the 1950s have failed to achieve their objective of radically improving the performance of the 'centrally planned economies'. Perhaps it is easier to understand the reasons for this when it is remembered that these countries never even managed to produce the statistical information that would have enabled the planners to compare the aggregate performance and efficiency of their economies with those of developing and highly industrialized countries (Kaser 1990).

The pretence of systemic 'superiority' could be sustained as long as it was possible to preserve insularity; and in an age of rapid technical advances that could not be expected to last for ever. The advances in communications, notably television, revealed to East Europeans the extent to which their standard of living and quality of life were below those in Western Europe. This created even more dissatisfaction and pressure on the governments to introduce reforms that would improve the range and quality of goods and services. At the same time, the arms race with the highly industrialized countries in the West moved to a much more advanced technical level. These two developments exposed both the relatively lower level of industrialization achieved in Eastern Europe and the limitations placed on further progress by the rigidity of its economic system.

The only way to overcome these disadvantages was to do the very thing that these countries had tried so hard to avoid: become involved to a greater extent in the international division of labour. The problem was that their highly centralized and politically controlled system, combined with the lack of managerial expertise, produced sub-optimal results even with imports of technology and capital equipment from the West. Finally, the energy crises, slower growth and protectionism in the West made it very difficult for a number of heavily indebted socialist economies to service and repay their debts. As a result, like other heavily indebted medium-income countries, they experienced sharp falls in their standard of living, high unemployment and increases in income inequality.

Economic stagnation in the 1980s, after several decades of rapid and sustained progress, increased social discontent and political instability around the world. However, in Eastern Europe these problems became particularly serious because the stagnation deprived the economies of the few advantages that they could claim over the much more advanced capitalist economies: the ability to secure economic stability, full employment and a fairly equitable distribution of income. Without them, there was nothing left to justify the system's continued existence. The time had come for its radical transformation.

Nevertheless, it is doubtful that the collapse would have been so rapid in the absence of such a close link between the economic and political aspects of the system, with the former entirely subservient to the latter. It was possible, therefore, to demolish the whole authoritarian political edifice by discrediting and reforming the inflexible, inefficient economic system that it controlled. But does this mean that there is no useful role left for the state to play in East European economies?

4.3 The management of a capitalist economy

Economic debate on the role of the state often confuses two important, fundamentally different questions. What is the optimum size of the public sector in an economy? And what role should the state play in a modern industrial society? The first question concerns what the public sector should do and how it should do it. The second, on the other hand, deals with what the government ought to do at the macroeconomic level and why. The two may, but need not be, related. It is not difficult to find in practice the government of a country with a small public sector playing a much more active part in the economy than the government of a country in which such a sector is large. As emphasized at the beginning of this chapter, government involvement in the economy will be determined by the country's level of industrialization, the structure of its economy and the nature of its economic system.

However, in one important respect the role of the state is always and everywhere of critical importance. Irrespective of the economic system, only the state can enact and enforce the laws, rules and regulations that ultimately determine the character of that system. Both *laissez-faire* and a command economy need an institutional framework within which to operate; and no one but the state has the authority and the means to create and safeguard such a framework.

Hence, to restate the obvious, whatever the exact form of the economic system that eventually emerges in Eastern Europe, it will be shaped by the state. It is equally certain that the system is not going to be uniform. As their cultural traditions, historical experience, resource endowments and ideological preferences differ, there are bound to emerge important variations in the way that these economies operate, including the role that the state plays in each. Capitalist economies, which is what they are all determined to establish, tend to differ – often markedly. Freedom stimulates creativity, which, in turn, produces diversity. There is, quite simply, no such thing as a single, universally applicable model of a capitalist economy!

Given its scale and uniqueness, it is fashionable to argue that the systemic change taking place in Eastern Europe represents completely uncharted territory. Although this is undoubtedly true of the nature and timing of specific decisions, it does not apply to certain basic principles that should guide these decisions. In managing the transition of their economies, and in developing an institutional framework that will enable them to play an important role in their performance afterwards, East European governments are in a position to learn from their own mistakes (such as those described in the previous section) and from the course of action adopted after the Second World War by West European and Japanese governments.

For instance, East European governments can make an important contribution to the short-to-medium-term performance of their economies by encouraging and assisting something that their predecessors worked so hard to prevent: a careful study of the various practices evolved by trial and error in the more advanced and successful economies. However, to be effective, such a borrowing of ideas, technology, management and administrative techniques has to be selective – concentrating on those aspects of Western knowledge and experience which are applicable in the conditions prevailing in the borrowing countries. Technical, like financial, assistance can easily be wasted unless it is directed towards the areas where it is likely to be most effective, which in turn depends chiefly on the recipients' ability to define their needs clearly – an area in which governments, in collaboration with the private sector, have played an important role since the beginning of the Industrial Revolution.

The contribution which East European governments make in this respect will depend to a considerable extent on how quickly they absorb what is probably one of the most important lessons from the West European experience after the Second World War: the way in which economic policy in these countries (unlike in socialist economies) was dominated by pragmatism rather than by ideology. As Myrdal (1960) observed towards the end of the post-war reconstruction period, government action in advanced capitalist economies that led to the creation of the welfare state after 1945 was the result of events not ideology. As a result, governments of different ideological persuasion pursued identical objectives. When their policies differed, the difference was the result of variations in national economic conditions and institutions, not their attachments to some utopian ideological blueprint (cf. Panić 1991a).

The importance of a realistic, pragmatic approach to problems of economic restructuring cannot be emphasized too strongly. To accomplish a successful transformation of their economies and socio-political systems, East European countries need more than a consensus for change (which they have). Equally important, they have to mobilize a consensus for the form that the change is ultimately to take, something that is clearly lacking at present. No course of action can lead to a successful conclusion unless it has at the outset a clearly defined objective. This is essential both to mobilize the resources required to achieve their desired goal and to ensure that the methods used in the process are not such as to make it ultimately unattainable. The state is the only form of organization at present that can articulate national aspirations in a complex modern industrial society as well as mobilize, when necessary, large-scale resources to realize them.

To be able to do this, a government needs to formulate national objectives in such a way as to reflect the aspirations of the majority of the population. However, although extremely important, that in itself is insufficient unless the country has the necessary productive resources at its disposal. This means that, normally, a clear distinction has to be made between the long-term goals (which reflect national aspirations) and the more modest short-term objectives (which reflect available resources). Given the danger of generating unreal, utopian aspirations of the kind described in the previous section, this is something to which East European governments should pay particular attention. Equally important, they should have learned from their history by now that there is a limit to sacrifices in welfare that people are prepared to tolerate for the sake of unspecified gains that they are promised in some distant future. Otherwise, like the communist governments before them, by encouraging unrealistic expectations they are likely to set in motion a sequence of events that is virtually certain to take them down a totalitarian road, not unlike the one they have just left.

The authorities in Eastern Europe are at a serious disadvantage in trying to perform such tasks, for the simple reason that there is very little confidence either in their willingness or in their ability to act in the national interest. With very few exceptions, governments in that part of the world have always tended, whatever their political colour, to be authoritarian, corrupt and incompetent. Hence, the state is unlikely to play a constructive role in the new order unless it depoliticizes the economic system. Strictly speaking, this is never entirely possible at the macroeconomic level because of the role that economic activity plays in the social and political life of a country, including its security and survival. However, it is both possible and desirable for precisely these reasons that decisions at the microeconomic level are the responsibility of individual enterprises acting in accordance with economic, not political, criteria. This means, of course, the privatization and decentralization of large sectors of the economy – a major task that only the state can perform. It also happens to be another task in which a pragmatic approach to the problems is of critical importance.

This applies to both the scope and timing of privatization and deregulation. It is difficult to think of anything more likely to discredit the experiment with a capitalist economy than attempts at 'overnight' transformation of the kind imposed in a number of these countries. Economic systems do not exist in a vacuum. For a capitalist economy to increase rather than diminish economic welfare it needs all those practices and institutions that are currently lacking in Eastern Europe: a legal framework of property and other rights and obligations, a financial system that can accommodate a wide diversity of needs and preferences, a proper system of accounting, a system of industrial relations, regulatory institutions to prevent market malpractice, a central bank and a ministry of finance capable of pursuing stabilization policies, and so on.

In the absence of all this, even if the means of production could be transferred without difficulty from the state to private ownership, it would require a miracle to make most of the newly privatized enterprises more efficient and responsive to consumer needs. The change in ownership is, of course, no guarantee of a change in the performance. Apart from the factors already mentioned, all these economies are desperately short of people with the managerial, administrative, legal, political and other skills needed to operate an advanced capitalist economy successfully. Consequently, given the size and market dominance of many enterprises in Eastern Europe, the most likely outcome of rapid deregulation and privatization is widespread bankruptcies, unemployment, growth of the 'black economy' and a ruthless exploitation of market power – leading to all the inefficiencies and distortions normally associated with monopolies. According to Kaser (1990), developments of this kind posed a serious threat to the 'Prague spring' in 1968 even before the Soviet tanks moved in.

Thus, instead of allowing the newly created 'market economy' to realize its full potential through efficient allocation of resources, the most probable outcome of hasty deregulation and privatization is a substitution of new price distortions for old ones. Even worse, it will give rise to the conditions which are ideal for powerful vested interest to take over effective control of the whole system (see, for instance, Clapham 1982) – making it virtually impossible to realize precisely those aspirations that were behind the 1989 revolutions: economic prosperity, social harmony and democracy.

As West European experience after 1945 shows, only the state has the power to prevent the substitution of one inefficient, brutal totalitarian system by another. But this requires a degree of self-confidence, public support and external assistance that is lacking in the much more economically and politically immature countries of Eastern Europe. The management of transition is an extremely important role that the state is unlikely – barring a miracle – to perform successfully in these countries without considerable external assistance.

Suppose, however, that they negotiate this particular hurdle in the foreseeable future and achieve the desired level of economic prosperity. Would the state have a useful role to perform then? Luckily, as before, the experience of the most successful capitalist economies provides a ready-made answer.

It is clear from the way that such economies have evolved that the state has an important role to play at high levels of industrialization. First, as there are a number of goods and services that only the state can produce satisfactorily in a modern society, the public sector tends to be large. Given its size, changes in public sector activity will have a significant effect on the rest of the economy: its output, employment, investment and income. (See, for instance, Ram 1986.)

Second, the higher the level of industrialization, the more complex is the division of labour. Tasks performed by individuals and groups become highly specialized and, consequently, interdependent. The success of any one course of action becomes, therefore, dependent on the collective response of a large number of individuals and groups, most of whom are completely ignorant of each other's existence. In the circumstances, it becomes essential for some institution to articulate collective goals and provide coherent signals to enable all these disparate activities to produce the desired overall end result. Otherwise, industrialization will increase the problem of uncertainty to such an extent as to make further progress more difficult and, eventually, impossible.

In theory, it is unnecessary for anyone to take on the role of the ultimate coordinator of economic activity, since 'the markets' can do it efficiently through prices. Prices provide the signals that enable all economic agents to act promptly and accurately so that their actions stabilize the economy, allocate resources efficiently and distribute income in a way that is socially acceptable. Although most of the decisions that enable advanced capitalist economies to achieve these objectives with considerable success are made at the microeconomic level, the overall outcome can fall short of the social optimum. (See Stiglitz 1994.)

There are a number of reasons for this. If prices are distorted by monopolies, externalities and imperfect information – all common in contemporary capitalist economies – they cannot provide 'correct' information, which means that they are unable to coordinate macroeconomic activity. Moreover, in an increasingly oligopolistic environment more and more adjustments are made in quantities, not prices.

It is hardly surprising, therefore, to discover that the overall outcome of actions taken independently at the microeconomic level can be suboptimal: for example, macroeconomic results of individual decisions can be contrary to the original intentions (Schelling 1978); cooperation that excludes government can create problems of 'the prisoner's dilemma' type (Vickers, 1985); and, as Keynes (1936) showed, markets lack the self-regulating properties capable of ensuring stable output and full employment. It is the last of these, the realization that various market failures can cause massive losses in economic welfare with disastrous social and political consequences, that in the end forced governments in capitalist economies to take on the role of the stabilizer, allocator and reconciler (redistributor) of last resort – with each of these functions encompassing more than purely budgetary activities of the kind described by Musgrave (1959).

All this is so familiar that it does not need elaboration. However, there are a number of reasons why these functions are likely to retain considerable importance in the East European context, making it essential for the governments to develop the institutional framework capable of discharging them effectively.

The ability to perform the role of the stabilizer of last resort satisfactorily is of particular relevance in Eastern Europe for two reasons. First, whatever their shortcomings, socialist economies did manage to sustain full employment. Hence, as developments in the former East Germany illustrate, people in these countries are unlikely to accept unemployment with equanimity. With heavy structural unemployment virtually inevitable, and the countries' limited capacity to provide the sort of welfare cushion common in Western Europe, it is important to take steps to minimize cyclical unemployment. Otherwise, there is a serious risk that (unfamiliar) job losses may eventually give rise to political instability and extremism of the kind common in Europe in the 1930s.

Second, as the systemic changes can be expected to produce enough uncertainty to discourage the investment needed to deal with problems of structural unemployment, it is essential not to compound the adjustment difficulties with policies that result in avoidable cyclical fluctuations. This is also one of the reasons why Eastern Europe should proceed slowly with the opening up of its economies, as rapid liberalization of trade and capital flows would make it even more difficult for their inexperienced governments to perform the stabilizing role.

For reasons analysed by Gerschenkron (1966), since the beginning of the Industrial Revolution governments have played an important role as the allocator of last resort, by encouraging and assisting investment in those areas where the private sector is either reluctant to commit resources or finds it difficult to mobilize them on the scale required. However, it is precisely because of their experience under socialism that this is an aspect of government activity that is now likely to find little favour in Eastern Europe with both governments and the public at large.

The problem is that many of the investments that these countries have to undertake urgently, such as those in infrastructure, fall exactly into those categories where government participation is essential because of their scale and the risks involved. Moreover, a good deal of uncertainty surrounds the ability of newly privatized enterprises to survive, let alone generate a satisfactory rate of return. Potential investors, domestic and foreign, are likely, therefore, to be highly reluctant to lend to such enterprises without government guarantees. For all these reasons, East Europeans would do well to study carefully the structure and performance of the Japanese financial system in this area before it was deregulated (cf. Corbett 1987 and 1990), as well as the extraordinary success of Japanese industrial policy (cf. Dore 1986). Whatever their ideological and political preferences, given the level of development that they have reached so far and the size of the task facing them, East European countries are unlikely to make much progress towards their long-term objectives without a successful government performance in the role of the allocator of last resort.

Finally, there are important reasons why East European governments should pay particular attention to their role as the reconciler (or income redistributor) of last resort. This is normally one of the most difficult areas of economic policy, not least because there are no absolute standards of equity and fairness. What matters in practice is what is regarded in any particular country as 'equitable' and 'fair'; and, as pointed out in the previous section, people in Eastern Europe are used to a good deal of equality in the distribution of their income and wealth. There is a strong possibility, therefore, that a significant widening of income differentials, as they move towards market economies, may create such resentment as to make it impossible to achieve the objectives that inspired the recent overthrow of the authoritarian governments.

The problem is practical rather than ethical. If the team effort, which is the key to modern economic success, is impossible without cooperation, willing cooperation is impossible without widespread approval of the existing form of economic and social organization. This ensures that the objectives towards which the effort is directed are widely shared. Diverse economic groups and interests will then cooperate in achieving them, as they all expect to benefit from the cooperation in a way that they regard as 'just'. As the final result will depend on the quality as well as the quantity of the collective effort, it is essential for the state, as the ultimate co-ordinator, to help ensure that *both* positive and negative freedoms (Berlin 1969) are diffused as widely as possible. In other words, optimum results are likely to be achieved when people are not only free to do something but also *able* to enjoy fully the benefits of freedom.

It is characteristic of all the most successful capitalist economies that their governments, whatever their ideological predilections, have made considerable efforts to try and reconcile equity with efficiency. Given that experience shows markets to be incapable of achieving this, East European governments will also have to pay special attention to what is one of the most sensitive issues in economic policy.

4.4 Conclusion

Contrary to the view currently in vogue, the state has an important role to play in the 'new' Eastern Europe. No doubt, some of the governments will perform the tasks analysed in this chapter better than others, for the same reasons that some public and private enterprises are more successful than others. At the same time, to paraphrase Tolstoy rather crudely, while unsuccessful economic organizations and systems may be inefficient for reasons that are specific to each, all successful ones tend to share, among other things, one characteristic: highly competent, publicly minded political leaders and administrators, able and willing to anticipate future events and act accordingly – backed by a strong national consensus for a particular course of action.

As things stand at present, East European countries are obviously short of both. The progress that they make in acquiring them will determine not whether their governments have an important economic role to play in the future but whether they perform it, in partnership with the private sector, in a way that increases rather than diminishes economic welfare.

Part III

The Origins of Globalization: Institutional and Spontaneous

5

Economic Development and Trade Policy*

National governments have been under greater pressure to liberalize their trade since the 1970s than ever before. The result, as this chapter shows, has been to break in many cases the long-standing link between economic performance and trade policy that could have important consequences for the existing international economic order.

The apparent break with tradition is particularly evident in the case of developing and transition economies. Trade liberalization has become one of the key conditions that they have to satisfy in order to qualify for financial and technical assistance from international organizations. As they rely heavily on these organizations for both, the failure to remove barriers to trade is bound to affect adversely their ability to achieve urgently needed improvements in economic welfare. The problem is that if they open up prematurely their economies, as demanded by outside donors, the long-term consequences for these countries may be equally damaging.

These developments, and the growing international hostility towards the World Trade Organization, make it necessary to re-examine in the light of historical experience the relationship between national economic performance and trade policy, as it has played such an important role in determining international economic and other relations. One question, in particular, is of critical importance at the moment: is it rational for countries at different levels of development to pursue the same, or even similar, trade policy?

The present chapter tries to answer this old and frequently debated question by analysing the *dynamics* of trade policies: the main reasons for their differences between countries and for their changes over time within countries. The analysis concentrates, therefore, on the most important arguments

---

* This is a slightly revised and expanded version of a paper orginally published as *DAE Working Paper No. 9006*, Department of Applied Economics, University of Cambridge, 1990.

for protection and the extent to which they have historically influenced commercial policies of a number of countries.

Although many of the arguments in the first two sections are familiar, the sections also contain a good deal of material that is new both in its content and analysis. The emphasis throughout is on dynamic considerations based on the experience of many countries *and* important developments in modern industry.

5.1   A very old controversy

For over two centuries now economists, politicians and, frequently, the public at large have been engaged in one of the most heated debates in economics: namely, whether free trade or protection is more likely to generate rapid economic development and thus make a greater contribution to economic welfare. Yet despite the time and effort invested, the vast theoretical output has at best produced 'ambiguous results' (Diaz-Alejandro 1975, Krugman 1987, Bhagwati 1989, Stern 1989). This is hardly surprising, as the most influential early protagonists set the debate on the wrong course by basing their arguments on fundamentally different premises (see Panić 1988, Chapter 7) – a practice followed to this day. The historical evidence is of no greater help to those looking for a conclusive answer, whether they analyse the effect of trade policy on economic development in the nineteenth century (Kravis 1970, Capie 1983, Bairoch 1989a) or more recently (Stern 1989).

The inconclusive nature of the empirical evidence is, in many ways, much less surprising than the 'ambiguity' of the theoretical models. Trade policy, after all, is only one of a wide range of policies pursued by individual countries in the course of their economic development. It is only to be expected, therefore, that as Corden (1975, p. 60) put it: "In relation to GNP, most policies other than macroeconomic ones have small effects ... [Hence] the effects of trade policy changes are often overrated". More recently, development economists have been emphasizing the fact that, although highly autarkic policies may slow down the rate of economic growth, there is no evidence that any particular approach to trade policy will lead to rapid growth (Chenery *et al.* 1986, Morris and Adelman 1988). Quantitative estimates (notoriously unreliable) of the effect of either free trade or protection on GNP tend to support this view. They are usually very small, amounting to no more than a few per cent of GNP. This seems to be true both in the nineteenth century (Kravis 1972, McCloskey 1980) and in the second half of the twentieth century (Corden 1975).

Not surprisingly, even some of the leading authorities in this branch of economics have admitted that the profession is in no position to provide satisfactory answers to a number of the key questions of economic policy (Corden 1975, Balassa 1975). For example, as things stand at present, it is far from clear why countries that pursue similar trade policies often achieve significantly different rates of growth. The same is true also of the fact that some countries are more protectionist than others. Why? Even more puzzling, why are some countries protectionist at some times but not at others? Or, why have some sectors been traditionally more successful than others in persuading their governments to protect them against foreign competition? Indeed, there is little unanimity even when it comes to answering such a basic question as: Why do countries actually protect their industries (see Corden 1975, pp. 83–4)? With so much uncertainty, even ignorance, concerning some of the most important aspects of trade policy, there is no guarantee that economists can be trusted to answer correctly questions of particular interest to policy makers such as: What is the most appropriate trade policy for a particular country? Or, what is the most appropriate mix of national trade policies for a viable and lasting international economic order?

It will be suggested in this chapter that satisfactory answers can be offered to most of these questions provided that we *start* with a well-known fact: that at any particular time not only efficiency and income levels but, more important, *the capacity for change* will vary significantly between countries, mainly as a result of differences in their level of economic development. Similar variations will also be apparent in a particular country over time – reflecting predominantly different phases of its development.

An explicit recognition of these differences at the beginning rather than at the end of analysis in this area is essential, because trade policy, like all policies, is formulated not in a vacuum but in response to specific problems. As a result, if the problems confronting two or more countries differ their policies will also have to differ. The same applies to a particular country during different phases of its development. Not surprisingly, other things being equal, economic analysis suggests and historical experience shows that it is the level of economic development (and thus, normally, the ability to reconcile internal and external balances without protection) that will be of critical importance in shaping national trade policies, rather than the other way round. (See Panić 1988, Part III.)

Some of this has, of course, always been recognized by economists, both classical and modern. Advocates of free trade have often accepted the need for protection under certain circumstances; and those urging protection have rarely failed to point out that they regarded it as a temporary measure, to be discarded as soon as the country was in the position to liberalize its trade without suffering losses in economic welfare (Panić 1988, Chapter 7, Bhagwati 1989). In other words, economists, at least the more pragmatic practitioners of the discipline, have always been aware of the fact that, although possible in theory, there is no such thing in practice as a unique, optimum, trade policy applicable at all times and places – for the simple reason that economic conditions differ, often markedly, from country to country.

5.2   Why countries resort to protection

There are certain types of trade restriction that are common to all levels of development. For instance, some activities will tend to be protected (through restrictions on imports and/or export subsidies) for strategic reasons. Historically, most countries have regarded it as a matter of national interest to preserve a high degree of self-sufficiency in agricultural products and in certain industries that supply armaments and other defence equipment. Retaliation by a country in response to new, or higher, import duties imposed against its exports is another frequent reason for protection. Lastly, protective measures can be introduced, or existing ones increased, purely for bargaining purposes: to force other countries to reduce their protection levels; or, alternatively, to counteract the monopoly power of foreign firms and force them to reduce prices (Shepherd 1978). However, the effectiveness of protection used for either of these purposes will depend very much on the size of the country concerned. Countries with large domestic markets obviously enjoy much greater bargaining power than those whose markets are small.

At the same time, there are four reasons why a country may resort to measures that restrict foreign trade which, unlike those just described, have their origin largely in its level of economic development relative to the rest of the world.

5.2.1   Administrative underdevelopment

The first reason common to subsistence economies and to countries in the early stages of industrialization, stems mainly from administrative limitations that make it difficult for the governments to raise adequate revenue. Unlike other forms of taxation, tariffs (in other words, taxes on imports) are relatively easy to collect. So also are taxes on exports. This is as true of certain low income countries today as it was of the now highly advanced economies before they started to industrialize. (See Davis and Legler [1966] for the importance of tariffs in US Federal Revenue in the nineteenth century.) Taxes on foreign trade are responsible, on average, for a third of tax revenue in developing economies. In some of the smaller countries the proportion exceeds 40 per cent of total government revenue (UNDP 1999, p. 92).

However, even in the case of these countries, there are likely to be considerable variations in the reliance on trade taxes. Some developing countries will have a much more advanced and efficient fiscal system than others. In addition, the responsibilities and needs of governments will vary a good deal from country to country; and so also, of course, will their ability to attract military and other grants from abroad. The last factor may, in fact, be of critical importance in this context, as the countries with underdeveloped administrative systems will almost invariably have a very limited capacity to raise loans on international capital markets.

As their ability to impose and collect domestic taxes is limited, premature trade liberalization will affect adversely more than the competence of governments in developing economies to assist in the setting up and growth of new industries. The reduction in their revenue, brought about by trade liberalization, will also restrict the governments' capacity to promote improvements in a number of areas of critical importance in economic development, such as health, education, transport and communications. What is more, many governments in developing countries will become unable to provide even a minimum 'safety net' for the people living on the borderline of absolute poverty – whose numbers may be increased by those who have lost their jobs and income as a result of trade liberalization. Their survival will then often depend on 'humanitarian aid' from the rest of the world.

5.2.2 Infant and transplant industries

As soon as they begin the process of sustained industrialization, countries will normally employ trade policies for quite a different reason: to facilitate the creation and growth of new industries either from domestic resources or by attracting foreign investment and firms.

In the first case, new ('infant') industries need to be protected until their comparative disadvantages are overcome through learning by doing. (The following argument need not apply, at least for as long as it has a clear lead over other countries, in those cases where technical breakthroughs enable a country to develop a completely new industry.) This would, of course, be unnecessary in a world of constant returns to scale, perfect competition and given technical knowledge. Firms would be small and have equal access to all existing and future knowledge. This would enable them to exploit with equal efficiency the comparative advantages characteristic of their country. Moreover, they would be in no position to prevent new entrants into their industry for the simple reason that they would lack internal ('firm-specific') advantages that would give them the market power to drive potential competitors out of business.

Economies of scale and technical progress change all that. The fact that costs decline with size means that no matter how many firms start a new industry, in the end there will be only a few of them left – giving the industry an oligopolistic structure. The surviving oligopolies will come to dominate their industry by possessing technical, financial, marketing and/or managerial advantages over other starters. It is these advantages that eventually enable them to achieve their size and dominance through internal growth, mergers and acquisition of their less enterprising competitors.

In other words, successful oligopolies achieve their superiority by developing advantages, specific to each firm, which make it possible for them to drive high-cost competitors out of business. That gives them an even larger share of the market and thus the ability to utilize further economies of scale. The newly acquired advantages can then be protected by discouraging or, if necessary, eliminating new entrants into the industry. The established firms can do this by using their accumulated knowledge and resources to reduce the price of their products to a level that a newcomer cannot match. Once the new firm is driven out of business, the prices can be raised back to their original level.

Early on in the development of a new industry, the process just described will be confined to one or, at most, a few countries. However, as the domestic market begins to be satisfied to the point where the rates of profit and investment start to decline, oligopolies will turn increasingly to exports; and, once this process begins, the existence of economies of scale and continuous technical progress will, in conditions of free trade and low transport and communications costs, eventually replicate at the international level the increase in concentration that had taken place within national economies. In other words, relatively few oligopolies, possessing distinct advantages over their foreign competitors, will drive these out of the industry, carving up the world market among themselves. The share of the market acquired in this way will then be protected by eliminating new entrants in other countries in exactly the same way as new firms at home were eliminated.

It is this ability of established foreign firms to destroy a country's new industries that makes it necessary for governments of developing countries to come to the aid of their fledgling firms either with subsidies or with tariffs and other forms of import control. For a long time this has been the instinctive national reaction, but is it rational? Is not a country's economic welfare irreparably damaged by protecting a new, high-cost domestic industry instead of allowing cheaper imports?

The answer would be firmly in the negative (that is, such policies would be irrational) if the advantages specific to certain firms and industries were also specific to the countries in which they had originated to an extent that could not be replicated elsewhere even in the long run. In fact, there are very few industries in which the reliance on raw materials, cheap labour or a large domestic market is so great that the advantages enjoyed by certain countries cannot be competed away in the long term by other nations through superior technical and organizational advances. As John Stuart Mill observed in the middle of the nineteenth century: "The superiority of one country over another in a branch of production often arises only from having begun sooner" ([1848] 1965, p. 918).

In other words, a country's *comparative* advantages in most 'branches of production' depend on the ingenuity, dynamism and accumulated skills of its citizens rather than on some inherent qualities that are beyond the reach of other countries. The problem faced by latecomers to industrialization is that it takes a long time to acquire the skills required at high levels of development as well as economies of scale internal and external to individual firms and industries.

That being the case, it is only natural that developing countries will wish to establish certain industries likely to improve their economic welfare in the long run despite the fact that, in the short run, their firms will be at a clear disadvantage compared to the existing foreign producers. Two types of industry will have particular attraction for most of them: those that generate external economies and those whose products enjoy a high income elasticity of demand – not least because, frequently, the same industry will share both these qualities. If successful, industries of this kind will not only accelerate domestic growth, through the multiplier process, but also ease the problem of reconciling internal and external balances (Panić 1988).

As economies of scale and learning by doing are common to such industries, it is hardly surprising that 'new' developments in the theory of international trade policy confirm something that has been clear for a long time from empirical observation. By offering subsidies to firms and restricting imports in 'strategic' industries, government policies will encourage their development under certain conditions by restricting foreign competition (see, for instance, Brander and Spencer 1983 and 1985, Krugman 1986). Alfred Marshall ([1920] 1959, p. 416) had made, in fact, the same point long before. The difference between private and social interests, he pointed out, is "less important with regard to those things which obey" the law of diminishing rather than the law of increasing returns to scale. Hence, "in the case of the latter, there is strong *prima facie* reason for believing that it might often be to the interest of the community directly or indirectly to intervene, because a largely increased production would add much more to consumers' surplus than to the aggregate expenses of production of the goods".

Eventually, these industries may achieve efficiency levels at least comparable to those of their foreign competitors, making further protection unnecessary. This argument is, in fact, consistent with the views of Hamilton ([1791] 1934) and List ([1841] 1885), the two most influential advocates of protection as a policy instrument in the *early* stages of a country's industrialization. Contrary to the view attributed to them in economic literature, neither Hamilton nor List argued for protection as a permanent instrument of economic policy (see Panić 1988, Chapter 7).

The key point made by the economists quoted above is that, in conditions of continuous technical progress, external economies, economies of scale and oligopolistic competition, protection of infant industries need not lead to the development of inefficient, inward-looking, autarkic economies (see also Krugman 1984). On the contrary, once these industries reach a level of efficiency and competitiveness equal to that existing abroad, the logic of oligopolistic competition will drive them to move into export markets for the simple reason that the domestic market will be too small to satisfy their constant need for growth in order to survive (Panić 1988). Consequently, although some countries, especially large ones, may start with an 'inward' rather than an 'outward-looking growth strategy', the more successful their industrialization is the more likely is this distinction to become blurred. That is, what starts as an 'inward looking' strategy will sooner or later become 'outward-oriented' in successful, rapidly expanding economies; and vice versa in the case of unsuccessful, stagnant economies. In other words, trade policy will depend in the long run on the success or failure of the overall economic strategy. The large welfare gains that are likely to follow trade liberalization in the former and create serious adjustment problems in the later (see Richardson 1989) will tend to ensure such an outcome.

Nevertheless, the likelihood of long-term success is greater in those countries that start their industrialization with an outward-looking economic strategy – that is, by copying the best practice techniques of production and organization from the leading economies. This is the way that the world's most advanced economies have achieved their current levels of efficiency and income. However, *without exception*, they protected their key industries until these managed to reach international levels of competitiveness – thus ensuring that trade liberalization did not cause serious losses in domestic economic welfare. As a result, in all these cases a highly successful outward looking economic strategy preceded for quite some time opening up of national economies to foreign competition. Policy makers in highly successful economies have been, irrespective of their ideological predilections, careful not to confuse economic 'openness' with an outward looking growth strategy. The three countries – Britain, USA and Germany – that have served as models to the rest of the world provide a classic example of this (see Panić 1988, Bairoch 1993, Deane 1965, Lazonick 1991, Goldstein 1993, Goldsmith 1995).

The alternative strategy to that of relying predominantly on domestic resources to develop infant industries – especially in countries with large, or potentially large, markets – is to use protection in order to attract foreign direct investment. In this case, when foreign firms are providing finance as well as technical, managerial and marketing know-how, the main purpose of protection is to force foreigners to set up production facilities in the country if they want to maintain access to its large, or rapidly growing, market. These were certainly the factors that influenced the direction of foreign direct investment before the First World War (Bairoch 1976b, Bloomfield 1968). More recently, barriers to trade, even threats of such barriers, have been one of the reasons for US and Japanese direct investment in the European Economic Community (Lunn 1980, Turner and Tuveri 1984).

As in the case of infant industries, these 'transplant' industries may be offered only temporary protection in countries whose general economic progress is such that their location-specific advantages rapidly become comparable to those that exist in the most advanced economies. Other things remaining equal, this will ensure that foreign firms continue their operations in such a country even when the barriers to imports are removed.

Clearly, the attractiveness of protection in the case of both 'infant' and 'transplant' industries is that it enables permanent benefits to be achieved either by imposing temporary restrictions on imports or by offering temporary subsidies. The snag is that, as already indicated, this generalization does not apply equally to all countries. As a result, disparities in their performance and circumstances will affect the level, extent and longevity of the protective measures that they pursue. *Ceteris paribus*, successful economies are likely to liberalize their trade much earlier. It is in their interest to do so, especially if their action encourages other countries to reciprocate.

There is, however, an important reason why even among highly successful countries some may liberalize trade much earlier than others: the size of their economies. For instance, a large country can restrict imports over a wide range of activities and over a long period for the simple reason that its domestic market is sufficiently large to enable firms to exploit economies of scale fully without the need to engage significantly in foreign trade. Such a policy may also, as mentioned above, attract foreign direct investment because of the country's large size. These advantages, plus the fact that a large country is likely to be well endowed with natural resources, will ensure that the rest of the world is of no more than marginal economic importance to it. Consequently, it will be under no pressure to pursue a liberal trading policy in order to encourage other countries to reciprocate. Access to foreign markets, although beneficial, is not of vital importance to its powerful economic interests – until their domestic market becomes saturated and the pace of technical progress slows down. It is at that stage, with the return on new investment falling, that firms from large countries will concentrate their attention on the global market as the key to their long-term success and survival.

A small country, on the other hand, depends heavily on foreign trade to satisfy its needs as well as to exploit economies of scale. Moreover, it can do the latter to a limited extent only, as the resources at its disposal force it to specialize within a narrow range of activities. The small size of its market will also limit the extent to which it can attract foreign direct investment unless it enjoys some important country-specific advantage. *Ceteris paribus*, these factors will tend to make its trade policy protectionist over a shorter period than the policy pursued by a large country – though the actual levels need not differ.

However, the ultimate success or failure of either infant or transplant industries will have much less to do with a country's trade policy than with the variations in all those factors that account for observed differences in the long-term economic performance of nations: the extent to which their social and political conditions stimulate or retard economic progress; the effectiveness of their educational and financial systems; their labour relations; and the managerial, technical, financial and marketing skills of those in charge of the new industries. In the absence of these factors, no amount of protection will enable infant industries to survive, let alone prosper, in the long run; nor can protective measures on their own be sufficient to attract foreign transnationals into a stagnant or declining economy. Moreover, significant differences even in one of these factors will probably be more than enough to produce noticeable disparities in the economic performance of two or more countries despite the fact that they are pursuing identical trade policies.

5.2.3   Declining industries

The third major reason why countries resort to protection is to shelter their declining or 'senescent' industries – the industries that find it increasingly difficult to compete internationally without import restrictions or subsidies. For obvious reasons, it has received a good deal of attention from proponents of free trade, anxious to show that protection leads to a serious misallocation of resources.

There are two problems with this argument. First, short-term misallocation of resources caused by their *under*-employment in declining industries is not necessarily more costly to the community, than the misallocation and the social costs that would arise from their long-term unemployment. Unless economies operate in the extremely unlikely conditions of perfect competition, it takes time for productive resources to be switched from declining to other industries. *Ceteris paribus*, the more advanced and specialized an economy the longer is this process likely to take. Second, although possible in theory, there is no empirical evidence that senescent industries can be protected indefinitely. The period over which protection has to be offered for this purpose will depend ultimately on the underlying economic and other conditions prevailing in a country. In general, it is likely to differ according to whether the economy in question is growing or stagnant.

The main aim of this type of protection in dynamic, rapidly growing economies is to rationalize, contract, even run down completely, declining industries without imposing too great a cost on the community (cf. Cheh 1974, Lavergne 1983). In other words, the aim is to protect employment and income during the transitional phase – a course of action that was strongly supported even by such influential advocates of free trade as Adam Smith and David Ricardo (see Panić 1988, pp. 123–4). According to Adam Smith, if the adjustment cost was likely to be significant "the freedom of trade should be restored only by slow gradations, and with a good deal of reserve and circumspection". Ricardo reached exactly the same conclusion because, in his view, sudden abolition of trade barriers could be "ruinous" to those whose livelihood depended on the sectors affected and thus turn out to be an "enormous evil".

In the *long* run the protection of declining industries saves neither the jobs nor the industries themselves either from a combination of major rationalization and modernization, or from terminal contraction (see, for example, OECD 1985). It does no more, therefore, than make the adjustment problems more manageable in the short run – a far from negligible function, as recent evidence shows that these problems may be substantial even in the most advanced economies and take years to solve (Richardson 1989, Wood 1994). In the process, protection also helps avoid social upheaval. The danger of this arises from the fact that the industries concerned are usually labour intensive, relying on low levels of skills and wages. Consequently, people made redundant are not very mobile and can therefore easily fall below what is regarded by society as an acceptable standard of living. This explains why measures to protect textile industries normally command so much public support (Anderson and Baldwin 1987, Ray 1981). In general, people attach considerably more importance to loss of income than to an equivalent gain (see Kahneman and Tversky 1979 and 1984). As the inter-war example of Germany illustrates, few developments are likely to be more destructive than a marked, permanent deterioration in the status and lifestyle of individuals and groups. What is more, as in the case of Germany, the destruction need not be confined to the country concerned.

The whole process of contraction is likely to take much longer in a stagnant economy, as the opportunities for alternative employment are far more limited. The intensity and the cost of protection may, therefore, increase over time until the burden of supporting the uncompetitive sectors reaches such proportions that the rest of the country refuses to tolerate it any longer. Conflicts of interest of this kind may well eventually cause serious economic problems and social, even political, unrest.

Implicit in this is an extremely important consideration, largely ignored in the theoretical literature. The overall stance of a country's trade policy tends to be determined mainly by the balance of power between its internationally competitive and uncompetitive sectors. It all depends in the end on their relative importance in the economy and on the extent to which the former regard their country's commercial policy to be against their interests, in the sense that it encourages other countries to pursue similar policies.

A classic example of this is provided in the nineteenth century by the conflict between agricultural and manufacturing interests in Europe, or more precisely between those in the UK and those on the continent (Helleiner 1973, Kindleberger 1978a). Continental landowners wanted free trade because they expected it to secure them entry into the lucrative UK market, as they were much more competitive than their UK counterparts. UK manufacturers advocated free trade for the same reason: they were confident that, thanks to their superiority over European manufacturers, it would give them easy access to the continental market. Not surprisingly, UK landowners and continental manufacturers were against free trade – though they were joined in the last quarter of the nineteenth century by continental landowners who changed their mind when cheap grain from North America and Russia began to flood their markets.

Furthermore, this and similar examples raise a question that is especially relevant today: what exactly does the concept of 'free trade' mean in conditions of oligopolistic competition and unequal development? (See also Chapter 6.) UK manufacturers and continental landowners were clearly expecting the benefits from trade liberalization to amount to more than a temporary access to foreign markets. They were confident that, with the barriers to trade removed, their cumulative advantages would be such as to prevent potential foreign competitors from achieving improvements in efficiency that would become a serious threat to their own long-term predominance. In other words, in promoting the cause of trade liberalisation they were advocating effectively *free trade protection* – protection of the advantages that they had acquired by starting, as Mill put it, 'sooner'.

This also explains why powerful US transnational corporations have been so active in promoting, through their Government and the World Trade Organization, liberalization of trade in developing and transition economies (see Korten 1995). Under the conditions of costly technological advances, economies of scale and oligopolistic competition trade liberalization may mean in practice no more than a switch in protection from those trying to acquire international competitive advantage to those who are already enjoying it.

5.2.4   Inadequate external finance

Finally, a country will resort to protection to improve its balance of payments and thus economize on its scarce reserves of foreign exchange. It needs little reflection to realize that, other things being equal, the need for this type of protection will be greater in the early stages of development than later – as the capacity to reconcile internal and external balances improves with industrialization (Panić 1988, Halevi 1971). However, even at lower levels of development, the need to economize on foreign exchange will be reduced if a country is able to attract, over a number of years, sufficiently large inflows of *long-term* capital to finance its current account deficits relatively easily.

That, of course, assumes that there is no change in the country's access to foreign markets for goods and services. This is important because a very sudden and adverse change in external conditions will increase the difficulty of reconciling internal and external balances by reducing the country's exports and, in this way, its capacity to acquire foreign exchange. (This is particularly true of small and medium-sized countries.) The problem can arise either because of a severe recession in the countries to which it exports or because the governments of these countries impose tariffs on its exports, or, frequently, both (see OECD 1985, IMF 1988). The result is a sharp deterioration in the country's balance of payments, accompanied by a fall in output and employment in its tradable sectors and, as a result, in the rest of the economy. The loss in welfare caused by external changes may leave the country little alternative but to introduce or increase its own tariffs in order to protect employment and income.

5.2.5 Protection and growth

It should be clear from the preceding analysis that there is no reason to expect protection levels to be correlated with rates of economic growth. Fast growing economies may resort to protection to nurture their infant and transplant industries, to achieve a sustainable balance of payments and, to a lesser extent, to avoid unacceptable economic and social costs while rationalizing and contracting their declining industries. Slow-growing economies, on the other hand, will want to protect their uncompetitive sectors in order to safeguard employment and income, to improve their balance of trade and, to a lesser extent, to create new industries. Hence, identical levels of protection can be associated with quite different rates of economic growth.

In contrast, there are several reasons why relative levels of economic development should influence a country's trade policy. The more advanced a country is the more sophisticated and effective will be its administrative apparatus for levying and collecting taxes, the smaller will be the proportion of both infant and declining industries relative to the rest of the economy and, lastly, the greater will be its capacity to reconcile internal and external balances without resorting to protection. Hence, *ceteris paribus*, the higher the level of development the lower should be protection levels.

Translated into dynamic terms, this means that over time a country's trade policy is likely to change with changes in its economic position and performance relative to other countries. Normally, it will start with a highly restrictive trade policy in the early stages of industrialization, liberalize it as its competitive position improves, reaching very low protection levels at the peak of its international competitiveness, but reverting to more restrictive policies if, or when, its relative position deteriorates. Long-term changes of this kind can be observed clearly from adaptations in UK and German trade policies since the early nineteenth century in response to changes in the countries' relative economic fortunes (Panić 1988, Chapter 8).

In general, trade liberalization tends to reflect the extent to which a majority of economic interests within a country feel confident that they will gain from greater international openness; and they will do so only when they are highly competitive internationally. Hence, as they gain ascendancy on world markets, employers will advocate trade liberalization in their own countries in order to use this to put pressure on other countries to reciprocate, making it easier for them to enter foreign markets. They will have the support of their employees, confident that freer trade will improve their employment and income prospects rather than cause unemployment and loss of income. Finally, consumers of the sectors' products will welcome trade liberalization, as it will increase their choice. For all these reasons, other things being equal, the more successful an economy becomes the greater will be the influence of these groups relative to those anxious to protect the existing order and, consequently, the more liberal will be its commercial policy.

In contrast, in a stagnant economy whose competitive strength is declining, the power relationships will be exactly the opposite of those described above so that the economy will tend to become more and more protected over time.

5.3   A taxonomy of protection

The main proposition developed in the preceding analysis – that it is the relative level of a country's economic development that determines its trade policy, not the reverse – is illustrated in Figure 5.1. The vertical axis shows levels of protection (T) and the horizontal axis levels of GDP per capita (Y). The former can range from zero (completely free trade) to 100 per cent (when all trade is controlled in one form or another). Income levels, on the other hand, start above zero (at some minimum level below which no population could survive) progressing up to the level achieved by the world's most advanced economy.

Given that both protection and income levels can differ widely from country to country, Tm and Ym indicate their median international levels. Hence, any country located along one of these lines has an average level of either protection or income; and a country located on the point at which the two intersect has (by world standards) average levels of both protection and income. All other countries will be found in one of the four areas into which Tm and Ym divide the diagram:

- I: countries with efficiency and income levels *below* and protection levels *above* the world average;
- II: countries with both income and protection levels *below* the world average;

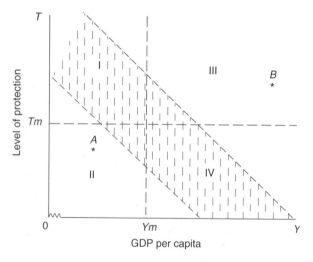

Figure 5.1   A taxonomy of protection levels

- III: countries with both income and protection levels *above* the world average;
- IV: countries with efficiency and income levels *above* and protection levels *below* the world average.

Figure 5.1 thus provides a very broad taxonomy of international trade policies. As countries start their economic development at different levels of productivity and income and then achieve unequal rates of economic growth, many of these disparities will remain, even increase, in the long term; and, according to the analysis in the preceding section, *ceteris paribus*, this will be reflected in their trade policies. Hence, if plotted in Figure 5.1, most countries should lie – at any one time – somewhere between the upper left-hand corner of I (the least advanced economies) and the lower right-hand corner of IV (the most advanced economies), roughly within the shaded area.

Over time, a country with a rate of growth above the world average will move from I to IV – though not necessarily along a smooth, downward path. It takes time for the tradable sectors of a late starter to reach levels of competitiveness comparable to those in the most advanced economies. Even longer is probably needed for influential economic interests connected with these sectors to feel confident that a more liberal commercial policy by their country would be to their advantage – in the sense that it would secure them easier access to lucrative foreign markets by encouraging other countries to pursue similar policies. Moreover, once such a consensus is reached nationally, subsequent trade negotiations between governments may be very lengthy, especially if they involve a number of countries. Hence, the transition from high to low levels of protection is likely to take place in a series of steps. Exactly the opposite process will be at work in a country which, having achieved a high level of development, goes through a long period of relative economic stagnation (with its productivity and per capita income growing well below the world average). If nothing is done to reverse the process, such a country will tend, in the very long run, to regress from IV to I – again in a series of steps.

The stepwise movements in both these cases are consistent with the proposition that the *rates* of economic growth are unlikely to be related in any systematic way either to levels or changes in protection. For economic, social and political reasons, adjustments in commercial policy will usually lag, often appreciably, behind changes in international competitiveness.

As economies capable of sustaining unusually rapid growth or stagnation over long periods are not common, many countries may remain in IV or I even in the long run. The reason for this is that although they may improve their economic welfare substantially – they will do so at the rates which will not alter their relative positions significantly. In the long run, Ym will shift to the right and Tm downwards, reflecting higher levels of industrialization and per capita incomes and lower levels of protection globally. But the combination of internal levels of development and trade policies will still place most countries within a range similar to that expressed in Figure 5.1 by the shaded area. In other words, the shaded area will shift to the right with *Ym* and become flatter as *Tm* moves downwards.

At the same time, there are always bound to be exceptions: countries in either II or III, well outside the shaded area. There are many reasons for this. For instance, *A* in II may represent a country rich in one or more natural resources. Although its levels of industrialization and per capita income are below the world average, its favourable resource endowment enables it to attract foreign investment as well as technical and managerial expertise. The steady inflow of foreign capital plus easy access to foreign markets makes it possible for *A* to reconcile its internal and external balances without the need to raise import duties. However, this is likely to change as soon as it embarks upon a sustained programme of industrialization. For reasons analysed in the previous section, it will then raise its protection levels – most likely moving into I before (if it manages to achieve and sustain a rate of economic progress above the world average) descending slowly into IV in the long run.

Alternatively, *A* might be a declining economy whose relative rate of growth, since reaching an advanced level of industrialization, has been so low that it has declined, over time, from IV to II. Nevertheless, it still persists with a commercial policy much more appropriate to its past than to its current level of development relative to the rest of the world.

Lastly, *A* may represent a country which, although at a relatively low stage of industrialization, is required by international treaties to follow a liberal trade policy completely inappropriate for its level of development. Some countries may enter willingly into such treaties by joining a trading block like the European Economic Community. More often, however, countries finding themselves in this position will be those lacking political and/or economic independence. Most Asian and African countries were forced to sign such treaties in the nineteenth century. More recently, as already mentioned, some of the countries (notably in Latin America and former socialist economies) heavily dependent economically on one or more of the leading industrial nations, or on international organizations controlled by these nations, have had to open their markets in exchange for external financial assistance.

Nothing could be further from this position than *B*, a country with both income and protection levels well above the world average. The most obvious example of this would be a very large, highly industrialized economy with a favourable ratio of natural resources to population. Since foreign trade is of no more than marginal importance to such a country, it is very difficult for the rest of the world to force it to reduce its high levels of protection. The task of mobilizing international consensus for this purpose will be made even more difficult by the fact that many countries of small, even medium, size may be heavily dependent on that country for one or all of these: access to its market, its exports of technical and managerial knowledge, or for its military protection against their more powerful neighbours. Consequently, *B* may remain indefinitely in III, or move into IV for political rather than economic reasons.

Another possibility is that *B* has such a favourable ratio of land to labour that it enjoys a high standard of living despite a relatively low level of industrialization. Protection is then used to enable it to develop its own industry – not least by ensuring that profits and real wages are so high as to attract foreign capital and labour, especially skilled labour.

Finally, it is implicit in the preceding analysis that, *ceteris paribus*, the dispersion of protection levels will be greater the greater is the international dispersion in efficiency and income levels. Put another way, other things being equal, countries with similar levels of industrialization and income per capita will tend pursue similar trade policies.

5.4 Historical evidence

The central proposition to emerge from the preceding two sections is straightforward enough: as underlying economic conditions vary significantly according to the stage of development reached, *ceteris paribus*, a rationally pursued trade policy – which is only one of a wide range of policies used – will largely reflect a country's level of economic development.

The important question now is whether available evidence about relative levels of development and trade policies is consistent with this proposition. Do national trade policies reflect the level of economic development? And, if this is the case, does it apply equally to all periods for which relevant data exist?

In principle, it should not be too difficult to answer these questions. All that is needed is some indicator of protection, such as tariffs, to be related to, say, estimates of GDP per capita as the most appropriate measure of relative efficiency and income levels. Table 5.1 shows that, as one would expect, there is a positive and statistically highly significant relationship between a country's ranking according to its level of industrialization (measured by the volume of manufacturing output per capita) and its ranking according to overall levels of economic development (indicated by GDP or GNP per head).

There are, however, a number of statistical problems. The most obvious is to find a reasonably adequate measure of aggregate protection. Estimates of tariff levels at different times exist for a number of countries. They normally show the revenue from custom and import duties expressed as a percentage of total imports. One problem with these data is that they may underestimate the extent and effectiveness of protection offered by tariffs. For instance, if new tariffs cause home demand to switch from foreign to

Table 5.1   Rank correlations of per capita levels of GDP/GNP and industrialization, 1913–80[1]

	r	t^2	Number of countries in the sample
1913[3]	0.73	4.45	19
1925[3]	0.83	6.73	22
1965[4]	0.93	10.43	20
1980[4]	0.70	4.14	20

Notes
[1] Appendices 5.A and 5.B give a full list of the countries included in these calculations, plus the sources of the data used.
[2] All the coefficients are statistically significant at the 5 per cent level.
[3] Excludes Argentina, Chile, Hungary, Indonesia, Peru, The Philippines and Thailand because indices of per capita levels of industrialization are not available for these countries.
[4] Turkey is excluded for the same reason.

domestic products, or from foreign products that are subject to import duties to those which are not, this may reduce the proportion of revenue from taxed imports to total imports. Consequently, the data will indicate that the country's trade policy has become more liberal when, in fact, exactly the opposite is the case.

The other problem is that the data normally refer to *nominal* rather than *effective* import duties, as they ignore dissimilarities in tariff levels imposed at different stages of production. There is always the danger, therefore, that in certain cases actual levels of protection may be seriously underestimated. In fact, although effective rates tend, on the whole, to be higher than nominal tariffs, empirical studies show that the ranking of countries and industries is virtually identical irrespective of which of these two measures is used (Balassa 1965, Grubel and Johnson 1971).

A much more serious problem is the uncertainty about the extent to which any *one* measure of protection really reflects the overall character of a country's commercial policy. Tariffs are only one of a wide range of policy instruments designed to restrict imports. Since the First World War at least, quotas and other direct forms of protecting domestic producers have been often more widespread and effective (League of Nations 1943, Page 1979, OECD 1985, World Bank 1987). In addition, devaluation or depreciation of a currency may also impose at least temporary barriers to imports as well as provide subsidies to exports (Corden 1982). Finally, some countries may restrict their exports either for economic reasons (to relieve shortages and inflationary pressures at home) or for political or strategic reasons.

The main problem in empirical research, therefore, is that no existing measure of protection includes all these barriers to trade. Consequently, one has to use whatever indicator is available internationally on a comparable basis – the practice adopted in this chapter. That has meant a heavy reliance on estimates of tariff levels – which are a more satisfactory indicator of trade policies for some periods than for others.

For instance, tariffs are almost certainly a fairly good indicator of the relative levels of protection in 1913. At that time, quantitative restrictions on trade in goods and exchange controls on capital flows were not in common use. Moreover, most of the countries included in the relevant tables and graphs in this section were on the gold standard, or pegged their currencies to those on the standard. Some of these considerations are also relevant in 1965. By that time, only a few of the less industrialized OECD countries included in the analysis were still relying extensively on non-tariff barriers to trade; and, although exchange controls were employed widely, exchange rates were fixed. 1925, 1931, 1974, 1975, 1979 and 1980 are less satisfactory in this respect because most of these controls were in use.

The disadvantage of relying on a single measure of protection in empirical analysis need not be as serious as it seems if it can be established that countries tend to employ at the same time and to a similar extent more than one form of trade barriers. This can be checked for the last four years analysed here by using not only tariff levels but also the indicators of 'managed trade' estimated by Page (1979). The figures refer to a country's trade in goods "that is subject to some non-tariff control, by exporter, importer or both" (Page 1979, p. 166). These include "quotas, anti-dumping duties, licences, certificates of origin or other administrative controls, price controls", voluntary export agreements and others (Page 1979, pp. 166 and 169). Ordinary correlations of tariffs and managed trade for 1974/5 and 1979/80 show that there is a positive, statistically significant relationship ($r = 0.51$ and $r = 0.45$ respectively) between the estimates of managed trade and those for tariffs for the 25 countries for which both these sets of data are available.

The results suggest that it is not unreasonable to assume that there is a tendency for countries to employ simultaneously and to a similar degree both tariff and non-tariff barriers to trade. At the same time, the coefficients are sufficiently low to indicate that many countries whose tariffs are relatively high will have relatively low other forms of trade management, and vice versa. Consequently, whenever possible, it seems advisable to use both these measures.

The choice of years has been dictated primarily by the availability of the indicators used in the analysis. However, it so happens that the years selected fall at or close to some of the turning points experienced by the world economy since 1900: 1913 (the last year of the much admired period of 'free trade' before the First World War); 1925 (the year in which a concerted effort to re-establish the gold standard began); 1931 (the collapse of attempts to recreate the pre-1914 international economic order, as even the most advanced economies increased barriers to trade); 1965 (a year towards the end of the extraordinary economic boom that followed the Second World War, and just preceding the great wave of trade liberalization in the second half of the 1960s); 1974 and 1975 (the beginning of the end of the long postwar boom caused, among other things, by the first oil shock, which also heralded the revival of protectionism, especially in industrial countries); and, finally, 1979 and 1980 (the years of the second oil shock, soon to be followed by the international debt crisis).

Finally, these problems, plus a few others explained below, account for the simplicity of the empirical tests used in this chapter.

It will be noticed that the results set out in all the tables, as well as the observations in one of the four graphs in this section, refer to country ranks – even though ordinary correlation coefficients and simple regressions were also estimated. Both of these produced results consistent with the main argument developed in this chapter, more so in fact than the rank correlations. Nevertheless, only the latter are reported.

There are several reasons for this choice. Some of them have to do with data problems while others are purely conceptual. Data showing international differences in GDP per capita, or levels of industrialisation, are no more than rough approximations (see Kravis *et al.* 1978, Bairoch 1982). Apart from differences in the coverage and accuracy of the original national estimates, the purchasing power of currencies is extremely difficult to assess adequately. There is therefore no guarantee that changes in the purchasing power of individual currencies are reflected in changes in their exchange rates (Isard 1977, Horne 1983). Hence, different estimates may show considerable variations in their relative levels of per capita GDP or industrialization even for the same group of countries. The *rankings* of countries obtained by researchers using these criteria, on the other hand, normally tend to show much more uniformity.

Differences in protection levels are also far from easy to assess accurately. Some of the problems associated with this were mentioned earlier. In addition, the fact that, say, tariff revenues account for the same proportion of imports in two countries does not necessarily mean that their barriers to trade are identical (even if they do not rely on any other protective device). The coverage of imports may be much more comprehensive in one of them than in the other; and, even if it is the same, tariffs imposed by one of these countries may be more restrictive.

Lastly, the various qualifications described in the preceding two sections suggest that international differences in protection levels at any particular time need not reflect fully measured differences in the levels of GDP or industrialization per capita. It all depends on the ease with which individual countries can reconcile their internal and external balances. Moreover, during a period for which relevant data are available, two or more countries may pursue trade policies that are much more consistent with their past (relative) position in the world economy than with their current position. Consequently, it seems reasonable to postulate quite simply, other things being equal, (a) that the higher a country's international ranking in GDP (or industrialization) level per capita the lower will be its ranking in protection levels; and (b) that there will be no statistically significant relationship between the rankings in protection and changes in the levels of GDP (or industrialization) per capita.

It is remarkable therefore that despite all these problems and so many shocks and far-reaching changes in the international political and economic environment between 1913 and 1980, including changes in the relative position of countries, most of the results reported in this section are consistent with the preceding analysis – though there are a number of notable and important exceptions.

To begin with, the simple tests of the second proposition are set out in Table 5.2. They consist of the four rank correlation coefficients between changes in per capita GDP and the levels and changes in (a) tariffs between 1965 and 1980 and (b) managed trade (that is, non-tariff barriers to trade) between 1974 and 1979. This particular analysis is confined to the two most recent periods for the simple reason that consistent estimates of protection levels are available for a number of countries for both the first and the end year of each period.

The results provide no support for the view held by the Bretton Woods organizations that countries with lower levels of protection will experience

Table 5.2 Rank correlations of growth of GDP per capita and levels and changes in protection (all imports), 1965–80[1]

	r	t^2	Number of countries in the sample
1965–80			
Percentage change in GDP per capita and tariff levels in 1965	0.26	1.18	21
Percentage change in GDP per capita and percentage change in tariff levels	−0.21	0.93	21
1974–79			
Percentage change in GDP per capita and levels of managed trade in 1974	0.22	1.52	45
Percentage change in GDP per capita and percentage change in levels of managed trade[3]	−0.06	0.33	32

Notes
[1] Appendices 5.A and 5.B list the countries included in these estimates and the sources of the data.
[2] None of the coefficients is statistically significant at the 5 per cent level.
[3] Excludes countries with 100 per cent managed trade in 1974 and 1979.

faster growth of GDP per capita. All the coefficients are statistically insignificant at the 5 per cent level. This is true irrespective of whether levels of tariffs or managed trade are used. Nor does it make any difference whether the changes in GDP per capita are correlated with the level of protection at the beginning of a period or changes in protection levels during the period. Using protection levels at the end of each period, or an average of the levels at the beginning and the end of the two periods, produced results that were virtually identical to those shown in Table 5.2. The obvious implication is that factors other than trade policy were far more important for the relative performance of the countries included in the analysis. These results are, therefore, consistent with the analysis in the previous two sections, and with the findings of the researchers quoted at the beginning of this chapter.

At the same time, the coefficients in Table 5.3 confirm an *inverse* relationship between rankings of countries by their levels of development and protection in almost all the years analysed. This applies equally to the

Table 5.3 Rank correlations of protection levels and per capita levels of GDP and industrialization, 1913–80[1]

	All imports and GDP[2]				Imports of manufactured goods and industrialization[2]		
	r[3]	*t*[3]	*N*[4]		*r*[3]	*t*[3]	*N*[4]
Tariffs							
1913 (a)	−0.02	0.10	26	(b)	−0.35	*1.36*	16
(b)	−0.41	*1.98*	21				
(b, c)	*−0.60*	*3.15*	20	(b, c, d)	−0.54	*2.22*	14
1925(a)	−0.07	0.34	28	(b)	−0.44	*1.96*	18
(b)	−0.36	1.77	23				
(b, c)	−0.54	*2.85*	22	(b, c)	*−0.67*	*3.53*	17
1931[5]				(a)	*−0.70*	*3.66*	16
(c)	*0.85*	*5.73*	15	(c)	*−0.88*	*6.60*	15
1965(a)	*−0.59*	*3.16*	21		n.a.		
1975 (a)	*−0.48*	*2.41*	21		n.a.		
1980(a)	−0.30	*1.36*	21		n.a.		
Managed trade							
1974 (a)	−0.32	*2.25*	45	(a)	−0.21	*1.03*	25
1979 (a)	−0.18	*1.24*	45	(e)	−0.21	*1.01*	25

Notes
[1] Appendices 5.A and 5.B list the countries included in these calculations, plus the sources of the data.
[2] (a) All countries; (b) excluding China, India, Indonesia, the Philippines and Thailand; (c) excluding the United states; (d) excluding Russia; (e) excluding Belgium.
[3] The figures in italics are statistically significant at the 5 per cent level.
[4] Number of countries in the sample.
[5] US tariffs on all imports are not available.

correlations involving levels of tariffs and managed trade. ('Tariff levels' refer, of course, to tariff revenues expressed as a percentage of the value of total imports.)

However, it will be noticed that not all the coefficients are statistically significant; and for the first two years (1913 and 1925) it is the inclusion of the United States and several low-income countries that makes significant difference to the results. Four of the five low-income countries (India, Indonesia, China and Thailand) were forced by colonial powers to adopt a policy of free trade, even though the last two were nominally independent (Bairoch 1989a, Maddison 1989). This is almost certainly the main reason for their position in the bottom left-hand corner of quadrant II in Figure 5.2. The Philippines, on the other hand, occupies a place in quadrant I, very much as one would expect from a country at its level of development. Nevertheless, it is excluded from the second group of correlations for 1913 and 1925 because, like the other four countries, the Philippines lacked the autonomy to pursue an independent tariff policy.

As can be seen from Table 5.3, there is a marked improvement in rank correlation coefficients between tariff levels and GDP per capita for both 1913 and 1925 when these five countries are excluded. But the coefficients

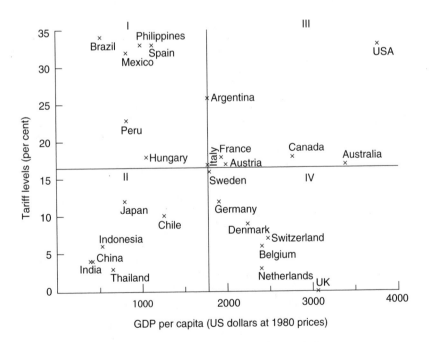

Figure 5.2 Tariff levels on all imports and GDP per capita, 1913
Sources: League of Nations (1927); Maddison (1989); Bairoch (1981).

become statistically significant at the 5 per cent level only when the United States is also left out. The exclusion of the United States is justified because its protection levels remained exceptionally high in the early part of the twentieth century despite the fact that by 1913 its per capita levels of GDP and industrialization were well ahead of those achieved by the other countries included in these calculations. For example, in 1913 only Brazil (34 per cent) among the countries in this particular sample (League of Nations 1927, Maddison 1989) exceeded the US tariff level (33 per cent). Yet the American level of industrialization per capita was eighteen times higher than Brazil's (Bairoch 1982) and its GDP per capita more than seven times higher (Maddison 1989). The US economy became even more protected during the inter-war period following the Fordney–McCumber Tariff of 1922, greatly increased subsequently by the Smoot–Hawley Tariff of 1930. (See Appendix 5.B for the sources giving these and other protection levels used in this chapter.)

Not surprisingly, as Figure 5.2 shows, the United States occupied in the early part of the twentieth century a position in the upper right hand corner of quadrant III. Australia and Canada were the other two countries with protection in excess of what one would expect from countries at their levels of income per head, though their tariffs were well below those in the United States. This explains why the results for 1913 and 1925 in Table 5.3 are highly significant statistically only when the United States is excluded.

There is a change, however, for 1931 when the correlation coefficients become highly significant statistically even with the US in the sample. (Data for tariffs on all imports are not available for the United States). The reason for this is not that American trade policy had become more liberal but that its increases in tariffs were matched, even exceeded, in 1931 by a number of countries confronted with the problem of sharply rising unemployment.

The correlation coefficient between country rankings according to their levels of GDP per capita and overall tariffs is also significant for 1965 when the US is included, but for a rather different reason. In the late 1940s, when the country dominated the world economy, the US Administration unilaterally reduced the country's tariffs (Anderson 1972). Subsequently, multilateral trade liberalization, which the US initiated and in which it participated actively, brought its tariff levels down further, so that by the mid 1960s they were below those of a number of OECD countries. This can be seen from Figure 5.3, the only occasion in the years covered in this chapter when US tariffs are below the median level of the countries for which relevant data are available. Thus in 1965 the US was located in quadrant IV, though, as Balassa (1967, p. 59) observed at the time, its economy was still more protectionist in the 1960s than those of major West European countries. Nevertheless, apart from the fact that the US trade policy in 1965 was at last beginning to reflect its relative level of industrialization, Figure 5.3 provides a good illustration of the negative, inverse relationship between levels of development and protection that is also shown by the data for

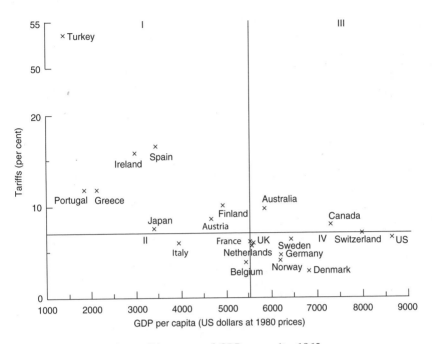

Figure 5.3   Tariff levels on all imports and GDP per capita, 1965
Sources: OECD (1985); Summers and Heston (1988).

1913, 1925, 1931 and 1975. In other words, for most of the twentieth century, industrialized countries, which form the bulk of the sample used for
each year, tended to liberalize their trade only when this was not likely to
affect adversely their economic welfare.

However, the nature of this relationship appears to have changed in the
second half of the 1970s. According to Table 5.3, the correlation coefficient
for 1975 is still statistically highly significant. However, although it has the
expected (negative) sign, the coefficient for 1980 is noticeably lower than
those for 1965 and 1975 as well as being statistically insignificant. The reason for this emerges when Figure 5.4 is compared with Figure 5.3. Clearly,
real GDP levels per capita rose appreciably during this period in all OECD
countries, with the median level shifting to the right from $5,536 in 1965
to $8,393 in 1980. At the same time, their tariff levels were reduced
substantially, with the median level of 1.72 per cent in 1980 compared to
6.93 per cent in 1965. But these reductions in import duties were far from
uniform. They were much greater in some of the poorest OECD countries
(Turkey, Ireland, Portugal) than in many of the most affluent members of
the organization (notably USA, Canada and Australia – with the last of these
being the only OECD country in which tariffs actually went up over the

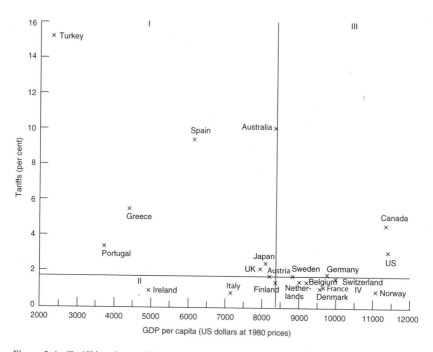

Figure 5.4   Tariff levels on all imports and GDP per capita, 1980
Sources: OECD (1985); Summers and Heston (1988).

period). Not surprisingly, the US is back in quadrant III of Figure 5.4, joined by West Germany. Japan is still in quadrant I, together with the UK (the exemplary upholder of free trade values and practice before 1914!) in long-term retreat from quadrant IV. Ireland and Italy, on the other hand, occupy quadrant II.

Rank correlations involving managed trade (that is, non-tariff barriers to trade) indicate a similar breakdown in the 1970s of the relationship with relative development levels. However, the reason is slightly different in this case. Unlike tariffs, levels of managed trade went up in the 1970s – especially in some of the largest and most industrialized countries (Page 1979, Nogues *et al.* 1986, Laird and Yeats 1988, Salvatore 1993). As a result, the location of countries in Figure 5.5, showing the relationship between managed trade in manufactured goods and per capita levels of industrialization in 1979, is similar to that in Figure 5.4. Again, some of the least industrialized countries for which relevant data are available (Brazil, Portugal, Ireland) are in quadrant II while three of the largest and most industrialized market economies – those of the United State, West Germany and France – are in quadrant III.

Finally, the description of empirical evidence has concentrated so far entirely on the cross-section comparisons in individual years even though

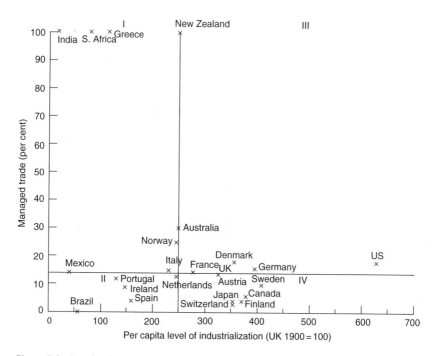

Figure 5.5 Levels of managed trade in manufactured goods and industrialization per capita, 1979

Sources: Page (1979); Bairoch (1982).

the analysis in the previous two sections was developed mainly in dynamic terms. The reason is that there are no time series for protection levels in various countries. Consequently, cross-section comparisons in several years for which the data covering a number of countries happen to be available are the best alternative to an analysis of the dynamics of trade policies.

There are, however, 15 countries for which relevant data are available for 1913, 1965 and 1980. As the values for either GDP per capita or overall tariffs in the last two years are not exactly comparable with those for 1913, Figure 5.6 plots the countries according to their ranking in each of these years. The ranks are drawn in such a way that 1 indicates the highest and 15 the lowest level of either GDP per capita or tariffs. Number 8 indicates the median rank in each case; and the four quadrant correspond again to those shown in Figure 5.1.

Figure 5.6 is, therefore, no more than a rather elementary exercise in comparative statics. Nevertheless, it still manages to reveal some of the long-term dynamics (and exceptions) described earlier. It will be noticed, for

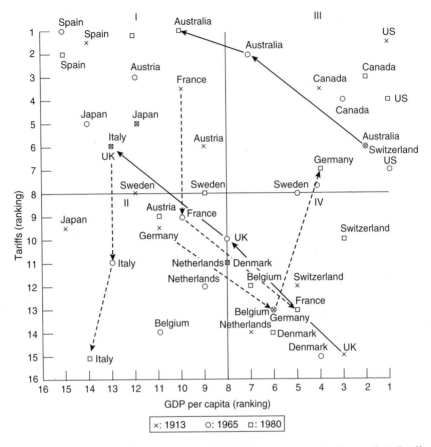

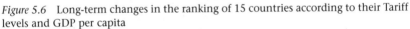

Figure 5.6   Long-term changes in the ranking of 15 countries according to their Tariff levels and GDP per capita

Sources: Bairoch (1981); League of Nations (1927); Maddison (1989); OECD (1985); Summers and Heston (1988).

instance, that with the decline in their GDP per capita relative to other countries, and thus in their international ranking, the UK moved from IV in 1913 to I in 1980, and Australia from III to I. France, on the other hand, experienced exactly the reverse movement: from I in 1913 to IV in 1980. So far as the rankings are concerned, the United States is consistently in the outer range of quadrant III; and the same is also true of Canada. Unlike in 1913, Japan was in quadrant I during the period of its 'economic miracle' after the Second World War. In the case of Italy, it is undoubtedly its membership of the European Economic Community that is responsible for the country's position at the bottom of quadrant II where, for the same reason, it was bound soon to be joined by Spain. In contrast, after moving from II in 1913 to IV in 1965, West Germany was the only European country in quadrant III in 1980.

What this evidence appears to indicate is that, for the first time in the last hundred years at least, the most advanced capitalist economies *as a group* have since the late 1960s/early 1970s imposed on a large part of the world a commercial policy which involves trade liberalization in many of the less advanced economies but a relative increase in their own protection. The difference would probably be even more marked if other forms of protection, such as subsidies, were included. The European Community has always subsidized heavily its agriculture; and the United States offers generous subsidies not only to its agriculture but also to its giant transnationals (see *Financial Times*, 25 January 2000, p. 7). In that sense, the pattern of global protection since the 1970s is increasingly resembling that imposed on the rest of the world by the colonial powers in the nineteenth century (see Bairoch 1993).

Whatever the motive, the initiatives for multilateral trade liberalization and harmonization of national commercial policies have clearly resulted in an international pattern of protection that could easily retard, or even reverse, the long-term improvement in global economic welfare achieved so far.

5.5 Conclusion

It is hardly necessary to point out again that the statistical tests of the basic propositions analysed in this chapter are very simple; or that there are numerous problems concerning the reliability and comparability of the data used in these tests. Nevertheless, the results are consistent with the main argument that, *ceteris paribus*, it is the relative level of a country's development that, for perfectly rational economic reasons, will tend to determine its trade policy rather than the other way round. Nothing illustrates this better than the policies pursued by the most advanced economies. Without exception, they liberalized trade when they felt ready to do so: when had they reached the level of industrialization and international competitiveness which ensured that greater integration into the world economy far from causing a loss in their economic welfare, would actually enhance it.

This does not mean, of course, that trade policy is irrelevant. On the contrary, it is an important tool of economic policy – but it is only *one* of a whole range of policy instruments employed in the course of economic development. This explains the frequently observed fact that countries with similar commercial policies often achieve significantly different rates of economic growth or, alternatively, that it is by no means rare to discover that countries with similar rates of growth pursue widely different trade policies.

This obviously has important policy implications. What constitutes optimum trade policy for a country should be determined on the basis of its level of economic development, the resources (real and financial) at its disposal, the size of its domestic market as well as the access to foreign markets and external finance that it is likely to secure in the foreseeable future. There is, quite simply, no 'general rule' here which is applicable to *all* countries irrespective of their particular circumstances. As Samuelson (1939, p. 195) pointed out, it is not possible to demonstrate "rigorously that *free* trade is better (in some sense) for a country than *all* other kinds of trade." In addition, the exact form of its trade policy should also be decided pragmatically. Although they have not been discussed in this chapter, the vast literature on the subject makes it clear that the instruments available are not equally appropriate under all conditions. Hence, policy makers have to choose whether to use tariffs, quotas or import licences; subsidies to exports, production or wages; special tax and credit preferences; selective government expenditure; or, most likely, a mixture of many of these.

All this means that international organizations and governments should beware of indiscriminate liberalization and harmonization of national trade policies. Such a harmonization represents a sensible long-term strategy only when the countries concerned are at a similar level of development. It is only then that, other things being equal, similarities in the factor endowments are likely to lead to factor price equalization rather than to an increase in international inequalities. This point was emphasized by Heckscher ([1919] 1949, p. 291) in his contribution to what became later known as the Heckscher–Ohlin model of international price equalization.

Otherwise, for reasons analysed in the early part of this chapter, by preventing individual countries from developing fully their productive potential, premature liberalization may well result eventually in widespread losses in economic welfare and a cumulative increase in economic inequality within and between countries. This, as international experience since the end of the nineteenth century shows, poses a major threat to an open and orderly global economic system. Improvements in global employment, efficiency and income levels are unlikely to be sustained for long within an open framework if the existing arrangements are clearly against the interest of many countries (see Panić 1988, Panić and Vacić 1995). In other words, universal retreat into economic insularity is the most likely outcome of international trade liberalization which ignores the ability of individual countries to reconcile their internal and external balances; and that, as the 1930s showed, would be extremely costly to all concerned.

Appendix 5.A   Countries included in the analysis

1913

All imports: Argentina, Australia, Austria, Belgium, Brazil, Canada, Chile, China, Denmark, France, Germany, Hungary, India, Indonesia, Italy, Japan, Mexico, Netherlands, Peru, Philippines, Sweden, Switzerland, Spain, Thailand, United Kingdom and United States.

Imports of manufactured goods: the above countries but *excluding* Argentina, Brazil, Chile, China, Hungary, India, Indonesia, Mexico, Peru, Philippines and Thailand and *including* Russia.

1925

All imports: all the countries listed in 'All imports' above, apart from Japan and with the addition of Czechoslovakia, Poland and Yugoslavia.
Imports of manufactured goods: as above, plus Hungary.

1931

All imports: Austria, Belgium, Bulgaria, Czechoslovakia, Finland, France, Germany, Hungary, Italy, Poland, Rumania, Spain, Sweden, Switzerland and Yugoslavia.
Imports of manufactured goods: the above countries plus the United States.

1965, 1975 and 1980

All imports: Australia, Austria, Belgium, Canada, Denmark, Finland, France, Germany (West), Greece, Ireland, Italy, Japan, Netherlands, Norway, Portugal, Spain, Sweden, Switzerland, Turkey, United Kingdom and United States.

1974 and 1979

All imports: Algeria, Argentina, Australia, Austria, Belgium, Brazil, Canada, Chile, Denmark, Egypt, Finland, France, Germany (West), Greece, India, Indonesia, Iran, Iraq, Ireland, Israel, Italy, Japan, Korea (South), Mexico, Morocco, Netherlands, New Zealand, Nigeria, Norway, Pakistan, Peru, Portugal, Singapore, South Africa, Spain, Sweden, Switzerland, Syria, Taiwan, Thailand, Tunisia, Turkey, United Kingdom, United States and Venezuela.

Imports of manufactured goods: Australia, Austria, Belgium, Brazil, Canada, Denmark, Finland, France, Germany (West), Greece, India, Ireland, Italy, Japan, Mexico, Netherlands, New Zealand, Norway, Portugal, South Africa, Spain, Sweden, Switzerland, United Kingdom and United States.

Appendix 5.B   Statistical sources

Tariffs

1913 and 1925: League of Nations (1927); Bairoch (1989b); Maddison (1989).
1931: Woytinski and Woytinski (1955); Bairoch (1989b).
1965 and 1980: OECD (1985).

Managed trade

1974 and 1979: Page (1979).

Per capita GNP or GDP

1913, 1925 and 1931: Maddison (1989); Bairoch (1981); Rostow (1980).
1965, 1974, 1979 and 1980: Summers and Heston (1988).

Per capita levels of industrialization

All years: Bairoch (1982).

6
Transnational Corporations and the Nation State*

The extraordinary growth of transnational corporations (TNCs) has probably been one of the most important developments in the world economy in the second half of the twentieth century. It is their actions that have been a major factor in linking national economies, especially those from the highly industrialized countries, to such an extent that the linkages are "beginning to give rise to an international production system, organized and managed by transnational corporations" (UNCTC 1992, p. 5). In the pursuit of narrow corporate objectives and strategies, a relatively small number of these enterprises have achieved such a command over global resources, and with it such an impact on the international economy, as to raise serious doubts about the long-term survival of the nation state as a form of political organization.

Unlike states, TNCs have no sovereign power. In other words, their decisions can be blocked and overturned by the states in which they operate. Nor can they prevent an independent state from exercising its sovereignty. What they can do is frustrate the exercise by making it costly in welfare terms, especially in the short to medium term. Consequently, national and international production, employment, distribution of income, trade, finance and policies – even the question of war and peace – cannot now be discussed meaningfully without taking the actions of TNCs into account, because of the far-reaching economic, social and political changes that these can set into motion.

In spite of all this, TNCs continue to be treated as something of a curiosity in economics, rather than as an important, integral part of the international division of labour and, thus, of the dynamics of sustained economic progress. Even textbooks on international and industrial economics rarely devote more than a few pages to them, with no attempt to incorporate TNCs

* This chapter was previously published in R. Rowthorn and R. Kozul-Wright (eds), *Transnational Corporations and the Global Economy*, Macmillan, London, and St Martin's Press, New York, 1998, pp. 244–76.

into the general analysis. The underlying assumption seems to be that there is nothing in the size, objectives, organization and behaviour of these enterprises that would justify a radical change in either micro- or macro-economic analysis.

The power of oligopolies to influence the environment in which they operate, rather than simply react to it in an easily predictable manner like the trusted perfect competitor, has never appealed to economists seeking unambiguous, clear-cut answers to complex questions. By operating at any one time in a number of different economic and political environments and, what is more, by exploiting these differences, TNCs are even more powerful and 'unpredictable' than oligopolies confined to a single country. This enables them to achieve particular objectives by means not available to mul-tiregional national enterprises, making them an awkward subject for formal analysis. It is this combination of power, mobility and adaptability that is probably the main reason why various attempts to develop theoretical mod-els explaining the origin and behaviour of TNCs have not been entirely suc-cessful (see Buckley 1985, Helpman and Krugman 1985, Ethier 1986). Given this background, one should not be surprised that the European Commission managed to produce two reports on the Single Market in the Community hardly mentioning the one form of organization, the TNC, whose actions had been largely responsible for making the creation of such a market pos-sible (Cecchini 1988, Emerson *et al.* 1988).

Outside the mainstream analysis, there is, of course, a vast literature on the subject, predominantly descriptive in character. It has produced a large amount of invaluable information on the history, number, size, geographi-cal and sectoral distribution, importance and activities of TNCs. But it has made little effort to analyse the extent to which the nature of international trade, factor flows and economic policy have been influenced by these enterprises in ways that purely *national* firms would never be able to do.

Using some of this information, it will be suggested in the sections that fol-low that a number of important aspects of international economic integra-tion and their consequences for economic policy – all of which have attracted a good deal of attention over the last twenty years – can be understood prop-erly only if one takes into account the special characteristics, objectives, resources and behaviour of TNCs. Moreover, if international economic inte-gration and interdependence are unavoidable in a process of continuous industrialization and technical and organizational changes (Panić 1988), so also is the most important conduit through which they take place at higher levels of development: the transnational enterprise. The first two sections deal, therefore, with the ways that TNCs can influence the process of inter-national integration, the nature of international trade and factors move-ments, and the long-term national and international adjustments. This is followed in the penultimate section by an analysis of the impact that TNCs can make on national economic policy.

6.1   The process of spontaneous integration and disintegration

The literature on international economic integration, both regional and global, has developed largely around the three basic concepts: openness, integration and interdependence. 'Openness' refers to an absence of various obstacles that restrict trade and/or factor movements between countries. 'Integration' indicates the extent to which two or more countries participate in the international division of labour through specialization and close links in their production, trade and financial structures. Finally, 'interdependence' describes a situation in which two or more economies are linked "to such a degree that economic developments in each of them are influenced significantly by policies and developments outside its borders" (Panić 1988, p. 5).

Clearly, each of these three concepts refers to a distinct aspect of the process of linking different economies. Nevertheless, they are often used interchangeably – a practice which is justified only if there is always and everywhere the same chain of events: from openness (removal of barriers to trade by governments) to integration (expansion of trade and linking of national economies following trade liberalization) to interdependence (the point at which the process of integration reaches such a level that it becomes impossible to solve economic problems of one country without the active cooperation of other countries).

The problem with this sequence of events is that it provides an accurate description of what would happen in a world consisting *entirely* of enterprises whose production and other facilities are confined to a single country. With factors of production mobile within countries – and completely immobile between them – the only way that two or more economies can become integrated and interdependent is through trade; and this is not possible if there are obstacles which restrict exchange of goods between countries. That, of course, is what happens in the world assumed in the traditional trade theory that still dominates much economic analysis and policy making.

However, once the assumption of international factor immobility is dropped, making it possible for national enterprises to operate simultaneously in two or more countries – thus transforming themselves into transnationals – the sequence of events described above changes radically. While it is still necessary for separate national economies to become integrated in order to be interdependent, this can be achieved now even if barriers to international trade continue to exist. The barriers can be divided into at least five major groups:

1. *Administrative*: tariffs, subsidies (and thus, at least in theory, exchange rate devaluation which combines the two), quotas, exchange controls and restrictions on labour mobility. An economy becomes more open when they are reduced or abolished and less so when they are introduced or raised.

2. *Geographic*: distance and/or inaccessibility. Improvements in transport and communications will open up such economies.
3. *Cultural and religious differences*: major variations in lifestyles, preferences and patterns of demand. These barriers to international specialization and trade can be removed only by greater international cultural uniformity.
4. *Inequalities of income and wealth*: large disparities in income and wealth per head between and within countries are a major factor in determining the size of national markets. Like (3), this particular obstacle to greater international integration can only be reduced, or even significantly removed, in the long run.
5. *Corporate barriers*: price discrimination and output allocation between different parts of an enterprise and markets, tied sales, collusive tendering, exclusive dealing, cross-subsidies, transfer pricing and similar practices designed to prevent entry into an industry. Barriers of this kind can be reduced by an effective competition policy.

It does not require much reflection to realize that each of these five types of barrier represents a more or less insurmountable obstacle to trade for national firms. They would be in no position to alter (3) and (4). To gain access to foreign markets, they would depend entirely on governments to at least reduce (1) and (5); and they would have no alternative but to wait for technical breakthroughs to solve the problem of (2) to the point where it became profitable for them to trade with distant and/or previously inaccessible countries.

In contrast, instead of being an obstacle, most of these barriers provide TNCs with an incentive to locate their activities in a country protected by them. If a market is large, or growing so fast that it is confidently expected to reach in the near future the size which will make it profitable for them to establish production facilities there, TNCs will make use of their ownership specific advantages (managerial, financial, technical and/or marketing) to do precisely that. As a result, they will enter foreign markets despite administrative and geographical barriers and, by mobilizing local expertise and skills, in many cases they can also overcome cultural and religious differences. Corporate barriers involving TNCs are more difficult to overcome without direct state action, in the sense that it is dangerous for firms in sectors where they exist to risk a price war that could fatally weaken all of them – making it easier for TNCs outside the industry to enter it and corner a large share of the market.

Exchange controls are also ineffective in preventing TNCs from spreading their operations globally rather than in the home country. One reason for this is that they can borrow easily on international markets. This is particularly true of large TNCs, many of which have a higher credit rating on world capital markets than most national governments. In addition, they can use internal, transfer prices to move funds from their home base to other countries without the national government even realizing that this is happening.

Significant disparities in productivity, income and wealth are the one type of barrier that transnationals are likely to avoid, though not completely. Markets in countries with low incomes are too small to tempt TNCs. Even if they are growing fast, it will take some time for them to attract foreign direct investment on a large scale. At the same time, compared to the highly industrialized countries, their labour skills and productivity are likely to be low and the infrastructure inadequate. In other words, costs of production will be high, especially as the scope for economies of scale is too low to promise return on capital comparable to profits that can be earned in the most affluent countries. The exception will be countries rich in natural resources and/or with an abundant supply of labour on subsistence wages. In the absence of significant administrative barriers in the rest of the world to their exports, both will attract TNC activities with a high raw material or labour content and low value added. Hence, many low-income countries will also become integrated into the international economy, though to a much lesser extent than the countries whose productivity and income levels are high (Panić 1988, Chapter 2). The latter offer opportunities with which TNCs are familiar, as most of them originate in such countries.

Given the ability of TNCs to overcome obstacles to entry into different markets, the moment they begin to play a prominent part in the international economy, the integration sequence can be started either by governments or by these enterprises. In the first case, governments take steps to open up their economies and TNCs respond to the opportunities that such policy changes offer by increasing their level of specialization as well as by rationalizing their operations in different countries (*officially* induced integration). In the second case, that of *spontaneous* integration, the spread of TNC facilities in different countries integrates their economies and makes them so interdependent that the governments are left with no alternative but to respond to the pressure from transnationals to open up their economies. It is no secret that executives from a number of prominent TNCs in Europe played a major role in the 1980s in persuading leaders of the EC countries to remove the remaining obstacles to the creation of a single internal market.

The impact of TNCs will be increased by the fact that sooner or later they will transfer sectoral interdependence within countries to the international level. Once firms from one sector acquire the advantages which make it possible for them to operate in more than one country, enterprises that have over many years developed close economic links with them in their country of origin will follow – as these links will, in turn, give the latter important advantages, enabling them to spread their own operations globally.

There will be a strong incentive for them to do so. By following their long-established business partners across national frontiers, they will prevent firms in other countries from becoming major suppliers of goods and services to the TNCs – eventually threatening the original suppliers' position even in their own countries. This explains why the growth of manufacturing TNCs in sectors producing final goods stimulates internationalization of businesses in the components industries, retail and wholesale trade, banks, insurance companies, advertising agencies, etc. Eventually, many of them may transfer the bulk of their operations from their country of origin to some other country where the market is larger and expected to remain so in the foreseeable future.

In the process, TNCs are also likely to rationalize their operations within and between countries – especially if the barriers to trade and factor movements analysed earlier become negligible. They will reduce, even close down, production and other facilities in some countries and establish or expand them in others. As a result, Viner's distinction of trade creation and trade diversion (Viner 1950) becomes as relevant to trade between regions of a country as between countries. In other words, greater *international* economic integration and interdependence may well be accompanied by *national* economic disintegration and, thus, a weakening of the links between the regions of a country. The result is a widening gap in regional economic performance and income levels within the same country, while there is an equalization of efficiency and income levels between the regions in different countries which are favoured by transnationals.

Although such developments can have important political consequences in the long run, governments may not even be aware that anything of the kind is taking place until they are confronted with major adjustment problems and political crises.

6.2 How free are international trade and factor movements?

Most countries have participated actively since the 1950s in a concerted international effort to liberalize foreign trade in the belief that this will enhance their *national* economic welfare. Consequently, as pointed out in Chapter 5, by the mid 1980s administrative barriers to trade were even lower than during the heyday of free trade in the nineteenth century. The geographic barriers have also come down dramatically, thanks to revolutionary improvements in transport and communications since the Second World War. Cinema and television may not have eliminated cultural barriers to trade, but they have helped create a greater uniformity of international tastes, aspirations and demand patterns than ever before. The increase in this uniformity was also influenced significantly by a marked reduction in income differentials over the period 1950–80 between industrial countries and between them and the middle income countries (see Panić 1988, Chapter 10). More recent data and studies (cf. Chapter 1) indicate a reversal of this trend in the 1980s, though not to such an extent as to affect international trade and capital flows adversely (Panić and Vacić 1995, UNCTAD 1994, Walter 1993). Since the 1970s many countries have also either reduced or, in a number of cases, abolished exchange controls.

Judged by these criteria, international trade ought to enjoy a greater degree of freedom now than ever before; and capital flows, although not as unrestricted as before 1914, are probably subject to less stringent controls at present than at any other time since the First World War. Yet, despite these changes, it is far from clear that foreign trade and factor movements are as free as the more liberal national attitudes and policies imply. The growth of TNCs, the concentration of a wide range of activities within them and the increasing practice of international corporate alliances – all point to the possibility of more extensive corporate barriers to free trade than before. Moreover, it is by no means certain that gains from the more liberal trading regime that has evolved since the 1960s have accrued to all countries, even less that they have benefited all sections of the population within any one of them. According to the doctrine of free trade, supported since the eighteenth century by the vast majority of economists, this is the main justification for opening up national economies.

The doctrine of free trade is both logically consistent and deceptively simple. By removing barriers to trade, countries become able to specialize and thus exploit fully their absolute (Adam Smith) as well as their comparative (Ricardo) advantages. They will maximize gains from trade by exporting to countries where prices for their goods are highest and import from countries whose products are cheapest. More specifically, producers will benefit from free trade as specialization improves efficiency, lowers costs of production and increases profits. Consumers will gain as free trade widens the choice and, by stimulating competition, lowers prices. Hence, the benefits of a more liberal trading regime are widely diffused between and within countries. In the long run, identical goods and factors of production will command the same price (when adjusted for transportation costs) around the world.

It is not all plain sailing, of course, as the transition to free trade is bound to involve adjustment costs. That much has been realized from the beginning. Where economists have differed is in the assumptions that they make about the scale of the required adjustments and the time that it would take to achieve them.

Those who, like Adam Smith, take a highly optimistic view of the whole process have in mind a world in which foreign trade accounts for a relatively small proportion of total economic activity, the existing levels of technical knowledge and specialization are low and the structure of industry is highly competitive. In conditions of perfect competition, not an unreasonable assumption in the eighteenth century, it is relatively easy for firms, capital and labour to move from declining to growing sectors of an economy within a relatively short period. The existing firms do not enjoy any of the advantages that would make it difficult for new enterprises to enter their industry, attracted by the possibility of earning abnormal profits. (Exactly the same equality of skills and opportunity applies to owners of capital and labour. This explains also why they are immobile internationally, as the lack of special skills and small income differentials between countries offers them no greater opportunities abroad than at home.) In other words, specialization may improve producers' efficiency. But it does not provide a few of the firms with that competitive edge which would enable them to make full use of economies of scale, secure a large share of the market and, in so doing, raise the cost of entry to a level that would make it difficult for new firms to join the industry. It is interesting that in the course of the Industrial Revolution, as methods of production became more complex and conditions of entry more demanding, there was a noticeable change in the views of the classical and neoclassical economists concerning the adjustment costs and the time that it might take to re-establish equilibrium (Panić 1988, Chapter 7).

Whatever else it may resemble, the environment in which TNCs operate has little in common with the highly competitive model just described. Much of this is also true, of course, of competition among national oligopolies. The important difference is that, by being confined to a single country, the latter are in no position to influence the nature and direction of foreign trade in the ways open to TNCs.

Thanks to the ability to allocate various aspects of their operations across national frontiers – linking activities in different countries through vertical and horizontal integration – transnationals internalize a considerable part of the process of international specialization and exchange. International integration and interdependence at the end of the twentieth century are, therefore, increasingly something that takes place within individual TNCs according to the role allocated by the overall corporate strategy to each affiliate belonging to the enterprise. This is particularly true of the largest TNCs which, as UNCTAD (1994, pp. 5 and 8) points out, "exercise considerable impact on home and host countries' output, demand patterns, trade and technology flows, employment and labour practices. They also influence the structure and pattern of competition of their industries."

That being the case, is it possible that the great effort made since the 1960s to liberalize international trade and capital flows has achieved no more than a substitution of the control of international allocation of resources by TNCs for the control previously exercised by the state? And what proof is there that decisions by individual TNCs, each acting in its own corporate interest, are more likely to improve national economic welfare than decisions made by individual governments, each pursuing policies it believes to be in the national interest?

The problem with answering either of these questions is that there is very little direct evidence which would make it possible to compare the extent to which actions concerning trade, factor movements and prices taken by TNCs differ from those that would have been made by national oligopolies. Most of this information is confidential and, consequently, no firm is either prepared or normally required to make it available to outsiders. In fact, only a relatively small number of senior executives of a TNC are likely to know the reasons behind key decisions and the extent to which any particular outcome could be attributed to them. All that an outsider can do, therefore, is use some of the piecemeal information that is available to obtain a rough idea of the scale of resources controlled by TNCs and the effect that this may have on developments between and within national economies.

In the early 1990s there were about 37,000 parent TNCs controlling 206,000 affiliates (UNCTAD 1994, p. 4). The value of foreign direct investment stock owned by parent TNCs was estimated in 1992 at $2.1 trillion and sales of their foreign affiliates at $4.8 trillion. The latter was equal to one-fifth of the world GDP at factor cost. It was also about 60 per cent higher than total world exports of goods and non-factor services excluding intra-firm trade of TNCs (*ibid.* p. 20). In the same year, transnationals employed around 73 million people: 60 per cent of them in parent companies at home and the rest in foreign affiliates, more than half of them in developed countries (*ibid.* p. 175).

It is clear even from these estimates, which refer to the primary and secondary sectors only, that TNCs control a significant proportion of world resources, most of them acquired since the 1970s. The number of TNCs from major industrial countries went up from 7,000 in 1970 to 24,000 in 1990 (UNCTAD 1993, p. 1). The stock of foreign direct investment was almost seven times greater in 1992 than in 1975 and the number of people employed by TNCs increased by over 80 per cent over the same period (UNCTAD 1994, p. 175). Trade within TNCs (excluding intra-firm transactions in services) went up as a proportion of world trade from 20 per cent in the early 1970s to at least one-third in the early 1990s (*ibid.*, p. 143). Seventy per cent of all US receipts from royalties and licence fees and 50 per cent of all such payments "represented intra-TNCs transactions" (UNCTAD 1993, p. 164).

The growth of international financial activity has been even more impressive. Between 1964 and 1991 the size of gross international banking market increased from 1.2 per cent to 37.0 per cent of world output, 12.4 per cent to 215.6 per cent of world trade and 10.3 per cent to 270.9 per cent of gross fixed domestic investment (UNCTAD 1994, p. 128). In less than two decades, since the early 1970s, cross-border inter-bank liabilities went up from $455 billion to $5560 billion; cross-border bank credit to nonbanks from $54 billion to $1708 billion; and cross-border bank deposits of nonbanks from $75 billion to $1695 billion (*ibid.;* see also US Congress 1993, Chapter 6).

Transnational activities are, of course, as common in banking and finance as in primary production and manufacturing. In 1985, the world's largest 100 banks had a foreign network of 4,660 offices (UNCTC 1988, p. 114). As a result, a high proportion of international financial transactions must now be taking place within individual institutions and corporations.

Given such rapid growth of TNCs of all types, and the fact that most of them come from developed economies, it is hardly surprising that they play an extremely important role not only in many small countries but also in some of the world's largest and most industrialized economies (see Dunning 1992). In the United States, the value of gross product of TNC parent firms and foreign affiliates operating in the country was equal to over one-third of total US output and almost three-quarters of the manufacturing output. In Japan, the comparable figures were one-quarter and slightly over one-third (UNCTAD 1993, p. 159. See also US Congress 1993, Chapter 3). At the end of the 1980s, the share of intra-firm trade in the two countries was (Japan in brackets): 34 (33) per cent in total exports and 41 (29) per cent in total imports (UNCTAD 1994, p. 143). Foreign affiliates accounted for 38 per cent of exports from the United Kingdom in 1989 and 26 per cent of French exports in 1982 (UNCTC 1992, p. 330). In many of the most advanced economies foreign companies are responsible for 20 per cent or more of their insurance industry (UNCTC 1988, p. 466) and most of their largest advertising agencies are foreign owned (*ibid.* p. 465). Though far from negligible, these figures, nevertheless, seriously understate the dominant role of TNCs in trade of individual industries (Casson 1986) and national economies, including that of the United States (Hipple 1990).

Even more remarkable is the extent to which vast international resources seem to be controlled by a relatively small number of TNCs. According to UNCTAD (1993, p. 2), no more than 370 transnationals (1 per cent of all parent TNCs) control half of the world's stock of foreign direct investment (that is, around $1 trillion). In 1992 the largest 100 firms (excluding those in banking and finance) owned global assets worth $3.4 trillion – almost 40 per cent ($1.3 trillion) of which were held outside their home countries (UNCTAD 1994, p. 5). They also employed 12 million people, around five million of them in their affiliates abroad (*ibid.* p. 176). Fifty TNCs "accounted for more than one-quarter of all United States patents granted to firms during the 1980s" (UNCTC 1992, p. 4). In 1990, total R&D expenditure by the largest 20 US and non-US transnationals exceeded by a large margin national R&D expenditure of all the leading industrial countries except the United States and Japan (UNCTC 1992, pp. 136–7). In many sectors a few TNCs are responsible for anything from 25 per cent to over 60 per cent of world output (Dunning 1981, p. 4 and 1992, p. 45). Finally, and contrary to the information quoted earlier from UN reports, according to a World Bank study, by the early 1980s "intrafirm trade within the largest 350 transnational corporations (TNCs) contributed about 40 per cent of global trade" (World Bank 1992, p. 33). The growth of corporate alliances in recent years must have increased further the degree to which relatively few TNCs either control directly or influence indirectly international production, employment, investment, trade and distribution of income.

The importance of all these changes in the structure of the international economy is that the rise of transnationals is likely to have a profound effect on the international division of labour and the distribution of gains and losses that result from it. The latter cannot be emphasized too strongly. Unequal gains from global specialization are likely, as past experience shows (Panić 1988, Part III), to lead to the breakdown of an internationally integrated system. Yet this important condition is normally brushed aside in economic literature by assuming either perfect competition in commodity markets or, like Helpman and Krugman (1985), *perfect* mobility of labour and capital once administrative barriers to trade are removed.

The existence, size and market power of TNCs could hardly provide a more visible demonstration of the irrelevance of such assumptions. In doing so, they also raise serious doubts about the extent to which a removal of administrative barriers to trade and factor movements will, *ceteris paribus*, lead to a more efficient allocation of resources and a more equitable distribution of income between and within countries.

Globally, the strategies of transnationals are likely to evolve around two broad objectives: protection of the existing market and entry into new markets with the aim of achieving as large a share there as possible. To realize these goals, TNCs may have little alternative but to engage in restrictive business practices both internally and in relation to their competitors. Not surprisingly, according to Dunning (1992, pp. 438–9) primary and secondary industries are "replete with examples of [transnationals] attempting to limit competition". As a result, even if the first four types of protection were to disappear completely, the outcome could be quite different from what would happen to international trade in the absence of TNCs, especially if corporate barriers to trade remain undetected and unrestrained.

For example, unlike national companies, transnationals will not export to a market where prices are high if they already have affiliates operating in that market, earning high profits which are used to subsidize one or more of the group's less profitable facilities in some other part of the world. This restricts exports, output, employment and income in other countries where these transnationals operate. The same problem is likely to arise also if affiliates of a TNC in country X are more efficient than those in country Y but are not allowed to export there because this would drive the less efficient affiliates operating in Y out of business, which would be against the overall corporate interest. There are, of course, welfare losses in both these cases in the importing countries as well, especially if resources from the less efficient affiliates could be transferred relatively easily to some other sector. Moreover, as part of the overall corporate strategy, affiliates in a country may be forced to import products from other affiliates in the same group despite the fact that they are much more expensive than comparable goods and services available on the home market.

Corporate strategies of this kind are probably the main reason for the important differences in prices that remain between countries of the European Community over a wide range of products (Glejser 1972, Cecchini 1988, Emerson *et al.* 1988) even though administrative barriers to trade were abolished within the Community in the 1960s. Moreover, according to a study, cartelization among leading TNCs in the heavy electrical equipment industry resulted in an increase in global prices by almost a quarter compared with what they could be under more competitive conditions (Epstein and Newfarmer 1982). Nor has much greater freedom of international capital flows led to "narrowing of differences in rates of return on capital investment in the major industrial countries, or in real long-term interest rates." (Akyüz 1993, pp. 51–2).

International allocation of resources and the welfare of countries are also likely to be influenced by decisions of parent TNCs concerning the choice of production methods for individual affiliates as well as by their preference for R&D activities to be concentrated mainly in the parent's country of origin. In both cases, the outcomes may appear to be perfectly rational from the point of view of individual TNCs. However, the former may prevent a country from realizing fully its comparative advantages, and the latter may stifle development of those inventive and innovative skills which are essential if a country is to achieve higher levels of industrialization.

Attempts by national companies to enter an industry in which profits are high can easily be undermined by the threatened TNCs. They can either take over the intruding firm and prevent its further expansion, or use their vast resources to subsidize activity in this industry, underprice the national firm, drive it out of business and then raise prices to their original level. It is probably no coincidence that the only sectors in which even the much admired Japanese industrial policy failed to create successful indigenous firms happen to be those in which US transnationals managed to establish a firm foothold early on (Magaziner and Hout 1980).

If trading strategies of TNCs can, following the abolition of administrative barriers, perpetuate misallocation of resources, their investment decisions may create serious adjustment problems in some countries. As already pointed out, trade liberalization will provide TNCs with an opportunity to rationalize their activities by reducing, or even closing down completely, their operations in some countries and increasing, or starting them, in others. (See Panić 1991b.) The result will be a fall in output, employment and income in the former and an improvement in all of them in the latter. In addition, the balance of payments will deteriorate in the first group, as the goods or services that used to be produced at home will now have to be imported. The countries' external position will worsen further if some of those products were exported, as the overall foreign earnings will fall by the amount equal to these exports. In contrast, the overall balance of the second group will improve, since their exports will rise and imports fall. If enterprises that have had traditionally close links with the TNCs which are rationalizing their operations do the same, the difference in economic performance of the two groups of countries will become even more pronounced, as the processes of cumulative decline in one case and cumulative growth in the other unfold. Unchecked, the unequal gains from freer trade and factor flows will sooner or later become a serious obstacle to greater international openness and integration and may, eventually, reverse the whole process.

It is perfectly true, of course, that some of these problems could arise following trade liberalization even in the absence of TNCs. It has always been recognized that once they are exposed to foreign competition, inefficient domestic producers will go out of business, unless they improve their products and production methods significantly. To do this, they need time or, at least, adequate forewarning of any major change in their country's commercial policy. This was the rationale behind the argument for protection put forward by Hamilton and List in the eighteenth and nineteenth centuries and recognized as necessary by such prominent advocates of free trade as Ricardo, Mill and Marshall (Panić 1988, Chapter 7). It also explains why, traditionally, most countries have tended to liberalize their trade gradually.

In contrast, changes involving rationalization of international operations by TNCs may come unexpectedly, be implemented rapidly and involve closure of facilities which are by no means uncompetitive internationally (see US Congress 1993, pp. 28n and 67). Hence, the adjustment problems imposed on a country may be sudden, large and, from a national point of view, unnecessary. At the same time, considerable advantages will accrue to the countries to which the TNCs transfer their operations.

Once the processes started by investment and reallocation decisions of TNCs set in they are difficult to reverse in conditions of economic openness. According to the conventional wisdom, if wages were flexible investment flows between the two groups of countries contrasted above would reverse automatically. Wages would fall in the declining economies, making it more profitable for TNCs to invest there, and vice versa in the case of expanding economies.

There are three serious flaws in this argument. First, low wages are not necessarily synonymous with low wage costs. Higher wages can be offset by higher productivity and other advantages that economies with high efficiency and income levels can offer (such as collective experience and skills, organized in a multitude of highly specialized institutions). Besides, in many of the industries in which TNCs are most prominent wages account for a relatively small proportion of total costs. Second, a general reduction in wage levels would mean a reduction in the size of a country's market. This would be a major disincentive to TNCs to invest there as, other things being equal, the size and growth of a market are among the most important factors influencing their decision where to allocate their core activities (Dunning 1992). *Ceteris paribus*, if they have the option of investing in two similar markets, one of which is contracting while the other is expanding, all available evidence indicates that they will choose the latter. Finally, it is impossible for a high- or a medium-income country to reduce its wages to a level that would enable it to compete on equal terms with low-wage countries without major social and political upheavals. It is difficult to think of anything that would frighten off TNCs more effectively!

Even attempts by governments to offer generous incentives to transnationals as well as a programme of extensive deregulation may, at best, produce no more than partial success. What matters in the end to them is a country's *relative* economic performance in the past and its future prospects compared to those of other countries. Hence, a developing or declining economy is unlikely to attract TNCs in sufficient numbers to transform its productivity and income levels unless it somehow manages *first* "to improve domestic economic performance in general and, in particular, to increase demand growth and to improve infrastructure and human resources" (UNCTC 1991, p. 88). Not surprisingly, as one writer observed, "[f]oreign capital typically lags rather than leads industrial development" (Amsden 1993, p. 76).

What the analysis in this section suggests is that in a world of TNCs and independent, sovereign states, both the concept and predictions of the familiar free trade model need to be revised. Is trade 'liberalized' if reductions in administrative barriers are offset and, perhaps, nullified by greater corporate barriers? Can the liberalization and deregulation under these conditions guarantee improvements in economic welfare in all countries participating in this if transnationals – according to Dunning (1981, p. 3) one of "the most powerful economic institutions yet produced by the capitalist system" – continue their nomadic existence in the pursuit of narrow corporate goals, irrespective of the effect that this may have on the countries in which they operate? The conflict between the corporate and national interests is bound, therefore, to have far-reaching implications for economic policy in general, well beyond the relatively simple issue of trade policy.

6.3   The economic goals of TNCs vs. the political responsibilities of national governments

One of the most difficult problems that the international community has been trying to solve since the 1960s stems precisely from that conflict: how to reconcile the international preoccupations of transnationals with the national responsibilities of governments. The issue would not arise if *all* enterprises were confined to single nation states, in the sense that any regional imbalances caused by the actions of interregional corporations could be offset partly by labour mobility and partly by government redressing the imbalance through resource transfers. Exactly the same would happen, in theory at least, if the whole world were organized into a single supranational state, as in this case TNCs would be no different from multiregional national enterprises, and the supranational government would have the same powers as the government of a nation state. (As Chapters 10 and 11 show, it would be much more difficult than this in practice!)

The difference in preoccupations of TNCs and governments arises because of differences in their responsibilities. The duty of those running a TNC is to protect and enhance the value of assets under their control, and to maintain a satisfactory return on shareholders' investments. The international character of transnationals sooner or later produces a situation in which it is not quite clear what the national identity of a TNC is, and, with it, their concern for the 'national interest' of the countries in which they operate diminishes. The board of a TNC is expected to maximize corporate profits not the welfare of any of these countries. In fact, to identify with their national interest would limit the ability of a TNC to achieve its corporate objectives – especially if, as is very likely, there are important, often conflicting, differences in what various countries regard as 'national interest'. Their preferred ways of improving economic welfare may also differ significantly. TNCs do not set out deliberately to frustrate national aims and policies. But they are likely to do so if these make it difficult for them to achieve their own corporate objectives.

Improvements in national economic and social welfare were accepted as one of the main responsibilities of modern governments in the 1940s when, as a result of the inter-war experience, it became clear that they were closely linked to the more traditional responsibilities of the state, such as internal order, external security and personal liberty. After the Second World War, governments of different political persuasion took it as their duty to ensure that a number of important economic objectives were achieved: full employment, a satisfactory rate of growth (that is, the rate required to maintain full employment in a dynamic economy), price stability, a balance on external account and a more equitable distribution of income (Panić 1991a).

A number of interrelated macroeconomic instruments were employed to carry out these objectives. Roughly, fiscal policy was used to achieve and maintain full employment, industrial policy to promote growth, monetary and income policies to keep inflation under control, a mixture of trade and exchange controls and currency devaluation to balance external account, and taxation and social policy to realize a more equitable distribution of income.

The growth and ubiquity of TNCs in virtually every sector of a modern economy have progressively reduced the ability of national governments to pursue these policies successfully and, consequently, to realize the expectations of their electorates, which have changed very little over the last 50 years (see Johnston 1993, Taylor-Gooby 1993). The result has been growing social problems and unrest, and dissatisfaction with major political parties and governments. Some of these might have occurred in any case. But it is unlikely that they would have been as acute in the absence of TNCs.

The reason for this is that the existence of TNCs adds considerably to the degree of uncertainty, which is invariably present in macroeconomic management. Consider, for instance, likely responses to *fiscal policy* in an open economy in which they play an important role – starting with microeconomic reactions to reflation. National firms, which normally produce most of their output for the domestic market, will react to an increase in aggregate demand, stimulated by higher public expenditure and/or lower taxes, by first increasing output, then employment and finally, if the long-term demand prospects are satisfactory and the existing capacity is judged to be inadequate to meet them, by undertaking new investment. This sequence can be expected with some confidence because it represents the most rational course of action for them.

The same is not necessarily true of TNCs. Their response may differ from that of national firms even if most of their output is for the market in which they are located. If they expect economic recovery to be short-lived, or if capacity under-utilization happens to be much more severe in members of the same group operating abroad, it may be far more profitable from the overall corporate point of view for the increase in demand to be met with imports from foreign affiliates rather than by increasing domestic output.

Moreover, there is no guarantee that TNCs will undertake new investment in a particular economy even if they react to the fiscal stimulus by raising levels of output and capacity utilization. It may suit their long-term plans better to expand operations in another country where, in their judgement, demand prospects are more favourable and/or subsidies and other incentives offered by government are higher. What is more, they may use higher profits generated by economic recovery in one country to finance new investment in another part of the world, either overtly via direct investment or covertly through transfer prices. For similar reasons, a reduction in taxes on profits intended to stimulate new investment at home may, instead, lead to higher direct investment abroad. Consequently, the overall effect of a fiscal stimulus may turn out to be much weaker than the government expected, making only a modest contribution to reducing unemployment levels in either the short or the long term.

Similar uncertainties will also surround the outcome of deflationary policies implemented by one country to reduce aggregate demand by a combination of lower public expenditure and higher taxes. The reason for this is that TNCs may decide to minimize the impact of such policies on their costs and profits by expanding exports, thus maintaining – especially if the multiplier effect of their actions is large – higher levels of activity in the economy than those judged by the governments to be 'prudent'. Provided that the external environment remains unchanged, national firms may also increase their exports under these conditions. But the overall effect of their exports on domestic production and employment will be smaller for two reasons: (a) they normally sell abroad a much lower proportion of their output than TNCs and (b) they tend to account for only a small share of the total exports of a modern economy.

This explains also why national firms will rarely undertake new investment when domestic demand is low and capacity under-utilization high.

Apart from the fact that they have sufficient capacity to meet short-term increases in demand, recession will reduce their profits and, therefore, their ability to finance new investment from internal resources. At the same time, deflationary policies will ensure that the cost of external borrowing is high.

In contrast, none of these reasons need prevent TNCs from investing in times of recession if they judge this to be in their long-term interest. Internal finance, in particular, should not present a serious problem, as affiliates in any one country can borrow from other members of the same group operating around the world. Hence, the overall outcome of the deflationary package may turn out to be much weaker than expected.

The risk involved in demand management under the conditions described above is that the slow response to the original policies to expand/contract aggregate demand may, together with public pressure, force the authorities to introduce additional measures leading, eventually, to serious overheating of the economy in the first case and to a deep and long-lasting recession in the second – quite contrary to what the government intended.

The problems just described are also important because of the effect that they are likely to have on the ability of nation states to pursue a successful *industrial policy* in order to restructure and increase their productive capacity. This requires two important objectives to be achieved simultaneously: (a) to increase the level of investment which, in turn, requires a higher volume of savings; and (b) to allocate new investment in a way that will maximize the country's long-term economic welfare. Both may bring the state into direct conflict with TNCs operating on its territory.

For instance, transnationals may decide, on the basis of evidence available to them, that long-term prospects are much more favourable in some other country, or countries, than in the one trying to pursue an industrial policy. They may, therefore, transfer profits earned in the country to these alternative locations in order to finance their planned investment there. Hence, other things remaining the same, instead of increasing, the level of savings and investment in the country will be reduced, making it difficult to achieve the objective of expanding and modernizing its productive capacity. If the government now tries to raise the level of saving and investment through higher taxes, the result may be exactly the opposite if TNCs react to this by transferring even more of their profits and new investments to other countries. National firms can be prevented from investing abroad by introducing exchange controls and making sure that these are strictly observed. TNCs can avoid such controls by manipulating their internal transfer prices. Their ability to do this may increase the burden of taxation borne by national enterprises – with the result that industrial policy will become highly unpopular with the business community whose support and co-operation are essential for the policy to succeed.

The problem of allocating investment to those firms and sectors believed to be most likely to maximize the country's welfare is, if anything, even more difficult.

Much has been written in economics about the risks inherent in 'picking the winners', and whether this can be done correctly by anyone except those intimately involved in the production and distribution processes at the microeconomic level. Yet broadly based decisions of this kind (whether a firm or industry should be allocated more resources to expand and modernize its productive capacity) are made routinely by people who have anything but an intimate knowledge of the processes under consideration: financial institutions and boards of large corporations – national and transnational – with complex, highly integrated production and distribution networks.

Moreover, in every single advanced economy the state has traditionally been involved in some of the key decisions in this area, through either industrial or trade policies. The history of the world's largest corporations shows that not one of them has managed to develop to its current size and status without assistance of this kind (Ruigrok and Van Tulder 1995). Internationally, there are countless examples, therefore, of remarkable successes and costly failures at all levels of decision making in the allocative process.

In other words, industrial policy has been around for a long time and the levels of industrialization reached by high- and medium-income countries are a testimony to its success and endurance. At the same time, it has never been an easy policy to implement, and the existence of transnationals has introduced additional problems for reasons that are perfectly understandable from their point of view.

The opening up of national economies gives TNCs a chance to rationalize their international operations. Hence, they may want to pull out of precisely those activities in a country that the country would like to expand. For the same reason, attempts by national governments to minimize the effects of externally generated recessions on their economy, by diversifying the country's productive structure, are likely to come into conflict with the desire of TNCs to reduce corporate risks by diversifying their operations internationally rather than within individual countries.

Official efforts to set up new domestic firms to fill the gaps left by departing TNCs would require a number of difficult problems to be overcome. In the absence of tariffs and quotas, the new firms would face tough competition for quite some time from the long-established foreign TNCs. They would need, therefore, heavy subsidies, first to survive and, then, to reach the level of resources, expertise and efficiency enjoyed by the TNCs.

Finally, the pace of technical change and greater international competition has created new problems for both TNCs and governments. Rising R&D costs, shorter product cycles, economies of scale and a highly uncertain economic and political environment have forced many TNCs to pool risks by forming strategic alliances. This has increased both the flexibility and the complexity of the international production and distribution networks, making it even more difficult to implement industrial policy in a single country successfully.

There are also serious difficulties in implementing *monetary policy*. (See also Panić 1991b.) Suppose a central bank engages in open market operations to reduce the quantity of money in circulation in order to control inflation. Interest rates rise, discouraging demand for money for transaction purposes. As intended, the volume of transactions is reduced and, in this way, the level of economic activity. That, at least, is the way that the economy is expected to behave and in the absence of TNCs it is, more or less, what would happen. The policy could be frustrated, even nullified, if purely national enterprises were able to borrow with ease in international capital markets on more favourable terms. That, however, is an alternative open to very few, if any, of them. Potential foreign investors will be unfamiliar with such enterprises and, under the conditions assumed here, the government would be unwilling to overcome the problem by underwriting their external borrowing.

Transnationals can alter the effectiveness of monetary policy significantly for the simple reason that, as already pointed out, their sources of funds are not confined to a single country. All TNCs, especially larger ones, have relatively easy access to international capital markets. Hence, TNCs from the country pursuing a restrictive monetary policy will be able to borrow on these markets at interest rates that are lower than those prevailing in the country. In fact, they may be assisted in this by the country's banks and financial institutions operating in euromarkets – one of the ways in which the latter can escape restrictions on lending imposed in their own country. All this assumes, of course, that the TNCs need to raise external finance. But many of them may not have to do so, since their affiliates can borrow on favourable terms from members of the same enterprise located in other countries. What is more, they can use the funds acquired in this way to lend to national firms with which they have close business links, thus weakening the squeeze imposed by restrictive monetary policies.

Contrary to the policy of the central bank, the overall effect of external borrowing by the TNCs will be to increase the supply of money in the economy and, thus, improve the liquidity of the financial system. Nevertheless, the cost of borrowing to national enterprises will remain relatively high, forcing many of them (efficient as well as inefficient ones) to go out of business, with serious consequences for the country's output and employment. Their position may become even more desperate if, as a result of TNCs switching large funds into the currency in order to benefit from relatively high interest rates, the growth of money supply exceeds the targets set by government. Given that the authorities have no idea what proportion of the money held by the public is intended for transaction purposes, a government convinced that keeping the supply within pre-determined targets is essential for controlling inflation will react to 'excessive' demand for money by raising interest rates further in an attempt to reduce the supply. This may well turn a recession into an old-fashioned depression, as happened in the United Kingdom in the early 1980s.

The problem of greater unpredictability is not confined to restrictive monetary policies. Attempts by a central bank to stimulate the economy by increasing the supply of money and reducing interest rates may not prove to be more successful than the fiscal measures described earlier and for exactly the same reason: economic developments and prospects in the country pursuing such a policy are not as favourable as those in other countries in which the TNCs operate. Moreover, a more relaxed monetary policy may lead to a lower than expected increase in the money supply, as TNCs switch large funds into other currencies – partly to benefit from the relatively high interest rates prevailing in the rest of the world and partly to escape depreciation of the country's currency, which, of course, their own action will help bring about.

For all these reasons, the ultimate outcome of monetary policy is not necessarily more predictable than that of demand management described earlier. In fact, frequent resort to restrictive monetary measures 'to fight inflation' may well increase unpredictability and reduce the effectiveness of monetary policy instruments for the simple reason that, because of their unequal impact on national and transnational enterprises, it is likely to increase the relative importance of the latter in an economy.

The other policy instrument used after the Second World War to control inflation, *incomes policy*, is even more vulnerable to the growing importance of TNCs in national economies. To be effective, a policy of this kind needs widespread consensus. That, in turn, is most likely to be achieved if differences in productivity levels between firms are small. The reason for this is that under such conditions it is possible to reduce inflationary pressures (as increases in wages granted by one firm can be matched by the rest without an unsustainable increase in their unit costs) without seriously affecting allocation of resources (that is, making it difficult for efficient firms to attract labour of high-quality) or the distribution of income (either among wage earners or between wages and profits). The greater the differences in efficiency levels and growth of productivity the more likely are rigid wage guidelines to be resisted, as they will penalize employees in more efficient firms and industries.

Empirical evidence shows that, in general, productivity levels are higher in TNCs than in national firms, substantially so in less advanced economies. Their production methods tend to be capital-intensive, which means that they tend to have relatively low unit labour costs. Not surprisingly, they normally pay higher wages than national firms do (see Dunning and Morgan 1980) and their settlements frequently influence the rate and size of wage increases in the rest of the economy.

There is, however, more to this than their ability to pay higher wages. The cost of strikes and other interruptions to production is high in capital-intensive industries because fixed costs account for a significant proportion of total costs. Hence, worsening labour relations and strikes could easily offset the savings that TNCs might make by observing wage guidelines. This is one of the reasons why they will be hostile to incomes policies. The fact that such policies interfere with their global pricing and profit strategies as well as impede their ability to attract labour of high calibre from other sectors and countries will make TNCs unwilling to observe them for long.

As already mentioned, capital-intensive national firms face similar difficulties. However, unlike TNCs, they cannot easily transfer their operations abroad, with serious consequences for the country's output and employment. It is this bargaining advantage that makes it possible for TNCs to act as leaders in setting wages and, if it is in their interest, to discredit and frustrate government efforts to control inflation by means of prices and incomes policies. This is, in fact, what happened in the UK in the autumn of 1978 when Ford UK granted wage increases of 15 per cent, three times higher than the level set by government guidelines. Attempts to persist with the policy led to 'the winter of discontent', with widespread stoppages and strikes – and less than a year later to a change of government.

With administrative barriers to trade greatly reduced, even completely removed in certain parts of the world, the *exchange rate* remains, in theory at least, the only macroeconomic policy instrument capable of removing persistent current account imbalances without sacrificing output and employment. This is particularly relevant in the case of persistent deficit countries, as they are normally under pressure to do something about their imbalances.

In theory, these can be eliminated through currency devaluation/depreciation provided that the combined price elasticities of demand for a country's exports and imports satisfy the Marshall–Lerner condition: that is, that the sum of the two elasticities is greater than one. Although this tends to be the requirement widely quoted in the economic literature, there are, in fact, five other conditions that are essential if the exchange rate is to be an effective policy instrument.

First, the country devaluing its currency should be small and the only one experiencing external disequilibria. It will obviously never restore the balance by lowering its exchange rate if other countries respond by letting their currencies depreciate; and they are less likely to do so if they are in external equilibrium and the devaluing country is so small that changes in its exports and imports have no significant effect on their levels of activity. Second, foreign trade should form only a small proportion of the country's GDP. Otherwise, domestic wages and prices will sooner or later rise in response to higher import prices. As a result of this and their dependence on imported inputs, export prices will also go up, thus wiping out some, or even all, the gains from a lower exchange rate. Third, supply schedules in the country have to be highly elastic so that resources can be switched promptly into the sectors producing either exports or import substitutes. Fourth, wage earners must not respond to higher import prices by asking for higher wages, as this would trigger off an inflationary spiral offsetting the gains from devaluation. Finally, there should be no interaction between actual or anticipated exchange rate changes and capital flows, starting off a depreciation–inflation spiral.

The problem is that increases in the international division of labour are bound to influence all these conditions to a certain degree. Unless they have a good deal of spare capacity in relevant sectors, the more countries specialize the more difficult it becomes for them to expand exports in the short to medium run; and, in many cases, even under these conditions they may not be able to substitute domestic products for imports. Consequently, the price elasticities of their tradables will be reduced. Moreover, as increasing specialization decreases the level of self-sufficiency, trade will account for a growing proportion of individual countries' GDP. External development will, therefore, become more and more important in influencing their levels of activity, and changes in import prices will play an increasingly important role in domestic inflation rates and export prices. Capital flows in anticipation/response to exchange rate changes will both accelerate and intensify this process. The short-to-medium run effects of exchange rate changes may thus turn out to be quite different from those expected.

Given the increase in international integration and interdependence since the 1950s, it is hardly surprising that empirical data reveal a world which differs significantly from the one depicted by the conditions that need to be satisfied if exchange rate changes are to bring about the required external adjustments. Trade now either accounts for a high share of individual countries' GDP or, if that is not the case, the countries are so large that the rest of the world is unlikely to be indifferent to marked changes in the volume of their exports and imports (Maddison 1991, Panić 1988, Chapter 2). The relevant price elasticities fail to satisfy the Marshall–Lerner condition in the short run (Artus and Knight 1984); and wages and domestic prices respond to changes in import prices to such an extent that real exchange rates often bear little or no relation to movements in nominal rates (Goldstein 1980, Brown *et al.* 1980). Changes in absorption remain, therefore, the most effective way of correcting current account imbalances in the short run (Artus and Young 1979, IMF 1984).

These are the facts. But it would, of course, be wrong to attribute them entirely to the existence of TNCs. After all, as the traditional trade models show, under certain conditions national firms are capable of taking the international division of labour to a fairly high level. Nevertheless, it is inconceivable that national firms could ever influence the effectiveness of the exchange rate policy instrument in practice to the same degree as TNCs. It may not be possible to quantify the contribution of the latter to the observed facts. However, for a number of reasons, there can be no doubt that it has been very important.

First, as virtually all TNCs are oligopolies it is only natural that they transfer from national to international markets the basic code of behaviour among such enterprises: that of competing mainly in non-price terms. Price competition, which can easily accelerate in oligopolistic industries into price wars highly damaging to all, is, therefore, something that they will normally avoid.

Second, by providing, through vertical integration, secure markets for affiliates operating at different stages of production and distribution they can take the degree of specialization to a much higher level than national firms would ever dare risk. Hence, a good deal of intra-firm trade is likely to consist of goods and services specific to a particular TNC for which there are no ready-made substitutes on the open market.

Third, international responsiveness to relative price changes will be reduced further by the practice common to TNCs of dividing the global market among their affiliates selling similar products. The affiliates will be allowed to move into each other's market only in exceptional circumstances, to deal with a temporary crisis: for instance, if one of them is unable to fulfill orders in its market and, as a result, is in danger of losing a slice of the market to other TNCs.

Fourth, having invested heavily in physical and human capital in a certain location transnationals are unlikely to abandon it easily because of transient changes in the exchange rate. It is only in the long run that persistent improvement or deterioration in relative costs and prices may influence their decision whether to modernize or expand their facilities in a particular country or move them to a more favourable location.

Finally, as they are familiar with economic conditions and institutional arrangements in different countries and, normally, hold financial assets in a number of currencies, they can switch large funds at short notice from one currency into another, causing unsustainable movements in exchange rates – in the sense of increasing inflation or unemployment to the point at which they threaten the social fabric and political stability of a country. The readiness of TNCs to grant higher wages in order to prevent costly dislocation of their international production schedules may contribute further to these problems.

Clearly, there is nothing malicious in any of these actions. Each is perfectly rational from a corporate point of view. That, however, is not how governments may see it, as they find another major macroeconomic policy instrument failing to produce the expected result. Yet this is inevitable given that, as argued above and confirmed by Goldsbrough (1981), price elasticities are much lower for intra-firm than for conventional trade. As he showed, the former were not only generally statistically insignificant but also in most equations had the wrong sign. This was true of his estimates for both countries and industries. At the same time, he found that there was no difference in the responsiveness of the two types of trade to changes in demand: the relevant coefficients in both cases had the right sign and were statistically significant. The importance of these results lies in the fact that, as shown in the previous section, intra-firm trade now accounts for a high proportion of world trade. They are also consistent with the conclusion that the only way to eliminate large external imbalances on the current account is to lower levels of activity in the short run and/or undertake major structural adjustments in the long run (Panić 1988, Part II).

Finally, *social policy*, in the form of various social provisions, has played an important role in many countries since the Second World War in promoting social harmony and consensus. These, in turn, have made a major contribution to the countries' economic success, especially in the early postwar period, by demonstrating tangibly its benefits to all social groups. The policy was financed through different forms of (often heavy) taxation. Although never popular, the burden of taxation was made bearable by rapidly growing incomes, high levels of employment (which made it possible for the burden to be shared widely) and confidence that this state of affairs would continue indefinitely.

The rise of transnationals would have made it difficult to maintain social policies and the consensus even without the marked deterioration in the international economic environment since the 1970s. Although those running TNCs have to respect the customs and laws of the countries in which they operate, their allegiance to the corporation can be expected to take precedence over their allegiance to any particular country. This is essential if an enterprise operating in more than one country is to preserve its independent, transnational identity – with its diverse parts committed to common objectives and working in unison to achieve them. Many TNCs now recognize the need for organizations of their size and influence to assume wider social responsibilities and to reconcile them with their more traditional, narrow corporate ones. (See, for instance, UNCTAD 1994, Chapter 8.) Yet if there is a conflict between the two, it is not difficult to guess to which of them they would have to give higher priority.

Conflicts of this kind are often likely to arise out of differences in the background, traditions and values of those running TNCs and those in charge of national governments. Senior executives of a TNC will come predominantly from its country of origin. They will, therefore, be a product of its social attitudes and behaviour and, in general, will regard these as being superior to the traditions and institutions that they find in host countries. Hence, they will ensure that their values are enshrined in the 'corporate ethos', and foreign employees aspiring to positions of responsibility will have to embrace them if they are to realize their ambitions. The danger is that indiscriminate export of 'home' country attitudes and practices into widely different environments may produce outcomes which are against the long-term interests both of TNCs and of the host nations.

For instance, transnationals may succeed in persuading national governments, anxious to attract them, to introduce policies which lead to a steady downward pressure on wages, a lowering of unemployment and various social benefits as well as a relaxation of health, safety and environmental standards. Whatever the 'competitive' advantage of such policies in the short run, they may eventually prove to be highly costly to TNCs and to the states that adopt them if they produce deep social divisions, industrial strife and political instability. After all, a stable economic and political environment is one of the most important determinants of foreign direct investment.

In developing countries, the presence of transnationals may give rise to a number of problems, associated with the emergence of 'dual economies', which are particularly difficult to solve. Local citizens and firms associated with foreign corporations will tend to earn higher incomes and enjoy various privileges – often in sharp contrast to the rest of the population who continue to live in poverty, with many of them struggling to satisfy even the most basic needs. The result may be widespread resentment, increase in various forms of anti-social behaviour and the growing popularity of movements hostile to foreign influence and, in certain cases, to the process of industrial development itself. Yet, if TNCs do not reward those working for them with higher earnings and other benefits, which reflect at least to some extend their superior levels of productivity, they are likely to be accused of exploitation, especially if they keep repatriating the profits earned in these economies to the home country.

Those in charge of national firms may be close ideologically to their counterparts in TNCs, sharing at least some of the latter's attitudes to the welfare state and labour relations. At the same time, the survival and success of their enterprises, including their own livelihood and quality of life, depend on the maintenance of social order and political stability in their country of residence. Consequently, they will have little option but to accept the higher taxes and re-distribution of income needed to support the welfare state.

In contrast, TNCs are in a position to compare taxes and social conditions in different countries, selecting the most favourable location from their point of view. Given this flexibility, they may frustrate the social policies and institutional arrangements in a country in the knowledge that if their preferred alternatives lead to upheavals, making it difficult for them to achieve their overall corporate goals, they can move to another country. This will obviously involve real and financial losses, in some cases heavy losses, in the short term. But, unlike in the case of national enterprises, their survival and long-term success are not tied to operations in a particular country.

The other important fact, emphasized earlier in this section, is that – again unlike national enterprises – TNCs can minimize their tax liabilities by switching pre-tax profits to other countries. In doing so, they also shift the burden of taxation to national enterprises and individuals who may already be experiencing a reduction in their real income as a result of stagflation.

This may produce radical political changes either if taxes are raised to maintain social expenditure despite a shrinking tax base caused by higher bankruptcies and rising unemployment, or if social expenditure is cut to avoid tax increases. As developments of this kind have been common even in industrial countries since the early 1970s, it is hardly surprising that the welfare state, created to avoid a repetition of the socio-political upheavals of the 1930s, has been under continuous attack in recent decades.

It would, of course, be wrong to attribute these changes entirely to TNCs. Nevertheless, given the dominant position that they now occupy in most national economies, enabling them to exert considerable influence on government policies, there can be little doubt that they have contributed significantly to changes in economic and social policies in many countries. If this is correct, they have also contributed to the re-emergence of serious social problems and growing 'political dissent' even in the leading industrial nations (cf. Taylor 1992).

6.4 Conclusion

This chapter has focused on conflicts likely to arise between transnationals pursuing their narrow commercial objectives and national governments trying to discharge the wide-ranging economic, social and political responsibilities placed on them by their electorates. It has ignored, therefore, the important contributions that TNCs have made to both national and global economic welfare.

The vast resources at the disposal of TNCs and the key role which they increasingly play in the international allocation of resources, production and trade have important implications for both national and international economic policies and, ultimately, for the effectiveness of the nation state as a form of political organization. Consequently, even in open economies, economic policy cannot be treated now simply as a matter of inter-governmental attitudes and actions, ignoring transnationals.

Unlike the states in which they operate, TNCs have no sovereign power. However, as their resources are located in different countries, they can influence the outcome of international agreements, including attempts to co-ordinate national policies, producing results which may turn out to be quite different from those originally intended. If over 40 per cent of world trade consists of intra-firm trade within a relatively small number of large TNCs, what exactly do the concepts of 'trade liberalization' and 'free trade' mean? And if they do not mean exactly what is generally understood by them, do changes in trading regimes trigger off improvements/deteriorations of the kind predicted by traditional theory? Analysis in this chapter suggests that they may not do so. Moreover, it also implies that the impact of TNCs on national economic policies may be such as to undermine seriously the authority of the only institution, the 'nation' state, capable of providing the economic and political stability without which TNCs would find it difficult to function effectively and, consequently, to justify their existence.

This does not, of course, mean that TNCs have made government economic actions irrelevant, even less that they have affected all states equally. The governments of large countries still retain considerable freedom to pursue policies which are in their national interest for two basic reasons; (a) their economies are much more self-sufficient than those of small countries and (b) the size of their markets, combined with the institutional uniformity and greater independence and predictability of their policies, ensures that TNCs cannot afford to be excluded from them and will, therefore, be careful not to antagonize their governments. Moreover, although the effectiveness of each of the major macroeconomic policy instruments can be weakened by the actions of TNCs, their ultimate success will depend on the overall package of measures introduced by national authorities, the strength of national consensus for a particular course of action and the skill with which the policies are pursued.

Nevertheless, the ubiquity and economic power of TNCs raise important questions concerning the existing responsibilities of nation states and transnationals. Are electorates still justified in expecting national governments to discharge effectively the responsibilities for which a larger form of political organization seems to be required? Equally important, are national authorities right to demand no more from TNCs, in terms of wider economic and social responsibilities, than from small national enterprises? Developments over the last 30 years suggest the need for a fundamental re-appraisal of the capabilities and responsibilities of these two dominant forms of macro- and microeconomic organization.

Part IV

Globalization, Cooperation and Supranationalism

7
The Aspirations Gap, Interdependence and Global Inflation*

It has become something of a platitude to say that sharp, continuous increases in prices are one of the most serious economic problems of our time. Indeed, the problem is so great, we are told, that unless it is brought under control *inflation* will destroy the very fabric of the 'Western', 'industrial' or 'civilized' society – the exact scale of the 'destruction' depending on the author's capacity (or predilection) for taking a 'cosmic' view of such momentous happenings.

The argument developed in this chapter is rather different. It starts from the proposition that, far from being the *cause*, a high and accelerating rate of inflation is invariably a symptom of underlying socio-economic conflicts and tensions. These conflicts and tensions, in turn, are the result of modern economic progress or, more accurately, the form that it has taken over the last 200 years. Consequently, a proper understanding of price 'explosions' – such as the unprecedented rates of inflation experienced all over the world since the end of the 1960s – is extremely difficult without at least some understanding of the economic, social and political forces which make an inflationary spiral of this kind possible.

At the same time, it cannot be emphasized too strongly that this chapter is not intended to be – and, therefore, should not be interpreted as – a disguised attempt to discredit the idea of economic growth. There is far too much poverty, disease, social friction and political oppression in the world for 'anti-growth' theses to be either justified or justifiable. However, implicit in the analysis that follows is the notion that there are considerable potential benefits to be gained from a more rational approach to economic progress, particularly a more equitable distribution of its gains both nationally and internationally – and that these benefits are social and political as well as economic.

---

* This chapter was previously published as 'The Inevitable Inflation' in *Lloyds Bank Review*, July 1976.

Finally, I have used the statistical information available for a number of OECD countries to test tentatively some of the more important propositions. The choice was deliberately restricted to these countries because, with a few exceptions, they do not try to suppress underlying tensions and conflicts by force. Moreover, most of them produce relevant data that are reasonably comparable. They can be used, therefore, to verify empirically some of the propositions that follow, even though these are based on the experience of a far greater number of countries. For instance, although the data and the analysis refer explicitly to capitalist or 'market economies', much of the analysis is equally applicable to 'socialist' countries, at least those in Eastern Europe (see Panić 1978).

7.1   A global puzzle

The fact that since the end of the 1950s annual rates of inflation in excess of 2–3 per cent have become common all over the world is illustrated in Table 7.1. What is more, there has been a tendency for the rates to accelerate in each consecutive cycle, culminating in the unprecedented 'flare-up' in the early 1970s and the two worst recessions since the 1930s.

Table 7.1   Average annual increases in consumer prices, 1959–74

	1959–63	*1963–69*	*1969–74*	*1959–74*
Turkey	4.8	6.3	14.4	8.5
Spain	4.1	6.6	9.8	7.0
Japan	5.8	3.7	10.7	6.6
Denmark	4.4	6.1	8.6	6.5
Finland	3.5	6.0	9.0	6.3
UK	2.7	4.1	9.4	5.5
Italy	4.1	3.3	8.9	5.4
Netherlands	2.4	5.1	7.4	5.2
Norway	2.7	4.1	8.2	5.1
France	3.9	3.9	7.5	5.1
New Zealand	1.8	4.1	8.6	5.0
Sweden	3.4	3.9	7.5	5.0
Switzerland	2.7	3.4	7.1	4.4
Australia	1.5	3.0	8.0	4.3
Belgium	1.2	3.6	6.6	4.0
W. Germany	2.4	2.5	5.6	3.5
Canada	1.3	2.8	5.9	3.4
USA	1.3	2.1	6.3	3.3
Average	3.0	4.1	8.3	5.2

Source: IMF, *International Financial Statistics*.

The exact reasons behind the sharp acceleration in price increases since the end of the 1960s are still by no means clear. Economists will, no doubt, spend a good deal of time and effort in producing various explanations and arguing about their relative merits. Indeed, there is already quite an impressive list of alternative 'causes'. These include: large US deficits on the balance of payments, leading to excessive expansion of world money supply; growing synchronization of industrial countries' trade cycles and, as a result of this, severe pressure of demand for raw materials and other products; a somewhat mysterious breakdown in the unemployment–inflation 'trade-off'; the widespread abandonment of the system of fixed exchange rates; and so on. Yet, although there is some truth in all these explanations, the immediate reasons for the price acceleration are much less important than the underlying causes that make inflation of this kind both possible and sustainable over so many years, including periods of large-scale under-utilization of resources.

Table 7.1 illustrates also another important fact: that inflation has been experienced by countries with different political systems. This is highly relevant in relation to some of the more 'parochial' theories of inflation, such as those that single out *organized* labour as its main cause. However, if that were the explanation, how would we account for the fact that Spain and Turkey have had higher rates of inflation than, say, the UK? Or, taking the countries with well-organized and powerful labour organizations, why has the UK had a higher rate of inflation than West Germany or Sweden, the two countries with more powerful and highly influential trade unions? Clearly, there is something important here that has yet to be explained.

Lastly, the table suggests that inflation has been experienced by countries at different stages of industrialization. There is, however, a very important difference. The countries which have had the highest rates of inflation over the period and, consequently, occupy the upper half of the table are predominantly those with a relatively lower standard of living, such as Turkey, Spain and Japan. Conversely, at the bottom of the table, with the lowest rates of inflation, are countries such as the United States, Canada and West Germany, all of which have, as Table 7.2 shows, very high incomes per head. The real significance of this observation will become apparent later, after we have considered two inter-related questions. Why the difference? And how is it brought about?

7.2   The aspirations gap

Economic progress, like all progress, rests on a deep and continuous feeling of discontent with the *status quo*. It is this discontent and a strong desire to improve their standard of living which motivate people to work hard and accept sacrifices in terms of current consumption, without which sustainable economic growth is impossible. This is the 'constructive' aspect of the

Table 7.2   Level of income, income inequality and industrial strife

	GDP per capita, 1971 (US$)	Income inequality in the mid 1960s (Gini coefficients)	Social expenditure per capita, 1971 (US$)	Strikes: days lost per 1000 people employed (annual average, 1960–74)
USA	5118	0.34	411	1111
Sweden	4431	0.39	771	32
Canada	4316	0.34	439	1248
Switzerland	3842	0.37	559	4
W. Germany	3585	0.45	698	45
Denmark	3491	0.37	489	574
Norway	3260	0.35	422	111
Australia	3226	0.30	277	725
France	3175	0.50	577	300
Belgium	3007	0.41	550	276
Netherlands	2825	0.42	523	52
New Zealand	2544	0.38	296	265
Finland	2468	0.46	322	681
UK	2453	0.38	354	575
Japan	2176	0.39	134	248
Italy	1887	0.40	328	1501
Spain	1080	0.39	46	–
Turkey	350	0.56	7	–

Sources: OECD, *National Accounts of OECD Countries 1962–1973* (Paris: OECD); Paukert (1973); Wilensky (1975); International Labour Office (1972).

old and perfectly understandable human need to increase control over the economic environment. However, prolonged neglect of the less desirable social consequences of these aspirations can easily lead to pent-up frustrations, conflicts and thus a destructive social force of great potential. The world-wide tendency to accelerating rates of inflation can be interpreted to some extent as a relatively mild manifestation of these underlying conflicts, and perhaps even as an early warning of the much more unpleasant developments that could follow.

Basically, there are two types of human need, as Keynes, for instance, pointed out in his essay *Economic Possibilities for Our Grandchildren*: "those needs which are absolute in the sense that we feel them whatever the situation of our fellow human beings may be, and those which are relative in the sense that we feel them only if their satisfaction lifts us above, makes us feel superior to, our fellows" (Keynes [1930] 1972, p. 326). The important difference between the two is that, while the absolute needs could be met within a reasonable period of time, the relative needs, as Keynes observed, are probably insatiable.

Yet, economic progress has depended so far for its motive power, particularly in capitalist economies, predominantly on these relative, 'insatiable' needs. The result has been, for the reasons outlined briefly below, to create claims on resources that cannot be met from the world's existing productive capacity. Indeed, it is most improbable that we shall be able to meet them from any productive potential likely to be created in the foreseeable future. And, when claims are made on goods and services that exceed the productive capacity of an economy, social and economic tensions and conflicts follow, with inflation as one of the outcomes.

The importance of *relative* income, *relative* status and *relative* influence has been observed for some time now by economists and other social scientists. (The three usually, though not always, tend to go together and re-enforce one another.) This is true of nations as well as of individuals and groups within a particular nation. Briefly, there is an apparent tendency for people to feel worse off – even when their standard of living shows a clear improvement in absolute terms – if those with whom they normally compare themselves have done relatively better. For example, B's income may increase substantially. Nevertheless, B will feel 'worse off' if the gap between B and A (who is in front) has increased; or the gap between B and C (who is behind) has narrowed.

If that is the case, does it mean that A, B and C will remain indefinitely satisfied with improvements in their standard of living so long as there is no change in their relative position? The available evidence seems to indicate strongly that they are unlikely to do so. For instance, developing countries wish to emulate the material standard of living, status and influence of the leading industrial nations; in other words, to close the existing gap. Similarly, the less privileged groups in society have a strong desire to enjoy many of the advantages which go with higher income and status and, indeed, will tend to believe that, on the whole, 'social justice' demands that they do so. The problem is that they can achieve this only if they 'catch up' with the more privileged groups. Otherwise, irrespective of how much their absolute position improves, they will always remain 'poor' and 'underprivileged'. Beyond a certain minimum level, 'poverty', like 'wealth', is a relative concept.

It is this gap between the standard of living and the status that people have and those that they would like to have that I have called *the aspirations gap*. The size of the gap will depend on changes experienced by individuals, groups and nations relative to those of their 'reference groups'. Needless to say, the gap has always existed in some form; and, as already indicated, it has provided the 'motive power' for the economic growth achieved over the last 200 years. However, until a few decades ago this was confined to a relatively small section of the world's population. What has happened since then, particularly since the 1940s, is that people all over the world have become not only concerned about the gap but also determined to take action, constructive or otherwise, to eliminate or at least to reduce it.

This transformation can be traced to certain developments that have taken place over the last 50 years. However, the root of all this lies in a number of major, essential economic and social reforms which have brought the 'visible hand' of modern government and the vast resources which it can mobilize, both nationally and internationally, right into the centre of economic affairs. Full employment and economic growth became major goals of national economic policies, as indeed they should be. The changes led to a period of unprecedented improvements in the standard of living in industrial and semi-industrial countries, both 'capitalist' and 'socialist'. The immense psychological impact of this success is difficult to overestimate. It has demonstrated to lower-income groups all over the world that their position is not necessarily hopeless; and that a major co-ordinated effort, combining national and international resources on a large scale, could produce astounding transformations within a period of a few decades. In other words, success has not just increased the expectation of success. It has led to what has been called 'the revolution of rising expectations'.

Several important and interrelated developments have helped to spread this 'message'. First, a complex division of labour, on an international scale, also requires a complex system of communications. At the same time, improvements in communications do more than improve international intercourse. They also make people conscious of what is happening everywhere on the globe. Thanks to television and the cinema, people have become aware of something that many of them would have found difficult to imagine: the standard of living enjoyed in advanced industrial countries, including the lifestyle of the more affluent sections of society within these countries.

Second, since the 1940s there has been a massive improvement in literacy and educational facilities. Rapid economic progress and technological change require an educated labour force. Hence, demand for better educational opportunities is likely to come from various sectors of the economy, as well as from individuals who realize the economic and social advantages of more advanced education and entry into certain occupations. The role of education in widening the aspirations gap lies partly in increasing people's awareness of the importance of their skills in an increasingly complex economic process and, partly, in widening their horizons to the extent that they can question the rationality and justice of the existing socio-economic relationships, including their own place in the established hierarchical order.

Third, rapid economic progress and the international division of labour are dependent upon a highly developed, low-cost transport system to extend the size of the market. The advances made in this area since the 1940s have led to an unprecedented movement of people and ideas.

Finally, to the extent that it creates wants, advertising, which has expanded enormously since the 1950s, also helps create the aspirations gap. The cumulative effect of advertising, carried by transnational corporations to virtually every corner of the globe, goes beyond making people familiar with and attached to particular brands of goods and services. It promotes a certain life style and values that go with it. Hence, industry also plays an important role in creating the aspirations gap.

Once we accept the existence of the gap – and the findings of various social scientists leave little room for doubt – it requires little reflection to realise that the aspirations gap and the tension and potential conflict which can result from it are the unavoidable consequence of existing inequalities. The desirability of a higher standard of living (and the same is true of status and influence) is demonstrated to those who do not enjoy it by those who do. What is more, if the preceding analysis is correct, the greater the inequalities the larger the aspirations gap and, hence, the stronger the inflationary pressure as people make excessive demands on existing, limited resources.

There is, in fact, a relatively simple, rough test of this proposition. If lower income countries try to imitate levels of consumption achieved in the high income countries, they should experience higher rates of inflation – given their more limited productive capacity. There will, of course, be differences resulting from economic and social organization and traditions that vary from country to country. The same is also true of the means that those who would like to close the aspirations gap have at their disposal to do something about it. Nevertheless, the proposition should hold, particularly in the case of countries that are similar in terms of historic traditions and general economic philosophy.

This is basically true of the OECD countries included in the two tables. Hence, price changes in Table 7.1 can be related to the levels of income in Table 7.2. Admittedly, the figures for income per head have a number of weaknesses, including the problem of converting them into US dollars. Moreover, they show estimates of incomes rather than of consumption. Nevertheless, the estimates provide, on the whole, a fairly accurate picture of the relative standards of living and, therefore, we can assume, of the relative levels of consumption. A statistical comparison of the average annual price increases in 1959–74 with incomes per head in Table 7.2 shows that, other things being reasonably similar, the lower the average level of income in a country the higher tends to be its rate of inflation. As can be seen from the Statistical Appendix (see p. 190), the correlation coefficient for the period 1959–74 is −0.77, which is highly significant statistically. The correlation coefficient for the shorter period, 1969–74, is weaker (−0.55). Nevertheless, it is also statistically significant. (The results were confirmed subsequently using a much larger sample of countries, both industrial and developing. Cf. Panić 1978, Peacock and Ricketts 1978.)

However, incomes are distributed unequally not only between nations, but also between individuals and families within nations. Should a similar relationship hold here also? Again, there are statistical problems that make empirical tests rather difficult. Data for income distribution are often poor and unreliable. There is even disagreement about the most appropriate measure. However, one of the summary measures of inequality, the 'Gini coefficient', has become recently available for over forty countries (Paukert 1973). This is the indicator of inequality included in Table 7.2. Theoretically, the Gini coefficient can vary between *zero*, when all incomes are equal, and *one*, when all income goes to one recipient. Needless to say, neither extreme is likely to be found in practice. But they provide a useful criterion for judging the figures in Table 7.2, in the sense that the lower the coefficient for a country (that is, the closer it is to zero) the more equally are personal incomes distributed within the country. Thus, the distribution of incomes is appreciably more equal in Australia, for example, than in Turkey. As for the relationship between inequality and rates of inflation, the tables in the Appendix show that it is positive and statistically significant both in the short and in the long run. In other words, the greater the inequality of income distribution in a country, the higher is also likely to be its rate of inflation. (See Panić 1978 for a confirmation of these results using a larger sample.)

In fact, this finding can be examined from a slightly different angle. Social expenditure tends, on the whole, to be progressive, in the sense that lower income groups are likely to benefit more from it, at least in the short run. It can be assumed, therefore, that countries with high social expenditure per head are making a greater effort to reduce the aspirations gap by enabling those with low incomes to enjoy a standard of living in line with what is thought to be an 'acceptable standard' in these countries. The Appendix tables show that this is also one of the factors that affect significantly the rate of inflation both in the short and the long run. The implication is that a good deal of the inflationary pressure over this period came from low income groups. These groups have experienced serious falls in their levels of consumption as a result of large increases in the price of food and other essentials, particularly in the countries where social expenditure was relatively low.

The main conclusion of this section is therefore simple: the greater the national and international inequality of incomes the greater the aspirations gap and, consequently, actual and/or potential inflationary tendencies.

7.3   Coercive power

If the aspirations gap provides the motive power, the division of labour is the engine that, in the absence of appropriate institutional adjustments, transforms that power into the modern inflationary process. The joint presence of the two factors is essential. Otherwise, there would be either the motive without the means or the means without the motive.

The division of labour is one of the basic principles of economic organization and thus of economic progress. Indeed, the proposition that it depends on the size of the market, with which Adam Smith opened

The Wealth of Nations, is amongst the most celebrated in the history of economics. To us, reading it 200 years later, it is almost too obvious to need further elaboration. Expansion in the size of the market will enable people to divide more and more various tasks, specialize in them and master them to an extent which will lead to undreamt of improvements in productivity. These improvements will raise real incomes, increasing further the size of the market which, in turn, will bring about further division of labour, and so on. To paraphrase Adam Smith rather crudely, the upshot of all this is that, in an advanced industrial economy, people will be able to enjoy a very high standard of living thanks to countless individuals who have cooperated in producing their food, clothes, dwellings, furniture, fuel and light, the tools with which they work and the services which are essential for their work as well as for their relaxation and enjoyment.

These are the well-known advantages. Unfortunately, there are also potential dangers and it is these which, if neglected, become important in the inflationary process. The division of labour progressively reduces self-sufficiency and, in this way, increases peoples' dependence on other individuals and groups. Moreover, as roundabout methods of production and productivity increase so also does the complexity of the skills required to perform various tasks and the length of time necessary to acquire such skills. Consequently, there is an increase in heterogeneity and the non-substitutability of labour. The concept of an aggregate 'labour force' becomes increasingly meaningless as the 'non-competing groups' proliferate even within broadly defined occupations. Furthermore, it is often forgotten that the growing productivity of labour is both the consequence and cause of its growing relative scarcity over a wide range of occupational groups. This means that the higher the stage of the division of labour reached, the deeper and more prolonged unemployment has to be to reduce the underlying, structural scarcity of labour even on a temporary basis.

The importance of the growing 'scarcity' of certain types of labour is that it enables those who find themselves in this position to apply what I shall call *coercive power* – the ability to use the bargaining strength that this gives them in order to improve their relative position. They may or may not use it. But the potential power is there should they choose to exercise it. The danger that it will be used stems from the fact that division of labour can lead to the development of sectarianism and vested interests centred around specific activities: social oases with weak links within a tightly interwoven and complex social and economic framework.

Nor is labour the only factor of production to specialize and increase its coercive power. The same is also true of capital. In a dynamic economic environment, rapidly growing markets enable firms to specialize. By doing so they can increase the size of their operations and thus benefit from economies of scale – lowering the costs of production and, in this way, expanding their markets even further. In time, a relatively small number of firms will acquire sufficient resources to perpetuate their own growth through consolidations, mergers, acquisitions, the use of costly technologies and so on. The large size and relative importance that they eventually achieve gives these oligopolies considerable economic and political power. To begin with, they control large volumes of output and investment and in this way both short- and long-term employment. But that is not all. Their control of a significant proportion of the market gives them also the power to determine their own prices. This makes it possible for them to alter prices, irrespective of the state of demand, in order to cover costs and earn a 'satisfactory' (that is, target) short-term rate of return. All empirical evidence indicates that there has been an unprecedented growth in industrial concentration, particularly since the Second World War, in industrial and semi-industrial countries. This means that there has been an appreciable increase in the coercive power at the disposal of 'capital', though, as in the case of 'labour', that power may or may not be used.

Furthermore, oligopolies need access to larger and larger markets in order to grow, which means that most of them have to operate internationally. This is one of the factors that have been responsible for the unprecedented growth of world trade in manufactures and services in the second half of the twentieth century. A large proportion of this is due to the growth of intra-industry specialization and trade as a result of industrial diversification on a world scale. The increasing importance of this form of trade reflects, in fact, the extraordinary growth of transnational enterprises in all sectors of the global economy.

These developments have increased economic interdependence amongst countries, especially those in which the division of labour has progressed to a very high level. Not only do they depend heavily on primary producers for raw materials and foodstuffs, they also depend increasingly on one another, because each industrial country finds that other advanced economies are its most important market. Their purchasing power is such that they comprise by far the largest and the most significant part of the world market. The growing interdependence of these economies in particular is reflected, among other things, in the increasing synchronization of the business cycle on a global scale. More important, by increasing their interdependence, the international division of labour also increases the coercive power of nations, especially those with large economies.

Finally, the division of labour leads not only to growing interdependence in private sectors of different countries but also between the 'private' and 'state' sectors within each country. Economic growth cannot proceed very far without a major expansion of the infrastructure (transport, education, health, public administration, etc.). This, together with the more traditional areas of state responsibility, such as defence, makes vast claims on resources which can be provided adequately only by mobilizing *national* resources. Moreover, it has been recognized since the Second World War, even in capitalist economies, that the government has to manage the overall level of demand in order to prevent large-scale unemployment of the kind experienced in the 1930s. By appropriate fiscal and monetary policies governments can maintain high levels of aggregate demand. High levels of aggregate demand mean, of course, lower unemployment and higher real wages. They also ensure higher utilization of capacity, lower unit costs and, thus, higher profits. High utilization of capacity and improvements in profits in a capitalist economy encourage technological change and new investment – the only way to maintain longer-term profitability, full employment and continuous increases in real incomes. Not surprisingly, therefore, both 'labour' and the owners of real capital have a strong interest in the achievement and maintenance of a high level of economic activity, and there is an intense pressure on governments to secure this.

What the analysis in this section so far implies is that the division of labour, by increasing interdependence and sectarianism, introduces a built-in 'destabilizer' into modern industrial societies of a kind unknown to pre-industrial civilizations. Various groups of labour depend on one another for employment and income. Together, they have the same dependence on capital, and capital on them. The two together depend on the government for the achievement of their objectives: to provide them with the infrastructure essential for efficient work and civilized living, as well as for creating an appropriate institutional framework and a sufficiently high level of aggregate demand to help them enjoy full employment and high incomes. Government, in turn, depends on them for the attainment of certain 'national' objectives. Finally, the three together are dependent for the achievement of both sectional and national objectives upon the action of other nations.

This intricate and complex network of highly interdependent relationships provides almost limitless scope for the use of coercive power both nationally and internationally. There is no need, in fact, for formal organizations and negotiating spectaculars in full view of television cameras and eager journalists. Experience from the countries where such things do not exist shows that widespread dissatisfaction or feelings of injustice will be expressed in a lack of involvement in work and, consequently, low productivity and output. More direct pressure will come from management whose production targets are threatened. In these circumstances, the government has to respond by paying greater attention to improvements in real incomes and working conditions. It has little alternative. The more the decision-making process depends on a large number of individuals and groups – their expertise as well as their acquiescence – the less power those in authority have to impose for long their will upon the people over whom they exercise authority.

This means that the more advanced the division of labour, the less effective will authoritarian or even rigidly hierarchical forms of organization become. People will cooperate enthusiastically and efficiently in the attainment of those objectives that they have helped to formulate and which promise to satisfy their aspirations. Organized pressure groups, such as trade union (labour), cartels (capital) or, say, OPEC (countries) simply formalize and intensify a power which is already there. It is this coercive power which, as already pointed out, makes it possible for the aspirations gap and the socio-economic tensions to which it leads to be transformed into, among other things, a sustained and worsening rate of inflation.

7.4   The paradox

Clearly, given the high and increasing degree of economic interdependence, inflation can be triggered off in a number of ways and from a number of directions. What is more, the preceding analysis implies that it could be set in motion even in conditions of a general underutilization of resources. All that is necessary is for an important part of the intricate economic 'mechanism' to feel that its real income and/or relative position is threatened.

For instance, oligopolists can start an inflationary spiral by raising their prices as recession deepens and brings about a major fall in their capacity utilization and profits. A highly skilled and/or strategically placed group of wage or salary earners can set the process in motion by discovering that their relative position has deteriorated and taking 'appropriate' action to remedy it. A government can produce a similar effect by increasing taxes in order to reduce total demand and/or cover its own expenditure. Countries in possession of a strategically important commodity can start off the spiral internationally by increasing sharply the price of that commodity. Ultimately, whichever way the spiral starts, it is unlikely to remain a purely 'local' affair. The international division of labour has turned the aspirations gap and coercive power into international rather than national phenomena.

At the same time, it has also given rise to an important paradox. Following the arguments developed in the preceding section, it might be expected that coercive power and therefore socio-economic conflicts would be greatest in those countries which have achieved the highest levels of productivity and income, that is, in the countries in which division of labour has progressed the most. In fact, the position seems to be exactly the opposite. If we take the incidence of strikes as the most visible peaceful symptom of underlying frustration and conflict, the Appendix tables show that it is negatively correlated with the level of income. (The correlation coefficients are highly significant statistically both in the short and the long term.) In other words, the higher the level of income in a country, the lower, on the whole, will be the number of days lost in strikes – though these, as all the other results in this chapter, should be treated with caution because of data problems. For example, even in the sample of countries used here, data on strikes are either not available (Spain and Turkey) or quite different from those in the other

OECD countries (Canada and the United States where strikes are less widespread and less frequent, but last much longer).

Obviously, the potential power that exists is not used. The most plausible explanation for this seems to be that the aspirations gap is reduced as the level of income increases. To begin with, it is the countries with high per capita incomes that, with their levels of consumption, create the international aspirations gap. But that is only part of the story. The available evidence suggests that the distribution of income tends to become more equal at higher levels of productivity and income. Moreover, as their standard of living rises, other things being similar, countries tend to devote more resources to social expenditure. There is, of course, nothing fortuitous in this. They are reaping the benefits of their relative economic success and of changes in their institutions and policies that have taken into account the fact that economic growth inevitably causes profound changes in economic, social and political relationships. The apparent effect of all this is to reduce both open and hidden conflict and, in this way, also inflationary pressure. Hence the paradox: the countries in which factors of production have, potentially, the greatest coercive power are also the countries with the lowest rates of inflation. It is exactly opposite, of course, in the case of lower-income countries. The serious problem which they and, consequently, the world as a whole face, is that, although they can do a certain amount to minimize internal forces of conflict – no country, irrespective of its size, can do much on its own about existing world inequalities. These inequalities and, hence, the inflationary tendencies which stem from them are, therefore, a global challenge.

What gives a particular sense of urgency to this challenge is the growing realization in recent years that, given the size of the world population relative to available resources, it is highly improbable that we can achieve for everyone, say, a Scandinavian standard and style of living, even assuming that both world population and Scandinavian income per head stopped increasing. In fact, in the absence of far greater international co-operation, it is extremely unlikely that we shall even be able to solve the problem of absolute poverty in the foreseeable future. The potentially destructive forces that these failures may unleash – thanks to the combined forces of the aspirations gap and coercive power – are immense; and they pose an even graver danger because so few people seem to have grasped their real significance.

Early in the nineteenth century, David Ricardo ([1817] 1969, p. 1) argued that: "To determine the laws which regulate ... distribution [of income] is the principal problem of Political Economy". To the extent that the global inflationary tendencies anlysed in this chapter have become linked to the national and, even more, to the international distribution of income this has become itself a major problem of international *political* economy. As such, it cannot be solved by means of simple, mechanical expedients, such as those often advocated by economists, which ignore the social and political consequences of economic policies.

Statistical appendix

Correlation coefficients
(All the coefficients in bold are statistically significant at the 5% level)

Table A 1959–74

	Income	Inequality	Social expenditure	Strikes	Prices
Income	–	**−0.54**	**0.55**	**−0.61**	**−0.77**
Inequality	**−0.54**	–	0.34	−0.10	**0.56**
Social expenditure	**0.55**	0.34	–	−0.43	**−0.71**
Strikes	**−0.61**	−0.10	−0.43	–	0.30
Prices	**−0.77**	**0.56**	−0.41	0.30	–

Table B 1969–74

	Income	Inequality	Social expenditure	Strikes	Prices
Income	–	**−0.54**	**0.55**	**−0.57**	**−0.55**
Inequality	**−0.54**	–	0.34	−0.15	**0.48**
Social expenditure	**0.55**	0.34	–	**−0.48**	**−0.70**
Strikes	**−0.57**	−0.15	**−0.48**	–	0.45
Prices	**−0.55**	**0.48**	**−0.70**	0.45	–

Sources: Tables 7.1 and 7.2 and, in the case of strikes and prices, additional data for 1969–74. The coefficients for correlations between income, inequality and social expenditure are the same in the two tables because data for the last two were available for one year only.

8
International Interdependence and the Debt Problem*

8.1 Introduction

There is little doubt that the current levels and composition of developing countries' debts present a serious threat to the survival of the international financial system. Not surprisingly, the possibility of a global financial upheaval has inspired a large and rapidly growing literature covering a wide range of issues. Yet it is far from clear that the debate has been very successful in isolating the real origin of the problem. In the debt drama, as in a detective story, the real culprit is not necessarily one of the main suspects, even though the latter may be guilty of many serious offences.

Moreover, disagreement, even confusion, surrounds some of the key concepts used in the debate. For instance, 'adjustment' features prominently in the literature. What is not often clear is whether it means the short-term, macroeconomic demand corrections or the long-term, microeconomic structural changes in the volume and patterns of supply. Both processes require international financing, though, of course, of a different kind and duration.

Above all, there is still a tendency to ignore the consequences of international integration and to believe that the corrections, even the adjustments, can be achieved in isolation. Unfortunately, as the inter-war experience shows, the moment that individual countries begin – under external pressure – to apply national solutions to international problems is also the moment that the world economic system begins to disintegrate.

The almost frantic efforts by central and commercial banks, as well as by international institutions, to reschedule the debts have succeeded, so far, in

---

* This chapter was written jointly with Manmohan Kumar and was first published in S. Borner and A. Taylor (eds), *Structural Change, Economic Interdependence and World Development*, Proceedings of the Seventh World Congress of the International Economic Association, Macmillan, London, 1987.

averting a major international crisis. Nevertheless, there are growing doubts about the adequacy of all these actions to prevent a repetition of similar crises in the near future.

This raises a number of important questions about the behaviour of each of the major participants in the debt drama. Given the misjudgments and blunders common in a dynamic economy – especially in the early stages of industrialization – have developing countries been guilty of a failure to adjust? Or, have they suffered from adjustment failures brought about by external developments, mostly outside their control?

Next, the borrowing countries' government and other development programmes in the 1970s are judged now to have been unrealistic and too ambitious. Is this an *ex post* verdict or did they appear in the same light *ex ante*? If the latter is true, why did banks, generally regarded as well-informed and rational, fail to spot this at the time? Even worse, if they were aware of the borrowers' weaknesses, why did they continue to lend? In other words, has the debt problem arisen as a result of carelessness and failure on the lenders' part to assess the risks properly? Or have some developments outside the markets' immediate control completely altered the environment in which banks and other financial institutions operate?

Above all, what has been the role of industrial countries in the debt-creating process? They dominate the world economy in terms of production, trade and technical and managerial expertise. The banks which performed, according to one of the Governors of the Federal Reserve, the "absolutely amazing" feat of transferring quickly vast sums of capital to where it was "needed" (Wallich 1982, p. 247), come predominantly from these countries. Hence, the accusing finger is inevitably pointed at industrial nations, especially the larger ones, whenever the debt problem is attributed to low commodity prices, slow growth of world trade and high interest rates. What has gone wrong there? Has the debt problem been created by the quite unprecedented failure to adjust not in developing but in industrial countries?

The remainder of this chapter will deal briefly with some of these questions. To keep it within a reasonable length, it will be assumed that there is a general familiarity with the history and size of the debt problem (see, however, Table 8.1 for some aggregate data). For similar reasons, the analysis will concentrate on that part of the total debt (excluding export credits) which developing countries owe to private institutions – mainly banks – as this is where the recent difficulties have arisen. As Table 8.1 shows, the share of these debts in the total went up from 20 per cent in 1971 to 46 per cent in 1982. Finally, no systematic attempt will be made to differentiate between individual countries and banks according to the scale and seriousness of their problems, even though it is widely recognized that some developing countries are in a much more precarious position than others.

Table 8.1 Total debt disbursed at year end and debt service ratios, 1971–82

Country group	Total debt ($ billion)	Percentage borrowed in private markets	Debt service as percentage of exports[1]
Low-income countries[2]			
1971	18	2	12
1975	40	7	16
1980	86	6	17
1982	110	6	23
Middle-income countries[3]			
1971	24	14	16
1975	40	29	10
1980	107	38	12
1982	144	39	16
Newly industrialized countries			
1971	31	38	15
1975	72	60	15
1980	192	65	18
1982	266	67	24
Total non-OPEC[4] *(excluding centrally planned economies)*			
1971	73	20	15
1975	152	38	14
1980	385	44	16
1982	520	46	21
OPEC			
1971	14	15	6
1975	28	25	4
1980	79	37	7
1982	106	37	14
Centrally planned economies[5]			
1972	11	n.a.	n.a.
1976	48	60	29
1980	86	68	56

Notes
[1] Debt service includes interest and amortization. Exports include goods, services and private transfers.
[2] Includes countries with per capita income of less than $600 in 1980.
[3] Includes countries (other than newly industrialized and OPEC) with per capita income of more than $600 in 1980.
[4] Non-OPEC (excluding centrally planned economies) data exclude debts with a maturity of less than one year. The data for 1982 are estimates.
[5] Centrally planned economies include Bulgaria, Czechoslovakia, East Germany, Hungary, Poland, Romania and the USSR.

Sources: OECD (1982a), tables II.D.5 and II.D.8; IMF (1982), table 45.

8.2 The adjustment strategy of developing countries

There are two fundamentally different explanations for the developing countries' predicament. According to the first, the debt problem has arisen chiefly because of the borrowers' failure to pursue appropriate adjustment policies. The credit conditions in the international financial markets in the 1970s enabled the countries to finance their deficits relatively easily and thus encouraged them to postpone the necessary adjustments. The alternative explanation is that the problem has arisen mainly as a result of an abrupt deterioration, over the past few years, in the world economic environment, rather than the borrowers' failure to adjust (OECD 1982b, Treasury and Civil Service Committee 1983).

These opposing explanations reflect, of course, the fundamental disagreement that exists between the static and dynamic approaches to the problem of external imbalances. According to the first approach (which, for instance, the IMF is required to take by its Articles of Agreement), external imbalances are invariably temporary phenomena to be remedied by appropriate macroeconomic policies. The *status quo* can be re-established quickly if the authorities take the fiscal and monetary measures needed to correct what are basically unanticipated changes in absorption. This kind of reasoning rests on an important assumption: that there is a general satisfaction with the *status quo* so that its maintenance is essential for the existence of an open system of international economic relationships. 'Correction' or 'stabilization' – and not 'adjustment', in the sense of significant changes in productive capacity and patterns – are the proper descriptions of the policies and processes involved in this case.

Those who (like the OECD and the World Bank) are concerned with the dynamics of the system, that is, with 'adjustment' policies, tend to start from a different premise. External imbalances – both anticipated (long-term) and unanticipated (short-term) – arise precisely because many countries are dissatisfied with the status quo and are determined to change it by expanding and diversifying their productive potential. These countries have no alternative but to acquire foreign capital and technology, partly by exporting and partly by borrowing abroad.

There is nothing new or unusual in this. All the now industrialized countries have followed this strategy, and in many cases foreign investment formed a very high proportion of their fixed capital formation (Bloomfield 1968). The ability of the borrowers to repay and service their debts – and thus their creditworthiness – is bound to depend, therefore, on their capacity to earn foreign exchange. That capacity will be determined, partly, by the skill with which they undertake the microeconomic adjustment and, partly, by the policies pursued by creditor nations. Consequently, it is these two factors that have to be considered in any analysis of *adjustment* problems and policies.

It is, of course, true that foreign loans can be used, as has happened in a number of cases over the past decade, to sustain consumption rather than promote investment; or to finance investment in goods and services which cannot be exported. Nor is this all. "Sovereign borrowing [in the 1970s] was unfortunately in many cases unplanned and ill-considered – the residual outcome of numerous ad hoc decisions. … As is now becoming clear, all too often nobody was keeping a record of the total volume of debt involved, still less considering how the mounting total of debt could be serviced" (Treasury and Civil Service Committee 1983, p. xxv).

There is nothing new, however, in mistakes of this kind. The literature on economic development is full of similar complaints. Yet the world does not live permanently under the threat of banking failures and international financial crises. The important difference is between situations in which *some* countries experience difficulties in repaying and servicing their debts; and periods when the problem arises simultaneously in many countries with different productivity and income levels, pursuing different policies. (Cf. Kindleberger 1978b, OECD 1982b, Sachs 1982.)

In the 1970s a few, mainly low-income, countries needed to reschedule their (mostly official) debts. At the same time, a number of countries – predominantly NICs and East European economies – found it relatively easy to raise external finance from private sources because, in most cases, they were seen to be pursuing the necessary adjustment policies. Given the stagnation at that time in industrial countries, and the increasing uncertainty about their future policies, the relatively rapid growth in the semi-industrialized economies made investment there more attractive (OECD 1979). Worries about potential shortages of raw material increased further the flow of investment to these countries. The flows, in turn, enabled the borrowers to maintain the momentum of growth.

Many of them raised their savings and investment ratios significantly (Sachs 1981) and, as Table 8.2 shows, there was also a significant switch of resources in NICs into exports between 1973 and 1978. The switch was even more pronounced in the early 1980s. But, as the table shows, these efforts were offset by a large deterioration – appreciably greater than in the 1970s – in NICs and non-oil-developing countries' terms of trade.

The available evidence indicates therefore that, on the whole, external borrowing was used in a number of LDCs to create productive capacity and, in many cases, to follow an outward-orientated development strategy. The result of these "domestic policy measures" was that, just before the second oil shock, they "permitted the newly industrialized countries to reduce, and ultimately to eliminate, reliance on additional net external financing" (Balassa *et al.* 1981, p. 17). The same is not true, however, of the many low-income countries with inadequate capacity to adjust.

Why is it, then, that the strategies which were apparently producing desirable results in the 1970s, at least in the case of NICs, are judged now to have

Table 8.2   Growth and trade, 1968–82 (average annual percentage changes)

	1968–72	1973–78	1979–82
GNP			
Industrialized countries	4.7*	3.2	1.4
Newly industrialized countries	8.0	5.8	2.7
All non-oil-developing countries (excl. China)	6.0	5.2	3.1
Oil-exporting countries	9.0	6.5	−2.3
Exports (volume)			
Industrialized countries	9.0*	6.3	2.9
Newly industrialized countries	12.1	9.1	5.9
All non-oil-developing countries (excl. China)	8.6	6.2	5.4
Oil-exporting countries	n.a.	2.0	−15.8
Imports (volume)			
Industrialized countries	9.0*	6.0	1.0
Newly industrialized countries	13.3	7.5	0.6
All non-oil-developing countries (excl.China)	7.7	6.5	0.1
Oil-exporting countries	n.a.	18.5	13.4
Terms of trade			
Industrialized countries	0.3*	−1.6	−2.0
Newly industrialized countries	0.7*	−1.1	−3.7
All non-oil developing countries (excl. China)	0.3*	−0.2	−3.3
Oil-exporting countries	0.5*	24.1	20.1

* 1963–72.

Source: International Monetary Fund (1983).

been 'over ambitious' and 'mistaken'? The most obvious reason is that many of these economies are far too dependent on industrial countries to pursue their growth strategies in isolation. Hence, the extent to which they can benefit from a virtuous circle of internal adjustments and external borrowing depends on the policies of industrial nations as well as their own efforts.

Exports of goods and services form a high proportion of domestic output in many developing countries which have borrowed heavily abroad since the early 1970s (cf. Morgan Guaranty 1983). Moreover, almost two-thirds of their trade is with industrial countries (see Havrylyshyn and Wolf 1981). The oil crises produced little change in this respect in the 1970s. As a result, a slump in the activity and imports of industrial countries is bound to affect adversely both the adjustment process and the external financial position of developing countries in several ways. (See, for example, Goldstein and Khan 1982, Morgan Guaranty 1983, Khan and Knight 1982.)

First, it will reduce the volume of their exports, though the extent of this will depend on the type and competitiveness of their tradable goods and services. As Table 8.2 shows, there has been a sharp decline in the rate of increase of imports into industrial countries, especially in the early 1980s. Exports from NICs have suffered also from protectionist measures in industrial countries (Anjaria *et al.* 1981).

Second, recession in industrial countries invariably affects developing countries' terms of trade. The prices of manufactured goods are affected less by changes in demand than are those of primary products. Occasionally, as OPEC has shown, a cartel may stabilize the price of its commodity, but at the cost of large reductions in production and export volumes. However, normally, commodity prices react sharply to changes in world activity levels (Enoch and Panić, 1981) and, among oil-importing developing countries, even in the case of NICs primary commodities account for a high proportion of their exports. The combined effect of lower export volumes and unfavourable terms of trade has been to produce a serious deterioration in developing countries' external balances. This is true now even of oil-producing countries whose large surpluses, generated by the second oil shock, melted away rapidly.

Third, a widespread global recession reduces, at least in the short run, the ability of developing countries to minimize the effects of the fall in demand for their products in industrial countries by trading more among themselves. This is what they did to a modest extent in the 1970s (Havrylyshyn and Wolf 1981). However, given the precarious financial state of many oil-producing economies and NICs, the scope for expanding intra-developing country trade has been reduced greatly in recent years.

Fourth, high levels of employment in industrial and oil-exporting economies enables other developing countries to export labour to these countries and use the workers' remittances to increase domestic incomes. Again, deep and prolonged international recessions since the early 1970s have greatly reduced opportunities for this kind of international exchange.

Finally, the mounting financial problems are bound, sooner or later, to reach crisis proportions because tight monetary policies in industrial countries will raise the interest rate payments of developing countries at the very time when the volume and prices of their exports are falling. This is particularly true of the existing debt carrying floating rates of interest and of new borrowing. In the circumstances, a deterioration in their capacity to service the existing debt becomes unavoidable, as Table 8.3 shows. This is exacerbated by the fact that global economic stagnation is likely to reduce the volume of direct foreign investment and concessional finance available to developing countries, making their financial position even more critical.

Table 8.3 Non-oil-developing countries: trends in exports and interest payments on medium- and long-term debt (average annual percentage changes)

	1970–3	1973–8	1979	1980	1981[1]
Gross interest payments	20	27	40	48	31
Exports					
Receipts	23	19	28	25	5
Price	12	13	18	17	−5
Volume	10	6	9	8	10
Outstanding debt					
Newly-industrialized countries[2]	22	26	18	16	19
Middle-income countries	8	21	21	17	16
Low-income countries	17	21	15	13	10

Notes
[1] Estimated.
[2] Argentina, Brazil, South Korea, Mexico and Taiwan only.
Source: OECD (1982b), p. 6.

8.3 Banks: freedom, exuberance and … disorientation?

Recently, banks have been blamed increasingly for: failing to assess realistically the extent to which economic policies of borrowing countries were sustainable; allowing, in their eagerness to expand business, interest rate premia to fall far below the risks involved; ignorance about the ultimate location of their loans; and the fact that until 1982 they "had no satisfactory overall picture of international lending" (Treasury and Civil Service Committee 1983).

All this adds up to a rather formidable list of major errors. Yet, as in the case of imprudence and misjudgments by developing countries, the only thing that is new about them is their size. There is no other instance in history in which so many of the world's leading banks have found themselves in such a potentially extremely dangerous situation.

There are a number of important reasons for this. To begin with, the problem arises partly out of the very nature of concentration and oligopolistic competition, that is, attempts to maximize earnings and minimize risks in an increasingly complex economic environment (where collusion is only partially feasible). The importance of economies of scale and the market position of an enterprise in determining its competitive strength will, inevitably, lead to a preoccupation with growth, size and market share.

As soon as a few enterprises start to explore new opportunities or markets, others will follow in order to prevent their competitors from gaining an important long-term advantage. Such behaviour is common to oligopolies, both national and international (Knickerbocker 1973). Hence, bankers will tend to play it safe by staying with the 'herd', a tendency that has been re-enforced by the spread of syndicated lending (see Simpson 1981). Those who manage vast sums of money that belong to somebody else cannot afford to be either adventurous or uncommonly cautious. Their natural tendency will be to conform to the general pattern of behaviour.

Herd behaviour is encouraged also by the kind of data at the banks' disposal. Most banks will arrive at their assessments of country risks using similar information, obtained from similar sources, analysed within a similar, more or less well established, analytical framework. Not surprisingly, the volume of international lending to a country is determined mainly by bankers' evaluation of its creditworthiness according to a mixture of economic, financial and socio-political criteria. (See Mendelsohn 1982, Nagy 1978, Thornblade 1978, Kern 1981, Kumar 1982.) They will be reassured in the correctness of their adopted procedures by 'experts' who, invariably, regurgitate the same data and views at the numerous conferences and seminars that bank analysts either organize or attend so assiduously. As the data record past performances, the assessments will tend to favour the firms and countries with a relatively good past record. It is hardly surprising, therefore, that the ratings published twice a year by the *Institutional Investor* show (see Table 8.4) industrial countries to have the highest rating, followed by NICs, OPEC and East European countries – with LDCs forming the bulk of those with poor ratings. This is, of course, precisely the way that most corporate and bank investments are distributed internationally.

Like the borrowers from developing nations, banks can be accused of failing to anticipate correctly the duration and consequences of industrial

Table 8.4 Major banks' average credit ratings[1] of country groups, 1979–83

	1979 (S)[2]	1980 (M)[3]	1980 (S)	1981 (M)	1981 (S)	1982 (M)	1982 (S)	1983 (M)
All countries (95)[4]	55.6	53.6	53.0	52.0	50.5	48.6	46.9	45.2
Industrial countries (23)	79.7	79.4	78.8	79.3	78.5	77.3	76.3	75.1
Newly industrialized countries (17)	67.8	66.5	54.0	63.3	62.4	61.9	59.9	55.8
OPEC (8)	64.5	57.7	56.7	53.6	53.8	52.0	50.0	49.1
Centrally planned economies (7)	61.2	57.2	55.6	53.9	49.3	43.7	38.4	35.4
Low-income countries (40)	40.4	38.8	38.1	37.4	35.7	33.7	32.2	30.8

[1] Ratings range from 100 (perfect) to zero (default).
[2] S = September
[3] M = March
[4] The numbers in brackets are the number of countries in each group.

Source: Authors' computations based on statistics in the *Institutional Investor* (various issues).

countries' policies for their own as well as other countries' economies. Bankers have been among the most ardent and persistent advocates of the tough anti-inflationary policies adopted by the major industrial countries after the second oil shock. At the same time, they have used their increasing capacity to intermediate and create credit on a global scale in order to augment their earnings by financing growth in NICs and Eastern Europe. The oil surpluses and the slump in demand for investment funds in industrial countries – caused by tough anti-inflationary policies – made the pursuit of such a course of action relatively easy.

Ex ante, this difference in banks' reactions to the problems confronting industrial countries and those confronting developing countries was certainly not irrational. The banks stood to gain from a combination of high interest rates in the stagnant industrial economies and high rates of return on investments in the much more dynamic NICs. What they failed to recognize sufficiently – hardly surprising, given the uncoordinated nature of most of the lending – was that this strategy could succeed only if the individual economies were independent of each other, so that policies in one part of the world had very little effect on the rest. Unfortunately, given the existing degree of international interdependence, the rest of the world had no chance of escaping the adverse effects of the industrial countries' policies, and this was bound, sooner or later, to influence the capacity of many borrowers to service, let alone repay, their debts.

However, it could be argued in the banks' defence that very few people foresaw correctly the problems that the industrial nations and, consequently, the rest of the world would face in reconciling their internal and external policy objectives after the second oil shock in 1979. The annual reports of international organizations, governments, central banks and research institutes provide a lasting record of the persistent tendency, especially in recent years, to overpredict growth in industrial countries, and thus underestimate the financial problems of the rest of the world. For instance, in its 1979 Annual Report, the Bank for International Settlements (BIS) reassured everybody that: "We now know from experience that even large current account imbalances can be financed without too much trouble by the international banking system" (BIS 1979, p. 178). The World Bank (1979) and the OECD (1979) were of the same opinion. Two years later in 1981, the Federal Reserve (Dod 1981) and the IMF, among others, could still inspect the scene calmly because, as the IMF put it: "the overall debt situation ... does not give cause for alarm" (IMF 1981, p. 11).

Not surprisingly, the widely held view that there was 'no cause for alarm' was reflected in the attitude of the commercial banks. The state of the world economy has, invariably, an important bearing on the short-term liquidity and long-term solvency position of the borrowers, both countries and companies.

A combination of the freedom provided by international money and capital markets and the banks' ingenuity has, undoubtedly, prevented a much earlier and more severe decline in world economic activity. However, the growth of the markets has also loosened that link between banks and the authorities' policy intention that is provided in a national economy by its central bank. It is not simply a question, as Kindleberger (1978b) has argued, of the lender of last resort stepping in to save illiquid banks on the brink of disaster and, in this way, preventing major financial crises. Before that stage is reached, a central bank will provide adequate warning of the coming changes in the levels of activity and their likely effects on both banks and their customers by altering the conditions under which it is prepared to act as the lender of last resort. If the situation is serious, it may even impose direct controls. There is no international organization that can perform such a role globally. Hence, in an international environment of uncoordinated national policies, banks can easily delude themselves into believing that, as pointed out earlier, stagnation in one area will have little or no effect on expansion elsewhere. The unprecedented increase in prosperity since the Second World War, the absence of defaults, the development of syndicated loans, floating interest rates and other financial innovations have all combined to increase further a false sense of security.

8.4 The paralytic prime mover

The most unexpected development since the 1970s has been the apparent inability of industrial economies to regain their lost momentum. They have failed so far to achieve either some sort of *modus vivendi* with oil producers that would guarantee a significant and sustainable world economic expansion without large increases in oil prices, or substantial adjustments which would reduce greatly their vulnerability to another oil shock. Instead, the inability of industrial countries to reconcile their internal and external balances has produced a drift, as Table 8.5 shows, towards levels of activity and employment that are unsustainable in the longer term. There is a limit to how far the problem of inflation can be 'solved' at the price of continuously rising unemployment levels, or vice versa.

Despite a voluminous literature on the subject, there is still no agreement about the reasons for the apparent decline in the regenerating capacity of industrial economies. It certainly cannot be attributed to a sudden and widespread drying-up of technical inventiveness. The energy crisis, combined with advances in the field of electronics, provides an immense scope for new investment and change. However, the ability of established, let alone new, firms to alter radically their products and production methods is bound to diminish with the size of the required changes, particularly in a stagnant and uncertain world economic environment. Once firms commit their capital stock and expertise to certain products and production methods, it becomes difficult to do something radically different in the short or even medium term. Even more serious has been the rise of highly organized

Table 8.5 Increasing disequilibria in industrial countries, 1968–82

	1968	1968–73	1973	1974	1974–78	1978	1979	1979–82	1982
Major seven countries									
Growth of GDP									
Average (% p.a.)		4.8			2.7			1.4	
End years (%)	5.5		6.2	0.1		4.5	3.5		−0.4
Consumer prices									
Average (% p.a.)		5.3			9.4			9.5	
End years (%)	4.1		7.5	13.2		6.9	9.2		6.9
Unemployment									
Average (%)		3.3			5.0			6.2	
End years (%)	2.9		3.4	3.7		5.1	5.0		7.9
Current balance of payments									
Average ($ billion)		7.2			4.6			−13.1	
End years ($ billion)	5.7		8.1	−13.1		21.7	−10.7		−6.3
Other									
Growth of GDP									
Average (% p.a.)		5.3			2.3			1.5	
End years (%)	5.0		5.5	3.4		2.1	3.0		0.2
Consumer prices									
Average (% p.a.)		6.4			10.8			9.5	
End years (%)	4.6		9.9	12.4		8.5	7.8		9.7
Unemployment									
Average (%)		1.7			3.5			5.7	
End years (%)	2.4		2.1	2.2		4.6	4.4		6.4
Current balance of payments									
Average ($ billion)		0.8			−9.4			−20.4	
End years ($ billion)	−1.2		3.2	−9.3		−5.6	−14.6		−18.3

Sources: OECD (1983); IMF (1983).

vested interests with conflicting preferences and aims, and sufficient power to sabotage necessary institutional changes (see Olson 1982).

This seems to be particularly true of the major industrial countries. Their weight in the world economy is such that once they become incapable of generating sustained economic progress it is virtually impossible for the rest of the world to do so. Given the openness and interdependence of industrial economies, the combined effect of their actions on the rest of the world – either contractionary or expansionary – is now likely to be greater than intended (see OECD 1983). Developing countries have little chance, therefore, of adjusting their economies if stagnation in industrial countries drastically reduces their ability to earn foreign exchange. In the circumstances, a successful programme of economic reconstruction and development, far from solving, may increase – as recent experience shows – their liquidity *and* solvency problems. On past experience, industrial countries would probably have to sustain over a number of years an annual rate of growth considerably higher than the average for recent years in order to diminish the threat posed by the debt problem. Given their recent economic objectives and policies, it is extremely unlikely that they will achieve anything of the kind in the foreseeable future.

The alternative strategy of forcing developing countries to undertake extremely harsh stabilization measures cannot seriously be expected to provide a lasting solution to the debt problem. The most likely outcome of such a strategy will be to increase further the vicious circle of economic decline and financial problems to which it gives rise within the developing world.

The relatively small size and insularity of developing economies, compared with those of industrial nations, has led some experts to argue that changes in their levels of activity would have a very small effect on output and employment in industrial countries. However, the argument rests on an important assumption: that industrial countries can generate rapid and sustainable economic expansion, something that they have failed to achieve since the early 1970s (Cline and Associates 1981, p. 255).

In the absence of economic dynamism, a further decline in demand for their goods and services is bound to aggravate the already serious economic and social problems facing industrial nations. Most of the latter's trade is with each other. However, in 1979 a far from insignificant proportion of their exports (37 per cent in the case of the major seven countries) went to NICs, centrally planned, oil-exporting and low-income countries, most of which are now in serious financial difficulties. Hence, persistent economic stagnation in these countries is bound to affect adversely the most advanced economies. As Morgan Guaranty (1983, p. 7) put it: "The LDCs are a significant market for industrial country products, accounting for nearly 40% of US exports (nearly 3% of GNP) and 28% of OECD exports (over 4% of GNP)....A uniform 3% cutback in LDC growth, for example, is estimated to lower OECD growth by 0.8% and US growth by 0.5%." This, in turn, would increase further the financing problems of developing countries, especially NICs.

The impact of developing countries on the world, with the exception of OPEC, may not be very large. But it is worth remembering that financial problems of LDCs in the inter-war period, and the highly deflationary policies which they were forced to adopt at the end of the 1920s, were one of the factors which contributed to the breakdown of the international financial system in the 1930s.

8.5   Conclusion and some policy implications

There is little doubt that lack of coordination, excessive optimism and serious misjudgments both by the governments of developing nations and by banks have contributed to the size of the financial problems that many of these countries are experiencing. Consequently, developing economies will have to take much more into account in the future not only their own potential but also the likely effect of industrial countries' policies on their ability to adjust. The authorities will, therefore, have to pay far more attention to the volume and type of external borrowing. Economic development should *not* rely on short-term borrowing but on medium- and long-term finance raised, for example, by issuing long-term bonds. Many of the recent difficulties experienced by developing countries in servicing and paying off their debts have been caused by the unfavourable maturity distribution of their external borrowing.

The problem is that most developing countries find it difficult to raise long-term finance because of their low international credit ratings. It is here that the World Bank could develop further the 'lead' role that it has performed in the past. The Japan Development Bank performed a similar role in Japan very successfully after the Second World War. Thanks to its record in promoting investment, the mere fact that the Japan Development Bank provides long-term capital to finance a project – often a rather modest proportion of the required total – is sufficient to attract investment from private banks and other financial institutions.

Banks will also have to take into account much more the economic and financial implications of international and sectoral interdependence. The scale and type of their lending should be coordinated and controlled more tightly from the centre. This could be done both at the headquarters of individual banks and by central banks (see Chapter 9). Banks will, also, have to consider the extent to which the benefits that arise from their ability to operate internationally are offset by confusing signals about the most likely effects of macroeconomic policies coming from different authorities, each trying to pursue an 'independent' course of action.

All this should receive a good deal of urgent attention. However, the danger is that, by concentrating almost exclusively on the role of developing countries and banks in the debt drama, both experts and policy makers will continue to ignore one of the most important aspects of the problem: growing institutional paralysis and inability of industrial countries to achieve significant and sustained adjustments. Given their global importance, there is little likelihood of correcting the maladjustments and threats of financial collapse in the world economy so long as this paralysis persists. It is an illusion to believe that developing countries can adjust *independently*, even though they bear full responsibility for the character and success of such policies.

Under present conditions, with poor prospects for rapid, sustained growth in industrial countries, the financing of unanticipated deficits and the prevention of large-scale defaults has to become the dominant policy issue. No country that wants to modernize its economy and increase the standard of living of its population rapidly can afford to contemplate defaults with equanimity; such an action would simply be against its long-term interests.

Unfortunately, in a highly interdependent world economy, the policies of other nations may leave it little choice. Moreover, although the ultimate step may be risky for one country to take, once a few countries are driven to this course of action, others in a similar position may not find it so difficult to follow. It is for this reason that the rescheduling by commercial banks, together with bridging and other loans by central banks and international organizations, has to be undertaken in order to avoid a major international crisis. However, financial measures of this kind can do no more than provide a temporary solution by spreading debt service payments and allowing some of the 'stabilization' policies to be implemented. The underlying problem remains, to resurface again in a not too distant future. In fact, the long-term problem may become even more serious if, as has happened in the past, the rescheduling results in harsher terms than those on which the original loans were made and thus increases the cost of servicing the debts (see Sachs 1982).

There is also a limit to how far international organizations, such as the IMF, can be used to solve problems for which they were never designed. At best, the IMF can help some countries to finance and correct their external imbalances. However, what a large number of countries need at the moment is the time and loans which would enable them to adjust, that is, to restructure their economies. The IMF is no more in a position to assist such efforts now, despite the increases in quotas and some new facilities, than it was when help of this kind was needed for the post-war reconstruction, a process in which it played an insignificant part. Ideally, given the nature of the current problems, the IMF should act much more in tandem with the World Bank.

The need for the two to work closely together was emphasized in 1945 by the President of the American Banking Association at the time, who argued "that the objectives of Bretton Woods could be carried out best if there were but one international financial organization instead of two. ... Some stabilization programmes will call for long-term loans" (quoted in Dell and Lawrence 1980, p. 149). However, whether the two are allowed to act more frequently in this way, and the effectiveness of their actions, depends ultimately on their paymasters: the major industrial countries. The danger of pushing international organizations into a position where their actions are likely to create rather than solve long-term problems is that they will become completely discredited. This would be in nobody's interest, as an integrated world economy needs such institutions, even if their role is to remain marginal.

It is also doubtful whether a number of possible solutions, proposed in recent years, would be effective on their own. This is certainly true of 'the clean slate strategy', whose advocates believe that the debt problem could be eliminated fairly quickly either by writing off large proportions of developing countries' debts or by transferring them to, say, international organizations. A major weakness of the first approach is that, as it would be very costly to the lenders as well as affect adversely banks' capital, it would reduce bank lending both at home and abroad. In the absence of a major injection of official capital this would exacerbate economic stagnation, making the repayment and servicing of many of the remaining debts difficult. Similarly, the second option would require international institutions to possess resources far greater than those at their disposal at the moment (see, for instance, Laulan 1983). Adequate resources for the purpose, on the other hand, would give them a power and independence that the most influential nation states are still not ready to contemplate.

More important, for reasons analysed in this chapter, even if banks and other institutions continued lending to developing countries and the loans were used to restructure these economies – so long as industrial economies continued to stagnate the world would be confronted within a few years with another major debt problem and the threat of a serious financial crisis. In other words, the debt problem, like the energy crisis, will remain a threat to an open system of international economic relationships so long as institutional paralysis jams the wheels of economic progress in industrial countries.

Unfortunately, it is unlikely that the industrial countries will soon rediscover, by introducing appropriate institutional changes, their lost dynamism and resume rapid, sustainable growth. The debt problem, on the other hand, requires urgent action. Perhaps the most promising approach would be for the Group of Ten countries to establish an 'International Reconstruction Fund' to be managed by one of the existing international institutions. The fund could be used partly to fund the most troublesome proportion of the existing debts, and partly to provide the countries in difficulties with longer-term loans that would, by giving them more time, make their structural adjustment strategies more likely to succeed. However, as in the case of the Marshall Plan, it should be a condition that the loans are granted predominantly to those countries that produce careful, realistic stabilization and adjustment plans.

Actions of this kind require political rather than economic solutions. The technical tool kit for rebuilding the international financial system is well stocked with instruments developed over the past century. Which of them are used, when, and how, depends ultimately on the resolution of existing socio-political problems. Sooner or later, the governments of the industrial countries will have to stir themselves into action: either to stabilize the international financial system through a 'Reconstruction Fund', or to stem the tide of bank failures as more and more developing countries are forced to default.

More attention will also have to be paid to the form in which official capital is provided. A much clearer line needs to be drawn between 'grant economies' (that is, LDCs which cannot easily attract private foreign capital) and 'growth economies' (that is, semi-industrialized countries that can do so provided that the world economy is not in a state of prolonged stagnation).

The former should be assisted with international aid and the latter with loans. A consideration of this kind is particularly important now that, given the state of the industrial economies, most governments operate under serious budgetary constraints which are bound to limit significantly the flow of official funds to developing countries.

Perhaps the greatest contribution which economists can make towards solving the debt problem is to stop pretending that this can be achieved by adopting certain 'economic' measures irrespective of the institutional framework within which they would have to operate.

9
Banking Supervision in Conditions of Deregulation and Globalization*

9.1 Introduction

Far from being a new phenomenon, financial crises, which have received so much attention in recent years, have been a regular feature of the international economy every time that the nation states have opened their economies to trade and capital flows with other countries (cf. Kindleberger 1978b, Sprague 1910). What is new about the crises since the 1970s is their frequency and size, both of which have increased markedly over the period. Nor has this been confined to a few countries. The crises have involved banks from industrial, developing and transition economies, and from countries in virtually every part of the world.

In other words, serious crises tend to be avoided in conditions of economic insularity when there are extensive controls on external trade and capital flows, such as those that were common between 1914 and 1960. The insularity enables national authorities to regulate and supervise effectively actions of their financial institutions.

This has changed since the 1960s for several reasons. First, there has been an unprecedented growth of transnational enterprises, both industrial corporations and banks, as a result of rapid technical progress and industrialization in many parts of the world. This has made it possible to transfer relatively easily funds internationally, even in times of exchange controls, through internal transactions between the parent companies and their affiliates. Second, the oil crises of the 1970s caused a massive transfer of resources from oil importing to the oil-exporting countries. Most of these funds were deposited initially in transnational banks, making it both

* This chapter was written in 1999. It was funded by the Department for International Development (DFID) as part of UK Government's bilateral programme of technical assistance for the countries of Central and Eastern Europe. The views expressed are those of the author and should not, therefore, be attributed to the DFID or any other organization.

possible and necessary for them to intermediate globally. In this way, they played a major role in enabling oil-importing countries to finance their large balance of payments deficits – preventing even greater losses in economic welfare than those that occurred in the middle and at the end of the decade. Third, partly as a result of this experience, many countries either relaxed or removed completely exchange controls, thus accelerating the process of globalization in banking and other financial services. Finally, the process of liberalization was accompanied by deregulation. This increased the range of banking services through two inter-related activities: by expanding their operations in higher-risk areas that promised higher returns, and through innovation. The latter enabled banks to offer a wide range of new services in what was rapidly becoming a highly competitive industry operating in an increasingly unstable and, therefore, highly risky economic, financial and political environment.

The proliferation of banking crises since 1980, including the growth in their frequency and size, has coincided with these changes. According to an IMF study, between 1980 and 1996 almost three-quarters of its members (133 out of 181 countries) experienced major banking problems. In 36 countries these reached crisis proportions. As for the rest, they went through what the IMF experts classed as 'significant' problems. (Quoted in Goodhart *et al.* 1998, p. 1.) Since then, there have been serious financial crises in the emerging economies of the Southeast Asia and Russia. Not surprisingly, all studies on the subject agree that the incidence of banking crises has increased significantly in the last quarter of the twentieth century. Moreover, a study of the crises before and since 1950 concluded that the banking crises since the second half of the 1970s have been unprecedented in their size and frequency (Honohan 1996).

Given the importance of banks in national and international financial systems, and the role that they play in the 'real' economy, this has had a number of serious consequences for the countries involved. To begin with, the cost of resolving the banking crises has often been huge. It is estimated (see Goldstein 1997) that total losses/costs to individual countries in the period 1980–96 ranged, as a proportion of GDP, from 10 per cent (Japan, Hungary, Tanzania) to 55 per cent (Argentina). The overall resolution cost of banking crises in developing and transition economies during the period is put at around $250 billion (Honohan 1996). Although not on the same scale, the resolution cost of the US saving and loan fiasco in the 1980s is put at 2–3 per cent of its GDP (Goldstein 1997). As the US GDP at the time was in the region of $4.5 trillion, the sum is far from negligible in absolute terms: at least around $110 billion.

The few figures quoted in the previous paragraph indicate that, in terms of resources, the cost of banking crises is greater in developing than in industrial economies. The same is also true of the frequency of such crises. However, the growing importance of the emerging countries in the world economy has increased the risk that their banking problems will result in major spillover effects elsewhere, including industrial countries (Bank for International Settlements 1996). The reason for this is that there has been a significant increase in economic and financial integration and interdependence between industrial and developing economies, not least because most major corporations and banks from industrial countries also operate in the developing world.

Experience shows that large-scale bailouts of banks can impose heavy costs on public sector finances and macroeconomic stability, a problem that has been particularly serious in Latin America. According to Goldstein (1997, p. 6):

> research suggests that banking crises exacerbate downturns in economic activity, prevent savings from going to their most productive use, reduce the availability and increase the cost of credit to small-and medium-sized firms, and seriously constrain the flexibility of monetary policy (including, among other things, the willingness to increase interest rates to deal with large, abrupt shifts in international capital flows).

The economic and social cost can be devastating. For instance, the ILO estimated that between 10–20 per cent of the entire population in the countries worst affected by the Asian financial crisis in 1997 would fall into poverty, with major long-term social consequences (Lee 1998).

The changes described briefly above (deregulation, globalization, increase in the frequency and scale of banking crises, and the magnitude of economic and social costs to which they give rise) have, clearly, sharpened the division between private and social costs and benefits that they have brought about. This, in turn, makes it necessary to re-assess the scope and effectiveness of existing banking regulations and supervision, both national and international, introduced to prevent the recurrence of such problems.

Much has been written over the years about regulating/supervising banks. The literature, like the regulatory frameworks that it analyses, is invariably based on two assumption of critical importance in this context: namely, that those in charge of banks at the microeconomic level are in full control of the organizations that they manage; and that, as a result of this, they are in a position to ensure that the 'prudential' rules demanded by the community are fully observed.

This chapter will analyse briefly the issue of banking supervision by questioning validity of the two basic assumptions. The reason for this is that a number of highly publicized cases in the 1990s have revealed serious shortcomings in 'prudential supervision' (that is, management) at the microeconomic level. These examples of major business malpractice by relatively junior employees, and managerial failure to do anything about them until it was too late, raise important questions about the possibility of monitoring and supervising such institutions at the macroeconomic level. Can this be done successfully by either national or international regulatory authorities unless steps are taken to prevent some of these institutions from becoming increasingly, under competitive pressure, surrogate casinos? The analysis that follows is based on the experience of many economies: industrial, developing as well as those in transition. It also reviews in general terms some of the steps taken to prevent banking crises and failures in order to minimize the costly systemic risks that they can inflict, both on the countries in which the failures occur and on the countries with which they have close economic links.

9.2 Financial liberalization and the supervision and management of banks

Few students of the international financial history since the middle of the nineteenth century would disagree with the conclusion of a former Head of Financial Supervision at the Bank of England: "the case for some form of regulation of the financial services sector is unanswerable" (Quinn 1998a, p. 123).

Whatever the actual or potential problems and failings of public regulation, historical experience shows that in the absence of such regulation market failures of the private sector are even more serious for the economies and societies involved. The case for financial regulation normally rests, therefore, on the need to prevent the most obvious and costly forms of market failure or, when this happens, on the equally important need to limit the consequences of such a failure. One way to avoid the former consists of making sure that financial institutions do not use the resources and information at their disposal to gain monopolistic power in the market in which they operate and, in this way, exploit the customers. The other important reason for the regulation is the need to protect clients, especially smaller and less informed ones, from the effects of financial failure. This is essential to minimize systemic instability and risk: the likelihood that the failure of one financial institution may lead to the failure of others, causing (as happened in the 1930s) the collapse of national financial systems and then, as a result of this, of the economic system in general.

As the experience of the economies in transition shows, within highly integrated economic systems such risks are not confined to the financial sector. However, because of the range of activities in which financial institutions are normally involved, the domino effect of one major failure is likely to happen very quickly and have particularly adverse effects on the economic system as a whole. The larger the institution that fails the greater the risk.

This is particularly true of banks because of the strategic position that they occupy in all financial systems, national and international. Unlike other financial institutions, banks represent for a large number of borrowers the only source of finance. They are also the institutions that manage the payments system. Hence, if their viability is threatened, or appears in any way to be in doubt, there will be runs on banks, with far reaching consequences. No other institution, financial or non-financial, occupies such a position in a modern economy. Not surprisingly, bank failures may generate social costs far in excess of the private costs. Yet, like other microeconomic entities, banks are not required to incorporate social costs in their decision making process.

The societies in which they operate cannot afford to ignore such costs. Since the Great Depression of the 1930s – which saw widespread bank failures (for example, 20 per cent of all US banks suspended operations at the time) – central banks have developed various regulatory frameworks. These have, invariably, had two major purposes: to ensure soundness of individual banks and, more generally, to prevent national financial sectors from collapsing in times of economic crises. More specifically, the regulatory 'nets' have included prudential measures: (a) to maintain bank solvency; (b) to ensure that banks have adequate liquidity; (c) to provide official guarantees, such as deposit insurance for the safety of bank deposits, even in the case of the banks in difficulties, in order to preserve confidence in the banking system; (d) to make sure that insolvent banks are liquidated in an orderly fashion; and (e) to provide solvent banks experiencing a liquidity crisis with the cash needed to prevent their failure. As one would expect, the scope and effectiveness of these measures has varied greatly even among industrial countries.

The differences did not matter that much so long as national economies and their financial systems were largely insulated from banking failures outside their borders. The combination of globalization, deregulation and innovation since the 1970s has changed this radically. By increasing international financial interdependence it threatens frequently to turn national crises into international crises, and vice versa.

As a result, the task of implementing prudential measures of the kind listed above has become even more complex and difficult. One of the reasons for this is that the changes have increased the problem of moral hazard, unavoidable in all attempts to regulate and supervise banks. The more effective the safeguards provided by the authorities the greater the temptation for banks to engage in risky deals. Unequal effectiveness of regulatory frameworks between countries makes it easier for them to do this by expanding such activities in the countries where controls on their operations are less stringent. The more reluctant the countries are to harmonize their regulatory frameworks – and so far they have been very reluctant to do this – the greater the scope for engaging in risky operations in search of higher profits.

The problem of moral hazard is more serious now for another reason. The more banks expand into less familiar activities and countries the more they will become anxious to minimize the risk of failure by internalizing globally the various services through mergers and acquisitions. Size is a powerful weapon in dealing with, both, competitors and governments. The systemic risk ensures that governments will be much more reluctant to allow a large bank to fail. Hence, in an internationally integrated market they will tend to turn a blind eye to the growth of large financial institutions because that could put national banks at a competitive disadvantage compared to their foreign competitors. Moreover, the threat of large banks to move their operations to countries with less rigorous competition policies is another reason why governments will do little to prevent banks from growing beyond the size at which they are 'too big to fail'. This partly explains why it usually requires a major international crisis, or an imminent threat of such a crisis, to achieve some form of international cooperation (cf. Kapstein 1991).

However, there are also practical reasons why this may not be possible, at least in the short run. All of them are the result of different traditions, cultures and levels of development. For instance, secrecy laws make it difficult for national authorities to supervise their banks properly, creating problems for international harmonization of regulatory practices. Two important examples of this are Germany and Switzerland where the authorities were forbidden by law until the late 1990s to collect information about international operations of their financial institutions. This obviously reduced effectiveness of their supervisory systems for the simple reason that if a major foreign branch or subsidiary of a domestic bank became illiquid or insolvent, there could be serious repercussions for the whole bank and, if it happens to be large, for the domestic financial system. The experience of US banks is illustrative of the growing importance of foreign activities in banks' portfolios. By the early 1980s one- to two-thirds of all profits earned by US banks came from their foreign branches (Kapstein 1991, p. 3).

Moreover, there are important differences between countries in their accounting conventions, disclosure requirements and legal frameworks. In many cases accounting conventions are sufficiently weak to make it possible for banks and their borrowers to conceal the exact size of non-performing loans. There are also differences between countries in their definitions of what constitutes a non-performing loan. In some of them it is bank managers and not banks supervisors who set the criteria for classifying a loan as 'non-performing'. All this makes effective monitoring and supervision of banking activities extremely difficult for both the official supervisor and the private investor.

The problem is compounded by deficiencies in proper disclosure of information, such as: failure to provide relevant financial and prudential information on a globally consolidated basis, differences in accounting standards between countries, differences in domestic reporting requirements for banks, and inadequate penalties for providing or publishing inadequate information.

Legal constraints contribute further to this list of potential supervisory failures. These range from the laws that prevent banks from seizing or transferring loan collateral, or making it impossible to resolve bankruptcy cases quickly, to the failure of national legal systems to give adequate authority to bank supervisors to discharge their responsibilities properly.

For all these reasons, it will take a long time or a major global financial crisis for the international community to agree on a supranational regulatory and supervisory framework capable of dealing promptly and adequately with adverse effects of financial globalization. Some countries lack the experience and expertise to make a proper contribution to such a system. In others, the state is too dependent on powerful private interests convinced that an unregulated, crisis prone global economic environment is in their interest. Finally, with the proliferation of small, 'sovereign' states, there is an increasing number of countries that lack the resources to provide the required supervisory framework. The failure in 1991 of the Bank of Credit and Commerce International (BCCI), owned mostly by Abu Dhabi and based in Luxembourg, may yet be replicated many times in the twenty-first century.

In the absence of international consensus and an effective supranational framework, there is little alternative to 'national management of the international economy' (Panić 1988) in banking, as in many other areas of economic activity. In other words, there is no realistic alternative at present to banking supervision remaining the responsibility of *national* authorities. The problem is that the dynamics of globalization, deregulation, financial innovation and technical changes make this increasingly an inappropriate substitute for an international authority.

There are basically three reasons for the increase in frequency and size of banking failures since the 1970s: greater macroeconomic instability and shocks brought about by the absence of institutions and policies needed to prevent market failures in conditions of globalization; much more intense competition in the banking sector stimulated by deregulation and, as a result of this, willingness of banks to engage in risky activities; and an increase in managerial failure and fraud, as the world in which banks operate has become more risky and unprofitable. All of them make national regulation and supervision of banks much less effective in preventing costly bank failures and financial crises of the kind common since the 1970s.

One of the consequences of globalization has been the lack of reliable, up-to-date information about the scale of international private banking, including the extent of individual banks' exposure in different markets. This became soon obvious during the debt crisis of the early 1980s. The crisis revealed that even major banks from leading industrial countries had little or no information about the scale of their involvement in developing countries that were either defaulting or in danger of doing so. Similar complaints have accompanied all the subsequent banking crises, despite the fact that commercial lending to countries at relatively low levels of development and financial sophistication deserves special care.

The obvious reason for this is that in many developing countries even the most diligent and conscientious of bank managers is confronted frequently with the problem of inadequate information about would be borrowers. The problem is equally serious for domestic and foreign banks, irrespective of whether the latter operate in such countries. Under competitive pressure many banks have become heavily involved in high-risk countries, with their national supervisors unable to do anything about it. This must raise serious doubts about the ability of the existing regulatory frameworks, even in the most advanced economies, to perform their task adequately in the new international environment.

The job of national banking supervisors has always been difficult. Deregulation, as a former Head of Banking Supervision at the Bank of England has admitted, has added significantly to this by making financial markets much riskier (Quinn 1998a). The trend towards financial deregulation started in the 1960s, intensifying first in the 1970s and, then, even more so in the 1980s. The aim was to promote flexibility and efficiency of banks through greater competition. The result, as intended, was lower interest rate spreads and profitability. However, in achieving this, deregulation also led to something that, presumably, was not what the authorities intended: it increased the vulnerability of banks to insolvency. In search of higher profits, banks lent heavily to risky borrowers, such as developing countries and speculators (both domestic and foreign). The debt crisis of the early 1980s and the collapse of property markets involved banks in heavy losses that reduced, in many cases seriously, their capital base. In the process, the losses also increased the risk of insolvency. This, as mentioned earlier, has encouraged banks to do two things: diversify, through mergers and acquisitions, the services they offer, and innovate by introducing a wide range of new 'products'.

As the BCCI case shows, large transnational banking conglomerates make it impossible for any one national regulatory authority to be responsible for them. This, plus the fact that both national regulatory standards and the effectiveness with which they are implemented vary significantly between countries, makes proper supervision of such banks as a whole impossible. In the case of Barings, the UK part of the business remained sound. Nevertheless, the whole institution became insolvent as a result of the activities of its subsidiaries in the Far East.

Deregulation and innovation complicate the matters further by making it difficult to be sure whether the main reason for the new products developed by banks is to increase competitiveness rather than to evade supervision. In fact, even if their objective is the former, the specificity and variety of new products is bound to make monitoring of their operations difficult – both within individual banks and by the regulatory authorities. As a result, banks become more vulnerable to fraud and scandals of the kind that engulfed Banco Ambrosiano, BCCI and Barings.

Much of this should have been relatively easy for the authorities to anticipate and, consequently, to take appropriate steps to secure the benefits of globalization and deregulation while avoiding their most obvious and unacceptable costs. Instead, in most economies, industrial and developing, financial liberalization has been introduced without proper preparation. More liberal banking policies and reductions in banks' reserve requirements have made it possible for banks to satisfy pent up demand for credit, leading to rapid credit expansion. This may have contributed to higher real interest rates, as banks have engaged in more risky operations. The new, more liberal environment is made potentially even more unstable by the fact that many credit managers and bank supervisors lack the expertise to deal with new credit and market risks, or to understand full implications of some of the new financial instruments. In spite of this, it is still not unusual for banks and governments to pay insufficient attention to the training and provision of adequate resources for proper bank supervision, internal and external, under the new conditions. It is hardly surprising, therefore, to discover that 18 of the 25 banking crises included in a recent study occurred in countries where financial liberalization had taken place during the previous five years (see Goldstein 1997, p. 14). The changes described so far have, as already mentioned, weakened supervisory capacities of the national authorities as well as internal controls within banks. It was his concern with the latter that prompted the President of the New York Federal Reserve to warn in the mid-1990s that "virtually all of the most serious trade-related losses [by banks] have involved internal control breakdowns" (quoted in Kinsella 1995, p. 3).

There are a number of risks that are taken daily by those responsible for managing banks: *credit risk* (not being re-paid by a borrower), *liquidity risk* (running out of cash), *operational risk* (losing control over what is happening within a manager's/director's area of responsibility), *positional risk* (making a costly mistake in the dealing room) and *fraud* (being deceived by an employee or customer).

The relative importance of each of these risks changes with changes in the economic environment within which banks operate. For instance, although credit risk continues to feature high on the list of bankers' pre-occupations and concerns, liquidity risk has been greatly reduced by the existence of the lender of last resort. At the same time, there is little doubt that the other three risks present much greater threat to the viability and survival of individual banks at the beginning of the twenty-first century than they did for most of the previous one.

Two recent developments have increased significantly operational risks of banks: the growth of banking conglomerates and the heavy reliance on computerization of banking activities.

One of the advantages of conglomerates is that, as in other forms of economic activities, they reduce banking risks through diversification. The disadvantage is that the diversification increases managerial diseconomies of scale. Banking conglomerates offer a wide range of services, some of which are extremely complex. That inevitably reduces the ability of those in positions of responsibility to monitor and control actions of their subordinates. Their task is made more difficult by globalization, which spreads their operations over many countries. The usual problems of management are greatly exacerbated partly by the distances involved and partly by the diversity of corporate cultures of control, based on different views and traditions concerning 'business ethics'. BCCI provides a classic example of the dangers inherent in cultural differences that are not subjected to effective control.

Computerization increases operational banking risks in several ways. The information processing activities, which used to be dispersed throughout a bank, now become concentrated in the hands of relatively few members of staff. This increases the danger of computer related fraud. At the same time, the information stored on a computer system may become widely available through terminals and other computers. The risk inherent in such a system is that the information may be read and altered by unauthorized members of staff, leading to theft and embezzlement.

Both these possibilities for misuse of banks' funds require even more active monitoring and control by the senior management. The problem is that computer systems are not only complex but also constantly undergoing rapid changes and improvements. Senior managers, in particular, are unlikely to have the time to keep abreast of these changes and, consequently, may lack the technical competence to understand the significance of the changes and the potential risks involved. They may underestimate, therefore, the growing importance of internal control – with the result that inadequate resources will be allocated to what has become a vitally important organizational aspect of modern banking. Hence, the required standards of internal control at the operational level cannot be achieved and maintained without active involvement of the most senior managers. That is possible only if they have the skills needed to appreciate fully what is required and to shape internal organization and resources of banks in the way most likely to achieve the desired result.

Positional risk is closely related to the operational risk in the sense that it is influenced, both, by financial innovation and by the structural and technical changes described above. One of the consequences of financial innovation, most of which is tailored to the specific needs and preferences of the customers, is that a large number of decisions are taken down the hierarchical chain, by relatively junior members of staff, close to the customer. Huge bonuses and performance-related pay add to the temptation to engage in highly risky activities in search of improved corporate profits and personal rewards. As these changes make internal control and external supervision more difficult, they also increase the risk of fraud and error.

One of the forms of financial innovation that has received a good deal of attention in this respect is the new market in derivatives, as the very nature of these instruments is such that they are extremely difficult to monitor and control. Derivatives are basically hedging instruments developed in response to the growing volatility and risks that arise from changes in interest rates, exchange rates, and equity and commodity prices, all of which are the direct result of deregulation and globalization. The main argument in support of derivatives is that they make it possible to reduce (that is, 'hedge') various risks produced by these changes. The problem is that the risks can also be greatly increased by derivatives designed for speculative purposes in futures, options, and other derivative instruments. The increase in macroeconomic instability since the early 1970s has provided banks with the opportunity to earn high profits if they bet correctly on movements in prices of financial assets and commodities. However, as the long list of banking crises and failures over the period shows, this can also lead to heavy losses when the bets turn out to be wrong. In spite of this, there has been a phenomenal growth in the market for derivatives, with "derivatives related credit exposure" exceeding "by a factor of 2–4 the capital of the 10–15 most active players in the market" (White 1998, p. 315).

Two characteristics make derivatives potentially dangerous: their complexity and their ability to change risks within a very short period. Both make it very difficult for those who do not participate directly in the deals to understand and evaluate properly the risks involved. In other words, derivatives have increased greatly the risk of financial failure "by reducing the ability of both regulators and other market agents to interpret market signals, and to control risks adequately" (Goodhart 1998, p. 260).

Finally, all these changes may put banks at a risk also by attracting at operational levels a small proportion of the people who lack the integrity and a sense of responsibility that such jobs require. The danger is that the opportunity to place high bets with other people's money is likely to make jobs at operational levels in banks irresistible to compulsive gamblers (see Partnoy 1998) – providing them with a unique chance to become rich without risking even a minute fraction of their own wealth! The effect of this can be devastating for the unsuspecting customers and the banks themselves.

In conclusion, regulatory and supervisory functions, which are never easy, have, as a result of institutional changes and technical progress, become extremely difficult at all levels. This raises two important questions for policy makers. Can the various international agreements be effective if there are serious weaknesses in the supervisory frameworks erected at national levels, as well as in their implementation? And, can the latter be significantly improved if those responsible for the management of banks are experiencing increasing difficulties in monitoring and controlling what is going on within their own institutions?

9.3 Banking regulation: internal, national and international

This section describes some of the steps that many countries have either taken or are considering at the moment in order to minimize the risk of banking crises and failures. They refer specifically to measures to improve banking regulation and supervision in response to at least some of the problems described in the previous section. Many of these issues are controversial because, as Quinn (1998a, p. 123) has pointed out, while there is widespread agreement that some form of banking regulation is essential, there is far less consensus when it comes to "the more difficult question" concerning "the form that the supervision should take".

An important reason for this is the difference in national experiences, needs and priorities. For example, as mentioned earlier (p. 214), one of the factors that have contributed to the increase in banking crises and failures since the 1970s is much greater macroeconomic instability and shocks, caused by deregulation and globalization. As some countries have proceeded much further along this road than others, the macroeconomic environment has not deteriorated equally in all of them. The relevance of this in the context of banking supervision is that, although the instability threatens the soundness of banks, it does so as the direct result of economic policy in general. That, of course, lies completely outside the competence of banking regulators and supervisors. At the same time, national policies will have an important bearing on the scope and effectiveness of their actions.

The other reason for the difficulties experienced in harmonizing international attitudes to banking supervision, and the success with which it is implemented, is that banking expertise, sophistication and supervisory skills are much greater in some countries than in others.

However, despite such important differences in national economic performance and capabilities, deregulation, globalization, financial innovation and technical progress are creating a number of problems that all countries with banking and financial sectors either already share or will increasingly do so. As these problems arise at different levels (internal, national and international) future policies in this area will be effective only if they differentiate carefully between the levels at which they can be applied most successfully. That requires a clear distinction between regulation, supervision and control (or management within individual banks).

The purpose of *banking regulation* is to maintain the stability and confidence in the financial system, to ensure that financial markets operate smoothly and efficiently, and to protect retail depositors as well as borrowers and other users of banks. The objectives can be achieved only if there is a legal and administrative framework robust enough to prevent bank failures. The regulation has, therefore, to formulate and apply rules that uniformly cover all relevant institutions and individuals. The rules have to be specified clearly and in considerable detail. The sanctions that back them up must also be prescribed unambiguously and in advance.

Banking supervision is the process that involves monitoring of individual banks to ensure that they follow the prescribed regulations and, thus, do not behave imprudently. In other words, the supervision is concerned with the application of the banking laws and regulations. However, given the variety of banks and their operations, the supervisors have to be allowed a certain degree of discretion. It is unrealistic to expect banking regulation or law to be all embracing *ex ante*, especially in periods of rapid changes. The greater the degree of discretion the more important it is that banking supervisors, like the regulators, are publicly accountable for their actions.

The problem, and it is a rapidly growing problem, is that the sheer size, variety and complexity of modern banking activities is such that no outside supervisor can be expected to monitor or supervise all, or even most, of internal operations of banks. The more banks engage in derivatives trading the more difficult is the task of outside supervisors. Positions in this particular market change so rapidly that annual, quarterly or even monthly reporting may be totally inadequate to monitor and track them effectively. This puts special responsibility on senior executives of banks to ensure through *internal control* of day-to-day activities that prudential rules prescribed by the regulators are observed. More specifically, it is their responsibility to make sure that the main objective of financial innovation is not to avoid regulation – placing at risk the viability of banks and, in this way, economic welfare of the countries in which they operate.

These definitions suggest that banking regulation can be effective at both international (for common problems) and national (for country specific problems) levels. Supervision of banks can be carried out successfully only at the national level, though a supranational authority can monitor the extent to which individual countries are observing the commonly agreed rules and regulations. Finally, implementation of the laws and regulations can be made successfully only through internal control within individual banks. Hence, the success of banking regulation and supervision has become increasingly dependent (a) on the degree to which measures implemented at each of the three levels complement each other, and (b) on the extent of co-operation between the levels.

Traditionally, 'market forces' in banking have been regulated in four ways, most of which have now been either discarded or emasculated in many countries.

First, there is the price regulation, that is, control of interest rates. This has now effectively been abolished, at least in the industrialized world. The result is greater interest rate volatility, contributing to macroeconomic instability. Policy changes in this area obviously lie outside the responsibility of banking regulators and supervisors. Moreover, any attempt to reverse the trend towards greater deregulation and liberalization, begun in the 1970s, would receive little support from powerful financial interests and their governments.

Second, restrictions on cross-border financial flows are another way to make banking supervision more effective. That, however, is another regulatory instrument that has been abandoned in many countries with the abolition of exchange controls. As a result, speculative short-term capital flows have become easier, increasing the risk of banking crises and failures. (The Asian crisis of 1997 is the latest demonstration of this fact. See Hahm 1998.) One way to reduce the risk of this is to impose 'exit taxes' on the short-term inflows of capital, applied on a scale that falls progressively with the length of time that the funds stay in the country. The Germans and the Swiss used this form of control in periods of great currency instability in the 1970s. More recently, Malaysia introduced such a tax in September 1998.

Third, the regulation can take the form of restrictions on the range of activities that banks are allowed to engage in. The range has increased greatly as a result of deregulation and globalization, with banks, as pointed out earlier, becoming more and more involved in risky activities. This is probably an area that is likely to receive increasing attention from the regulators and supervisors. If this happens, the success of the regulatory initiatives will depend on the extent to which they are applied evenly to all banks both within individual countries and internationally. Otherwise, the highly risky activities will be transferred from the institutions that are required to observe the new restrictions to those that are not.

Finally, the regulations can be applied to the establishment of new forms of institutions whose sole purpose is to evade regulations. An example of this are derivative product companies set up by major US securities firms specifically to escape the regulatory rules, including those that relate to capital adequacy. Any system that regulates officially certain aspects of banking activity and allows others to be self-regulating is, in fact, deliberately failing to take proper steps to preserve the viability of banks and the financial system in which they operate. The failure of the Korean authorities to supervise the merchant banks in the same way that they supervised the deposit banks was one of the reasons for the Korean financial crisis in 1997 (cf. Chang *et al.* 1998).

It is clear from the preceding analysis that the environment in which banks operate has changed radically since the 1970s. Its main features now are high volume trading, highly sophisticated cross-market position taking, and increasingly complex relationship with large corporate customers. The complexity and the global nature of banking operations has attracted increasingly sophisticated, international fraudsters and money launderers. These developments, in turn, have led to greater demands made on banks by the regulatory authorities.

The complexity, diversity and speed of modern banking operations present the regulatory and supervisory authorities with formidable problems, making it increasingly difficult for them to apply general rules to all banks. The alternative, which appears to be more appropriate in the circumstances, is to rely instead on banks to develop their own methods of assessing risks and controlling actions of their employees, something that many of them are trying to do in any case.

It is obviously in the interest of banks that they should develop efficient methods of internal control. But it is far from clear that it is in the interest of the countries in which they operate to substitute self-regulation for official monitoring and control. Banks, especially smaller ones, may not have internal methods of control and assessing risks. Even if they have a very effective system of internal control on paper, there is no guarantee that they will actually monitor and enforce it. The failure may be the result of negligence, incompetence or a deliberate exploitation of the regulatory problems associated with moral hazard.

For these and similar reasons, it would be difficult for the state to delegate its regulatory responsibilities for prudential supervision to banks even when they pursue strict methods of internal control. Such controls may be in the interest of banks, their investors and depositors, and the rest of the society. But individual bank employees, including some of those in positions of responsibility, may find it in *their* interest to gamble with the funds entrusted to the banks. Moreover, not all of the staff with impeccable integrity has the necessary information, skills or the authority to prevent serious malpractice within their institution. The national authorities have, therefore, no alternative but to develop a supervisory framework that ensures that the systemic risk remains only a theoretical possibility.

It has always been recognized that it would be impossible to eliminate risk completely from economic activity, especially banking. As bankers would be the first to point out, without taking risks they could not 'make money'. Liberalization encourages them to take even greater risks by increasing their freedom of choice. There are many reasons for this including greed, ignorance, negligence, gullibility, naivety and stupidity. It is up to the authorities to decide which risks are likely to give rise to unacceptable social costs and, consequently, have to be outlawed. The important distinction that has to be made in this context is that between individuals who indulge in high-risk investments with their own wealth, and the individuals and the institutions who do so for any of the reasons listed above with other people's wealth. Banks, obviously, fall into the latter category.

It is, as mentioned earlier, impossible to prescribe a detailed package of controls that all banks have to follow. No two banks are likely to be identical in the services they provide, managerial competence and integrity, and their corporate culture. Nevertheless, this does not mean that it is beyond the competence of the authorities to demand certain general standards of practice that all banks should follow. These could, for example, include: position limits that traders should not be allowed to exceed, time limits within which bank offices should reconcile accounts, particularly risky type of dealings that bank employees must not engage in, who (according to experience and seniority) must be responsible for carrying out routine checks at different levels and, in case of the failure to do this, face penalties, including criminal liability. The rules could be formulated on the basis of past bank failures as well as on the experience of the best-practice banks.

The most successful in this respect are likely to be the authorities that take a proactive rather than a reactive attitude to banking regulation. The latter, by its very nature, will fail to go far enough to prevent a recurrence of banking crises and failures caused by practices which are not covered by the existing rules and regulations. In a rapidly changing banking environment of continuous financial and technical innovation reactive authorities will, therefore, constantly be solving past crises instead of preventing future ones.

To protect both private and national interests, the regulators need, therefore, to anticipate possible dangers and act accordingly. For instance, they should be able to specify clearly important criteria that banks are expected to meet (for example, capital adequacy) and the practices in which it would be illegal for them to engage (for example, certain types of derivatives, or setting up offshore institutions in order to avoid regulation). There also seems to be a strong case for stiff penalties to be imposed on senior executives of institutional investors, such as pension funds, whose employees enter, for personal gain, into highly risky deals with banks (cf. Partnoy 1998) – despite the fact that they are not supposed to do so.

Moreover, there is a clear need for special rules concerning 'connected lending', that is, lending to bank owners and managers, and their businesses. This kind of lending tends to lead to high concentration of risk. It also seriously interferes with an objective assessment of credit. A number of studies quote such practices as a major cause of banking crises since 1980 in, among others, countries such as Argentina, Brazil, Chile, Indonesia, Malaysia and Thailand. To make matters worse, in many developing countries bank auditors and supervisors lack the authority to trace the use of such funds.

To be effective, the rules ought to apply equally to private and state banks. The latter should, for example, be required to maintain strict standards of lending, to control costs and to innovate. It is also essential that they identify problem loans at an early stage to avoid losses. According to available evidence, loan losses by state banks have been in many developing countries worse than those experienced by private banks.

Whatever the type of bank, it is important for the regulators to specify clearly whose responsibility it is within individual institutions to ensure that the prescribed standards of internal control are observed. For instance, directors might be required to certify at specified intervals that their banks comply with the standards – making them legally responsible if the banks are discovered to have failed to do so. This would also insure that they devote adequate resources to internal control.

Considerations of this kind raise the important question of the most appropriate form of corporate governance for banks. Should it be similar to the governance of large corporations outside the Anglo-Saxon world where large shareholders and creditors are represented on the boards as monitors and supervisors? If the answer is in the affirmative, and to ensure that they do so, their responsibilities would have to be defined clearly by regulatory authorities. Failure to discharge them could then be liable to legal penalties. However, if this approach were adopted, it would apply only in those cases where they had the information that demanded action but failed to do so. In the cases where the bank withheld such information from them, its executive directors and senior management would become legally liable.

Finally, in order to attract high-calibre officials, it is important that banking supervisors enjoy the prestige that such a highly responsible task demands. They would also have to have the resources and the authority to perform their duties properly. Although this is essential at all times, highly skilled and conscientious supervisors are particularly invaluable when banks run into difficulties. This is the time when their reports are likely to be unreliable, increasing the danger that the insolvencies will not be discovered in time. According to de Juan (1996), this contributed to the severity of Spanish banking crises in the late 1970s and early 1980s.

The ultimate challenge that banking regulators and supervisors face is that no matter how conscientiously and effectively they deal with the issues analysed above, major banking failures may still occur because of international differences (a) in the regulatory standards and (b) in the ability of countries to implement international agreements. Transnational banks can exploit easily these differences by moving risky activities from the countries where they are proscribed to those that allow them. The Eurodollar market grew rapidly after the Regulation Q in the United States imposed limits on the interest rates that banks could pay on deposits. International differences in requirements concerning capital adequacy have been exploited in a similar way by banks. Hence, it is essential to avoid major inconsistencies in the application of the rules, or significant disparities in the practices adopted which allow banks to play off one country against another. Globalization and deregulation make, therefore, international cooperation unavoidable. Oil crises, inflation, economic stagnation, floating exchange rates, and highly volatile interest rates affect all countries.

Not surprisingly, it was in the 1970s that the need for greater international co-operation in this area became apparent. All the problems listed above occurred simultaneously, creating the worst economic and financial crisis since the Second World War. Inevitably, this was accompanied by a number of bank failures even in major industrial countries: Franklin National Bank of New York, Herstatt Bank in Germany and the 'fringe bank crisis' in London. With major banks operating on both sides of the Atlantic, and in many parts of the world, differences in regulatory standards were bound to pose a serious threat to the viability of individual banks and financial systems.

As a result, the G-10 countries formed the Basle Supervisors' Committee with the responsibility to co-ordinate banking regulations and supervisory practices. This was sealed with the Basle Concordat in 1975. Nevertheless, despite this and subsequent international initiatives, an important problem remains, perpetuated by the limited extent to which even countries whose financial systems are closely integrated are prepared to cooperate. A uniform international standard of regulation and supervision is likely to favour, at least in the short to medium term, the countries that already operate the rules and regulations similar to those incorporated into such a standard. Powerful interests in the countries where this is not the case may use this as an excuse to persuade their governments not to accept the standard, arguing that it would damage their and the country's ability to compete.

Not surprisingly, therefore, international agreements tend to be piecemeal, covering only some of the most serious problems that have already happened. For instance, the Basle Concordat failed to deal with an issue that was not too difficult to anticipate: who is responsible for foreign branches of a bank? The question became highly relevant only a few years later, in 1982, when Banco Ambrosiano, a large Italian bank, failed. The Italian authorities acted promptly to guarantee full backing for depositors of the parent bank in Italy. But they refused to extend the guarantee to the bank's subsidiary in Luxembourg through which the Banco Ambrosiano carried out its activities in the euromarket. A decade later, following the collapse of the BCCI, the Basle Supervisors' Committee was still trying to deal with the problem of cross-border banking establishments by setting "four minimum standards" that member countries had to observe (Quinn 1998b, pp. 452–3).

Equally important, it should have been clear from the start that differences in the deregulation would be reflected, among other things, in differences in capital adequacy ratios, and that it would not take banks long to exploit this. It does not demand great accounting skill to work out that banks could earn much higher profits by expanding their operations in the countries with the low requirements. There was a clear risk, therefore, that the capital adequacy of transnational banks would be affected adversely by deregulation. Nevertheless, it was only in 1988 that the Basle Accord was reached with the aim of achieving international convergence of supervisory regulations governing their capital adequacy. According to Kapstein (1991), this became possible only when, for reasons of domestic policy, the US Administration agreed to back it up. However, a decade later it became obvious that, as a result of financial innovation, the Accord was "less effective in ensuring that capital requirements match bank's true risk profile" (Basle Committee 1999, p. 4). Consequently, early in 1999 the Basle Committee published a consultative paper with proposals for a new capital adequacy framework.

The shortcomings of the original Accord are not entirely surprising if Kapstein (1991) is right that "most of the G-10 central bank governors were less than enthusiastic about discussing the convergence of banking standards". For reasons analysed in this and the previous section, without the 'enthusiasm' of central banks for proper international standards of regulation and supervision, neither national regulatory frameworks nor systems of internal control within banks are likely to operate effectively. If that is missing, the probability of avoiding future banking crises and failures, including the threat of systemic failures, is bound to remain low.

9.4   Conclusion

It has always been recognized that few, if any, economic institutions depend so much on public trust and confidence as those in the financial sector. This is particularly true of banks. Given their importance for efficient and orderly functioning of modern economies, the integrity and effectiveness of banks is essential for economic performance in general and thus, ultimately, for social harmony and political stability.

It is for this reason that all modern economies require a regulatory framework capable of ensuring that the trust and confidence on which banks depend are not compromised by illegal or imprudent practices. How well the regulatory bodies discharge their responsibilities depends normally on the competence of the legislators, ability and integrity of those who run the banks, and on the support that they receive from the state and from the financial community itself.

Hence, a regulatory system operates at two levels. At the macroeconomic level it functions within a universal framework provided and, when necessary, enforced by the state. At the microeconomic level, on the other hand, its effectiveness is determined, in addition to the generally applicable rules, according to the norms and 'corporate culture' that have evolved over time within each bank. The former depends on actions by those appointed by the state to monitor and supervise the whole banking system. In the same way, the latter is dependent on actions of those appointed by each bank to ensure, among other things, that members of staff for whom they are responsible do nothing that will be detrimental to the reputation and performance of the institution. That requires them to safeguard the interests of their investors and depositors, and to maintain the standards of business behaviour expected by the wider community.

The growth and global spread of banks, deregulation, financial innovation and technical changes have contributed to serious managerial diseconomies of scale. This has made effective monitoring and supervision of banks extremely difficult even at the microeconomic level. Not surprisingly, there has been an increase in both the frequency and scale of banking crises since the 1970s, the period during which radical changes in banking practices have taken place. As shown in this chapter, the sheer complexity of the changes and high social costs of bank crises and failures have created special problems and responsibilities for those responsible for monitoring and supervising banking activities at all levels: from bank managers and directors to the national and international regulatory authorities.

Consequently, in the new international economic and financial environment, bank failures and systemic crises can be avoided only if banks cooperate closely with national regulatory authorities *and*, equally important, if national authorities cooperate with one another. That demands careful development of effective complementary regulatory systems at three levels: that of individual banks, national and international. This may reduce individual freedom and national sovereignty. But it is the only way to minimize the risks that are, ultimately, against the interest of all: investors, depositors, bank employees and the whole community, both national and international. Given the extremely high private and social costs of banking crises and failures, the regulation and supervision of banks require far greater attention and resources now than ever before.

10
The Bretton Woods System: Concept and Practice*

The first (discouraging) thought that occurs to anyone asked to write about the Bretton Woods System is that there is nothing, no aspect of the subject, that has failed to attract careful and lengthy scrutiny over the last 50 years. The existing literature must be at least as voluminous as that on the Classical Gold Standard; and the number of devotees of the System is probably greater than the one that admired for so long its much-debated nineteenth-century precursor.

International financial crises since the early 1970s have frequently produced calls for 'a new' Bretton Woods System. The problem with this is that the system, like the gold standard, was a product of particular circumstances that cannot be reproduced easily. Moreover, it is never clear whether those who advocate a return to more orderly international economic relationships, such as those that existed in the 1950s and for most of the 1960s, mean the system as conceived at Bretton Woods or the system as it operated in practice.

Nevertheless, the conditions that inspired the search for a consensus in the conduct and control of economic relationships between nations in order to enhance their economic welfare, the solutions that were proposed in response to the specific problems that had destroyed in the 1930s the multilateral system of trade and finance created over the preceding half a century, and the obstacles that made it impossible to implement the whole of the Bretton Woods blueprint in practice – all have important lessons to offer to a world struggling with similar difficulties half a century later. Many of the problems that Keynes, White, and others tried to solve in the 1940s are still with us and will continue to lead to serious crises for as long as international economic integration and the growing interdependence to which it gives rise continue to increase in a world divided into a large number of independent states – all jealously guarding their national sovereignty.

* This chapter was previously published in J. Michie and J. Grieve Smith (eds), *Managing the Global Economy*, Oxford University Press, Oxford, 1995, pp. 37–54.

This chapter analyses, first, the extent to which the original plans for a new global monetary system were influenced by developments between the two world wars. After the principles, the chapter turns to the practice: the factors that made the system successful early on, but then progressively deteriorated, creating many of the difficulties which the architects of the Bretton Woods System tried to ensure would never happen again. It concludes with some suggestions why a Bretton Woods Mark II would have to be different from the old one and of the obstacles that make it unlikely on a global scale in the foreseeable future.

10.1   The supranational blueprint and its origins

As Machlup (1977) has shown, the idea of creating an international economic and monetary union has a long history. In spite of this, it remained for centuries only a dream for the simple reason that until the 1940s no government took a serious interest in any of the schemes proposed. For instance, in the 1920s a French economist, Nogaro, floated the idea of establishing an international bank to issue a new international currency (Gomes 1993, p. 215). A few years later, in 1929, Schacht, the President of the Reichsbank, proposed the creation of an international clearing union (Luke, 1985); and in 1930 Keynes ([1930] 1971, pp. 358–61) suggested a modified gold standard to be managed by a 'supranational bank' acting as the international lender of last resort. Nothing happened.

However, only a little over a decade later, both the Allies and the Germans were incorporating these suggestions into their plans for a new international economic order to be established once the war was over (Van Dormael 1978, Gardner 1980). Two important, inter-related developments, which took place in the intervening period, played a major role in contributing to this change in official attitudes. The collapse of the international economic system at the beginning of the 1930s, followed by the Great Depression, the rise of Fascism and the Second World War destroyed the old order created by trial and error before 1914 in response to growing international economic integration. Most contemporaries were convinced that each step in this sequence of events was a direct result of the one preceding it. The events also demonstrated the fact that industrial countries, in particular, were too advanced, specialized, and interdependent to contemplate genuine, lasting improvements in economic welfare after the war without re-establishing some sort of a new economic order. Moreover, the task was too important and urgent for the postwar recovery to be left to the slow, haphazard processes of the markets whose limitations had been exposed in the interwar period (Milward 1987a and 1987b). It had to be taken on, therefore, by governments; and the powerful vested interests that might have resisted this successfully were too shell-shocked and marginalized by the disastrous turn of events in the 1930s and early 1940s to put up an effective resistance to fundamental, far-reaching changes. Hence, such changes became not only essential but also feasible.

British, American, and other plans and, ultimately, the Bretton Woods blueprint for the postwar order reflect, therefore, these preoccupations rooted in the inter-war experience. They were the outcome of a pragmatic approach to the major challenges of the time adopted by a remarkable generation of public-spirited politicians, administrators, and experts, often of widely different ideological persuasions. However, they had one thing in common: most of them had lived through two world wars and the Great Depression; and it was this experience that made them determined to create economic and social conditions which would ensure that the world would never again have to live through similar man-made disasters.

The starting point, which made all the subsequent development possible, was the widespread acceptance of the fact that economic interdependence requires consensus and cooperation if countries participating in the international division of labour are to achieve their national objectives; and that many of the problems experienced between the two world wars could be traced directly to a failure in this respect. Even the rather informal financial arrangements that had existed under the Classical Gold Standard (see Eichengreen 1992) broke down as, confronted with unprecedented economic and social crises, each country tried to solve its problems in isolation. In spite of this, very few of them managed to stage a genuine economic recovery before the outbreak of the Second World War; and those that did (for example Nazi Germany and the Soviet Union) achieved economic success at exceptionally heavy social cost.

The lessons that this experience had taught those who attended the Bretton Woods Conference were summarized in the opening speech by the US Secretary of the Treasury, Morgenthau (US Department of State 1948a, p. 81):

> All of us have seen the great economic tragedy of our time. We saw the worldwide depression of the 1930s. We saw currency disorders develop and spread from land to land, destroying the basis for international trade and international investment and even international faith. In their wake, we saw unemployment and wretchedness – idle tools, wasted wealth. We saw their victims fall prey, in places, to demagogues and dictators. We saw bewilderment and bitterness become the breeders of fascism, and finally, of war.

The important conclusion, as Morgenthau pointed out to a much wider audience in a radio broadcast, was that: "We have come to recognise that the wisest and most effective way to protect our national interests is through international co-operation" (quoted in Eckes 1975, p. x). Keynes went even further in his closing speech at Bretton Woods (US Department of State 1948a, p. 1110): "We have been learning to work together. If we can so continue, this nightmare, in which most of us here present have spent too much of our lives, will be over. The brotherhood of man will have become more than a phrase."

What they had done 'working together' at Bretton Woods was to produce the first and, in many ways, the most ambitious blueprint for a global economic order ever attempted. It was designed to eliminate permanently a number of serious problems experienced in the inter-war period (and, indeed, before 1914) within a basically supranational, centralized institutional framework.

The first problem that they had to solve in setting up a new international monetary system was that of agreeing on (a) what should constitute liquid assets which would be universally acceptable in settling international debts and (b) how they were to be created. The practice from about the 1870s until the Second World War was to rely for this purpose on gold and one or two national currencies, with a few other currencies in a minor, supporting role. The snag, as those attending the Bretton Woods Conference knew from experience, was that the production of gold might fail to expand sufficiently to finance the growth of world trade and investment. This had happened before 1914 and to an even greater extent in the inter-war period, with the result that national currencies of the most important trading nations were used to fill the gap, effectively turning the international financial set-up into an extension of their national systems, mainly that of the dominant economy.

However, in a dynamic economic environment this only produces a temporary solution. In the medium to long term the relative position of countries in the international economy changes and with this the relative demand for their currencies. The once dominant country is overtaken by more dynamic economies whose firms become responsible for a larger share of international trade and investment. As a result, a high proportion of international exchange is conducted in its currency, in preference to that of the once dominant country. However, for the transition to be smooth, supporting a continuous expansion of world trade and investment, the authorities of the new leading economy have to be both willing and able to provide its currency in the quantity required. Otherwise, international trade, investment, and production will decline. The rate of decline may be slowed down for a time if the once dominant economy is determined to continue playing a major financial role and reduces the supply of its currency relative to the shrinking global demand for it, thus maintaining its exchange rate unaltered. The problem is that such a policy cannot be pursued for long because of its adverse effects on domestic output and employment.

All this is, of course, precisely what happened in the inter-war period, though there were already some signs of the changing roles of major economies and their currencies towards the end of the Classical Gold Standard. As Kindelberger (1973) has pointed out, after the First World War an economically weakened Britain was in no position to play the key role, and the United States, because of the virtually closed nature of its economy, was both unable and unwilling to take over.

Both the British and US plans, prepared for Bretton Woods, tried to deal with these weaknesses: the British by creating an international currency ('bancor') to be made available on demand; and the American by revising contributions to a new international organization at intervals according to changes in the relative size and importance of the countries in the international economy (US Department of State 1948b, pp. 1536–7). The latter also proposed an international monetary unit ('unitas') for the new global organization (*ibid.* p. 1543). In the end, it was the US 'contributory' plan (minus 'the unitas') that was adopted at Bretton Woods and enshrined in the IMF Articles of Agreement. Nevertheless arguments about the relative merits of the two plans continued for years. Yet, as will be shown later, each had serious deficiencies and, therefore, little chance of success. (Both plans are reproduced in US Department of State 1948b.)

The next problem that architects of the Bretton Woods System set out to solve – that of establishing an international lender of last resort – was also prompted by their past experience. Even under the Classical Gold Standard, a country with temporary liquidity difficulties depended on the self-interest of other countries to come to its rescue in order to prevent an international financial crisis (Eichengreen 1992, Bloomfield 1963). In other words, although, at least in the case of major countries, it was likely that other countries would help, there was no guarantee that they would do so. No central bank was under an obligation to act as a surrogate international lender of last resort, nor were there generally agreed rules according to which this should be done.

The British and US plans for, respectively, a 'Clearing Union' and an 'International Stabilization Fund' were intended to overcome these problems by creating a supranational institution that would act, effectively, as a central banks' Central Bank, by stepping in to help countries with temporary liquidity problems. The end result of these labours, the International Monetary Fund, was therefore instructed (Article I) to act in such a way as to enable countries "to correct maladjustments in their balance of payments without resorting to measures destructive of national and international prosperity". It was to do this (Article V.1) by dealing only with national monetary authorities (that is, central banks, ministries of finance, and stabilization funds).

Moreover, like national central banks, the IMF was to provide clearing facilities, as all central banks were to hold reserves with it. In addition, again like a national central bank, it was given the authority to ask a country applying for help to take certain corrective actions in order to qualify for assistance. (IMF Articles of Agreement are reprinted in US Department of State 1948a, pp. 942–84.)

All these powers were, in principle, both necessary and desirable. However, to be effective in practice, the institution had to have sufficient resources, independence of the influence of any one country, and undisputed authority to discharge its responsibilities. The founding fathers of the Bretton Woods System were in no position to provide this. Hence, their blueprint contained another serious deficiency that was to make it unworkable in the form intended.

Another important issue that the 44 countries participating at the Bretton Woods Conference were determined to resolve was that of preventing destabilizing capital flows and competitive exchange rate devaluations. Both were regarded – on the basis of pre-war experience – as a major obstacle to creating the viable system of multilateral trade and payments which they believed to be essential if they were to achieve high levels of output and employment after the war. For instance, Nurkse (1944) expressed a widely held view when he argued, in his analysis of international finance in the inter-war period, that floating exchange rates discouraged trade, led to misallocation of international resources, and encouraged destabilizing speculation. Hubert Henderson (1955, p. 291), another influential observer of economic disintegration in the 1930s, concluded that competitive devaluations were the least helpful policy instrument to the countries that employed them and most harmful to the rest.

Not surprisingly, both the British and US plans wanted member countries to hold a large proportion of their reserves with the new international organization. That would make it possible for the organization to clear external imbalances and thus avoid destabilizing flights of short-term capital from one financial centre to another, as happened in the 1930s. To ensure this, it was also essential – in the British but not the American view – to impose controls on international capital flows, especially those of a short-term, speculative nature. Keynes certainly believed, as Churchill explained in a letter written in 1941, that "the exchange regulations and controls imposed during the war" would have to be maintained "for some considerable time" (quoted in Van Dormael 1978, p. 10). Experience had taught him that only in this way would it be possible to sustain over a long period a system of fixed exchange rates in which all currencies would be pegged to the new international currency advocated in the British plan (see Moggridge 1986). At the same time, both British and American plans contained a provision for countries with persistent balance of payments difficulties to devalue their currency.

In the end, most of these proposals were incorporated into the IMF Charter. The Fund was given responsibility "to promote exchange rate stability" and "to avoid competitive devaluations" (Article IV.4a). Its members were allowed to devalue only "to correct a fundamental disequilibrium" (Article IV.5a) – although no attempt was made either then or subsequently to define this concept (see Solomon 1982). If a member changed the par value of its currency despite the Fund's objections it would become "ineligible to use the resources of the Fund unless the Fund otherwise" determined (Article IV.6).

What is more, a persistent offender in this respect might be required to withdraw from the IMF (Article XV).

There is obviously consistency and logic in these arguments and provisions. The problem is that their effectiveness depended critically on the Fund's ability to appropriate a significant part of member countries' national economic sovereignty. This was a much more important aspect of the Bretton Woods agreement than the often discussed fact that the system was a variant of the gold standard, as all the currencies were fixed to the US dollar which, in turn, was fixed to gold. The IMF, after all, was empowered to increase international liquidity, if its larger members approved, by altering the par values of members' currencies relative to gold (Article IV.7).

A system of fixed exchange rates, strictly and scrupulously observed, should in itself be sufficient to ensure that all countries participating in it have no alternative but to follow rigid stabilization and adjustment rules. That was certainly true of countries belonging to the Classical Gold Standard – even though, for various reasons, the system was much more flexible than is generally believed (Panić 1992). However, the risk with a quasi-monetary system (that is, a system of fixed exchange rates) is that there is no guarantee that when confronted with a serious internal imbalance a country will stick to the rules rather than change its exchange rate; or, alternatively, that a country earning current account surpluses will not simply increase its reserves rather than expand domestic activity and imports, invest abroad, or allow the rate of exchange to appreciate to the point at which it eliminates the surpluses.

All these practices had become so common in the inter-war period that the British plan included a provision empowering the new international organisation ('the Clearing Union') to impose penalties on both deficit and surplus countries (US Department of State 1948b, pp. 1554–5). The idea was that the organization should charge extra interest: in the first case if a country's reserves fell over a period of a year or so below a certain minimum; and in the second case if the reserves held by a country at the Clearing Union over a similar period were persistently over a specified maximum.

The Americans made no similar proposal – hardly surprising, as everyone expected them to be by far the most important surplus country for a long time after the war. Nevertheless, they agreed at Bretton Woods that a 'scarce currency clause' should be included in the IMF Charter. If there were a general scarcity of a currency, the Fund would try first to borrow it from the country concerned. However, if excess demand for the currency persisted, the Fund would declare it 'scarce' and start to ration it (Article VII.3a). The moment this happened, any member would have the right, after consulting the Fund, to impose restrictions on transactions with the country whose currency had been declared 'scarce' (Article VII.3b) – for as long as the scarcity lasted. The restrictive measures were to be discontinued only when the Fund declared the currency no longer scarce (Article VII.3c) – in other words, after the country had taken appropriate steps to balance its external account.

In this way, the IMF was given extraordinary powers to force even its largest and most influential members to observe the stabilization/adjustment rules. It could do so in the case of a deficit country when asked to act as the lender of last resort; and in the case of a surplus country by declaring its currency scarce.

All the problems, proposals, and policy decisions described so far were designed to deal with the short-term aspects of economic activity: international financial measures needed to facilitate high levels of activity and trade without which the most important policy objective that industrial countries were determined to pursue after the war – that of high levels of employment and income – could not be achieved. However, there was another important factor that had contributed to the disintegration of the international economy in the 1930s: the unprecedented collapse of international long-term capital flows (see Bairoch 1976b, and Panić 1988, Chapter 9).

The three nations which provided most international investment before 1914 – the United Kingdom, France, and Germany – were in no position to play this role after the First World War. The Americans, on the other hand, had the resources but no inclination to take over the role on the scale required. Their financial institutions had little experience of investing abroad, as all but a small proportion of the country's savings were used to finance domestic investment. Moreover, those who borrowed from the United States found it difficult to service and repay their debts because of the country's highly protectionist policies.

It was this experience that led US Treasury officials, under Harry White, to propose the creation of a new institution whose task would consist of providing the long-term capital that would be required for the postwar reconstruction. The problem was obvious enough: after the war, economic and political uncertainties could be expected to be so great that private investors would be most unlikely to provide such finance, at least in the initial stages of postwar reconstruction. In the circumstances, as White put it: "Only an international, non-profit institution with enormous resources can afford to undertake the task of supplying adequate amounts of capital on the gigantic scale that will be necessary after the war" (quoted in Eckes 1975, p. 52).

The International Bank for Reconstruction and Development was created, therefore, to perform the function of an international allocator of last resort. Its Charter, agreed at Bretton Woods, makes it clear that the Bank's task was to assist and supplement private international investment, not to supplant it. This is emphasized in Article III.4 which, among other things, specifies that the Bank would lend mainly if the funds could not be obtained from other sources on reasonable terms. The Bank's Charter was also specific about the ways in which it would either make loans from its own resources or underwrite loans ("in whole or in part"), including those made "by private investors through the usual investment channels" (Article IV.1a). The role intended for the Bank is, in fact, reminiscent of that played by the Japan Development Bank in the extraordinary growth and modernization of the Japanese economy after the Second World War. (The IBRD Articles of Agreement are reprinted in US Department of State 1948a, pp. 98–1014.)

Equally important for a *World* Bank, serving countries at different levels of development and with different political systems, the IBRD was not allowed (a) to specify in which country the proceeds of its loans should be spent (Article III.5a) and (b) to interfere in the political affairs of a country, or to be influenced in making its decisions by the political system of the member or members concerned (Article IV.10).

By agreeing on the Charters of the two institutions, delegates at the Bretton Woods Conference managed to achieve something that the world had never even attempted before: to create the basic framework of supranational institutions required to manage the economic and financial behaviour of a large number of nation states whose economies were closely integrated. As Keynes, White, and others involved in producing the Bretton Woods blueprint realized – and were to be proved right by subsequent events – the only viable, lasting framework for an integrated world economy is one that is managed by supranational organizations. For reasons that had become obvious during the inter-war period, dependence on a single, dominant country could not be expected to guarantee long-term improvements in global economic welfare of the kind planned by national governments after the war.

The problem that they could not solve at Bretton Woods was the one central – then as now – to the effective running of an internationally integrated economy: how to ensure in the absence of a world parliament and government that supranational institutions perform the role that such a system demands. It was this, in fact, that made the system which operated from the late 1940s until the early 1970s depart significantly in a number of respects from the blueprint produced at Bretton Woods.

10.2   The revival and fatal flows of a system managed by a dominant economy

Contrary to popular belief, the 'Bretton Woods System' never operated as intended by those who created it. Instead of being managed by the two supranational institutions, it was run by the dominant economic power after the Second World War: the United States. In that sense, its fortunes, like those of the Classical Gold Standard, were directly linked to those of the relative economic performance and policies of the country responsible for the largest share of world industrial production, trade, and finance at the time – precisely the outcome that those attending the Bretton Woods Conference had been anxious to avoid.

As there are already numerous accounts of how the post-war system actually operated, important lessons for the future can now only be gained by discovering the reasons why it departed from the original blueprint.

Warning signals that the system was unlikely to function as agreed at Bretton Woods were there from the start. For instance, a common complaint in the literature is that the founding fathers seriously underestimated the scale of the postwar reconstruction effort and the time that it would take; and that, as a result of this, the two international institutions were provided with totally inadequate resources to play the role for which they had been created. There is some justification in this, in the sense that it was commonly believed at the time that the postwar recovery would be accomplished within 5 years. In fact, in most cases it took 10 to 15 years (cf. Panić 1991a). As for the financial resources given to the IMF and the IBRD, it was agreed at Bretton Woods that they should receive $8.8 billion and $10 billion respectively (US Department of State 1948a, pp. 976 and 985). The two figures, although quite large at the time, would have been sufficient to cover the amounts provided in different forms to Western Europe and Japan by the United States (see Milward 1987a) during the first six or so years after the war. But there would have been very little left for other countries or purposes – even if the IMF and the IBRD had been in a position to spend every dollar, or its equivalent in other currencies and gold, allocated to them.

In fact, political considerations and economic realities ensured that the sums that the two institutions could actually use were considerably smaller. When the World Bank started its operations after the war it had effectively only $570 million (that is, the US contribution) available for lending – less than 6 per cent of the resources that it was supposed to have (Spero 1981, p. 36). Moreover, it could advance loans only in those cases where it was assured of repayment. IMF currency dealings between 1947 and 1952 amounted to no more than $850 million (Kenwood and Lougheed 1983, p. 255). As its responsibility was limited to short-term stabilization, it refused to come to the aid of countries with serious adjustment (that is, reconstruction and development) problems even when it was in a position to help them. Not surprisingly, in 1947, soon after they had started their operations, the two organizations expected to be the pillars of the Bretton Woods System admitted that they had inadequate resources to deal with the mounting international economic problems (Mason and Asher 1973, pp. 105–7 and 124–35).

There were basically two reasons for this. First, in agreeing on contributions to be made by individual countries to the IMF and the IBRD the founding fathers had to consider carefully what would be acceptable to national parliaments, especially the US Congress, and the powerful interests that they represented. (See, for example, Mickesell 1994.) The agreed quotas reflected this as much as what was thought to be either necessary or within the ability of individual countries to contribute. Second, it was important for political reasons to treat at Bretton Woods all national currencies as if they were of similar importance and would, therefore, be equally in demand after the war. To distinguish 'key' currencies from others would have made it virtually impossible to achieve the consensus needed to create the postwar system. At the same time, it was clear that only a few countries – in particular, the United States – would be able to provide the goods and services needed for postwar reconstruction, for the simple reason that the economies of the remaining nations were either destroyed and dislocated by the war, or not sufficiently industrialized. To make things worse, the grossly uneven productive capacities and competitive strength of individual countries made it essential for almost all members of the two institutions to continue with the inconvertibility of their currencies after the war in order to avoid major financial crises of the kind experienced by the United Kingdom in the summer of 1947 (see Milward 1987a). The outcome was that the IMF and the IBRD had at their disposal a large stock of currencies that were for all practical purposes unusable.

The two supranational institutions were, therefore, in no position to manage the international financial system – the task for which they had been created in 1944. Not surprisingly, the supranational edifice that represented the Bretton Woods System as originally conceived collapsed almost as soon as it was created in 1946/47. The 'Bretton Woods System' that soon afterwards rose from the ashes was something quite different: managed by the United States because of its dominant economic position in the world, its fortunes were bound to be tied closely to that country's ability to maintain this supremacy. The problem is that no country can realistically be expected to sustain such a position for long in a dynamic world economy. Consequently, no international monetary system dependent on a dominant economy is likely to have more than a relatively short life span.

At the end of the Second World War, the United States accounted for half of world manufacturing output, half of world shipping, one-third of world exports and 61 per cent of total world reserves of gold (Kennedy 1989, p. 461). In 1950 its reserves were 2.73 times greater than its liquid liabilities (Milner and Greenaway 1979, p. 271). The dollar was not only fixed to gold but also, as an official reserve asset, convertible into it. In these circumstances, it is inconceivable that the bancor or any other international currency could have displaced the dollar as the international medium of exchange, unit of account, and store of value unless its creation had coincided with the abolition of all national currencies. Even in the 1960s the dollar accounted for more than two-thirds of the official reserves of all countries, with its share rising to over 77 per cent in the early 1970s when the 'Bretton Woods System' finally collapsed (cf. Walter 1993, p. 187).

With the US economy and currency in such a commanding position, it was also inevitable that it would be the US authorities and financial institutions that would manage the international system rather than the two supranational institutions created at Bretton Woods for the purpose. In other words, as before 1914, the international monetary system became effectively an extension of the dominant country's system. It could hardly have been otherwise, as it was that country's authorities and financial institutions that determined the supply of the world's key currency – influencing the ability of other countries to reconcile their internal and external balances at desired levels of output and employment. Consequently, it was the US authorities and financial institutions that had a major influence on the stability and growth of the world economy; and, under the global economic conditions that existed for a quarter of a century after the Second World War, no supranational institution would have been able to challenge this influence. Hence, the position occupied by the United States under the 'Bretton Woods System' was very similar to that played by the United Kingdom under the Classical Gold Standard – in contrast to the original Bretton Woods concept and blueprint which were designed to provide a more permanent solution.

Initially, the system worked extremely well after the advent of the Cold War left the United States with little alternative but to take over its management in 1947 in order to prevent a major international economic and political crisis. US policies ensured a steady injection of dollars into the world economy, making it possible for imbalances in international payments to be adjusted in an orderly fashion, without imposing serious welfare costs either on the countries concerned or on their trading partners. In this way, the United States also helped preserve the system of fixed exchange rates, at least among industrial economies, for more than two decades.

Massive US economic assistance to other countries started with the European Recovery Programme (Marshall Aid) and other official transfers in the late 1940s. However, as the remarkable success of the programmes in Western Europe and Japan became apparent, official grants and loans for this purpose were reduced after the early 1950s without adversely affecting the supply of international liquidity provided by the United States. The reason for this was that the reduction in official transfers coincided with increases in the country's military expenditure and long-term investment abroad which, together, offset its large, persistent surpluses on trade in goods and services (cf. OECD 1964). In that sense, the United States, like the United Kingdom before 1914, provided other countries with its currency on a scale that facilitated the growth of world output, trade, and investment without compromising the confidence that the dollar enjoyed internationally. It performed, therefore, the role of a surplus, creditor country in a way that benefited the rest of the world and would have made it unnecessary for the IMF to apply the scarce currency clause against the dollar even if it had been able to do so.

However, unlike the British in the inter-war period and to a lesser extent before 1914, the Americans were unwilling to sacrifice any of their major economic and political objectives when their economic supremacy and, thus, their position at the centre of the 'Bretton Woods System' began to wane. As the rate of growth of the economy accelerated in the 1960s and unemployment levels fell, US current account surpluses decreased progressively. At the same time, the country's military expenditure and investment abroad continued at high levels, producing large deficits on the basic and overall balance of payments. The result was a sharp deterioration in the ratio of US reserves to liquid liabilities: from 2.73 in 1950 to 0.92 in 1960 and 0.31 in 1970 (Milner and Greenaway 1979, p. 271). Not surprisingly, the dollar became vulnerable to speculative attacks, as doubts increased around the world about the country's ability to maintain the value of its currency fixed to gold at the existing parity ($35 to one ounce of pure gold).

The first run on the dollar occurred in 1960 when international speculators began to exchange it for gold on the London market. The general unease about US ability to manage the System and maintain the exchange rate of the dollar continued throughout the decade, intensifying after sterling's devaluation in November 1967. There was also increasing resentment in Europe that the Americans were deriving 'seigniorage' benefits from the role played by their currency and institutions under the 'Bretton Woods System'.

Clearly, to deal with these problems and complaints, the United States needed either to tighten macroeconomic policies to boost its surpluses on trade in goods and services, or to reduce its military expenditure and investment abroad. However, for domestic reasons, the successive administrations found it difficult to do either. Instead, they made some attempts in the mid-1960s to control capital outflows, tie foreign aid to orders from the United States, and introduce various schemes to encourage exports. Yet, despite the country's apparent determination to keep the dollar at the centre of the international system, no attempt was made to take the required stabilization/adjustment measures because of their potentially adverse effects on domestic output and employment.

In the end, as in the British case 40 years earlier, the conflicting objectives and policies could not be sustained. In August 1971, the Nixon Administration first abandoned convertibility of the dollar into gold and imposed a 10 per cent surcharge on imports; and a few months later, as part of the Smithsonian Agreement, devalued the dollar by 10 per cent – signalling, in effect, the end of the 'Bretton Woods System'. For the second time within a century, after initial success, a dominant country had failed to secure a viable, lasting international monetary system. The reason was the same in both cases: the inability of the country at the centre of the system to maintain its economic supremacy and, with it, the capacity to fulfil its international role without sacrificing domestic welfare. No international system can survive if the country responsible for managing it is unwilling to observe its basic rules. One of the consequences of this is that international consensus will start to break down precisely at the moment when it is needed most: that is, when it becomes apparent that no country is capable of managing the system on its own.

The Americans played a major role in rebuilding international cooperation after the war, especially among the countries of Western Europe (see Milward 1987a, Panić 1991a). Marshall Aid was given on condition that the countries receiving the Aid cooperated in implementing it through the Organization for European Economic Cooperation (set up in 1948). The United States actively promoted intra-European trade and the clearing of external imbalances by helping create the European Payments Union in 1950. The success of these and other initiatives made an important contribution towards the greater European integration that is still in progress. Later on, in the early 1960s, there was an increase in collaboration among the central banks of industrial countries in supporting each other's currencies in times of speculative attack. The 1960s also saw a significant liberalization of international trade.

However, as the decade progressed there were serious disagreements among industrial countries about the policies required to deal with the growing disparities in their external balances and who should bear the main responsibility for taking steps to correct them: deficit countries, such as the United States and the United Kingdom, or surplus countries of the European Community, notably West Germany. In other words, neither side was prepared to observe the rules of the international stabilization/adjustment game when they began to come in conflict with their national objectives and policies.

This could have only one outcome: greater uncertainty and, consequently, international financial instability – especially as the weakening of consensus and cooperation among the major industrial countries coincided with rapid growth of international investment flows.

The scope for such flows was limited until the second half of the 1950s by two factors: tight controls of capital exports, practised by almost all industrial countries; and, where this was not the case (the United States), the risks and uncertainties associated with investing in economies struggling to recover from the economic and other damage and dislocation caused by the war. However, with the success of the recovery, the narrowing down of international income differentials, and improvements in transport and communications, there came a rapid growth of transnational corporations followed by transnational banks and other financial institutions.

By 1971 the value of liquid assets held by the top one hundred US transnational corporations (TNCs) exceeded the combined reserves of the largest industrial countries (Robbins and Stobaugh 1974, pp. 182–3). The growth of transnational banks (TNBs) was even more rapid. Between 1965 and 1974 the value of assets held abroad by branches of US banks had risen from $9 billion to $125 billion. Foreign banks operating in the United States held, in 1974, assets worth $50 billion (United Nations 1981, p. 34). The gross size of eurocurrency deposits (that is, including inter-bank deposits) went up from $19 billion in 1964 to $210 billion in 1972 (Pilbeam 1992, p. 312).

Given the resources at their disposal, it was sufficient for these transnationals to switch a relatively small proportion of their assets from one currency to another to cause a major exchange rate crisis. The growing discord among industrial countries provided them with the incentive to do precisely that in order to protect the value of their assets. Yet, although their actions interfered increasingly with the ability of different countries to achieve their economic objectives, the fact that transnationals operated globally made it, as Chapter 6 shows, more and more difficult for any one government to control their actions. (See also Panić 1991b).

A system of fixed exchange rates cannot survive for long under these conditions, as Keynes and his contemporaries learned from experience, particularly when there are noticeable differences in the ability of different countries – including those whose currencies are used widely in international transactions – to reconcile their internal and external balances. Of the two reserve currencies, sterling was the first to be subjected to persistent pressure until it was devalued in 1967. The dollar followed four years later. The 'Bretton Woods System', resuscitated and managed with great success for a number of years by the United States, was no more.

An international monetary system, using a single global currency and run by supranational institutions, could have avoided the financial (though not the economic!) problems described in this section. As a result, it would probably be functioning even more effectively now than in the 1940s. Keynes and many of his contemporaries realized this. Unfortunately, like all visionaries, they were far ahead of their time.

10.3   Conclusion: is the world ready for a 'New Bretton Woods'?

The 'collapse' of the 'Bretton Woods System' in the early 1970s has been mourned ever since. However, as suggested in the previous section, the change has not been as dramatic or as complete as seems to be widely believed. The return of floating exchange rates – unavoidable in a world of massive capital flows – destroyed the quasi-monetary union (that is, the regime of fixed parities) that had existed from the late 1940s until the early 1970s. To that extent, the demise of the postwar system has increased economic uncertainty considerably by relaxing (though not removing!) the obligation to observe the well-known stabilization/adjustment requirements and, thus, weakening the need for international cooperation which such a system demands.

That has obviously imposed welfare costs on all countries. But the costs have been kept down by the fact that the industrial countries in particular have been careful to avoid competitive devaluations and other protective devices of the kind that caused so much damage in the 1930s. Thus, the Bretton Woods spirit of international cooperation has survived, though mainly in a negative form: national governments have, in general, taken considerable care not to repeat the worst mistakes of the inter-war period, but have not made a genuine effort to create a new world economic and financial order. In the same spirit, the two international institutions created at Bretton Woods have not been abolished mainly because, as recognized in the 1940s, an integrated world economy needs supranational organisations. Although much more prominent since the 1970s than before, neither has been at the centre of international economic developments. This is neither surprising nor new. They had not been allowed to manage the international financial system during the preceding 25 years either.

All this may be unsatisfactory, but what is the likelihood of doing better by restoring a much needed order and predictability in international economic and financial relationships under a 'Bretton Woods Mark II'?

As I have argued elsewhere (Panić 1988), the basic economic requirements of such a system are straightforward enough and, from a technical point of view, relatively easy to implement. The reason for this is that, in principle, they are not different from those that have been applied for many years in the most successful industrial countries, especially those with federal constitutions. Hence, if the world had a single political authority the same blueprint could be implemented globally – by fiat if necessary.

The problem is, of course, that the day when nation states are ready to hand over sovereignty to a world authority, because it is much more likely to satisfy the economic and social aspirations of their citizens, belongs to a very distant future. Consequently, the critical issue in creating an effective supranational institutional framework is still the same as in 1944: how to make it worthwhile for a large number of countries at different levels of development, often with widely different problems and priorities, to collaborate in a way that makes all of them noticeably better off than they would have been otherwise.

Given that there are even more sovereign states now than at the time of the Bretton Woods Conference, with huge differences in their efficiency and income levels, global consensus and active cooperation of a lasting nature are extremely unlikely. The best that one can hope for are mini 'Bretton Woods' at regional levels. Arrangements of this kind should be easiest to achieve among industrial countries with similar problems and objectives – though the European Union, the most promising candidate for a successful regional grouping, has been demonstrating in recent years the difficulties involved.

The familiar alternative, a global system managed by a dominant economy whose actions have a marked effect on the welfare of other countries, appears to be a thing of the past. No single country currently in existence is in a position to exert such an influence either at present or in the fore-seeable future.

As a result, it is inconceivable that the global economy can be managed now either supranationally (as intended at Bretton Woods) or by a dominant economy (as practised effectively for a time after 1945 by the United States). A truly international currency ('son of bancor') is, therefore, as unlikely as it was 50 years ago; and it is even less realistic to expect a single national currency to fill globally the gap as successfully as sterling did before 1914 and the dollar after 1945. Nevertheless, given the size of the US economy, the dollar is bound to remain a major asset in settling international debts for quite some time, with its relative importance determined by the size and survival of regional blocs.

The existence of a number of major currencies – in a world in which transnational corporations and financial institutions can switch vast funds from currency to currency at short notice – makes return to a global system of fixed exchange rates extremely unlikely in the foreseeable future. As Keynes argued, controls of capital flows are essential for the viability of a global monetary union in a world of independent national currencies. Effective control of transnational enterprises is virtually impossible at a time when so many countries are desperate to attract their capital as well as their technical and managerial expertise. This, in turn, means that a global sys-tem of fixed exchange rates (that is, a global quasi-monetary union) would be unsustainable in the near future.

For all these reasons, the most likely prospect for quite some time is that of growing financial disorder, such as the world economy has been experi-encing since the end of the 1960s. A new Bretton Woods – whatever aspect of the original model or the way that it was applied in practice this repre-sented – is not a practical proposition. But regional groupings, such as the European Union, though very much a second best, are more likely, if organized properly, to enhance global economic welfare than almost two hundred squabbling countries of varying degrees of impotence.

Whether or not regional groupings materialize and survive long enough to provide in the long run a stepping-stone to a truly global system of the kind contemplated at Bretton Woods will depend on the extent to which those forming them respect the guiding principle which prompted that remarkable conference in 1944: that international integration and, ulti-mately, world peace are unsustainable without close collaboration between independent, sovereign states directed towards improvements in economic welfare, widely diffused within and between countries.

11
The End of the Nation State?*

11.1 Introduction

It is generally recognized that international economic links are more extensive now than ever before, making it difficult for individual countries to achieve their economic and social objectives in isolation. It is perfectly rational, therefore, to wonder, as an increasing number of people have been doing in recent years, whether the nation state has reached the end of its useful existence.

The question may be topical, even deserve our urgent attention, but it is not new. Twenty-four centuries ago Aristotle (*Politics*, Book VII) defined the optimum size of a state according to the level of its self-sufficiency. Modern theories of optimum currency, or policy, areas are saying in effect something very similar (Ishiyama 1975, Panić 1988). If this is correct, then in reducing the self-sufficiency of existing states the international division of labour has also made it necessary to examine seriously the possibility of creating larger forms of political organization in order to cope with the economic and social consequences of greater international interdependence.

It is considerations such as these that led Robert Schuman, one of the architects of the post-war European economic integration, to argue in the 1940s that the nation state had become "an anachronism, a nonsense, a heresy" (quoted in Milward 1992, p. 326). Yet more than half a century later, with international economic interdependence far greater than at any time during Schuman's long life, the nation state still remains the most effective form of macroeconomic organization – a fact which, contradictory though it may seem, would not have come as a surprise to Schuman. Although he was convinced that existing nation states were incapable by themselves of improving the economic welfare of their citizens – a view which he shared with many of his contemporaries – Schuman was sufficiently a realist to recognize that "[o]ur European States are a historical reality; it would be impossible to make them disappear" (quoted in Milward 1992, p. 329).

---

* Abridged from *Structural Change and Economic Dynamics*, May 1997, pp. 29–44.

In fact, according to one eminent political scientist, there is an important practical obstacle to developing an alternative, more effective form of political organization in place of the nation state. "Even at its most ideologically pretentious the [human] species has not yet *conceived* a practical form in which to transcend the nation state" (Dunn 1993, p. 66). In other words, the real problem is that even if we wanted to go beyond the nation state we would lack a realistic blueprint for a viable, effective alternative.

In what follows, I shall suggest that there are perfectly rational reasons for our reluctance 'to transcend the nation state'. Successful multinational, multiregional 'nation' states, especially those with federal constitutions, provide a ready-made institutional framework for developing *practical* forms of supranational organization (Panić 1988). The problem is not, therefore, that we lack the blueprint for such a form of organization. The real obstacle to creating it is that we have yet to be convinced that the welfare gains that could be realistically expected within a supranational framework would be equal to, let alone greater than, those that we believe to be attainable nationally.

These issues have assumed considerable practical importance in Europe since 1991 when, at their meeting in Maastricht, members of the European Community committed themselves, effectively, to the objective of an economic, monetary and, ultimately, political union.

11.2   Economic integration and economic sovereignty

The effort needed to establish a successful, lasting, framework of supranational institutions, rules and conventions – capable of conducting macroeconomic policy more effectively than the nation state – is justified only if the level of international economic integration and interdependence is such that existing states find it impossible to achieve their most important economic objectives without the active cooperation of the countries with which they have close economic ties.

It is, of course, indisputable that, whatever the criterion used for historical comparison, the degree of economic interdependence (especially among the industrialized countries) is greater now than during any other period for which relevant data are available.

For instance, measured at constant prices, exports accounted for a much higher percentage of GDP in all industrial countries at the end of the 1980s than in 1870, 1914 or during the intervening period (Maddison 1991). The degree of international specialization and trade is particularly high among the countries of Western Europe and North America. Moreover, a high proportion of imports of manufactures in many sectors consists of intermediate products (see Panić and Vacić 1995). In other words, as foreign products form a significant input in domestic production, levels of economic activity are influenced now by external supply as well as demand conditions. This is, of course, in addition to the dependence of all economies, once they begin to industrialize in earnest, on imports of primary commodities. Some of these, as the energy crises of the 1970s demonstrated, have become of strategic importance for the world economy as a whole (Panić 1988, Part IV).

In the financial sector a combination of deregulation, innovation and massive redistribution of world income in the 1970s and 1980s has resulted in international capital flows whose size easily exceeds the combined foreign exchange reserves of the leading industrial countries. As a result, it has become impossible for these and other economies to pursue independent monetary policies without incurring unacceptably high costs in either inflation or stagnant output and employment. (See Chapters 6 and 9.)

Moreover, the overall figures, although high, almost certainly understate the extent to which key economic decisions are now interrelated at the microeconomic level. The reason for this is that most of them are controlled by transnational corporations (TNCs) operating in two or more countries and therefore basing their corporate strategies on relative developments and prospects in different economies.

The combined effect of TNC activities, in themselves the channel through which international integration takes place, has been, among other things: (a) to decrease the effectiveness of national economic policies and thus the ability of individual countries to achieve important economic and social objectives (Chapter 6, Panić 1991b); (b) to reduce the expected benefits of trade liberalization by preserving price differences in integrated markets (Emerson *et al.* 1988); and (c) to put pressure on countries to harmonize their institutions and policies (UNCTC 1992, p. 45), even when this could clearly be contrary to the interests of those involved.

The changes are obviously far-reaching. But do they add up to an erosion of national economic sovereignty to such an extent that the nation state in its present form, has in effect, lost its *raison d'être*? To answer this question in the affirmative is to imply that the level of international economic interdependence is not only high but also *irreversible*. In other words, the implication is that the countries involved lack the means to retreat into a more autarkic economic existence even if they were convinced that a *lower* degree of international specialization would allow them to achieve and maintain a higher degree of economic welfare in the long run.

However, although there is little doubt that individual countries, especially those in the industrialized world, have progressively lost since the 1950s effective control over their economies, there is no evidence that they have also lost their economic sovereignty. This distinction is important because the meaning of 'sovereignty' in economics is no different from what has been understood by the concept in political theory since the sixteenth century when Bodin, the French political philosopher, defined it as the *supreme* authority to make and enforce laws (Bodin [1575] 1992). More specifically, sovereignty is exercised by that institution which has the power to make and implement decisions that *cannot* be overturned or obstructed by any other institution. What this means in practice is that so long as a country maintains its parliament, armed forces and police there is really nothing, in the absence of war and conquest, that any outside power can do to force it to implement new, or persist with old, policies that it considers to be against its national interest.

The last point cannot be emphasized too strongly. International laws and agreements depend on consent to a far greater extent than the agreements and laws reached and applied within individual countries; and neither rational individuals nor independent sovereign states are likely to consent to something that is clearly going to damage their interests. Hence, the extent to which a state allows a certain degree of intrusion into its national sovereignty depends on the effect that greater involvement in international economic specialization and trade is expected to have on the welfare of its citizens. (See Panić 1996.)

A high and growing level of international integration will be tolerated, therefore, only so long as it clearly demonstrates to those participating in it that the economic benefits of closer links with other countries outweigh those that it could achieve in isolation, or, if this is not the case, that the apparent costs (economic, social and political) of the international division of labour are still lower than those that would be incurred by a retreat into autarky. The moment a continuing deterioration in the ability of individual countries to reconcile their internal and external balances reaches the point at which the costs of integration are judged to be unacceptably high, and there is no satisfactory solution in sight, the pressure for international disintegration may become too strong for any government to resist. That, of course, is exactly what happened in the 1930s. (See Panić and Vacić 1995.)

In other words, international economic treaties and agreements – including those which are regarded as 'irrevocable' – will be observed only as long as they live up to the expectations that brought them about. Otherwise, no matter how long they may have exercised self-restraint in using it, nation states will reassert sovereign authority in order to enable their governments to assume whatever degree of control over their economies is thought to be in the national interest. In the case of countries that play an important role in the world economy, the threat of such action represents a safeguard, ensuring that the rest of the international community does not disregard their interests.

11.3   The problem of achieving and sustaining international economic cooperation

Two important conclusions follow from the analysis above. No responsible national government can disregard for long the unfavourable welfare consequences of international economic integration. At the same time, if necessary, every independent nation state can make full use of its economic sovereignty in order to reduce its links with the rest of the world. It is these two facts that explain why, historically, it has proved so difficult to maintain international economic cooperation over long periods even when it is generally recognized that it is essential if interdependent economies are to achieve their objectives.

There are three ways in which the governments of two or more interdependent economies can cooperate. First, they can exchange important information. This enables them to become aware of each other's problems and preferred courses of action. The snag is that the willingness to exchange information does not commit those doing it to anything else, including measures to minimize the risk of conflict that would make some, or even all of them, worse off. Second, economic cooperation assumes a more active form if each country takes into account the aims and actions of other countries in formulating its own objectives and policies. In this case, general uncertainty is reduced to the extent that they all pursue policies that are mutually consistent. Finally, they can agree on joint action in order to achieve certain common objectives. Such an agreement is, of course, superior to the other two forms of cooperation. However, even in this case, serious uncertainties remain, in the sense that there is always the risk that if the coordination turns out to be disadvantageous to one or more countries they will renege on the original agreement and adopt a policy stance damaging to other nations.

Economic cooperation between states can come to an abrupt halt for several reasons. First, some governments may discover that they have misjudged the relative seriousness of the problems confronting them and consequently have no option but to change the original priorities and policy. The same outcome may also result from a change of government, or from some countries being much more successful in achieving the original aims than the rest. In other words, effective policy coordination is possible only if, or while, the countries which undertake a joint course of action have similar problems and priorities.

Second, countries will not progress very far with the active coordination of policies if they have dissimilar institutional frameworks, making it difficult for them to implement chosen policies with equal effectiveness. The more dissimilar the institutions, the smaller will be the range of policy options that they can pursue jointly.

Third, international cooperation will break down if the agreed policy package is 'incorrect', that is, if it consists of a combination of policy instruments that is incapable of achieving the objectives that the cooperating countries have set themselves.

Fourth, attempts by governments to coordinate their policies will come to an end if, in selecting a particular policy stance, they fail to ensure either that powerful corporate interests support it or, if this is not the case, that those interests are prevented from acting in such a way as to make effective intergovernmental cooperation impossible.

Fifth, as the coordination of specific policies is unlikely to involve *all* economies, it will not last long if countries outside the group are not only hostile to what these economies are doing but, even more important, are also in a position to sabotage their effort for economic or political reasons.

Finally, policy cooperation and coordination will break down if those participating in it are convinced either that it is not beneficial to them or, equally important, that their benefits are noticeably smaller than those enjoyed by other members of the group. Lasting international cooperation is possible only if it enjoys broadly based popular support in the countries involved.

It requires little reflection to realize that if all these problems and pitfalls could be avoided all the time, international coordination of policies would represent the natural order of things. All well-informed, rationally run governments would independently choose economic objectives and policies that were compatible in their intent and execution with those pursued in other countries. There would be no need, therefore, for formal agreements to cooperate, even less for supranational organizations to ensure that their members follow the agreed policies, designed to improve the welfare of all concerned. In such a world the overall effect of actions taken by individual states would not differ in its character, timing, direction and intensity from those actions that would be pursued by a single supranational government (Panić 1988, Part V). The inherent, lasting similarity of the nation states would ensure a high degree of international consensus automatically and thus an appropriate, effective degree of international coordination of policies.

The problem is, of course, that there are significant differences in economic and social conditions, historical traditions, ideological preferences, objectives, institutions and policies even among the highly industrialized capitalist economies which, superficially, appear to be very similar in all these respects. Inevitably, government attitudes and policies, especially in democracies, will reflect such differences, as well as the interests and aspirations of powerful economic groups. Hence, contrary to the rather simplistic view often expressed by economists, not all governments that keep changing their policies and thus find it difficult to fulfil their international obligations are irrational, weak, irresponsible or 'lacking the willpower to pursue correct policies', especially when they are struggling to achieve objectives which enjoy strong popular support.

It has always been the responsibility of governments to act in the national interest. In an interdependent world this can be done successfully only by recognizing and respecting the interests of other nations, a fact that has been recognized by politicians, philosophers and economists for centuries (Machlup 1977). Nevertheless, the inability of nation states to achieve and sustain international cooperation has a long history.

Back in the nineteenth century, attempts by countries to coordinate their trade policies by reducing duties on imports – fairly widespread between

1860 and 1880 – were never made uniformly. Some countries adopted free trade while others continued with protection, with policy in both cases largely determined by levels of industrialization and international competitiveness (Panić 1988, Chapter 8). The differences became even more marked after 1880 when the trend towards trade liberalization in Europe was reversed. This was a deliberate response to the depression of 1873–9, imports of cheap grain from the United States (which caused serious adjustment problems in agriculture and industry) and the need to raise government revenues to help the process of industrialization (Bairoch 1989a, Panić 1988 and 1992). The retreat into protection may have also been influenced by the fact that international income inequalities increased sharply between 1860 and 1880. They were reduced over the following 30 years, indicating that not all countries benefited equally from a more liberal trading regime (Panić 1988, Chapter 10).

Nor was trade the only area in which there were clear limits to the readiness of individual states to break with their mercantilist tradition and policies. For example, a conference was held in 1867 with the aim of introducing 'universal money' in order to assist international trade and travel (Kindleberger 1984, pp. 66–7). Nothing came of this particular initiative, although its objectives were partially realized soon afterwards under the Classical Gold Standard that operated between 1880 and 1914. All countries that adopted the standard had to coordinate closely their monetary and exchange policies. However, quite a few states never tied their currencies to gold and, among those that did, a number went off the standard when they found the cost to be unacceptably high (Bloomfield 1959, Panić 1992).

The breakdown in international cooperation reached its peak in the 1930s when the Great Depression created stabilization and adjustment problems of exceptional severity. The gold standard, restored in the late 1920s by many countries, collapsed in 1931. Instead of coordinating their monetary and exchange rate policies, even leading industrial nations engaged in competitive devaluations in an attempt to gain temporary advantage over other countries (Kenwood and Lougheed 1983, Nurkse 1944). In addition, tariffs were raised and quotas and exchange controls introduced. The extent of protection varied from country to country, depending on the scale of their problems and the authorities' ability to cope with them.

In contrast, there was an unprecedented degree of international cooperation among industrial countries after the Second World War, when most of them were confronted with massive problems of postwar reconstruction and the threat to their economic and political system posed by the Soviet Bloc. Nevertheless, despite pressure from the United States, which provided generous assistance of critical importance to their postwar reconstruction effort, there was a clear limit beyond which the countries of Western Europe were not prepared to cooperate (Panić 1991a).

The 'Bretton Woods System', whose existence was dependent on the coordination of macroeconomic policies by independent nation states, operated for almost a quarter of a century much better than anyone could have expected in the 1940s, although not in the way that the founding fathers intended (see Chapter 10). However, even during this period, countries broke the rules when faced with major economic problems: for example, Canada for several years in the 1950s (when it allowed its currency to float); and the United States in 1971 (when it introduced its 'New Economic Policy', which heralded the end of the System, without either consulting or informing the International Monetary Funds as the Articles of Agreement that the country had ratified in the 1940s required the US government to do).

The attempt by leading industrial countries in December 1971 to revive a more flexible form of the Bretton Woods System, under the Smithsonian Agreement, collapsed within 15 months, as they found it impossible to defend the agreed exchange rate parities without aggravating their internal disequilibria. Moreover, post-war efforts to liberalize world trade were partly reversed after the first oil shock in 1973–4, which caused the worst global recession since the 1930s. More recently, in 1992, confronted with the dilemma of introducing policies that would have created unacceptably high levels of unemployment or abandoning the European Exchange Rate Mechanism, the United Kingdom and Italy opted for the latter. In doing so, they almost destroyed the experiment by members of the European Community of coordinating their monetary and exchange rate policies, something that most of them had been doing fairly successfully since 1979.

Yet even during periods of international economic disintegration there were odd oases of successful cooperation, invariably involving small groups of countries with close trading links and common interests. For example, although the attempt to create 'universal money' in the 1860s failed, a small number of European countries formed the Latin Monetary Union which "worked reasonably well" (Kindleberger 1984, p. 66) between 1865 and 1867. In the 1930s, with economic warfare at its most destructive, some long-standing trade partners tried to safeguard the existing links through bilateral trade arrangements, commodity agreements and regional cooperation (Kenwood and Lougheed 1983, Chapter 13). Finally, it was at the end of the same decade, the 1970s, which had opened with the collapse of the Bretton Woods System that the European Monetary System (EMS) was created. Although conceptually similar to the System agreed at Bretton Woods, it survived through a very turbulent period partly by being much more flexible and partly by consisting of a small number of European countries with close economic ties. In fact, the EMS has done more than 'survive' for over twenty years. In 1999 it was transformed into something much more ambitious than either the Classical Gold Standard or the Bretton Woods System: European Monetary Union, with a single currency and a single central bank.

What all these cases illustrate is the fact that international economic diversity (a) limits the scope for successful cooperation and (b) makes it very difficult to sustain such cooperation over long periods in a dynamic economic environment. It is this same diversity that also explains the difficulties that are traditionally experienced in trying to create effective supranational institutional frameworks.

11.4 Would supranational states do better?

The main purpose of all organizations – economic, social and political – is to coordinate the behaviour of individuals and groups, making it possible for them to achieve goals that would otherwise be beyond their reach. The exact size and form of an organization ought to reflect, therefore, the over-all objective that the individuals and groups comprising it set themselves and the number of those whose participation is required to achieve the objective.

What is true of organizations in general is also true of the state. However, the responsibilities of those running it are much more wide-ranging and complex. They include political, economic and social functions, for the sim-ple reason that the three are closely linked. Thus a democratically elected government is expected these days to protect the life and property of its cit-izens, guarantee their liberty and promote collective action to improve their welfare through the provision of basic necessities such as education, health care, decent housing and unemployment and other benefits. Consequently, whatever their ideological preferences, modern governments find it impos-sible to avoid responsibility for certain aspects of economic activity, since economic failure will undermine internal order and external security – the two basic conditions for the survival of the state as a viable form of politi-cal organization. The reason for this is that persistent failure to satisfy demand for improvements in economic welfare will increase scarcity and therefore a general feeling of deprivation. As a result, the failure will threaten the social status of individuals (through high or rising unemploy-ment), create a sense of insecurity and uncertainty about the future and, since not all groups will be affected equally by these changes, exacerbate social antagonisms and divisions.

To make things worse, in an economically interdependent world these conditions cannot be confined to a single country. Sooner or later, economic failure, and with it social and political instability, will be transmitted from country to country; and, if the existing institutions in all these countries repeatedly fail to find solutions to the problems created by conflicting demands on public resources, influential groups will begin to regard the nation state as an anachronism, incapable of protecting their interests and therefore not worth defending in its existing form. Widespread dissatisfac-tion of this kind, common during the 1930s, was probably as much respon-sible as German military superiority for the rapid military collapse in a number of European countries at the beginning of the Second World War (Milward 1992).

There is, therefore, much more to the argument for economic cooperation and coordination than the mechanics of deciding on appropriate production, employment or inflation targets and then persisting with the 'correct' policies until they produce the desired result. Hence, if the existing nation states find it virtually impossible to meet either or both of these conditions collectively and are too small to do so individually, it becomes essential to consider whether supranational states would be more successful in achieving widely demanded improvements in economic welfare.

There are, at least in theory, three basic macroeconomic functions that a supranational state could perform more effectively.

First, by creating a unified institutional framework at the overall, federal, level it would have a political and administrative apparatus with direct responsibility for reconciling national differences in objectives and policies in a way that was not open to the governments of the same group of countries separately. The main duty of national governments, as those who elect them see it, is to look after the well-being of their country by reconciling the interests of its various constituent groups. What happens in other countries concerns them only to the extent that it significantly affects, or is likely to affect, *their* national interest. Even then, short of war and conquest, they have no direct means of influencing events outside their borders. This changes the moment they form an economic and political union, as the supranational authorities now assume both the responsibility to reconcile the diverse national interests in order to advance the common good *and* the instruments of power to achieve this.

Second, as a result of these constitutional changes, supranational authorities would be able to persist with a specific macroeconomic policy stance for as long as it was required to achieve particular objectives. Deprived of its sovereign powers, no national group within such a state would be in the position to break ranks and introduce policies that would be to its advantage, disregarding the interests of the other groups.

Finally, the supranational state would be able – by using its powers to introduce and enforce laws – to alter institutions, rules and conventions in such a way as to promote the general welfare rather than the interests of a particular national group.

These arguments look convincing except for one major problem: *ex ante*, it is impossible to provide the firm evidence needed to convince the citizens of individual nation states that they would be better off within a supranational economic and political union. In fact, it is even difficult to show empirically that coordination of national economic policies is of more than a marginal advantage to the countries that engage in it (McKibbin and Sachs 1991). In the absence of such evidence, *a priori* reasoning can be used to advance equally convincing arguments for and against a supranational state.

It all depends, in the end, on how far the countries creating such a state are able, collectively, to solve a number of problems so as to make stabilization and adjustment policies within a larger union *significantly* more effective than they are at the national level. Past experience shows that particularly important in this respect is the ability to exercise economic sovereignty without incurring unacceptable welfare costs. To do this effectively, the supranational state should be able to create an efficient macroeconomic institutional framework, to mobilize consensus for a specific course of action and thus implement appropriate policies, and, lastly, to attract people of high calibre to run supranational institutions. (See Chapter 3.)

One way to examine the problems likely to arise in each of these cases, adopted in the rest of this section, is to analyse the conditions that have to be met and the reasons why this is difficult to achieve in practice. To illustrate the latter, a few examples of attitudes and preferences within the European Union will be used. Reactions within these countries are instructive because the European Community represents the most successful experiment in international economic integration ever attempted by a group of independent, sovereign states. Moreover, economically, socially, politically and culturally they appear to be more similar than almost any other group of countries in the world.

The ability of a state to exercise its *economic sovereignty* will depend on three things: political independence, size and degree of openness. A supranational state will obviously be larger than the national units comprising it and, consequently, considerably more self-sufficient. As a result, the authorities of such a state will be in a much better position to pursue particular objectives and policies than their smaller, national, counterparts. Moreover, supranational state can reinforce its economic independence relatively easily through trade barriers. It is relatively easy for this type of state to be highly protectionist to enable its firms to benefit fully from the economies of scale made possible by a large, unified market. As it is less dependent on foreign trade than other countries, it is not under the same pressure as smaller states to offer access to its market to foreign producers in order to encourage their governments to provide similar privileges to its exporters. This is one of the reasons why, for instance, the United States has been traditionally more protectionist than other industrial countries (see Chapter 5). What is more, given its size and resources, a supranational state will have considerable bargaining power in international economic negotiations. All this would enhance even more the ability of such a state to exercise its economic sovereignty.

In principle, economic independence should increase political independence, which in turn should make the exercise of economic sovereignty even easier. It should be much more difficult to force a large supranational state to alter its objectives and policies than a small nation state, and so far as outside pressure is concerned, this is no doubt true. However, internally, various constitutional limitations placed on supranational institutions by member states may seriously reduce the effectiveness of these institutions. The greater the differences in problems and priorities between the regions and nations of a supranational state, the more likely this is to happen, as those forming the state will lack confidence in the overall, federal, institutions to look after their interests. If the citizens of a democratic nation state are dissatisfied with their own institutions and political leaders, they are likely to trust even less those running a large political entity over whom they have considerably less control.

This could prove to be for many years a major obstacle to the creation of an effective supranational framework of institutions in the European Union. Surveys of public opinion in member countries show that, with one or two exceptions, most people are dissatisfied with the way that the Union is run (Waller 1995). The fact that many of them believe that their country is contributing most to the Community while benefiting least (Hewstone 1986, pp. 130–2) is probably the main reason for this dissatisfaction.

There are also considerable practical difficulties in creating an effective supranational *institutional framework*, even within such a relatively homogeneous group of countries as those forming the European Union. It may not be easy to reconcile the German preference for a loose federal structure with the highly centralized traditions of countries such as France and the United Kingdom.

Given these differences, how independent from political control will the European Central Bank really be? How effective will it be in discharging its responsibility for anti-inflationary policies when there are clearly important divisions of opinion between member countries as to what their citizens (a) expect from governments (Taylor-Gooby 1993) and (b) think about the power that government should have to realize these expectations (Johnston 1993)? To complicate matters further, there are clear disagreements concerning the need for a European monetary union between the business leaders, who even in the United Kingdom are in favour (Andersen Consulting 1995), and the population at large, which is in most of the countries strongly against the idea (Waller 1995).

More generally, there seem also to be important ideological divisions in Western Europe, reflected in the attitude towards public and private ownership. Surprisingly, they appear to be in evidence both within the business community (Harris Research 1994) and within the wider population (Taylor-Gooby 1993). In a democratic political system, divisions of this kind are bound to have a major influence on the nature and effectiveness of supranational institutions.

The organization and character of these institutions are also important for the success and survival of a supranational state because of another potentially contentious issue that those setting it up have to resolve. Although most nation states are clearly too small now to pursue effective macroeconomic policies, they are, in most cases, too large to respond quickly and adequately to the adjustment problems that arise at industry and regional levels. It is essential, therefore, to decentralize the decision-making process by delegating more responsibility and power to regional authorities. They are better placed to formulate and implement microeconomic policies appropriate to their areas of the country.

Supranational institutions and governments would be at an even greater disadvantage in this respect than their counterparts at the level of nation states because of the size of such a state and, consequently, their more limited knowledge of regional conditions and needs. The creation of a supranational state is bound for this reason to increase the power of regional authorities by giving them a wider range of responsibilities for their region. As a result, whatever is left of the nation state will be emasculated further and, in the long run, squeezed out of existence. Whether the citizens and various powerful groups of the existing nation states are prepared to allow the demise of the one institution on which they rely to protect their interests, especially when in difficulties, will depend on how confident they are that the new supranational and regional institutions will promote and defend their interests effectively, both within and outside the superstate. This will be particularly relevant in those cases where the regions have strong *national* identities.

In other words, the extent to which such a state proves to be a better form of political organization than the nation states that form it will depend ultimately on the degree of *consensus* for key economic and other priorities and policies. Enough has already been said in the preceding analysis to suggest that this may be far more difficult to achieve within a supranational state, as the differences in efficiency and income levels, needs and resources are bound to be greater.

Hence, if a 'harmony of interests' and consensus are difficult to achieve nationally, they are likely to prove even more elusive internationally. Take, for instance, a major policy issue such as unemployment. There are important differences in the support for higher government spending to create more jobs between European countries and the United States and Australia, between individual European countries and between the two recently united parts of Germany (Johnston 1993). Even business leaders from these countries are divided. Those in Belgium, the Netherlands, Spain and France are in favour of the European Union giving a high priority to reducing unemployment, in contrast to their counterparts in Germany and the United Kingdom, who attach a low priority to this policy objective (Harris Research 1994). Similar divisions of opinion also emerge when people in different countries are asked about the economic and social responsibilities that ought to be discharged by the state. There is much stronger support in the United Kingdom, Italy and Ireland than in West Germany for the idea that the state should provide health care, decent pensions, housing, unemployment benefits and assistance for industrial adjustment, as well as pursue policies which reduce income inequalities. However, as in the case of unemployment, East Germans appear to disagree significantly with their countrymen in the West (Taylor-Gooby 1993).

What international surveys of the kind quoted here seem to indicate is that "there is no clear trend towards [international] ideological convergence, even within the EC" (Taylor-Gooby 1993, p. 99). This is bound to make the task of those running a supranational state extremely difficult. The greater the economic and social differences among the countries forming a supra-national state, the harder it is to achieve a consensus on resource transfers. Yet the transfers are essential to reduce the inequalities and create a unity of interests and purpose without which such a state could not survive (Panić 1992). Failure to do this is likely either to lead to large-scale labour migra-tion or, if this is not possible, to exacerbate the existing problems, possibly to an extent that can be easily translated into political conflicts and, eventually, a break-up of the state.

With such ideological and practical differences in economic and social pri-orities and expectations concerning the role of the state, it becomes virtu-ally impossible to mobilize consensus in support of effective, sustainable *economic policies*. The disagreements will intensify in conditions of economic stagnation and rising unemployment or an accelerating rate of inflation – all of which will affect different individuals, sectors and regions differently.

Persistent economic failure tends to increase income disparities (especially if the better-off groups refuse to pay higher taxes to finance increases in pub-lic expenditure) and to contribute to the growth of crime and the incidence of various illnesses, with the result that public discontent will spread. Hence, as differences in economic performance, efficiency and income levels are likely to be significantly greater within a supranational state than within the nation states comprising it, the authorities of such a state may turn out to be less, rather than more, successful in pursuing appropriate economic policies than were the national governments before unification (Hicks 1978, Panić 1992).

Finally, in addition to the factors described above, the success of a state in achieving its major objectives depends also on the *administrative and politi-cal competence* of those running it. In theory, this should work in favour of a supranational state, as it would have a larger pool of talent from which to choose its political leaders and administrators. In practice, the result may be quite different, especially if there is a diversity of nationalities, religions or races.

To avoid accusations of bias and to maintain a 'correct' mix of represen-tatives of such groups at the federal level, many people may come to occupy key positions in a supranational state on the basis of criteria other than abil-ity. (Similar problems arise also in many multinational 'nation' states, but the diversity of nationalities, etc. is likely to be greater in a supranational state.) Even then, it may be difficult to avoid accusations of favouritism, dis-crimination and unfair treatment of different groups if the states, regions or national groups that benefit most from certain policies happen to be those whose representatives are responsible for these policies at the federal level.

Alternatively, if the outcome turns out to be exactly the opposite, the representatives will be branded 'traitors' by the regions or groups that they represent and will be accused of 'selling out' to the other groups. As, in the absence of perfect economic and social equality, it is inevitable that some regions and groups will benefit more from any one policy decision than others, persistent or, even worse, growing economic and other inequalities will sooner or later be exploited for political purposes. The work of populists and demagogues will be made easier by the fact that, for historical reasons, different national groups tend to be concentrated in different regions of a country. Failure to redress such grievances may eventually lead to the economic and political disintegration of the state.

11.5   Conclusion

For all these reasons, it seems very unlikely at present that the nation state will be superseded in the near future by a supranational state, either in Europe (where the logic of trying to achieve even higher levels of economic interdependence increasingly requires such a change) or anywhere else. Moreover, even if a supranational state is created, the prevailing conditions do not appear to favour its long-term survival – unless those creating it can overcome the kind of problems described in the previous section.

It is relatively easy to develop theoretical models 'proving' that supranational states would be closer to the ideal of an 'optimum policy area' than the existing nation states. However, as the analysis in this chapter has shown, there are serious practical problems that need to be solved if they are to be viable. The great diversity in economic performance, efficiency and income levels, ideological preferences, historical traditions and institutions between countries and regions, that makes international cooperation so difficult to sustain, would, given its size, become even more intractable in a supranational state. It is hardly surprising, therefore, that there is such reluctance in most countries in Western Europe to abandon the existing nation state, despite the fact that if the European Monetary Union is to last the creation of a supranational political authority is unavoidable. In fact, if globalization, in the sense of close economic and cultural ties between countries around the world, is to survive more and more countries will be faced with exactly the same dilemma in the future.

Bibliography

Acheson, D. G. (1969) *Present at the Creation: My Years at the State Department* (New York: Norton).

Aghion, P., Caroli, E. and Garcia-Penalosa, C. (1999) 'Inequality and Economic Growth: The Perspective of the New Growth Theories', *Journal of Economic Literature*, December.

Akyüz, Y. (1993) 'Financial Liberalisation: The Key Issues', in Y. Akyüz and G. Held (eds), *Finance and the Real Economy* (Santiago, Chile: S.R.V. Impress).

Aldcroft, D. H. and Morewood, S. (1995) *Economic Change in Eastern Europe since 1918* (Aldershot: Edward Elgar).

Alesina, A. and Perotti, R. (1996) 'Income Distribution, Political Instability and Investment', *European Economic Review*, June.

Amsden, A. H. (1993) 'East Asian Financial Markets: Why So Much (and Fairly Effective) Government Intervention?', in Y. Akyüz and G. Held (eds), *Finance and the Real Economy* (Santiago, Chile: S.R.V. Impress).

Andersen Consulting (1995) *The Impact of European Economic and Monetary Union on UK Industry* (London: Arthur Andersen).

Anderson, J. E. (1972) 'Effective Protection in the US: A Historical Comparison', *Journal of International Economics*, February.

Anderson, K. and Baldwin, R. E. (1987) 'The Political Market for Protection in Industrial Countries', in A. El-Agra (ed.), *Protection, Co-operation, Integration and Development* (London: Macmillan).

Angell, N. (1912) *The Great Illusion* (London: Heinemann).

Anjaria, S. J., Iqbal, A., Perez, I. L. and Tseng, W. S. (1981) 'Trade Policy Developments in Industrial Countries', *IMF Occasional Paper No. 5* (Washington, DC: IMF).

Armstrong, H. and Taylor, J. (1985) *Regional Economic Policy* (London: Philip Alan).

Artus, J. R. and Knight, M. D. (1984) 'Issues in the Assessment of Exchange Rates of Industrial Countries', *IMF Occasional Paper No. 29* (Washington, DC: IMF).

Artus, J. R. and Young, J. H. (1979) 'Fixed and Flexible Exchange Rates: A Renewal of the Debate', *IMF Staff Papers*, December.

Atkinson, A. B. (ed.) (1973) *Wealth, Income and Inequality* (Harmondsworth: Penguin).

Atkinson, A. B. (1975) *The Economics of Inequality* (Oxford: Clarendon Press).

Atkinson, A. B. (1999) 'Is Rising Inequality Inevitable? A Critique of the Transatlantic Consensus', *WIDER Annual Lecture No. 3* (Helsinki: UNU/WIDER).

Atkinson, A. B. (2002) 'Globalization and the European Welfare State at the Opening and the Closing of the Twentieth Century', in H. Kierzkowski (ed.), *From Europeanization of the Globe to the Globalization of Europe* (London: Palgrave Macmillan).

Atkinson, A. B. and Micklewright, J. (1992) *Economic Transformation in Eastern Europe and the Distribution of Income* (Cambridge: Cambridge University Press).

Atkinson, A. B. and Stiglitz, J. E. (1980) *Lectures on Public Economics* (Singapore: McGraw-Hill).

Atkinson, A. B., Rainwater, L. and Smeeding, T. M. (1995) *Income Distribution in OECD Countries: Evidence from the Luxembourg Income Study* (Paris: OECD).

Bairoch, P. (1976a) 'Europe's Gross National Product: 1800–1975', *Journal of European Economic History*, Fall.

Bairoch, P. (1976b) *Commerce Extérieur et Développement Economique de l'Europe au XIX Siècle* (Paris: Ecole des Hautes Etudes en Sciences Sociales).

Bairoch, P. (1981) 'The Main Trends in National Economic Disparities since the Industrial Revolution', in P. Bairoch and M. Levy-Leboyer (eds), *Disparities in Economic Development since the Industrial Revolution* (London: Macmillan).

Bairoch, P. (1982) 'International Industrialisation Levels from 1750 to 1980', *Journal of European Economic History*, Spring.

Bairoch, P. (1989a) 'European Trade Policy, 1815–1914', in P. Mathias and S. Pollard (eds), *The Cambridge Economic History of Europe. Vol. VIII. The Industrial Economies – The Development of Economic and Social Policies* (Cambridge: Cambridge University Press).

Bairoch, P. (1989b) 'The Paradoxes of Economic History', *European Economic Review*, vol. 33.

Bairoch, P. (1993) *Economic and World History* (Brighton: Wheatsheaf).

Bairoch, P. and Kozul-Wright, R. (1998) 'Globalisation Myths: Some Historical Reflections on Integration, Industrialisation and Growth in the World Economy', in R. Kozul-Wright and R. Rowthorn (eds), *Transnational Corporations and the Global Economy* (London and New York: Macmillan and St. Martin's Press).

Balassa, B. (1965) 'Tariff Protection in Industrial Countries – An Evaluation', *Journal of Political Economy*, December.

Balassa, B. (1967) *Trade Liberalisation among Industrial Countries* (New York: McGraw-Hill).

Balassa, B. (1975) 'Trade Protection and Domestic Production – A Comment', in P. B. Kenen (ed.), *International Trade and Finance – Frontiers for Research* (Cambridge: Cambridge University Press).

Balassa, B., Barsony, A. and Richards, A. (1981) *The Balance of Payments Effects of External Shocks and of Policy Response to These Shocks* (Paris: OECD).

Bank for International Settlements (BIS) (1979) *49th Annual Report* (Basle: BIS).

Bank for International Settlements (BIS) (1986) *Recent Innovations in International Banking* (Basle: BIS).

Bank for International Settlements (BIS) (1996) *66th Annual Report* (Basle: BIS).

Basle Committee on Banking Supervision (1999) *A New Capital Adequacy Framework – A Consultative Paper* (Basle: BCBS).

Bator, F. (1958) 'The Anatomy of Market Failure', *Quarterly Journal of Economics*, August.

Berle, A. A. and Means, G. C. (1932) *The Modern Corporation and Private Property* (New York: Macmillan).

Berlin, I. (1969) 'Two Concepts of Liberty', in I. Berlin, *Four Essays on Liberty* (Oxford: Oxford University Press).

Bertola, G. (1993) 'Models of Economic Integration and Localised Growth', in F. Torres and F. Giavassi (eds), *Adjustment and Growth in European Monetary Union* (Cambridge: Cambridge University Press).

Bhagwati, J. (1989) 'Is Free Trade Passé After All?', *Weltwirtschaftliches Archiv*, band 125.

Bloomfield, A. I. (1959) *Monetary Policy Under the International Gold Standard: 1880–1914* (New York: Federal Reserve Bank of New York).

Bloomfield, A. I. (1963) 'Short-Term Capital Movements under the Pre-1914 Gold Standard', *Princeton Studies in International Finance* (Princeton, NJ: Princeton University Press).

Bloomfield, A. I. (1968) 'Patterns of Fluctuations in International Investment Before 1914', *Princeton Studies in International Finance* (Princeton, NJ: Princeton University Press).

Bodin, J. ([1575]1992) *On Sovereignty: Four Chapters from the Six Books of the Commonwealth* (Cambridge: Cambridge University Press).

Boltho, A. (ed.) (1982) *The European Economy – Growth and Crisis* (Oxford: Oxford University Press).

Bourguignon, F. and Morrisson, C. (1999) 'The Size Distribution of Income Among World Citizens: 1820–1990', mimeo, June.

Brander, J. A. and Spencer, B. A. (1983) 'International R&D Rivalry and Industrial Strategy', *Review of Economic Studies*, vol. 50.

Brander, J. A. and Spencer, B. A. (1985) 'Export Subsidies and International Market Share Rivalry', *Journal of International Economics*, vol. 18.

Brebner, J. B. (1962) 'Laissez-Faire and State Intervention in Nineteenth Century Britain', in E. M. Carus-Wilson (ed.), *Essays in Economic History*, vol. iii (London: Edward Arnold).

Brown, R. N., Enoch, C. A. and Mortimer-Lee, P. D. (1980) 'The Relationship between Costs and Prices in the United Kingdom', *Bank of England Discussion Paper No. 8* (London: Bank of England).

Buckley, P. J. (1985) 'A Critical View of Theories of the Multinational Enterprise', in M. Casson (ed.), *The Economic Theory of the Multinational Enterprise* (London: Macmillan).

Burchell, B. (1992) 'Changes in the Labour Market and the Psychological Health of the Nation', in J. Michie (ed.), *The Economic Legacy 1979–1992* (London: Academic Press).

Cain, P. J. and Hopkins, A. G. (1980) 'The Political Economy of British Expansion Overseas, 1750–1914', *Economic History Review*, November.

Cairncross, A. (1985) *Years of Recovery – British Economic Policy 1945–51* (London: Methuen).

Capie, F. (1983) 'Tariff Protection and Economic Performance in the Nineteenth Century', in J. Black and A. L. Winters (eds), *Policy and Performance in International Trade* (London: Macmillan).

Casson, M. C. (ed.) (1986) *Multinationals and World Trade* (London: Allen and Unwin).

Cecchini, P. (1988) *The European Challenge 1992 – The Benefits of a Single Market* (Aldershot: Wildwood House).

Chandler, A. D. (1962) *Strategy and Structure: Chapters in the History of the Industrial Enterprise* (Cambridge, Mass.: MIT Press).

Chandler, A. D. (1977) *The Visible Hand: The Managerial Revolution in American Business* (Cambridge, Mass.: Belknap Press of Harvard University Press).

Chang, H. J. (2002) *Kicking Away the Ladder – Policies and Institutions for Economic Development in Historical Perspective* (London: Anthem Press).

Chang, H. J., Park, H. J. and Chul, G. Y. (1998) 'Interpreting the Korean Crisis: Financial Liberalisation, Industrial Policy and Corporate Governance', *Cambridge Journal of Economics*, November.

Cheh, J. H. (1974) 'United States Concessions in the Kennedy Round and Short-run Labour Adjustment Costs', *Journal of International Economics*, vol. 4.

Chenery, H. B., Robinson, S. and Sirquin, M. (1986) *Industrialisation and Growth – A Comparative Study* (Washington, DC: World Bank).

Chester, D. N. (1951) 'The Central Machinery for Economic Policy', in D. N. Chester (ed.), *Lessons of the British War Economy* (Cambridge: Cambridge University Press).

Clapham, C. (ed.) (1982) *Private Patronage and Public Power* (London: Frances Pinter).

Clark, I. (1997) *Globalization and Fragmentation – International Relations in the Twentieth Century* (Oxford: Oxford University Press).

Cline, W. R. and ASSOCIATES (1981) *World Inflation and the Developing Countries* (Washington, DC: The Brookings Institution).

Coase, R. H. (1937) 'The Nature of the Firm', *Economica*, November.

Cohen, S. S. (1969) *Modern Capitalist Planning – The French Model* (Cambridge, Mass.: Harvard University Press).

Corbett, J. (1987) 'International Perspectives on Financing: Evidence from Japan', *Oxford Review of Economic Policy*, Winter.

Corbett, J. (1990) 'Policy Issues in the Design of Banking and Financial Systems for Industrial Finance', *European Economy*, March.

Corden, W. M. (1975) 'The Costs and Consequences of Protection: A Survey of Empirical Work', in P. B. Kenen (ed.), *International Trade and Finance – Frontiers for Research* (Cambridge: Cambridge University Press).

Corden, W. M. (1982) 'Exchange Rate Protection', in R. N. Cooper, P. B. Kenen, J. B. de Macedo and J. van Ypersele (eds), *The International Monetary System under Flexible Exchange Rates* (Cambridge, Mass.: Ballinger).

Cornish, W. R. (1999) *Intellectual Property: Patents, Copyright, Trade Marks, and Allied Rights*, 4th edn (London: Sweet and Maxwell).

Cosh, A., Hughes, A. and Singh, A. (1990) *Takeovers and Short-termism in the U.K.: Analytical and Policy Issues in the U.K. Economy* (London: Institute for Public Policy Research).

Davis, D. R. (1998a) 'Does European Unemployment Prop Up American Wages? National Labour Markets and Global Trade', *American Economic Review*, June.

Davis, D. R. (1998b) 'Technology, Unemployment and Relative Wages in a Global Economy', *European Economic Review*, November.

Davis, L. and Legler, J. (1966) 'The Government in the American Economy 1815–1902: A Quantitative Study', *Journal of Economic History*, December.

Davis, L. A. and North, D. C. (1971) *Institutional Change and American Economic Growth* (Cambridge: Cambridge University Press).

Deane, P. (1965) *The First Industrial Revolution* (Cambridge: Cambridge University Press).

De Juan, A. (1996) 'The Roots of Banking Crises: Microeconomic Issues and Regulation and Supervision', in R. Housman and L. Rojas-Suarez (eds), *Banking Crises in Latin America* (Washington, DC: Inter-American Development Bank and John Hopkins University Press).

Dell, S. S. and Lawrence, R. (1980) *The Balance of Payments Adjustment Process in Developing Countries* (New York: Pergamon Press).

Deraniyagala, S. and Fine, B. (2001) 'New Trade Theory versus Old Trade Policy', *Cambridge Journal of Economics*, November.

Diaz-Alejandro, C. F. (1975) 'Trade Policies and Economic Development', in P. B. Kenen (ed.), *International Trade and Finance – Frontiers for Research* (Cambridge: Cambridge University Press).

Dod, P. D. (1981) 'Bank Lending to Developing Countries', *Federal Reserve Bulletin*, September.

Dollar, D. and Svensson, J. (2000) 'What Explains the Success or Failure of Structural Adjustment Programmes', *Economic Journal*, October.

Dore, R. (1986) *Structural Adjustment in Japan 1970–82* (Geneva: International Labour Office).

Dowrick, S. and Nguyen, D. (1989) 'OECD Comparative Economic Growth 1950–1985: Catch-up and Convergence', *American Economic Review*, December.

Dunn, J. (1993) *Western Political Theory in the Face of the Future* (Cambridge: Cambridge University Press).

Dunning, J. H. (1981) *International Production and the Multinational Enterprise* (London: Allen and Unwin).

Dunning, J. H. (1992) *Multinational Enterprise and the Global Economy* (Wokingham: Addison-Wesley).

Dunning, J. H. and Morgan, E. J. (1980) 'Employee Compensation in US Multinationals and Indigenous Firms: An Exploratory Micro/Macro Analysis', *British Journal of Industrial Relations*, July.

Easterlin, R. A. (2001) 'Income and Happiness: Towards a Unified Theory', *Economic Journal*, July.

EBRD (1999) *Transition Report 1999 – Ten Years of Transition* (London: European Bank for Reconstruction and Development).

Eckes, A. (1975) *A Search for Solvency – Bretton Woods and the International Monetary System, 1941–1971* (Austin, Texas: University of Texas Press).

Eichengreen, B. (1992) *Golden Fetters: The Gold Standard and the Great Depression, 1919–1939* (Oxford: Oxford University Press).

Einaudi, M., Bye, M. and Rosi, E. (1955) *Nationalisation in France and Italy* (Ithaca, NY: Cornell University Press).

Eiteman, D. K. and Stonehill, A. I. (1989) *Multinational Business Finance*, 5th edn (Reading, Mass.: Addison-Wesley).

Emerson, M., Aujean, M., Catinat, M., Goybet, P. and Jacquemin, A. (1988) *The Economics of 1992* (Oxford: Oxford University Press).

Enoch, C. A. and Panić, M. (1981) 'Commodity Prices in the 1970s', *Bank of England Quarterly Bulletin*, March.

Epstein, B. and Newfarmer, S. (1982) 'Imperfect International Markets and Monopolistic Prices to Developing Countries', *Cambridge Journal of Economics*, March.

Erickson, R. E. (1983) 'A Difficulty with the 'Command' Allocation Mechanism', *Journal of Economic Theory*, October.

Ethier, W. J. (1986) 'The Multinational Firm', *Quarterly Journal of Economics*, November.

European Commission (1977) *Report of the Study Group on the Role of the Public Finance in European Integration*, 2 vols (Brussels: European Commission).

European Commission (1991) 'Fair Competition in the Internal Market: Community State Aid Policy', *European Economy*, September.

European Council (1992) *Treaty on European Union* ('The Maastricht Treaty') (Luxembourg: Office for Official Publications).

Feldstein, M. (1998) 'Refocusing the IMF', *Foreign Affairs*, March/April.

Field, S. (1990) *Trends in Crime and their Interpretation* (London: HMSO).

Fieldhouse, D. K. (1981) *Colonialism 1870–1945* (London: Weidenfeld & Nicolson).

Foster, R. and Kaplan, S. (2001) *Creative Destruction* (London: Prentice-Hall).

Frey, B. S. and Stutzer, R. (2000) 'Happiness, Economy and Institutions', *Economic Journal*, October.

Frieden, J. A. (1991) 'Invested Interests: The Politics of National Economic Policies in a World of Global Finance', *International Organisation*, Autumn.

Friedman, M. (1962) *Capitalism and Freedom* (Chicago, Ill.: Chicago University Press).

Gardner, R. N. (1980) *Sterling–Dollar Diplomacy in Current Perspective: The Origins and Prospects of Our International Economic Order* (New York: Columbia University Press).

Gellner, E. (1998) *Nationalism* (London: Phoenix).

Gerschenkron, A. (1966) *Economic Backwardness in Historical Perspective* (Cambridge, Mass.: Belknap Press of Harvard University Press).

Giddens, A. (1998) *The Third Way – The Renewal of Social Democracy* (Cambridge: Polity Press).

Glejser, P. (1972) 'Empirical Evidence on Comparative Cost Theory from the European Common Market Experience', *European Economic Review*, vol. 3.

Goldsbrough, D. J. (1981) 'International Trade of Multinational Corporations and its Responsiveness to Changes in Aggregate Demand and Relative Prices', *IMF Staff Papers*, September.

Goldsmith, A. A. (1995) 'The State, the Market and Economic Development: A Second Look at Adam Smith in Theory and Practice', *Development and Change*, vol. 26.

Goldstein, J. (1993) *Ideas, Interests and American Trade Policy* (Ithaca, NY, and London: Cornell University Press).

Goldstein, M. (1980) 'Have Flexible Exchange Rates Handicapped Macroeconomic Policy?', *Princeton Papers on International Finance*, June.

Goldstein, M. (1997) *The Case for an International Banking Standard* (Washington, DC: Institute for International Economics).

Goldstein, M. and Khan, M. S. (1982) 'Effects of Slowdown in Industrial Countries on Growth in Non-Oil Developing Countries', *IMF Occasional Paper No. 12* (Washington, DC: IMF).

Gomes, L. (1993) *The International Adjustment Mechanism – From the Gold Standard to the EMS* (London: Macmillan).

Goodhart, C. (1998) 'Financial Globalisation, Derivatives, Volatility and the Challenge for the Policies of Central Banks', in C. A. E. Goodhart (ed.), *The Emerging Framework of Financial Regulation* (London: Central Banking Publication).

Goodhart, C., Hartmann, P., Llewellyn, D. and Rojas-Suarez, L. (1998) *Financial Regulation – Why, How and Where Now?* (London: Routledge).

Goodin, R. E., Heady, B., Muffels, R. and Dirven, H. J. (1999) *The Real Worlds of Welfare Capitalism* (Cambridge: Cambridge University Press).

Gordon, S. (1991) *The History and Philosophy of Social Science* (London: Routledge).

Gray, J. (1999) *False Dawn – The Delusions of Global Capitalism* (London: Granta).

Grossman, G. M. and Helpman, E. (1991) *Innovation and Growth in the Global Economy* (Cambridge, Mass.: MIT Press).

Grossman, G. M. and Helpman, E. (1994) 'Endogenous Innovation and the Theory of Growth', *Journal of Economic Perspectives*, Winter.

Grubel, H. and Johnson, H. G. (1971) *Effective Tariff Protection* (Geneva: GATT and Graduate Institute of International Studies).

Hahn, J. H. (1998) 'Financial System Restructuring in Korea: the Crisis and Its Resolution', *KDI Working Paper No. 9802* (Seoul: Korea Development Institute).

Halevi, N. (1971) 'An Empirical Test of the 'Balance of Payments Stages' Hypothesis', *Journal of International Economics*, vol. 1.

Halm, G. N. (1968) *Economic Systems*, 3rd edn (New York: Holt, Reinhart & Winston).

Hamilton, A. ([1791]1934) 'A Report on Manufactures', in S. McKee (ed.), *Papers on Public Credit, Commerce and Finance* (New York: Columbia University Press).

Hare, P. J. (1990) 'From Central Planning to Market: Some Microeconomic Issues', *Economic Journal*, June.

Harris Research (1994) *Can European Business Compete in Global Markets* (London: Harris Research Centre).

Havrylyshyn, O. and Wolf, M. (1981) 'Trade among Developing Countries: Theory, Policy Issues and Principal Trends', *World Bank Staff Working Paper No.479* (Washington, DC: World Bank).

Hayes, R. H. and Abernathy, W. J. (1980) 'Managing Our Way to Economic Decline', *Harvard Business Review*, July–August.

Heckscher, E. ([1919]1949) 'The Effect of Foreign Trade on the Distribution of Income', in A.E.A., *Readings in the Theory of International Trade* (Philadelphia: Blackiston).

Hefleblower, R. B. (1960) 'Observations on Decentralisation in Large Enterprises', *Journal of Industrial Economics*, November.

Helleiner, K. F. (1973) *Free Trade and Frustration: Anglo-Austrian Negotiations, 1860–1870* (Toronto: Toronto University Press).

Helm, D. (1986) 'The Assessment of the Economic Borders of the State', *Oxford Review of Economic Policy*. Summer.

Helm, D. (ed.) (1990) *The Economic Borders of the State* (Oxford: Oxford University Press).

Helpman, E. and Krugman, P. R. (1985) *Market Structure and Foreign Trade* (Brighton: Wheatsheaf).

Henderson, H. D. (1955) *The Interwar Years and Other Papers* (Oxford: Clarendon Press).

Hewstone, M. (1986) *Understanding Attitudes to the European Community: A Social–Psychological Study in Four Member Countries* (Cambridge: Cambridge University Press).

Hicks, U. (1978) *Federalism: Failure and Success – A Comparative Study* (London: Macmillan).

Hipple, F. S. (1990) 'The Measurement of International Trade Related to Multinational Companies', *American Economic Review*, December.

Hirschman, A. O. (1982) *Shifting Involvements – Private Interest and Public Action* (Princeton, NJ: Princeton University Press).

Hirst, P. and Thompson, G. (1996) *Globalization in Question* (Cambridge: Polity Press).

Hobsbawm, E. J. (1977) *The Age of Capital* (London: Weidenfeld & Nicolson).

Honohan, P. (1996) 'Financial System Failures in Developing Countries: Diagnosis and Perspectives', unpublished manuscript (Washington, DC: International Monetary Fund).

Horne, J. (1983) 'The Asset Market Model of the Balance of Payments and the Exchange Rate: A Survey of Empirical Evidence', *Journal of International Money and Finance*, vol. 2.

Huntington, P. S. (1997) *The Clash of Civilisations and Remaking of the World Order* (London: Simon & Schuster).

IMF (1981) 'External Indebtedness of Developing Countries', *Occasional Paper No. 3* (Washington, DC: IMF).

IMF (1982) *International Capital Markets* (Washington, DC: IMF).

IMF (1983) 'World Economic Outlook', *Occasional Paper No. 14* (Washington, DC: IMF).

IMF (1984) 'Exchange Rate Volatility and World Trade', *Occasional Paper No. 28* (Washington, DC: IMF).

IMF (1988) *World Economic Outlook* (Washington, DC: IMF).

IMF (1997) *World Economic Outlook* (Washington, DC: IMF).

Inman, R. (1987) 'Market, Government and the 'New' Political Economy', in A. J. Auerbach and M. Feldstein (eds), *Handbook of Public Economics*, vol. 2 (Amsterdam: North-Holland).

International Labour Office (1972) *The Cost of Social Security – Seventh International Inquiry, 1964–1966* (Geneva: ILO).

Isard, P. (1977) 'How Far Can We Push the 'Law of One Price'?', *American Economic Review*, December.

Ishiyama, Y. (1975) 'The Theory of Optimum Currency Areas: A Survey', *IMF Staff Papers*, July.

Johnston, M. (1993) 'Disengaging from Democracy', *International Attitudes – 10th BSA Report* (Aldershot: Dartmouth).

Jones, C. I. (1997) 'On the Evolution of the World Income Distribution', *Journal of Economic Perspectives*, Summer.

Kahneman, D. and Tversky, A. (1979) 'Prospect Theory: An Analysis of Decision under Risk', *Econometrica*, vol. 47.

Kahneman, D. and Tversky, A. (1984) 'Choices, Values and Frames', *American Psychologist*, vol. 4.

Kaldor, N. (1978) *Further Essays in Applied Economics* (London: Duckworth).

Kant, I. ([1784]1984) 'Idea for a Universal History with a Cosmopolitan Purpose', in H. Reiss (ed.), *Kant's Political Writings* (Cambridge: Cambridge University Press).

Kapstein, E. B. (1991) 'Supervising International Banks: Origins and Implications of the Basle Accord', *Princeton Essays in International Finance* (Princeton, NJ: Princeton University Press).

Kaser, M. (1990) 'The Technology of Decontrol: Some Macroeconomic Issues', *Economic Journal*, June.

Kaspar, W. (1972) 'Stabilisation Policies in a Dependent Economy: Lessons from West German Experience of the 1960s', in E. Claasen and P. Salin (eds), *Stabilisation Policies in Interdependent Economies* (Amsterdam: North-Holland).

Kennan, G. F. (1967) *Memoirs, 1925–1950* (Boston, Mass.: Little, Brown).

Kennedy, P. (1989) *The Rise and Fall of the Great Powers* (Glasgow: Fontana Press).

Kenwood, A. G. and Lougheed, A. L. (1983) *The Growth of the International Economy 1820–1980* (London: Allen and Unwin).

Kern, D. (1981) 'The Evaluation of Country Risk and Economic Potential', *Journal of the Institute of Bankers*, June.

Keynes, J. M. (1936) *The General Theory of Employment, Interest and Money* (London: Macmillan).

Keynes, J. M. ([1930]1971) *A Treatise on Money*, vol. 2 (London: Macmillan).

Keynes, J. M. ([1930]1972) 'Economic Possibilities for Our Grandchildren', in J. M. Keynes, *Essays in Persuasion* (London: Macmillan and Cambridge University Press).

Keynes, J. M. ([1926]1972) 'The End of Laissez-Faire' in J. M. Keynes, *Essays in Persuasion* (London: Macmillan and Cambridge University Press).

Khan, M. and Knight, M. D. (1982) 'Some Theoretical and Empirical Issues Relating to Economic Stabilization in Developing Countries', *World Development*, September.

Kindleberger, C. P. (1973) *The World in Depression, 1929–1939* (London: Allan Lane).

Kindleberger, C. P. (1978a) *Economic Response – Comparative Studies in Trade, Finance and Growth* (Cambridge, Mass.: Harvard University Press).

Kindleberger, C. P. (1978b) *Manias, Panics and Crashes: A History of Financial Crises* (New York: Basic Books).

Kindleberger, C. P. (1984) *A Financial History of Europe* (London: Allen and Unwin).

Kinsella, R. (1995) *International Controls in Banking* (Dublin: Oak Tree Press).

Knickerbocker, F. T. (1973) *Oligopolistic Reaction and Multinational Enterprises* (Cambridge, Mass.: Harvard University Press).

Knight, F. H. (1921) *Risk, Uncertainty and Profit* (Boston, Mass.: Houghton Mifflin).

Kornai, J. (1990) *The Road to a Free Economy* (New York: Norton).

Korten, D. C. (1995) *When Corporations Rule the World* (London: Earthscan).

Kowalski, L. (1989) 'Major Current and Future Regional Issues in the Enlarged Community', in L. Albrechts, F. Moulaert, P. Roberts and E. Swyngedouw (eds), *Regional Policy at the Crossroads – European Perspectives* (London: Jessica Kingsley).

Kravis, I. B. (1970) 'Trade as the Handmaiden of Growth: Similarities between Nineteenth and Twentieth Centuries', *Economic Journal*, December.

Kravis, I. B. (1972) 'The Role of Exports in Nineteenth Century United States Growth', *Economic Growth and Cultural Change*, vol. 20.

Kravis, I. B., Heston, A. and Summers, S. (1978) *International Comparisons of Real Product and Purchasing Power* (Baltimore, MD: Johns Hopkins University Press).

Krueger, A. O. (1998) 'Why Trade Liberalisation is Good for Growth', *Economic Journal*, September.

Krugman, P. R. (1984) 'Import Protection as Export Promotion: International Competition in the Presence of Oligopoly and Economies of Scale', in H. Kierzkowski (ed.), *Monopolistic Competition and International Trade* (Oxford: Clarendon Press).

Krugman, P. R. (ed.) (1986) *Strategic Trade Policy and the New International Economics* (Cambridge, Mass.: MIT Press).

Krugman, P. R. (1987) 'Is Free Trade *Passé*?', *Journal of Economic Perspectives*, vol. 1.

Krugman, P. R. (1991) *Geography and Trade* (Cambridge, Mass.: MIT Press).

Krugman, P. R. (1995) 'Increasing Returns, Imperfect Competition and the Positive Theory of International Trade', in G. M. Grossman and K. Rogoff (eds), *Handbook of International Economics*, vol. 3 (Amsterdam: Elsevier).

Kumar, M. S. (1982) 'Overseas Operations of International Banks, Lending and Foreign Direct Investment: Theory and Empirical Evidence', study prepared for the International Trade and Capital Flows Division of the World Bank (Washington, DC).

Laird, S. and Yeats, A. (1988) 'Trends in Non-Tariff Barriers of Developed Countries, 1966–1986', *World Bank Working Paper No. 137* (Washington, DC: World Bank).

Laulan, Y. (1983) 'A New Approach to International Indebtedness', *The Banker*, June.

Lavergne, R. (1983) *The Political Economy of US Tariffs – An Empirical Analysis* (New York: Academic Press).

Lavigne, M. (1999) *The Economics of Transition*, 2nd edn (London: Macmillan).

Lazonick, W. (1991) *Business Organisations and the Myth of Market Mechanism* (Cambridge: Cambridge University Press).

Lazonick, W. and O'Sullivan, M. (2000) 'Maximising Shareholder Value: A New Ideology of Corporate Governance', *Economy and Society*, February.

League of Nations (1927) *Tariff Level Indices* (Geneva: League of Nations).

League of Nations (1943) *Quantitative Trade Controls* (Geneva: League of Nations).

Lee, E. (1998) *The Asian Financial Crisis – The Challenge for Social Policy* (Geneva: International Labour Office).

List, F. ([1841]1885) *The National System of Political Economy* (London: Longman).

Lowe, R. (1978) 'The Erosion of State Intervention in Britain, 1917–1924', *Economic History Review*, May.

Luke, R. (1985) 'The Schaht and the Keynes Plans', *Banca Nazionale del Lavoro Quarterly Review*, March.

Lunn, J. (1980) 'Determinants of US Direct Investment in the EEC: Further Evidence', *European Economic Review*, vol. 13.

Machlup, F. (1977) *A History of Thought on Economic Integration* (London: Macmillan).

Mackee, T. and Rose, R. (1991) *International Almanac of Electoral History* (London: Macmillan).

Maddison, A. (1964) *Economic Growth in the West* (London: Allen and Unwin).

Maddison, A. (1989) *The World Economy in the 20th Century* (Paris: OECD).

Maddison, A. (1991) *Dynamic Forces in Capitalist Development* (Oxford: Oxford University Press).

Maddison, A. (1995) *Monitoring the World Economy 1820–1992* (Paris: OECD).

Maddison, A. (2001) *The World Economy – A Millennial Perspective* (Paris: OECD).

Magaziner, I. C. and Hout, H. M. (1980) *Japanese Industrial Policy* (London: Policy Studies Institute).

Marglin, S. A. and Schor, J. B. (eds) (1990) *The Golden Age of Capitalism – Reinterpreting the Postwar Experience* (Oxford: Clarendon Press).

Marshall, A. ([1920]1959) *Principles of Economics*, 8th edn (London: Macmillan).

Martin, R. (1999) 'The New 'Geographical Turn' in Economics: Some Critical Reflections', *Cambridge Journal of Economics*, January.

Mason, E. S. and Asher, R. E. (1973) *The World Bank since the Bretton Woods* (Washington, DC: The Brookings Institution).

Mathias, P. and Pollard, S. (eds) (1989) *The Cambridge Economic History of Europe. Vol. VIII. The Industrial Economies – The Development of Economic and Social Policies* (Cambridge: Cambridge University Press).

McCallum, J. (1983) 'Inflation and the Social Consensus in the Seventies', *Economic Journal*, December.

McCallum, J. (1986) 'Unemployment in OECD Countries in the 1980s', *Economic Journal*, December.

McCloskey, D. N. (1980) 'Magnanimous Albion: Free Trade and British National Income, 1841–1881', *Explorations in Economic History*, vol. 17.

McKibbin, W. and Sachs, J. (1991) *Global Linkages: Macroeconomic Interdependence and Co-operation in the World Economy* (Washington, DC: The Brookings Institution).

Mendelsohn, M. S. (1982) *How Bankers See the World Financial Market* (New York: The Group of Thirty).

Mickesell, R. F. (1994) 'The Bretton Woods Debate: A Memoir', *Princeton Essays in International Finance* (Princeton, NJ: Princeton University Press).

Milanović, B. (2002) 'True World Income Distribution, 1988 and 1993: First Calculations Based on Household Surveys Alone', *Economic Journal*, January.

Mill, J. S. ([1848]1965) *Principles of Political Economy* (London: Routledge).

Milner, C. and Greenaway, D. (1979) *An Introduction to International Economics* (London: Longman).

Milward, A. S. (1987a) *The Reconstruction of Western Europe 1945–51* (London: Methuen).

Milward, A. S. (1987b) *War, Economy and Society 1939–1945* (Harmondsworth: Penguin).

Milward, A. S. (1992) *The European Rescue of the Nation State* (London: Routledge).

Moggridge, D. E. (1986) 'Keynes and the International Monetary System 1909–1946', in J. S. Cohen and G. C. Harcourt (eds), *International Monetary Problems and Supply-Side Economics: Essays in Honour of Lorie Tarshis* (London: Macmillan).

Moore, B. (1967) *Social Origins of Dictatorship and Democracy* (Harmondsworth: Penguin).

Morgan Guaranty Trust Company (1983) *World Financial Markets*, June.

Morris, C. and Adelman, I. (1988) *Comparative Patterns of Economic Development 1850–1914* (Baltimore, MD: Johns Hopkins University Press).

Musgrave, R. A. (1959) *The Theory of Public Finance* (New York: McGraw-Hill).

Myrdal, G. (1957) *Economic Theory and Underdeveloped Regions* (London: Duckworth).

Myrdal, G. (1960) *Beyond the Welfare State* (New Haven, CT: Yale University Press).

Nagy, P. (1978) 'Quantifying Country Risk: A System Developed by Economists at the Bank of Montreal', *Columbia Journal of World Business*, Fall.

Nakamura, T. (1981) *The Postwar Japanese Economy – Its Development and Structure* (Tokyo: Tokyo University Press).

Nicol, W. and Yuill, D. (1982) 'Regional Problems and Policy', in A. Boltho (ed.), *The European Economy* (Oxford: Oxford University Press).

Nogues, J. J., Olechowski, A. and Winters, A. (1986) 'The Extent of Non-Tariff Barriers to Imports of Industrial Countries', *World Bank Staff Working Paper No. 789* (Washington, DC: World Bank).

Nove, A. (1983) *The Economics of Feasible Socialism* (London: Allen and Unwin).

Nurkse, R. (1944) *International Currency Experience: Lessons of the Interwar Period* (Geneva: League of Nations).

OECD (1964) *Statistics of Balance of Payments* (Paris: OECD).

OECD (1979) *Collective Bargaining and Government Policies in Ten OECD Countries* (Paris: OECD).

OECD (1982a) *Development Cooperation – 1982 Review* (Paris: OECD).

OECD (1982b) *External Debt of Developing Countries – 1982 Survey* (Paris: OECD).

OECD (1983) *OECD Economic Outlook*, July.

OECD (1985) *Costs and Benefits of Protection* (Paris: OECD).

OECD (1998) *Open Markets Matter: the Benefits of Trade and Investment Liberalisation* (Paris: OECD).

OECD (1999) *Principles of Corporate Governance* (Paris: OECD).

Ohmae, K. (1990) *The Borderless World – Power Strategy and the International Economy* (London: Collins).

Ohmae, K. (1995) *The End of the Nation State – The Rise of Regional Economies* (London: HarperCollins).

Olson, M. (1982) *The Rise and Decline of Nations* (New Haven, CT: Yale University Press).

Olson, M., Sarna, N. and Swamy, A. V. (2000) 'Governance and Growth: A Simple Hypothesis Explaining Cross-Country Differences in Productivity Growth', *Public Choice*, March.

Oules, F. (1966) *Economic Planning and Democracy* (Harmondsworth: Penguin).

Page, S. A. B. (1979) 'The Management of International Trade', in R. Major (ed.), *Britain's Trade and Exchange Rate Policy* (London: Heinemann).

Panić, M. (1978) 'The Origin of Inflationary Tendencies in Contemporary Society', in F. Hirsch and J. H. Goldthorpe (eds), *The Political Economy of Inflation* (London: Martin Robertson).

Panić, M. (1988) *National Management of the International Economy* (London and New York: Macmillan and St Martin's Press).

Panić, M. (1991a) 'Managing Reforms in the East European Countries: Lessons from the Postwar Experience of Western Europe', *UN/ECE Discussion Paper No. 3* (New York and Geneva: United Nations).

Panić, M. (1991b) 'The Impact of Multinationals on National Economic Policies', in B. Bürgenmeier and J. L. Mucchielli (eds), *Multinationals and Europe 1992* (London: Routledge).

Panić, M. (1992) *European Monetary Union – Lessons from the Classical Gold Standard* (London and New York: Macmillan and St Martin's Press).

Panić, M. (1996) 'Monetary Sovereignty Under Different International Systems: A Historical Comparison', in I. D. Davidson and C. Taylor (eds), *European Monetary Union – The Kingsdown Enquiry* (London: Macmillan).

Panić, M. and Vacić, A. (1995) 'International Economic Integration and Disintegration: An Overview', in M. Panić and A. Vacić (eds), *Economic Integration in Europe and North America* (New York and Geneva: United Nations).

Partnoy, F. (1998) *F.I.A.S.C.O.* (London: Profile Books).

Patrick, D. L. and Scambler, G. (1986) *Sociology as Applied to Medicine*, 2nd edn (London: Baillière, Tindall).

Patterson, G. (1966) *Discrimination in International Trade – The Policy Issues 1945–66* (Princeton, NJ: Princeton University Press).

Paukert, F. (1973) 'Income Distribution at Different Levels of Development: A Survey of Evidence', *International Labour Review*, August–September.

Peacock, A. P. and Ricketts, M. (1978) 'The Growth of the Public Sector and Inflation', in F. Hirsch and J. H. Goldthorpe (eds), *The Political Economy of Inflation* (London: Martin Robertson).

Pekkarinen, J., Pohjola, M. and Rowthom, B. (eds) (1992) *Social Corporatism – A Superior Economic System?* (Oxford: Clarendon Press).

Persson, T., Roland, G. and Tabellini, G. (2000) 'Comparative Politics and Public Finance', *Journal of Political Economy*, December.

Pilbeam, K. (1992) *International Finance* (London: Macmillan).

Polanyi, K. (1944) *The Great Transformation* (New York: Rinehart).

Porter, M. E. (1990) *The Competitive Advantage of Nations* (New York: Free Press).

Porter, M. E. (ed.) (1992) *Capital Choices – Changing the Way America Invests in Industry* (Washington DC: Council on Competitiveness).

Pritchett, L. (1997) 'Divergence, Big Time', *Journal of Economic Perspectives*, Summer.

Quinn, B. (1998a) 'Rules v. Discretion: The Case for Banking Supervision in the Light of the Debate on Monetary Policy', in C. A. E. Goodhart (ed.), *The Emerging Framework of Financial Regulation* (London: Central Banking Publication).

Quinn, B. (1998b) 'The Bank of England's Role in Prudential Supervision', in C. A. E. Goodhart (ed), *The Emerging Framework of Financial Regulation* (London: Central Banking Publication).

Ram, R. (1986) 'Government Size and Economic Growth: A New Framework and Some Evidence from Cross-Section and Time-Series Data', *American Economic Review*, March.

Ray, E. J. (1981) 'The Determinants of Tariff and Non-Tariff Restrictions in the United States', *Journal of Political Economy*, vol. 89.

Reich, R. B. (1991) *The Work of Nations* (London: Simon and Schuster).

Ricardo, D. ([1817]1969) *The Principles of Political Economy and Taxation* (London: Everyman's Library).

Richardson, J. D. (1989) 'Empirical Research on Trade Liberalisation with Imperfect Competition: A Survey', *OECD Economic Studies*, Spring.

Robbins, L. (1952) *The Theory of Economic Policy* (London: Macmillan).

Robbins, S. W. and Stobaugh, P. B. (1974) *Money and the Multinational Enterprise – A Study of Financial Policy* (New York: Basic Books).

Roberts, J. and Postlewaite, A. (1976) 'The Incentives for Price-taking Behaviour in Large Exchange Economies', *Econometrica*, January.

Robinson, E. A. G. (1935) *The Structure of Competitive Industry* (Cambridge: Cambridge University Press).

Robson, W. A. (1960) *National Ownership and Public Industry* (London: Allen and Unwin).

Rodrik, D. (1993) 'Trade and Industrial Policy Reform in Developing Countries: A Review of Recent Theory and Evidence', in J. Behrman and T. Srinivasan (eds), *Handbook of Development Economics*, vol. iii (Amsterdam: North-Holland).

Rodrik, D. (1994) 'The Rush to Free Trade in Developing World: Why so Late? Why Now? Will It Last', in S. Haggard and S. Webb (eds), *Voting for Reform* (New York: Oxford University Press and the World Bank).

Rodrik, D. (1996) 'Why Do More Open Economies Have Bigger Governments?', *NBER Working Paper 5537* (Cambridge Mass.: NBER).

Rodrik, D. (1997) *The New Global Economy and Developing Countries: Making Openness Work* (Washington, DC: Overseas Development Council).

Romanis Brown, A. (1975) 'The Role of Incomes Policy in Industrialised Countries since World War II', *IMF Staff Papers*, March.

Romer, P. M. (1986) 'Increasing Returns and Long-Run Growth', *Journal of Political Economy*, October.

Roskamp, K. W. (1965) *Capital Formation in West Germany* (Detroit, Mich.: Wayne State University).

Rostow, W. W. (1978) *The World Economy – History and Prospects* (London: Macmillan).

Rostow, W. W. (1980) *Why the Poor Get Richer and the Rich Slow Down* (London: Macmillan).

Ruigrok, W. and Van Tulden, R. (1995) *The Logic of International Restructuring* (London: Routledge).

Sachs, J. (1981) 'The Current Account and Macroeconomic Adjustment in the 1970s', *Brookings Papers on Economic Activity*, no. 1.

Sachs, J. (1982) 'LDC Debt in the 1980s: Risk and Reforms', in P. Wachel (ed.), *Crises in the Economic and Financial Structure* (Lexington, Mass.: Lexington Books).

Salvatore, D. (ed.) (1993) *Protectionism and World Welfare* (Cambridge: Cambridge University Press).

Sampson, A. (1981) *The Money Lenders* (Dunton Green: Hodder and Stoughton).

Samuelson, P. A. (1939) 'The Gains from International Trade', *Canadian Journal of Economics and Political Science*, May.

Samuelson, P. A. (1967) *Economics – An Introductory Analysis*, 7th edn (New York: McGraw-Hill).

Sauter, C. (1982) 'France', in A. Boltho (ed.), *The European Economy* (Oxford: Oxford University Press).

Sawyer, M. (1982) 'Income Distribution and the Welfare State', in A. Boltho (ed.), *The European Economy* (Oxford: Oxford University Press).

Schelling, T. C. (1978) *Micromotives and Macrobehaviour* (New York: Norton).

Schumpeter, J. A. ([1943]1961) *Capitalism, Socialism and Democracy* (London: George Allen & Unwin).

Semmell, B. (1970) *The Rise of Free Trade Imperialism* (Cambridge: Cambridge University Press).

Sen, A. K. (1999a) 'Human Rights and Economic Achievements', in J. R. Bauer and D. A. Bell (eds), *The East Asian Challenge for Human Rights* (Cambridge: Cambridge University Press).

Sen, A. (1999b) *Development as Freedom* (Oxford: Oxford University Press).

Shepherd, A. R. (1978) *International Economics: A Micro–Macro Approach* (Columbus: Charles E. Merrill).

Sideri, S. (1970) *Trade and Power: Informal Colonialism and Anglo-Portuguese Relations* (Rotterdam: Rotterdam University Press).

Smith, A. ([1776]1976) *An Inquiry into the Nature and Causes of the Wealth of Nations* (Oxford: Clarendon Press).

Solomon, R. (1982) *The International Monetary System, 1945–81*, 2nd edn (New York: Harper and Row).

Solow, R. M. (1956) 'A Contribution to the Theory of Economic Growth', *Quarterly Journal of Economics*, February.

Soros, G. (2000) *Open Society – Reforming Global Capitalism* (London: Little, Brown).

Spero, J. E. (1981) *The Politics of International Economic Relations*, 2nd edn (London: Allen and Unwin).

Sprague, O. M. W. (1910) *History of Crises under the National Banking System* (Washington, DC: US Government Printing Office).

Stein, J. C. (1988) 'Takeover Threats and Managerial Myopia', *Journal of Political Economy*, February.

Stern, N. (1989) 'The Economics of Development – A Survey', *Economic Journal*, September.

Steuart, J. (1966) *An Inquiry into the Principles of Political Oekonomy*, 2 vols (Edinburgh: Scottish Economic Society).

Stiglitz, J. E. *et al.* (1989) *The Economic Role of the State* (Oxford: Basil Blackwell).

Stiglitz, J. E. (1994) *Whither Socialism?* (Cambridge, Mass.: MIT Press).

Stiglitz, J. E. (2001) 'More Instruments and Broader Goals: Moving Towards the Post-Washington Consensus', in J. H. Chang (ed.), *Joseph Stiglitz and the World Bank – the Rebel Within* (London: Anthem Press).

Summers, R. and Heston, A. (1988) 'A New Set of International Comparisons of Real Product and Prices: Estimates for 130 Countries, 1950–1985', *Review of Income and Wealth*, March.

Supple, B. (1973) 'The State and the Industrial Revolution, 1700–1914', in C. M. Cipolla (ed.), *The Fontana Economic History of Europe. Vol. III. The Industrial Revolution* (Glasgow: Fontana Collins).

Swank, D. (2002) *Global Capital, Political Institutions, and Political Change in Developed Welfare States* (Cambridge: Cambridge University Press).

Swoboda, A. (1976) *Capital Movements and their Control* (Leiden: Sijthoff).

Taylor, C. R. (1992) *Growth, Inequality and the Politics of Discontent in the Industrialised Countries* (New York: Group of Thirty).

Taylor-Gooby, P. (1993) 'What Citizens Want from the State', *International Social Attitudes – 10th BSA Report* (Aldershot: Dartmouth).

Thornblade, J. B. (1978) 'A Checklist System: The First Step in Country Evaluation', in S. H. Goodman (ed.), *Financing and Risk in Developing Countries* (New York: Praeger).

Treasury and Civil Service Committee (1983) *International Monetary Arrangements – International Lending by Banks*, vol. 1 (London: HMSO).

Tsuru, S. (1994) *Japan's Capitalism – Creative Defeat and Beyond* (Cambridge: Cambridge University Press).

Turner, P. and Tuveri, J. P. (1984) 'Some Effects of Export Restrictions on Japanese Trading Behaviour', *OECD Economic Studies*, Spring.

UNCTAD (1993) *World Investment Report – Transnational Corporations and Integrated International Production* (New York: United Nations).

UNCTAD (1994) *World Investment Report – Transnational Corporations, Employment and the Workplace* (New York and Geneva: United Nations).

UNCTAD (1997) *Trade and Development Report – Globalisation, Distribution and Growth* (New York and Geneva: United Nations).

UNCTAD (1999) *World Investment Report – Foreign Direct Investment and the Challenge of Development* (New York and Geneva: United Nations).

UNCTAD (2000) *World Investment Report – Cross-border Mergers and Acquisitions and Development* (New York and Geneva: United Nations).

UNCTC (United Nations Centre for Transnational Corporations) (1988) *Transnational Corporations in World Development – Trends and Prospects* (New York: United Nations).

UNCTC (1991) *World Investment Report – The Triad in Foreign Direct Investment* (New York: United Nations).

UNCTC (1992) *World Investment Report – Transnational Corporations as Engines of Growth* (New York: United Nations).

UNDP (1999) *Human Development Report* (New York: Oxford University Press).

United Nations (1965) *Economic Planning in Europe* (Geneva: United Nations).

United Nations (1981) *Transnational Banks – Operations, Strategies and their Effects in Developing Countries* (New York: United Nations).

United Nations (2000) *World Economic and Social Survey 2000* (New York: United Nations).

United Nations (2001) *2001 Report on the World Social Situation*, May.

US Congress, Office of Technology Assessment (1993) *Multinationals and the National Interest – Playing by Different Rules* (Washington, DC: US Government Printing Office).

US Department of State (1948a) *Proceedings and Documents of United Nations Monetary and Financial Conference – Bretton Woods, New Hampshire July 1–22, 1944*, vol. 1 (Washington, DC: US Government Printing Office).

US Department of State (1948b) *Proceedings and Documents of United Nations Monetary and Financial Conference – Bretton Woods, New Hampshire July 1–22, 1944*, vol. 2 (Washington, DC: US Government Printing Office).

Van Dormael, A. (1978) *Bretton Woods – Birth of a Monetary System* (London: Macmillan).

Vickers, J. (1985) 'Strategic Competition among the Few', *Oxford Review of Economic Policy*, Spring.

Viner, J. (1950) *The Customs Union Issue* (London: Stevens & Sons).

Waller, R. (1995) 'Taxing Polls', *New Statesman and Society*, 26 May.

Wallich, H. C. (1982) 'Rescheduling as Seen by the Supervisor and the Lender of Last Resort', in P. Wachel (ed.), *Crisis in the Economic and Financial Structure* (Lexington, Mass.: Lexington Books).

Walter, A. (1993) *World Power and World Money* (London: Harvester Wheatsheaf).

Weiss, L. (1998) *The Myth of the Powerless State – Governing the Economy in a Global Era* (Cambridge: Polity Press).

White, W. R. (1998) 'Systemic Risk and Derivatives: Can Disclosure Help?', in C. A. E. Goodhart (ed.), *The Emerging Framework of Financial Regulation* (London: Central Banking Publication).

Wilensky, H. (1975) *The Welfare State and Equality* (Berkeley, CA: University of California Press).

Wiles, P. J. D. (1962) *The Political Economy of Communism* (Oxford: Basil Blackwell).

Williamson, J. (ed.) (1994) *The Political Economy of Policy Reform* (Washington, DC: Institute for International Economics).

Williamson, J. G. (1998) 'Globalization and the Labour Market: Using History to Inform Policy', in P. Aghion and J. G. Williamson, *Growth, Inequality and Globalization – Theory, History and Policy* (Cambridge: Cambridge University Press).

Williamson, O. E. (1971) 'The Vertical Integration of Production: Market Failure Considerations', *American Economic Review – Papers and Proceedings*, May.

Williamson, O. E. (1975) *Markets and Hierarchies* (New York: The Free Press).

Williamson, O. E. (1979) 'Transaction-Costs Economics: the Governance of Contractual Relations', *Journal of Law and Economics*, October.

Williamson, O. E. (1981) 'The Modern Corporation: Origin, Evolution and Attributes', *Journal of Economic Literature*, December.

Wood, A. (1994) *North–South Trade, Employment and Inequality – Changing Fortunes in a Skill-Driven World* (Oxford: Clarendon Press).

World Bank (1979) *World Development Report 1979* (Washington, DC: World Bank).

World Bank (1987) *World Development Report 1987* (Washington, DC: World Bank).

World Bank (1992) *Global Economic Prospects and the Developing Countries* (Washington, DC: World Bank).

World Bank (1997) *Private Capital Flows to Developing Countries – The Road to Financial Integration* (Oxford: Oxford University Press).

Woytinski, W. S. and Woytinski, E. S. (1955) *World Commerce and Governments – Trends and Outlook* (New York: Twentieth Century Fund).

Young, A. (1928) 'Increasing Returns and Economic Progress', *Economic Journal*, December.

Index of Names

Subject Index